D1577907

Kant's Theory of Mind

KANT'S THEORY OF MIND

An Analysis of the Paralogisms of Pure Reason

KARL AMERIKS

CLARENDON PRESS · OXFORD

OXFORD

UNIVERSITY PRESS

Great Clarendon Street, Oxford OX2 6DP

Oxford University Press is a department of the University of Oxford.
It furthers the University's objective of excellence in research, scholarship,
and education by publishing worldwide in

Oxford New York

Athens Auckland Bangkok Bogotá Buenos Aires Calcutta
Cape Town Chennai Dar es Salaam Delhi Florence Hong Kong Istanbul
Karachi Kuala Lumpur Madrid Melbourne Mexico City Mumbai
Nairobi Paris São Paulo Singapore Taipei Tokyo Toronto Warsaw

and associated companies in Berlin Ibadan

Oxford is a registered trade mark of Oxford University Press
in the UK and in certain other countries

Published in the United States
by Oxford University Press Inc., New York

First published 1982
This edition first published 2000

British Library Cataloguing in Publication Data

Data available

Library of Congress Cataloging in Publication Data

Data available

ISBN 0-19-823896-7
ISBN 0-19-823897-5 (pbk.)

Printed in Great Britain
on acid-free paper by
Biddles Ltd.,
Guildford and King's Lynn

Preface to the Second Edition

1. Kant's Theory of Mind Twenty Years After: A New Landscape

The first edition of *Kant's Theory of Mind: An Analysis of the Paralogisms of Pure Reason* (1982) was the first book in English devoted to its topic. After the ice was broken, a torrent of studies soon followed. Books by Andrew Brook, Quassim Cassam, Patricia Kitcher, Heiner Klemme, Rudolf Makkreel, Georg Mohr, C. Thomas Powell, Alejandro Rosas, and Dieter Sturma provided detailed investigations amplifying on the themes of Kant's Paralogisms.[1] Important studies of Kant's views on the mind were also incorporated in new writings by Henry Allison, Richard Aquila, Reinhard Brandt, Wolfgang Carl, Manfred Frank, Paul Guyer, Rolf-Peter Horstmann, Ralf Meerbote, Robert Pippin, Udo Thiel, and other leading Kant experts of the last two decades.[2] Their work has come to complement that of the still influential generation of major philosophers whose discussions of Kant were central to my original volume: Jonathan Bennett, Roderick Chisholm, Dieter Henrich, Gerold Prauss, Wilfrid Sellars, and P. F. Strawson. Beyond the work of these well-known figures, there have been dozens of other useful studies. For orientation one can start with the helpful reviews of the newer literature by Günter Zöller and Eric Watkins,[3] and the overviews contained in several new collections with essays focusing on Kant's notion of the self.[4]

In current systematic work on topics in the philosophy of mind, there has also been an enormous regeneration of interest in Kantian perspectives on issues such as consciousness, intentionality, self-reference, personal identity, and autonomy. The literature here is often connected with Kant's own texts only by brief references, but it is highly relevant to assessing the ultimate value of Kant's ideas; it is also enormous in extent and leads into so many different directions that even an overview is impossible. Names such as Thomas Nagel, John McDowell, Hector-Neri Castañeda, Colin McGinn, Donald Davidson, and Christine Korsgaard may give some indication of the diverse nature of the ever-growing influence, direct and indirect, of Kant's non-reductive approach to the mind.[5] Kant's criticism of some central features of the Cartesian tradition has also been a major force (although one that is still largely unexplored directly) behind the striking rebirth of interest in post-Kantian German thought, especially in areas concerning themes such as imagination, aesthetics, and the development of romanticism and 'postmodernism'.[6]

In the meantime, I have devoted several essays to a discussion of many of these new studies of Kant.[7] In addition, there are a number of very important but extremely recent books on Kant and the mind that no one has had a chance to comment on yet.[8] Given all these developments, the opportunity arising with this new edition of *Kant's Theory of Mind* presents a great temptation for expanding my earlier work on many fronts. For a number of reasons, I have chosen to resist this temptation as much as possible, and to modify the original edition in only a few ways. There are some frequently discussed aspects of Kant's discussions of the mind that, for the most part, I still abstract from in this study. As noted in the first edition (see below, p. 2), I minimize attention to the general cognitive activity of the self as subject, since that topic can be treated elsewhere and involves the entirety of Kant's theory of knowledge rather than the self as such. In addition, I abstract from direct treatment of the general issue of self-reference (but see below, p. 176, n. 103); there are many intriguing paradoxes here that some of Kant's statements generate, but it is not clear that the topic as it is discussed today was central to his main interests. Some of my own discussion may involve anachronistic concerns (e.g., in the account of contemporary perspectives on personal identity in Ch. IV. B below), but this is an ever-present danger in trying to relate a historical figure to new strands of current literature. No doubt, much of the literature that I engaged has been superseded in some way, but it does not seem appropriate to me to cut down my earlier collection of references. Some of the references may appear peripheral, but there can be some value in being reminded of discussions that are often unfairly forgotten now just because they are at a middle distance, neither in the limelight of the present nor the hallowed aura of the distant past. Readers can in any event consult the extensive references provided in the new material, and the bibliography that has been expanded and updated by a section with appropriate new references for the main topics of each of the old chapters.[9]

To the text itself, I have added only this Preface and a Postscript chapter, and otherwise there are no significant modifications to the content of the work. The Preface elaborates on what most readers appear to have regarded as the most distinctive feature of my book, namely, its special attention to the historical background of Kant's work. In particular, I recount some highly significant developments since 1982 concerning relevant materials in the new Academy edition volumes of Kant's lectures. I also respond to a few points in the most extensive new German study of the topic, Klemme's invaluable *Kants Philosophie des Subjekts* (1996). The Postscript, in contrast, is an essay devoted more to a systematic defence of major themes of my interpretation, and especially of the claim that Kant, despite all his criticisms of rational psychology, retains an unusual but still significant form of immaterialism. I defend this position by reacting to some recent remarks on Kant by Andrew Brook and Colin McGinn. My treatment of Brook and McGinn (as well as of Klemme) is tailored to the purpose of clarifying my own controversial and sometimes misunderstood reading of Kant's position. It does not aim to do justice to the detail of Brook's study of Kant on the mind, which is now the most extensive one in English, or to McGinn's general position, which is one of the most interesting in current philosophy of mind. Given that there is no point in even attempting to react in one place to all of the immense range of significant work on the topic in the last couple of decades, I have decided to focus on only a few recent but central discussions, and in this way to present an updated but relatively concise formulation of the key points of my position. For further indications of my views on related issues, readers can consult several other recent essays, and especially a new overview of the Parologisms that I have done for a recent collection,[10] as well as the more general picture of the Kantian and post-Kantian era that I have presented in another book.[11]

Several reviewers expressed the view that my original study was overly ambitious in trying to be succinct and yet, all at once, historically detailed, thoroughly evaluative, and attentive to the current literature on each topic. No doubt some things might have been done more effectively if fewer things had been attempted. At the time, however, I was very concerned with trying to challenge standard approaches in Kant research, and with provoking discontent with the common practice, more current in those days than now, of writing on Kant in a piecemeal fashion, that is, either for relatively unambitious exegetical and historical purposes, or for fairly narrow analytic and contemporary purposes. I still believe that, with classical works of the past, philosophers today should attempt, at least on some occasions, to give attention to all the dimensions of a major thinker's work. It is not easy to find the proper organization and style for such an effort, and I am sadly aware of the deficiencies that remain in my work. But I am also heartened by the thought that, after all this time, its content seems for the most part as relevant as ever, and Kant's own views on the mind are clearly of even more interest now than would have been expected years ago.

In the remarks that follow, I will first review the most important recent development in the study of Kant, namely, the new availability of numerous notes from his lectures (Section 2). I will then explain specifically how the lectures on metaphysics bear on the central issues concerning the self as interpreted in my earlier work (Section 3; readers with no acquaintance with the first edition can look at these pages as a quick preview of the main themes of the book). I will conclude by responding to some typical criticisms of my treatment of these issues as they are presented in Klemme's work (Section 4).[12]

2. New Material Concerning Kant

Recent decades have brought a remarkable addition to information available about Kant's philosophy through notes taken from his lectures. Batches of important lecture courses on ethics, logic, anthropology, and metaphysics have become available only recently in the Academy edition, and in some partial but lengthy translations that involve amendments of that edition.[13] Since these lectures come in multiple versions and cover a wide range of years, it has been possible to compare them against each other and with other evidence. Their general reliability has been confirmed, although of course they can never have the same claim to authenticity as work that Kant wrote or published himself. They serve none the less as a highly intriguing and convenient tool for studying the development of Kant's views—especially since, much more than his published writings, they tend to maintain a very similar organization and to list common topics over several decades. The materials from Kant's lectures on metaphysics were a major source of the research I conducted in the late 1970s in the process of drafting *Kant's Theory of Mind*. I relied heavily on lectures from the so-called Pölitz collection of the 1770s,[14] which was one of the few versions of these lectures that had been available prior to the publication of two massive books of vol. 28 in the Academy edition: vol. 28, First Half (1968, pp. 1–524), and Second Half, First Part (1970, pp. 525–987). These books contained notes from many lecture sets that had never been available before.[15] It is a startling fact of the time that, although metaphysics was obviously Kant's own prime concern, there had been no translation at all in English for these lectures, whereas material from lectures on other areas, such as ethics, logic, and anthropology, had long been made available. This failing may have been in part a reflection of ideological influences. Although a metaphysical school of Kant interpretation, influenced in part by the Pölitz lectures, had developed in Germany in the early twentieth century, in English the dominant approach to Kant (as to philosophy in general, at least until the recent resurgence of formal work on modal issues) remained largely opposed to traditional metaphysics. Thus, although Kant's philosophy as a whole continued to receive considerable attention in English, most interpretations of it, whether in theoretical or practical philosophy, tended very much to play down traditional metaphysical issues in favour of epistemological and ethical concerns

connected with the empiricist tradition.[16] This tendency was
reinforced no doubt by the intimidating complexity of Kant's
doctrines here, and also by the well-known fact that he was
famous for being quite a critic of many metaphysical arguments himself.

All the same, one would have expected that at least within
the German tradition there would have continued to have
been a lively discussion of Kant's metaphysics, and at least
some thorough treatment of the newly published lectures. But
this expectation was in vain. Perhaps the 'lively discussion'
did not occur because of the immediate post-war hegemony
of anti-metaphysical approaches stemming from the late
Heidegger, Nietzsche, and critical theory. Perhaps the 'thorough treatment' did not occur because of worries concerning
the sensitive issue that the editing of the lectures occurred in
less than ideal circumstances in Berlin. For whatever reason,
the task of trying to make something out of the 'metaphysical
Kant' for current philosophy was a rather lonely project when
I took it up in the late 1970s, with a sense of risk overcome
only by what seemed to be the clear and neglected force of
the evidence itself, especially in the overlapping treatments of
issues in the lecture notes.

Conditions changed with the remarkable find of two
lengthy and well-preserved additional lecture sets, the
Metaphysik Mrongovius (1782–3) and Vigilantius (1794–5),
published hastily in an extra Academy book of metaphysics
lectures: vol. 29, First Half, Second Part (1983, pp.
743–1188). These independent and mutually reinforcing notes
put to rest any remaining suspicion about the notes from the
metaphysics lectures as a valuable source of Kant's own
views. At about the same time, classical philosophy of mind
(like philosophy of religion) took on a resurgent form in analytic philosophy, with metaphysical approaches regaining
influence through figures such as Chisholm, Kim, Burge,
Kripke, Lewis, etc. But, while some general studies of Kant
in English turned to putting more weight back on metaphysical issues (e.g., in Guyer, van Cleve, Wood, Findlay, G.
Nagel, Melnick, Bennett's *Kant's Dialectic*), the newer studies
specifically on his philosophy of mind (e.g., in Brook and
Kitcher) maintained an approach that, on the whole,

remained more typical of mainline empiricist work. The topics in focus had changed; interpreters now looked in some
detail at Kant's published discussions of the mind's substantiality, simplicity, identity, etc., but the emphasis remained on
celebrating Kant's criticisms of dogmatic rationalism and on
exploring broadly empiricist projects such as parallels
between recent cognitive science and Kant's 'neutral' studies
of the mind's functions. Studies of Kant's historical background, and of the significance of the newly available lectures, now over a decade and a half old, continued to be an
exception.[17]

None the less, in addition to the availability of extra materials, there have been two significant international trends that
may eventually lead to a return to a much more widespread
appreciation of the full historical—and I would still say
rationalist—context of Kant's philosophy of mind and metaphysics in general.

One trend concerns the Kantian concept of freedom. This
concept is absolutely central to Kant's ethics, which is the
part of his philosophy that always seems to be growing in its
impact on philosophers and the public at large. Discussions in
English, where work is especially vibrant because of the enormous influence of Rawls, continue for the most part to seek
a Kantian practical philosophy that would work without any
ontological considerations, and often even without substantive
commitments to a concept of the good, or to deep objectivity in ethical theory as such. None the less, the recent work
of sympathetic critics such as Thomas Nagel and Jerome
Schneewind[18] is a sign of a growing awareness that there are
many ways in which Kant's own ethical position may not be
independent of the tradition of substantive metaphysics. At
the same time, the ever more fine-grained historical explor-
ations of German scholars such as Josef Schmucker and
Dieter Henrich[19] may eventually force all philosophers to
take much more account of Kant's early work, his
Reflections, and other evidence that ties him in essential ways
to a broader tradition than can be done justice by the contemporary preoccupation with formal issues such as an
abstract 'categorical imperative procedure'.[20] Above all, one
can expect that discussions elsewhere about the concept of

freedom as such, which is at the centre of intense metaphysical debates in contemporary philosophy, will eventually force themselves on the agenda of even overburdened Kant scholars.[21] For Kant, morality clearly requires freedom, and this requirement and its preconditions, one can now learn easily enough, have their first and most remarkable discussion in Kant's pre-critical lectures.

A second issue that connects Kant's complex background and recent philosophy is the fact of consciousness. Consciousness itself was a lost topic for a long time in analytic philosophy of mind, being passed over by studies of higher order functions such as intentional behaviour, perception, assertion, and 'cognitive processing'. But a basic phenomenon does not disappear simply because a generation of writers tends to be attracted to more specific and manageable issues. The so-called 'hard problem' of consciousness has come back into philosophical literature with a vengeance now,[22] and, although it may recede from the centre of attention just as quickly as it got there, it is difficult to imagine that the problem will ever disappear entirely. One aspect of it is guaranteed always to make Kant's approach appear especially valuable, namely, the close connection between human consciousness as such and the peculiarities of self-reference and self-consciousness, that is, the inescapable themes of Kant's revolutionary doctrine of apperception. In German scholarship, the topic of consciousness has for a longer time been much more at the centre of attention, in large part because of work by Dieter Henrich. On the one hand, Henrich has developed an elaborate reconstruction of what he takes to be Kant's own 'Cartesian' account of our consciousness; on the other hand, he has outlined a theory of his own and used it to criticize (what he takes to be) the Kantian approach from the perspective of later idealists such as Fichte and Hölderlin, who he suggests were closer to a more accurate account of the full complexity of the self.[23] Klemme's book, like much of my own earlier work, is an attempt to recover a more sympathetic picture of Kant's notion of consciousness, one that builds on some aspects of Henrich's work but holds back from any preference for post-Kantians.

The topics of freedom and self-consciousness overlap more

in Kant's philosophy than anywhere else. It is a central and unique claim of his pre-critical lectures and Reflections that absolute spontaneity and the ability genuinely to say 'I' are completely certain and provide prime evidence for each other. If matters could have been left at this point, a deep unity of theoretical and practical philosophy might have been proclaimed, and perhaps Kant would not have thought he had to write more than one *Critique*. But of course he did write the later *Critiques*, and he clearly qualified his earlier views in all sorts of ways. He did not take them back completely, though, and thus, in our own time, prominent writers such as Allison, Pippin, Korsgaard, and Prauss can come back, again and again, to the Kantian idea that we at least 'must take' ourselves to be free in both theoretical and practical contexts.[24] Obviously, if one is to evaluate such views and to determine how consistent they are with Kant's own critical strictures, it would be helpful to look not only at prime critical texts on the self and spontaneity, but also to examine very closely how they contrast with other materials such as the pre-critical ideas found in the lectures. These ideas are expressed there in the traditional terms that Kant himself was most familiar with, and that he surely meant to distance himself from eventually in some way. The difficult task is to come out with just the right account of that distance. For this reason, close attention to the pre-critical work, and a comparison of it with the rest of Kant's lectures and writings, remains essential. Without knowing each side of a chasm well, it is hardly possible to measure properly the bridge needed to cross to the other side.

3. The Significance of the Metaphysics Lectures

All these recent developments seem to me to provide a strong confirmation of my original hypothesis that the data provided by notes from Kant's lectures are worthy of close scrutiny. It may help to give a full presentation here of the passages that, from the beginning, provided the distinctive motivation of my study. Right at the start of the Rational Psychology section in the L1 (= 'Pölitz') lectures, one finds these four topics listed:

1. that the soul is a substance;
2. that it is simple;
3. that it is a single substance; and
4. that it is a spontaneous agent, simply speaking.[25]

These points are introduced as 'transcendental concepts according to which we consider the soul as such'. Very soon, however, they turn out to be not merely concepts that we think in terms of; they become parts of metaphysical assertions that are backed by unquestioned arguments. The notes continue:

We will thus cognize a priori no more of the soul than the I allows us to cognize. But I cognize of the soul:

1. that it is a substance, or: I am a substance. The I means the subject, so far as it is no predicate of another thing. . . . Consequently the I, or the soul through which the I is expressed, is a substance.
2. The soul is simple, i.e., the I means a simple concept. Many beings together cannot constitute an I. If I say: I think, then I do not express representations which are divided among many beings, rather I express a representation that takes place in one subject. . . . accordingly the soul must be a simple substance.
3. The soul is a single soul (the oneness, the unity of the soul), i.e., my consciousness is the consciousness of a single substance. I am not conscious of myself as several substances. . . . I am conscious of myself as one subject.
4. The soul is a being which acts spontaneously, simply speaking, i.e., the human soul is free in the transcendental sense. . . . this means absolute spontaneity, and is self-activity from an inner principle according to the power of free choice. . . . the I proves that I myself act; I am principle, and no thing which has a principle, I am conscious of determinations and actions, and such a subject that is conscious of its determinations and actions has absolute freedom. . . . When I say: I think, I act, etc., then either the word is applied falsely, or I am free. Were I not free, then I could not say *I* do it, but rather I would have to say: I feel in me a desire to do, which someone has aroused in me. . . . I do, as action, cannot be used otherwise than as absolutely free. All practical objective propositions would make no sense if human beings were not free.[26]

The next section continues with an argument that states:

But we have already demonstrated that the soul is a substance, and then that it is a simple substance. From that Wolff believed already to have proved immateriality; but that is false; immateriality does not yet follow from simplicity. . . . But one still has a ground for immateriality. . . . if the soul were material, then it would at least have to be a simple part of matter (because it is already proved that it is simple). But now no part of matter is simple, for that is a contradiction; thus the soul is also not material, but rather immaterial.[27]

And later, another important distinction is introduced:

An immaterial being that is gifted with consciousness of itself (from which it already follows that it is a rational being) is a spirit. From spirit must be distinguished that which is spiritual. Spiritual beings are those which are indeed connected with a body, but whose representations, whose thinking and willing, can continue even if they are separated from the body. . . . Now what can we cognize a priori of spirits? We can think of spirits only problematically. . . [28]

These passages already indicate most of the ideas that are at the core of my 'rationalist' interpretation. They should be very surprising for readers who know only of Kant's critical views. In the *Critique* (A 344/ B 402; see the beginning of Ch. II below) the first three arguments of the lectures reappear in order and almost verbatim, but now as the first three paralogisms, i.e., as illustrations of fallacies that are the object of Kant's famous attack on rational psychology. At first glance, then, it would seem that at the end of his silent decade Kant had come to nothing less than a total reversal of his pre-critical position. And yet, although it cannot be denied that there is a dominant new critical direction in his later treatment of mind, I believe matters are much too complicated to be forced into the all too easily assumed story of a '*total* reversal'. It is important to know that Kant was very familiar with the *full* list of issues indicated above, for he lectured on them year after year. Hence, wherever there are specific points on which he did *not* explicitly reverse himself, or where he maintained explicit qualifications, or clearly chose to avoid some questions, or did not even attempt certain kinds of criticisms against some arguments that he did use against others, one cannot help but assume that there were underlying reasons. When these reasons are all spelled out, they reveal a transition that I believe looks much more like a partial than a total reversal.

It is quite clear that these pre-critical notes are not an anomaly or passing fancy. Given earlier publications such as the *Inaugural Dissertation*, as well as the Reflections (Kant's incidental and marginal notes, not published in his lifetime) and lectures on anthropology and related topics in this period, the notes reflect pretty much the view that one should have expected of Kant at the time, that is, somewhere around the mid-1770s. They include criticisms of Wolff and Baumgarten on many points, so a *totally* rationalist position is *never* maintained. The criticisms are expressed within the framework of a position that is still broadly Cartesian, but that also reflects a commitment to some never withdrawn conclusions about the self that go beyond traditional philosophical psychology to original metaphysical, ethical, and epistemological claims. The rejection of a theoretical philosophy of spiritual monads goes hand in hand with a unique defence of features such as apperception, absolute freedom, and a non-material form of ultimate reality. These features of the subject are emphasized by Kant throughout the many complex shifts in the critical era as well, even though the grounds for their assertion and the interpretation of their meaning often differ significantly over time, especially after the period of the early lectures.

It is very important to keep an eye out for the nuances in Kant's later reaction to the various positions expressed in the lectures. Rational psychology encompasses a long list of issues, each issue has a multiplicity of meanings, and many of the arguments that employ them receive different kinds of treatment at different times. In the passages cited above, one should distinguish at least three broad groups of topics. First, there is the set of 'core' metaphysical claims about our substantiality, simplicity, and singleness (this third feature is discussed later in terms of oneness over time, i.e., personal identity, or at least its underlying condition).[29] Secondly, there is the central claim about absolute spontaneity, which is explained at great length (in a way that the brief citations cannot reveal), and is tied most directly to the distinctive capacities of the human subject as a genuinely theoretical and practical agent, i.e., as a being with judgement and will.

Thirdly, there is the classical problem of modern metaphysics concerning what kind of 'stuff' the human mind consists of, a topic that is obviously undertaken with an eye towards those who tried to build from the first sets of claims to a priori arguments for our independence from the body and for personal immortality.

In sum, Kant's pre-critical discussions of the human subject indicate that the self is, in the strictest sense, (*a*) substantial (etc.),[30] (*b*) free, and (*c*) non-material, but (*d*) that all of this still does not give us any ground for saying that it is a 'spiritual' being that can maintain itself in existence after the demise of the body. In other words, at this point Kant *already* has in hand the *main* negative claim he chooses to emphasize throughout the whole critical treatment of rational psychology. According to that claim, no matter how things go with more basic metaphysical issues, there is no prospect at all of success for the allegedly all-encompassing aim of previous philosophical psychology (even, for example, in such late and relatively cautious practitioners as Mendelssohn), namely the theoretical proof of a personal afterlife. From this perspective, Kant's views on issues such as our mere substantiality sink to strictly academic significance, and it is perhaps not surprising that, even though in the two editions of the *Critique* Kant revised the Paralogisms at greater length than any other part, and he provided new formulations of the specific arguments on the traditional 'core' topics, he did so without indicating that he had come to what he regarded as any fundamentally different position on the soul as such.

Matters on the issue of freedom are even more complicated. Whereas on the first issue, substantiality, there is a very explicit but ultimately not so crucial shift between the earlier and later Kant ('not crucial' precisely because on the last issue of spirituality there is explicitly no shift at all), for the middle (or 'keystone') issue of freedom there is quite a crucial shift, since it moves from being the most extensively treated topic to one that is put completely outside the main discussion in the *Critique of Pure Reason*. Without any indication of this banishment, Kant removes the whole topic of the self's agency from the four-part framework of the paralogisms of rational psychology, and he inserts in its place a separate discussion of the issue of our relation to external objects. Some of his haste and perplexity here is revealed by the fact that the first edition of the *Critique* approaches this issue in terms of the *epistemological* question of the 'proof of the external world', whereas the second-edition version of this section undergoes the most extensive revision within the Paralogisms chapter, and is redirected again towards the *metaphysical* issue of the mind's partial dependence on other things. Remarkably, nowhere in the first *Critique* does Kant directly evaluate the bold and central argument given in the lectures from the general power of judgement to the conclusion of absolute spontaneity. There is one well-known and ambiguous passage[31] that is left in about 'knowing' oneself through apperception as a 'purely intelligible object' (the term *erkennen* is used, and one can wonder whether here it means real knowledge, or just acquaintance and conception), and thus independently of sensibility, but the topic of the self's spontaneity is given no basic place in the Paralogisms, and the discussions of it in the Antinomies and the Canon refer only very indirectly to theoretical considerations in favour of our freedom and fall far short of endorsing them. What is most striking is the obvious fact that, if Kant had really lost confidence in the argument to our spontaneity in just the same way that he had for the other arguments of rational psychology cited earlier, then it would have been very easy for him to construct a paralogism for this topic just as he had done for the others.[32] The simplest explanation for his not taking such a route is to presume that, although by the 1780s spontaneity had become an issue Kant took to be more important than ever, it was not one for which he had settled upon an approach. His perplexity is revealed in the many key changes in his remarks about freedom that can be traced through the time of the two editions of the first *Critique* (1781, 1787) and the transition from the *Foundations of the Metaphysics of Morals* (1785) to the second *Critique* (1788).[33] The fact that his old argument for freedom was intertwined with considerations about apperception only complicated matters more, since it was a reformulation of his discussion of this topic that demanded his other major efforts in revising the first *Critique*, and especially in rewriting the Transcendental Deduction.

Note that without the pre-critical lectures we might have had no appreciation for the depth of Kant's shifts here, of the great struggle that he was going through on the issue of our absolute freedom, and that he was unable to express clearly even in a negative way as late as the first edition of the *Critique of Pure Reason*. Altogether, the lectures allow us to mark the distance that Kant had come by the 1780s: he was now (*a*) willing explicitly to retreat from (theoretically) arguing for our substantiality; while (*b*) he was reaffirming his innovative view that even with many concessions to rationalism there is no hope for its arguments for our spirituality; and, at the same time, (*c*), on the topic of our spontaneity, he was shifting in the most unclear and complex way, moving from an initial special enthusiasm about a theoretical proof, to a period of silence and ambiguity on it, and ending finally with a firm conviction in the second *Critique* that proof was possible only from a unique moral-practical 'fact of reason'.

One lesson I drew from all these developments is that, even at a fairly late stage in his work, Kant was quite capable of having a very unsettled position on key issues, and that he was especially gifted at deflecting attention from the limitations (in range and in value) of his position. I applied this lesson in working through all the various meanings and arguments concerning the traditional issues treated in the lectures on rational psychology. Some of my main conclusions were fairly radical, and still encounter considerable misunderstanding and resistance.

On the bundle of core issues concerning substantiality, simplicity, and identity, I noted that, although the later Kant can be seen as quoting and rejecting the positive arguments on these issues that the pre-critical lectures had clearly approved, he maintained a tendency not to make clear what the exact fallacy of the arguments was. This weakness has often been overlooked because contemporary readers tend to be so sympathetic to the general idea of rejecting rational psychology that they assume that there just could be no valid a priori ground for conclusions such as that the self is a substance. Sometimes they blithely repeat that Kant's general epistemological doctrines demonstrably rule out any such 'transcendent' and substantive synthetic a priori claims, as if it were not incumbent upon someone holding such bold doctrines to explain precisely why a relevant argument does not rather amount to a counter-example. This is especially remarkable since the arguments in question long had the sympathy of Kant himself, as well as of some of the greatest minds in the history of philosophy, and they can hardly be assumed to be transparent failures.

Many contemporary readers even tend to assume that Kant came to reject the *conclusions* of the arguments, although there are many reasons for believing that even the later Kant was willing to endorse the original conclusions themselves, as long they are not inflated and are understood as receiving their most important ground and meaning through our pure practical reason. Moreover, I believe there are sympathetic ways to understand these arguments even in a theoretical way, such that they need not transcend experience altogether but can be taken simply to characterize the general structure of the subject of experience, just as the principle of apperception is supposed to give a synthetic a priori characterization of how such a subject must function (there is, after all, no reason why rational psychology has to be conceived in an entirely transcendent sense, even though of course it often did appear in such a form). If synthetic 'functional' propositions (e.g., that the manifold of intuition in knowledge must be synthesized *by a subject*) are allowed, why are 'constitutive' ones (e.g., that the subject is immaterial) to be automatically ruled out? It is remarkable that when one actually looks at the *Critique*'s extensive first-edition discussions of the rationalist arguments for substantiality, simplicity, and identity, what Kant *emphasizes* time and again is only what he had said already in the lectures, namely, that one cannot 'make use' of the conclusions in ways that would accomplish the supposed end of rational psychology, that is, the a priori theoretical demonstration of our spiritual and immortal status. From this perspective, if *some* of the old arguments for our mere substance, or simplicity, or identity were still allowed, very little would follow 'that ultimately matters', although of course the general Kantian programme of restricting a priori claims would not be so neat. But in fact the published works that carry out this programme never do provide anything like the systematic coverage of topics outlined in the metaphysics lectures; only a complete metaphysics could provide the full determination of issues that Kant promised but never delivered in print (since he never published a full system). Philosophy of mind is not the only area that receives an incomplete treatment. If one studies sections of the *Critique* such as the second Antinomy, one will look in vain for a full rebuttal to the traditional general argument that is presented for the existence of simple beings. As long as one does not inflate one's commitment to these simples into claims that they are necessarily mental, or spiritual, or physical atoms, or grounds to which spatio-temporal phenomena can be reduced, one will find it very hard to see exactly what Kant himself has to say against them, other than that their existence is merely academic, and does not automatically affect nearly as many issues, theoretical or practical, as had been supposed before.

Such 'academic' points, prefigured, for example, already in the pre-critical passage quoted above concerning the fact that simplicity does not immediately prove immateriality,[34] constitute some of Kant's most valuable and under-appreciated gifts to the future. This is a legacy that is squandered by contemporary readers who themselves become dogmatic in their 'anti-dogmatism'[35] and assume Kant must have conclusively proven or even believed that no one could ever have any reasons for thinking that the self is, in some very bare sense, a substance or a simple being. Recognizing this legacy is consistent with allowing that Kant showed how the old proofs could be taken in many ways that do rest on demonstrable fallacies. We would be wrong, as he notes, to infer straightaway that mere apperception proves our permanent, or even extended existence, or that the unity of a thought entails by itself that the being having the thought could not later be divided.

In sum, the lesson I drew from a close study of the rationalist arguments in the lectures is that, despite the typical and overblown general claims that accompanied his discussion of them (Kant was forever saying his system solved practically all problems forever; yet people seem to have believed him only in areas such as psychology and theology where they already had their own deep preconceptions) in his later critical and published works, Kant did not accomplish a total or even explicit refutation of many of these arguments, but rather simply intensified his earlier insistence that they could not establish various specific kinds of simplicity and substantiality of 'human interest'. I did not go so far as to say that Kant actually meant to continue to endorse the old arguments for substantiality, simplicity, and unity; that would be dogmatic and not modest rationalism. I did emphasize, however, that his attitude towards these arguments as such was very unclear, and it took an especially long time for the problems with the argument to spontaneity to get sorted out. Above all, Kant's basic rationalist commitment to an attack on materialism was not only continued after the lectures but was even intensified in the critical period. Thus, if one were to define the main metaphysical battleground between modern rationalists and anti-rationalists as the issue of materialism vs. immaterialism—which certainly is not an unusual way of looking at it historically—then on my interpretation the most constant feature in Kant's work here is that he comes down clearly on the side of the immaterialists, and hence the rationalists, once these are distinguished from the spiritualists. What is new after the *Critique* is that Kant says not only, as in the passage cited from the lectures, that he has 'an' argument 'for' immaterialism; by the time of the *Metaphysical Foundation of Natural Science* [36] he is willing to fill out his system in such a way that there are conclusive considerations that, once they are added to the doctrine of the ideality of space and time, explicitly entail the ideality of the matter that fills space. Hence, immaterialism is not only an encouraged practically grounded position (like the other rationalist doctrines), or one for which there are some unchallenged theoretical grounds; it is a position that is considered evidently necessary, and as irresistible as basic doctrines about space and time, the denial of which Kant believes leads to contradiction.

In saying all this, I did not mean to endorse many of Kant's positions, and I hardly carried out an exhaustive evaluation of all their complex arguments. But I was very clear *not* to suggest that Kant was committing himself to the old *spiritualist* arguments of his successors; on the contrary, the whole point of his work in this area was to explore the possibility of a 'moderate' mere immaterialism that would be free of unwarranted supplements (see the Postscript below). This would leave him with narrow 'academic' results, matters of *Schulphilosophie*—but that is only fair for what are, after all, academic questions. In sum, although on my reading Kant is, to be sure, basically critical in the 1780s, in *some* ways he also looks more like the pre-critical lecturer than most contemporary readers would ever want to believe. But my interpretation has not gone unchallenged, so at this point I shift to a consideration of the extensive historical investigations recently completed by Klemme. I will concentrate not on Klemme's positive theses but rather on points where he takes himself to be departing from my interpretation, because these points express a perspective that is typical of many reactions that my work has received.

4. A Rejoinder to Common Criticisms

Unlike other critics, Klemme has exhaustively researched the development of Kant's study of mind—through the lectures and Reflections, as well as both editions of the *Critique*. None the less, at times his criticisms seem to overlook much of the nuanced and moderate rationalism in Kant that I had laboured to unearth. For example, from the beginning Klemme contends: 'At no point in his philosophical development did Kant regard rational psychology as a discipline that can dogmatically expand the knowledge we have already obtained about the nature of the soul through empirical psychology. For [*sic*!], its proper goal, the immortality of the human soul, can on no account be reached in this way.'[37] Later he asserts that my claim that Kant was a theoretical immaterialist would mean 'there would be no need anymore for the practical postulate of immortality'.[38] Such an approach misses the distinction that I had stressed in Kant between the claims of immaterialism and spiritualism (cf. the last passages from the lectures cited above), and it ignores the value of distinguishing the critiques of arguments for immortality from other philosophical arguments about the mind. Imagine someone similarly dismissing all contemporary metaphysics of mind simply because little was being done in it to prove our immortality!

Klemme's perspective on the pre-critical work is complicated by a controversial conception of one of the most difficult aspects of the first *Critique*. He concedes that even 'in the first edition of the *Critique* it is still allowed to say that the soul is a simple substance, without thereby falling prey to the concept of soul in rational psychology, but this is fundamentally excluded by the rules of language in the new determination of the relation of categories and forms of judgement in 1787'.[39] In other words, whereas supposedly it still was allowed, even in the original version of the *Critique*, to speak *meaningfully* in a general way, although perhaps without any theoretical *justification*, of non-spatio-temporally schematized possibilities such as 'simple substance', all such talk was supposedly eliminated by a new insight by Kant in the late 1780s, which legislated all such general claims into being either altogether meaningless or something that stands for a merely formal, syntactic category (i.e., the subject of a judgement). This is a not entirely uncommon interpretation, and there are some difficult Kantian passages that may encourage it, but there are also many texts (and the weight of common sense and charity) still pointing in another direction.[40] The interpretation has the terrible burden of foisting upon Kant a move towards a very extreme view that is intrinsically unattractive and quite unneeded, indeed antithetical to his own purposes. We know that Kant held that typical moral and religious assertions about some kind of non-spatio-temporal causation and substance are at least meaningful enough to discuss, for otherwise it would make no sense even to ask whether, for example, a superhuman power might arrange things so that our non-spatio-temporally characterized moral self can have a chance at the highest good it might deserve. Once again, the detailed evidence of the pre-critical lectures, especially now that it is clear that on so many points they overlap seamlessly with numerous later lectures in repeatedly going over such topics, reinforces the conclusion that Kant knew full well that it would always be possible for us at least to speak intelligibly about such matters as permanent souls even if the outlook is in principle bleak for our saying much that has a chance of being theoretically convincing about such things. And Klemme's interpretation is in more difficulty than most here, since it at least concedes that even Kant's original presentation of the *Critique* was not locked into a claim that the positions of traditional rationalism were wholly senseless (similarly, Kant's reaction to traditional theodicies was that they could be meaningfully distinguished and discussed even if it was hard to see how they might be theoretically assessed), as if the literal consideration of them was a passing fancy of pre-critical notes.

At times, however, Klemme resists ascribing some 'pre-critical' ideas even to the Kant of the 1770s, and he claims that the intuition of the self spoken of in that period is still 'by no means to be misunderstood as a medium for knowing ourselves in the strict sense of the word as souls, thus of being able to formulate synthetic a priori propositions about them'.[41] Here he seems to want to distinguish early claims about the intellectual intuition of the self as a moral being, as well as merely formal clarifications about 'intelligible' beings as such (who can reflect, be purely practical, etc.), from material claims about human selves, which have the specific characteristic of being 'souls' in the technical sense that they are not 'mere intelligences' but rather minds that are in some relation with sensibility. But as far as I can see, none of these distinctions excludes the fact that one and the same kind of being, namely a human being, could be both a soul and an intelligence, even if it is not a 'mere' intelligence. I take this to mean that the pre-critical arguments in the rational psychology of the lectures, which start from the general point that human subjects exist as intelligences and conclude that they are substantial, free, etc., do amount to synthetic a priori claims that could be true about beings like us who have the specific feature of being souls. The fact that Kant later definitely decided to reject inferring such claims (this is a major point of the Paralogisms) from our mere capacities as an intelligence is no sign that he did not endorse these kinds of arguments earlier.

Similarly, although it is certainly correct to say that, when Kant still speaks in the *Critique* of our necessarily 'regarding' ourselves as subject,[42] this *can* be understood 'purely functionally', it does not follow that we know Kant 'discovered' some magical doctrine that proves that the notion of subjectivity *cannot* have any implications for the nature of the subject that carries out various functions. The possibility of such implications can still be allowed, even if at the same time Kant can be praised for finally distinguishing, in his critical work, between inner sense and apperception, and for thereby indicating that so-called immediate intuitions of the self cannot be just *assumed* to have the Cartesian implications about our ultimate nature that had been accepted by many modern philosophers (including himself). Kant combined these critical insights with other doctrines that seem much less appealing but are none the less central to his final system and deserve some examination. Kant's relatively unstressed but constant thought about the *possibility* of noumenal assertions concerning souls should not be *totally* ignored, any more than one can ignore, even it seems ultimately unacceptable, his much more radical (but at least often discussed) transcendental idealist doctrine that the details of our ordinarily self-knowledge *necessarily* reveal *only* how we appear.

There is another aspect of Kant's transcendental idealism that I especially stressed in my account of the residual rationalism in Kant's philosophy of mind because it is a basic doctrine that bridges his pre-critical and critical periods. This is the doctrine of our immateriality. Interpreters such as Klemme[43] prefer to say that Kant's doctrine of the phenomenality of space, time, and matter implies only the *non-materiality* of all things in themselves, including our selves, but that this is not tantamount to asserting that the self is *immaterial*. Now it is certainly true (as I made a point of emphasizing) that many of Kant's statements about our immateriality have to be read in a restricted way. Sometimes he means only that the self does not immediately *appear* to itself as material, or only that as an item of ordinary *phenomenal* knowledge it does not fit in with our descriptions of material things; or only that in principle, given the limitations of *scientific* accounts from the specific properties of matter alone, no 'explanation' of the mind is to be expected from crude versions of materialism. These statements are limited in important ways, but they do not entail, or even encourage the thought, that Kant himself

fell short of also holding that the mind ultimately is not material in a basic metaphysical sense. Klemme seems to presume
at one point[44] that the argument I have in mind here is one
that connects the assertion of immateriality with simplicity—
although I stress that it is precisely one of Kant's virtues,
demonstrated throughout the pre-critical lectures, to see that
these two claims are not immediately connected.[45] Kant's
ultimate position rests rather on the general critical argument
noted earlier for the transcendental ideality of matter, an
argument that, if accepted, does show that the self, whatever
its ultimate constitution, definitely cannot be material. This
specific kind of argument is not one that Kant used in the
pre-critical lectures, but it is closely related to them and its
conclusion is entirely consistent with all his views in the
period after the *Inaugural Dissertation*.

It is an awkward and complicated fact that the conclusion
of Kant's argument for immaterialism does seem to amount
to an existential claim about the nature of things in themselves, but I see no way of getting around it. One can say that
such negative knowledge is not 'knowledge proper' and does
not tell us full out what the self is 'like', let alone that it must
have any of the spiritual properties that rationalists had
hoped to derive from it. But to say—as Kant (like any normal person) clearly thinks we can with certainty—that we
exist, in some unqualified and not merely phenomenal
sense,[46] *and* that in that sense we are not possibly material
beings (in any ordinary spatio-temporal sense), is, I believe, to
say precisely all that practically any metaphysician now would
ordinarily *mean* by the claim that we are immaterial beings in
a strictly philosophical sense. In this situation it seems to be
just wordplay to resist this conclusion by saying that, even if
it is conceded that we are *not material* beings, that does not
mean that we are *immaterial* beings. It is true, of course, that
when we say, for example, that a mathematical proof is not
green, that does not mean the proof (as opposed to its incidental expression) is something that is some other colour,
something we might call 'non-green'. Such a point is persuasive simply because the original thought of a proof as itself
literally green does not even make sense, and is a category
mistake, since proofs as such are the kinds of things that we

understand cannot be considered to be literally coloured. But we do at least understand the claim that the self exists and might be material, and many people are even strongly committed to it, and on these grounds we can say that the denial of that claim just is what it means to say the self really is immaterial, and not something beyond the whole category of materiality and its contrary. Kant's anti-materialism, even though it is from the beginning meant to fall far short of spiritualism, is still not a neutral or agnostic position; for him, it is an important and meaningful thesis: mere immaterialism, nothing more, nothing less.

The meaning of such statements does presuppose that Kant has some kind of notion of meaning for propositions and categories even when these are not tied to sensible experience. As has been noted, Klemme, like some other interpreters, rejects such a notion,[47] but it is hardly an unusual idea in Kant scholarship or one that is intrinsically unattractive. Kant's own pre-critical work gives many examples of a non-sensible use of the categories that involve purported real determinations, and are not merely an expression of 'functions of thinking'. Later Kant did not reject that work, or his practical propositions, as wholly unintelligible, but rather argued that they lack strict theoretical justification, or even a framework for such justification that human beings can foresee ever being able to use. Klemme is right to emphasize that it surely is a mistake to hypostatize a function of thinking into a determination of a real object, to assume, for example (as Kant himself did for a while) that the fact that we refer to ourselves via subject terms entails that we can exist only as subject. But such mistakes do not *mean* that the only true subjects are spatio-temporal objects, and that it never could be correct to conclude that we are immaterial things.

Moreover, it would be an astounding objection to traditional *rational* psychology to point out that such a characterization does not give us an *empirical specification* of the self—since the whole point of such psychology is to make *non*-empirical claims. It is true that, in the process of stressing his new critical direction, Kant does like to underline the empirical limitations of traditional psychology, as if that is all there is to say (A 349), but this is a rhetorical strategy from which

Kant eventually makes a clear retreat (in B). Unfortunately, the complexity of this strategy has misled many interpreters, including Klemme in his typical analysis of the A edition first paralogism about substance.

After citing Kant's claim that considering the self as a subject does not disclose that it must endure or be permanent, Klemme insists, as if it were obvious that this settles everything: 'But that is what the goal of the proof of rational psychology consists in.'[48] But why should a rationalist, of all people, have to assume that philosophical success rests entirely on such a goal, or, for that matter, on any empirical, temporal result? Klemme directly questions my claim that Kant's first-edition first-paralogism discussion 'presents no *direct argument against* our *mere substantiality*',[49] but instead of spelling out an argument in the paralogism itself (for such a 'direct' argument) Klemme helps himself to the heavy presumption that the category of substance *can* apply *only* to things that endure permanently.[50] This is not an 'argument' against the paralogism as stated, but is rather an external and dogmatic subreption, one of the very sort Kant had warned against in his *Dissertation*, and one that a rationalist would hardly need to accept. Even if one also accepts all of Kant's earlier discussion of substance in the *Critique*, all that immediately shows, at most, is that permanence is *one* way (a way needed to organize experience) of schematizing substance, not that it is the only way the term might apply; consider Kant's own talk about God, or the fact that the Second Analogy offers agency also as a sign of substantiality, and that the premisses of the paralogism, if granted, could be taken precisely as an expression of agency.

Klemme goes on to interpret the first paralogism (in A) as using for its minor premiss a purported *intuition* of the I as subject. He insists that there is no such intuition, or, more precisely and remarkably, that there is no *empirical* intuition of permanence—as if this were somehow what the rationalist must have been meaning to maintain.[51] Klemme thus locates the 'formal falsity' of the paralogism in a transition from a transcendental major premiss (the I, as subject, is thought as substance) to an 'empirical' minor premiss (the I is intuited empirically as a substance). Such a transition would be invalid, but note that this point can appear relevant only on the basis of a very unfair imputation of a (minor) premiss that is not at all the sort of consideration that a traditional rationalist need actually present. Moreover, the alleged minor premiss is by no means given in the direct language of the argument itself; the paralogism 'proof' does not actually make any reference to intuition. Furthermore, if such a premiss were given to the arguer, then at that point the conclusion of the argument that Klemme (though not a traditional rationalist) is interested in actually would follow, immediately and validly—for if I really do intuit that I am an empirical substance, then it is only logical for me to conclude that I am an empirical substance. Rather than revealing a relevant 'formal falsity', all the analysis has offered is a *material* challenge (of a most unusual sort, since there is no evidence that the claim being challenged is one that is being made, let alone invalidly inferred) to the truth of one of the premisses. This still leaves us, just as I contended, with 'no direct arguments *against* mere substantiality' (i.e., nothing that gives reasons for saying one is not a substance).[52]

The lesson I draw from all these complexities is that most interpreters continue to fail to note the full significance of the lecture materials and arguments of the pre-critical tradition—and to appreciate the meaning of Kant's own inability to counter these arguments effectively until he significantly reformulated his analysis in the second version of the *Critique*. More generally, I feel more strongly than ever that the arguments of Kant's *Critique* (and the true value of his critical turn) will never be understood properly until their exact relation to pre-critical materials is thoroughly examined. Unless interpreters properly appreciate the background of what Kant left unsaid in his later work, they will not be able to see how much of what was unsaid there—but still preserved in notes—frames what was actually written. Fortunately, it is now possible to hope not only that my original arguments will be re-examined, but also that the relevant and extensive lecture material (now that so much more of it has been made readily available) that they utililized will finally receive the serious attention that it deserves.[53]

Notes to Preface to the Second Edition

[1] Andrew Brook, *Kant and the Mind* (Cambridge, 1994); Quassim Cassam, *Self and World* (Oxford, 1997); Patricia Kitcher, *Kant's Transcendental Psychology* (New York, 1990); Heiner Klemme, *Kants Philosophie des Subjekts* (Hamburg, 1996); Rudolf Makkreel, *Imagination and Interpretation in Kant* (Chicago, 1990); Georg Mohr, *Das sinnliche Ich: Innerer Sinn und Bewusstsein bei Kant* (Würzburg, 1991); C. Thomas Powell, *Kant's Theory of Self-Consciousness* (Oxford, 1990); Alejandro Rosas, *Kants idealistische Reduktion*. *Das Mentale und das Materielle im transzendentalen Idealismus* (Würzburg, 1996); and Dieter Sturma, *Kant über Selbstbewusstsein*. *Zum Zusammenhang von Erkenntniskritik und Theorie des Selbstbewusstseins* (Hildesheim/Zurich/New York, 1985).

[2] See Henry E. Allison, *Kant's Transcendental Idealism: An Interpretation and Defense* (New Haven, 1983), *Kant's Theory of Freedom* (Cambridge, 1990), and *Idealism and Freedom: Essays on Kant's Theoretical and Practical Philosophy* (Cambridge, 1996); Richard Aquila, *Representational Mind: A Study in Kant's Theory of Knowledge* (Bloomington, 1983); Reinhard Brandt, 'Rousseau und Kants "Ich denke"', *Kant-Forschungen*, 5 (1994), 1–18; Wolfgang Carl, *Der schweigende Kant. Die Entwürfe zu einer Deduktion der Kategorien vor 1781* (Göttingen, 1989); Manfred Frank, 'Fragmente zu einer Geschichte der Selbstbewusstseinstheorien von Kant bis Sartre', in *Selbstbewusstseinstheorien von Fichte bis Sartre*, ed. by Manfred Frank (Frankfurt, 1991), pp. 415–599; Paul Guyer, *Kant and the Claims of Knowledge* (Cambridge, 1987), and *Kant and the Experience of Freedom* (Cambridge, 1993); Rolf-Peter Horstmann, 'Kants Paralogismen', *Kant-Studien*, 84 (1993), 408–25; Ralf Meerbote, 'Kant's Functionalism', in *Historical Foundations of Cognitive Science*, ed. by J. C. Smith (Dordrecht, 1989), pp. 161–87; Robert Pippin, 'Kant on the Spontaneity of Mind', *Canadian Journal of Philosophy*, 17 (1987), 449–75; Udo Thiel, 'Between Wolff and Kant: Merian's Theory of Apperception', *Journal of the History of Philosophy*, 34 (1996), 213–32.

[3] Günter Zöller, 'Main Developments in Scholarship in the *Critique of Pure Reason*', *Philosophy and Phenomenological Research*, 53 (1993), 445–66; Eric Watkins, 'Recent Developments in Kant Scholarship: Kant's Philosophy of Mind', *Eidos*, 12 (1995), 83–107.

[4] See, e.g., the collections: *Self and Nature in Kant's Philosophy*, ed. by Allen Wood (Ithaca, 1984); *Theorie der Subjektivität*, ed. by K. Cramer, H. Fulda, R.-P. Horstmann, and U. Pothast (Frankfurt, 1987); *New Essays on Kant*, ed. by B. den Ouden (New York, 1987); *Kant: Analysen-Probleme-Kritik*, vol. 3, ed. by Hariolf Oberer and Gerhard Seel (Würzburg, 1988); *Kant's Transcendental Deductions*, ed. by Eckart Förster (Stanford, 1989); *The Cambridge Companion to Kant*, ed. by Paul Guyer (Cambridge, 1992); *The Modern Subject: Conceptions of the Self in Classical German Philosophy*, ed. by Karl Ameriks and Dieter Sturma (Albany, 1995); *Figuring the Self: Subject, Absolute, and Others in Classical German Philosophy*, ed. by David Klemm and Günter Zöller (Albany, 1997); *Immanuel Kant: Kritik der reinen Vernunft*, ed. by Georg Mohr and Marcus Willaschek (Berlin, 1998); *Philosophie in synthetischer Absicht: Synthesis in Mind*, ed. by Marcelo Stamm (Stuttgart: Klett-Cotta, 1998).

[5] See, e.g., the introductions, articles, and bibliographies in the collections *Self-Knowledge*, ed. by Quassim Cassam (Oxford, 1994); and *Analytische Theorien des Selbstbewusstseins*, ed. by Manfred Frank (Frankfurt, 1994).

[6] See, e.g., discussions of Kant in volumes such as Paul De Man, *Aesthetic Ideology* (Minneapolis, 1996); Richard Eldridge, *On Moral Personhood: Philosophy, Literature, Criticism, and Self-Understanding* (Chicago, 1989); *Who Comes After the*

Subject?, ed. by Eduardo Cadava, Peter Conner, and Jean-Luc Nancy (London, 1991); and the collections, *The Reception of Kant's Critical Philosophy: Fichte, Schelling, and Hegel*, ed. by Sally Sedgwick (Cambridge, 2000); and *The Cambridge Companion to German Idealism*, ed. by Karl Ameriks (Cambridge, 2000).

⁷ On Chisholm and Prauss, see my 'Contemporary German Epistemology', *Inquiry*, 25 (1982), 125–38, and, on Prauss, see my review, *Review of Metaphysics*, 38 (1984), 136–9; on Frank, see my 'The Ineliminable Subject: From Kant to Frank', in *The Modern Subject*, pp. 217–30; on Guyer, see my review, *Philosophy and Phenomenological Research*, 55 (1995), 361–7; on Henrich and Guyer, see my 'Kant and Guyer on Apperception', *Archiv für Geschichte der Philosophie*, 65 (1983), 174–86; on Henrich and Sturma, see my 'Kant and the Self: A Retrospective', in *Figuring the Self*, pp. 55–72; on Kitcher and Powell, see my 'Understanding Apperception Today', in *Kant and Contemporary Epistemology*, ed. by P. Parrini (Dordrecht, 1994), pp. 331–47; on Powell, see my review, *International Studies in Philosophy*, 26 (1994), 143–4; on Makkreel, see my review, *Man and World*, 25 (1992), 227–34; on Pippin, see my review, *International Studies in Philosophy*, 18 (1986), 74–6; on Allison, see my reviews, *Topoi*, 3 (1984), 181–5; *Ethics*, 102 (1992), 655–7; *Philosophy and Phenomenological Research* 49 (1999), 825–8; and also my articles comparing his approach with Guyer and Wood, in 'Kantian Idealism Today', *History of Philosophy Quarterly*, 9 (1992), 329–42; and 'Kant and Hegel on Freedom: Two New Interpretations', *Inquiry*, 35 (1992), 219–32.

⁸ See especially David Carr, *The Paradox of Subjectivity* (New York, 1999); Klaus Düsing, *Selbstbewusstseinsmodelle* (Munich, 1997); S. L. Hurley, *Consciousness in Action* (Cambridge, Mass., 1998); Pierre Keller, *Kant and the Demands of Self-Consciousness* (Cambridge, 1998); and James Van Cleve, *Problems from Kant* (Oxford, 1999).

⁹ Because of what seems to have been a mix-up in the delivery of the proof corrections while I was travelling on a research trip in 1981, there were more than a few printing errors that were not caught in the first edition. An attempt has been made to correct these now while keeping the old text and pagination intact. The changes are minor, except for p. 59, line 7 from bottom, where two occurrences of 'immaterial' have been corrected to 'material'.

¹⁰ See my 'The First Edition Paralogisms of Pure Reason', in *Immanuel Kant: Kritik der reinen Vernunft*, pp. 369–88. Cf. Dieter Sturma, 'Die Parologismen der reinen Vernunft in der zweiten Auflage', in ibid., pp. 391–411; and Sturma, 'Self-Consciousness and the Philosophy of Mind', in *Proceedings of the Eighth International Kant Congress 1995*, ed. by H. Robinson (Milwaukee, 1995), vol. 1, pp. 661–74.

¹¹ *Kant and the Fate of Autonomy: Problems in the Appropriation of the Critical Philosophy* (Cambridge, 2000).

¹² The full (and quite appropriate) title of Klemme's book is: *Kants Philosophie des Subjekts: Systematische und entwicklungsgeschichtliche Untersuchungen zum Verhältnis von Selbstbewusstsein und Selbsterkenntnis*. It appears as vol. 7 in the series *Kant-Forschungen*, brought out by the Marburg Kant Archive. Citations to the book will use the abbreviation *Subjekt*.

¹³ For extensive historical and textual details, see the introductions to *Lectures on Metaphysics/Immanuel Kant*, ed. and tr. by Karl Ameriks and Steven Naragon (Cambridge, 1997), and to the new vol. 25 of *Kant's gesammelte Schriften* (Berlin, 1900–) = Section 4, *Vorlesungen*; Book 2, *Vorlesungen über Anthropologie* (Berlin, 1997), ed. by Reinhard Brandt und Werner Stark, First Half (pp. cli + 728), Second Half (pp. 729–1691); as well as my review in *Journal of the History of Philosophy* 37 (1999) 368–70. The most important corrections to the Academy edition concern a mistake in the order of the pages of the Metaphysik

Mrongovius. See Miroslaw Zelazny and Werner Stark, 'Zu Krystof Celestyn Mrongovius und seinen Kollegheften nach Kants Vorlesungen', *Kant-Forschungen*, 1 (1987), 279–97. See also Steve Naragon, 'Die Metaphysikvorlesungen Kants in der Akademie-Ausgabe', in *Kants Gesammelte Schriften (Akademie-Ausgabe)—Eine Kritische Bestandsaufnahme* (forthcoming); the introduction by Monique Castillo to the French edition of the Pölitz metaphysics lectures, in *Immanuel Kant: Leçons de métaphysique*, tr. by Monique Castillo (Paris, 1993); the introduction by J. Michael Young to *Lectures on Logic/Immanuel Kant*, ed. and tr. by J. Michael Young (Cambridge, 1992); the introduction by Allen Wood to Kant's *Lectures on Philosophical Theology*, tr. by Allen Wood and Gertrude Clark (Ithaca, 1978); the introduction by J. B. Schneewind to *Lectures on Ethics/Immanuel Kant*, tr. by Peter Heath (Cambridge, 1997); and Reinhard Brandt, *Kritischer Kommentar zu Kants Anthropologie in pragmatischer Hinsicht* (Hamburg, 1998).

[14] Pölitz's edition was published originally in 1821, and was mixed with materials from other times. Cf. Klemme, *Subjekt*, p. 102, and the Introduction to the English translation of the lectures.

[15] Not long after writing *Kant's Theory of Mind*, I had the fortunate opportunity to begin translating (with Steve Naragon), almost in their entirety, these extensive neglected materials which I had cited only in numerous short excerpts in my book. The translation project ended up being much more complicated than expected because of many problems with the Academy version of the lecture notes, especially in the new material of vol. 29 that came out only in 1983. Here we had to rely heavily on help from the Marburg Kant Archive. See above, n. 13.

[16] This approach, especially at that time, dominated not only interpretations by independently well-known philosophers such as Bennett and Strawson, who obviously had traditional empiricist concerns, but also very influential Kant scholars such as Lewis White Beck and Robert Paul Wolff. Wilfrid Sellars, as an interpreter, was an unusual exception; while his own philosophical views were empiricist, he kept them clearly distinct from his exceptionally balanced and original Kant interpretations.

[17] Among the exceptions is Gary Hatfield, 'Empirical, Rational, and Transcendental Psychology: Psychology as Science and as Philosophy', in *The Cambridge Companion to Kant*, pp. 200–27; cf. Vladimir Satura, *Kants Erkenntnispsychologie in den Nachschriften seiner Vorlesungen über empirische Psychologie* (Bonn, 1971).

[18] See Nagel's criticisms in 'Universality and the Reflective Self', in *The Sources of Normativity*, ed. by Christine Korsgaard et al. (Cambridge, 1996), pp. 200–9, and cf. Gerald Cohen, 'Reason, Humanity, and the Moral Law', in ibid., pp. 167–88; and the concluding chapters of J. B. Schneewind, *The Invention of Autonomy* (Cambridge, 1997).

[19] See Josef Schmucker, *Die Ursprünge der Ethik Kants in seinen vorkritischen Schriften und Reflexionen* (Meisenheim, 1961), and, for the most extensive selection (with a very helpful introduction and bibliography) of his works in English, Dieter Henrich, *The Unity of Reason: Essays on Kant's Philosophy*, ed. by Richard Velkley (Cambridge, Mass., 1994).

[20] See, e.g., innovative recent work by interpreters such as Allen Wood, 'Kant's Historical Materialism', in *Autonomy and Community*, ed. by Jane Kneller and Sidney Axinn (Albany, 1998), pp. 15–37; Susan Meld Shell, *The Embodiment of Reason* (Chicago, 1996); and the contributors to the volume *Feminist Interpretations of Immanuel Kant*, ed. by Robin May Schott (University Park, Pa., 1997). The 'CI procedure' comes from the highly influential work of John Rawls. See his 'Themes in Kant's Moral Philosophy', in *Kant's Transcendental*

Deductions, ed. by Eckart Förster (Stanford, 1989), pp. 81–113, and 'Kantian Constructivism in Moral Theory', *Journal of Philosophy*, 77 (1980), 515–72.

²¹ See, e.g., recent work by Harry Frankfurt, *The Importance of What We Care About* (Cambridge, 1988); Peter van Inwagen, *Metaphysics* (Boulder, 1993); and R. Jay Wallace, *Responsibility and the Moral Sentiments* (Cambridge, Mass., 1996).

²² See especially work by Thomas Nagel, Colin McGinn, and Manfred Frank. The topic of the 'hard problem' of consciousness has been stressed by David Chalmers, *The Conscious Mind* (Oxford, 1996). For an overview, see Joseph Levine, 'Recent Work on Consciousness', *American Philosophical Quarterly*, 34 (1997), 387–404.

²³ See again Henrich, *The Unity of Reason*, and, for some criticisms, see my 'Kant and the Self: A Retrospective'. On the importance of the pre-critical account of consciousness, cf. Carl, *Der schweigende Kant*.

²⁴ The parallels (concerning theoretical and practical spontaneity) in the lectures were emphasized first in my 'Kant on Spontaneity: Some New Data', in *Proceedings of the VII International Kant-Kongress 1990* (Berlin, 1991), pp. 436–46.

²⁵ *AA*, vol. 28, p. 265. For Kant's lectures here, I use my own translation and the German pagination, which is provided with the English text (see above, n. 13), and for Kant's works, the usual reference to the Academy edition (= *AA*) except, as is customary, for the A and B editions of the *Critique of Pure Reason*. In these excerpts I have added my own emphases. Passages with similar conclusions, but from the different perspective of empirical psychology, can be found in *AA*, vol. 28, pp. 224–6, and now also in the anthropology lectures; cf. Klemme, *Subjekt*, pp. 76–7 f. The arguments of the empirical and rational psychology are overlapping, since they each rest on the basic proposition, 'I think', but the empirical psychology stresses the intuitive nature of the evidence for the proposition, and the rational psychology investigates the proposition explicitly in terms of its relation to various 'transcendental' predicates. The empirical psychology thus focuses on starting from a particular self, whereas rational psychology focuses on claims about subjects in general. Cf. Klemme, *Subjekt*, p. 114.

²⁶ *AA*, vol. 28, pp. 266–9.

²⁷ Ibid., pp. 272–3.

²⁸ Ibid., p. 277.

²⁹ Klemme (*Subjekt*, p. 303, n. 69) suggests that I am saying that the paralogism is about being a person over time as opposed to being about an intelligence. In fact, all I say (see below, p. 129) is that, although sometimes Kant expresses the topic as having to do with our being an intelligence, it needs to be kept in mind that this capacity, unlike traditional discussions of 'personal identity', does not immediately involve a reference to temporality. A being can be an intelligence already in virtue of a capacity for reflection that it has independently of how this is extended over time.

³⁰ In his analysis of these passages, Klemme finds the arguments 'irritating' (*Subjekt*, p. 82).

³¹ A 546/B 574; cf. *Foundations of the Metaphysics of Morals*, *AA*, vol. 4, p. 452. Klemme suggests that I use the passage of the *Critique* as a 'theoretical proof for the freedom of the soul' (*Subjekt*, p. 124, n. 163; cf. p. 125, n. 165), but in fact my discussion (see below, pp. 190–1 f.) uses that passage simply as a reminder of Kant's ongoing rationalist concerns, and my argument rather goes on expressly to focus on developments after the first edition of the *Critique*, at the time of the *Foundations*, when a 'theoretical proof' from apperception is directly considered. The passage in the *Critique* is on all accounts perplexing (my hypothesis is that Kant really means to speak about how we regard the self, not how

we demonstrably know it); Klemme says the passage is only about the self as 'intelligence' and not as 'soul', but this alone is not decisive because the dogmatic pre-critical passages had also expressed their claims in terms of the self as 'intelligence'. At another point, Klemme imputes to me the idea that in the first paralogism of the A edition *Critique* Kant is making a 'cognitive judgment in the sense of rational psychology' (*Subjekt*, p. 274, n. 12)—but in fact I do not say that Kant is there asserting that he knows we are substances (see below, p. 67). Rather, I just point out that he says we can 'allow the sentence the soul is a substance' (A 356), and the mere fact that he points out that such a sentence expresses 'a pure category', and not an empirically determined concept, does not mean that the sentence must be taken to have a merely logical, in the sense of syntactical, understanding of the subject. On the contrary, the paralogism makes use of an existential assertion about the I, that as a being it is an 'absolute' subject. Until Kant clarifies explicitly, as he does in his reformulation in the B edition, that this does not amount to a categorical claim about a being, but only a claim about how the self is merely thought in a certain way, there is no ground given for denying the 'realistic' construal of the meaning of the proposition ('the soul is a substance') that Kant says we can 'allow'. For more on the interpretation of the first paralogism, see also the references in n. 10 above, and the discussion in Section 4 below.

[32] Klemme focuses instead on the idea that at this time Kant had not developed the categories of modality, and that freedom could be displaced anyway since it is not a category (*Subjekt*, pp. 112–13). This interpretation, among other things, misses the point that freedom, like agency, could still be discussed appropriately under the category of causality (as it is in the Antinomies), whether or not a discussion of modality was added.

[33] See below, Ch. VI.

[34] *AA*, vol. 28, p. 272. See at n. 27 above.

[35] See, e.g., 'it is settled from the start that a categorial inference of reason, in which the major premise of the inference makes a transcendental use of the categories, must be either analytic or meaningless' (Klemme, *Subjekt*, p. 308).

[36] *AA*, vol. 4, pp. 505–10.

[37] Klemme, *Subjekt*, p. 8.

[38] Ibid., p. 329.

[39] Ibid., p. 10.

[40] Here interpreters may have misread the implications of what is admittedly a very significant fact, namely, that Kant went out of his way at the time of the B edition to show that our justified theoretical knowledge requires not just any sort of representations (e.g., a bare notion of ourselves as 'intelligible', spontaneous, etc.) but rather a combination of inner sense and outer sense, and thus concrete spatial notions, in order to warrant specific determinate claims (see below, p. 216, and the many references in the Index to the role of spatiality in Kant's theory of self-knowledge). This is an important fact, but it can encourage misinterpretations by readers misled by Kant's tendency to say something is wholly 'without meaning', or 'significance', when what he means is merely that it does not provide knowledge. Similarly, Kant sometimes says a claim is a matter of 'faith' rather than knowledge when he means only what we would express by saying that it does not rest on sheerly theoretical arguments. Kant often uses words in a way that corresponds to casual and colloquial usage rather than to doctrines of meaning that have the sophistication of current theories, where many different senses of meaning have been distinguished. Sometimes, though, he does explicitly correct himself—see, e.g., A 247/B 304 (and cf. A 286/B 342), where, as Kemp Smith notes, Kant made a note to him-

self that 'no employment at all' should be filled out as 'for the knowing of any-thing'.

[41] Klemme, *Subjekt*, p. 125.

[42] Cf. A 349, and Klemme, *Subjekt*, p. 135. It was for this very reason that I introduced and repeatedly emphasized distinctions between many senses here for Kant's use of terms such as substance: an appearance sense, a phenomenal sense, a noumenal sense, a regulative or scientific sense (see below, pp. 33–4).

[43] Klemme, *Subjekt*, p. 21, n. 40; cf. p. 328. See also the Postscript below.

[44] Klemme, *Subjekt*, p. 328.

[45] See below, Ch. II, p. 50. Kant had long been concerned with the possi-bility of simple but material beings, i.e., a 'physical monadology'.

[46] Klemme deflates B 429, where Kant speaks of the 'Wesen selbst', or 'being itself', that we are given in thought. He questions my reading (*Subjekt*, p. 383, n. 18) of it as referring to an 'underlying reality' (see below, p. 72) that we are acquainted with even if we do not know its determinations. I do not follow this common criticism, since, whatever abstractions Kant wants to warn us about, it is hard to imagine that he (or any rational person) is denying (rather than precisely emphasizing) that we are certainly acquainted with the fact of our own existence, however that is to be understood. Klemme concludes with a note from the 'Preisschrift', where, when Kant talks about a subject 'in itself', he notes contradictions in claims about 'knowing oneself as one is and not as one appears [as temporal]' (*AA*, vol. 20, pp. 271, 338). But the contradiction Kant refers to is not in the mere notion of our existence or even that of an underlying self but rather in equating the determination of that self with how one appears in time.

[47] Klemme, *Subjekt*, p. 268.

[48] Ibid., p. 312.

[49] Ibid., p. 314, n. 95; the quotation is from my original text (see below, p. 198), but I have added emphases here.

[50] Klemme, *Subjekt*, p. 324.

[51] Ibid., p. 314: 'Nun wird zwar in der Tat in der Minor des Schlusses mit dem Ich-Subjekt ein absolutes Subjekt eingeführt, von dem behauptet wird, dass wir von ihm eine Anschauung hätten.' But in fact the minor claims ('behauptet') nothing about intuition but says simply: 'I, as thinking being, am the *absolute subject* of my possible judgments, and this representation of myself cannot be employed as predicate of any other thing' (A 348).

[52] Precisely because of the obvious oddity of this situation, one can under-stand why in the second edition Kant rewrote his whole treatment of the first paralogism; see below, p. 70. The problem noted in the B argument has to do with a rationalist argument form involving a minor premiss that is faulted pre-cisely for *not* making use of *any* intuition (rather than for making an intuitive claim whose truth is being challenged).

[53] For reaction to work on these topics over the years I am especially indebted to Eric Watkins, Steven Naragon, and Manfred Kuehn. For reactions to material in the original version of parts of this Preface, I am indebted to the participants at a conference in Naucelle (France) in 1998, and especially to its organizer, Alfred Denker, and the hospitality of his family. I thank Thomas Rockmore for his work on editing the volume that grew out of the conference; see my paper in *Kant's Pre-Critical Philosophy* (forthcoming). Thanks also to Georg Mohr, Marcus Willaschek, and others at the Münster conference on the *Critique*, and to Reinhard Brandt and Werner Stark and others at the Marburg confer-ence on the Academy edition.

Acknowledgements

Work on this book was made possible by grants from the Alexander von Humboldt Foundation, West Germany, the American Council of Learned Societies, and the University of Notre Dame. The first draft of the work was completed during a sabbatical leave spent in Cologne with the very helpful cooperation of Prof. Gerold Prauss. Special thanks are also in order to C. S. Evans, Richard Foley, Gary Gutting, Ed Kenar, Michael Loux, S. C. Patten, Robert Pippin, W. D. Solomon, R. C. S. Walker, and Michael Washburn. I am grateful to the editor of the *Journal of the History of Philosophy* for permission to reprint material in Chapter VI that appeared in an earlier version in that journal, vol. 19 (1981). The editors of *Idealistic Studies* have kindly allowed me to use material from my 'Chisholm's Paralogisms' (vol. 11 (1981), pp. 100-108), and the publishers of *Akten des 5. Internationalen Kant-Kongresses: Mainz 4.-8. April 1981*, edited by Gerhard Funke, in collaboration with Manfred Kleinschnieder, Rudolf Malter, and Gisela Müller, have kindly allowed me to use material from my 'Kant's First Paralogism' (vol. 1, pp. 485-492, Bouvier Verlag Herbert Grundmann, Bonn 1981).

For the second edition I thank Peter Momtchiloff for many helpful suggestions on behalf of Oxford University Press and I thank Patrick Frierson for his assistance at Notre Dame. Permission to reprint materials from the following is also gratefully acknowledged: 'Kant and Mind: Mere Immaterialism', *Proceedings of the Eighth International Kant Congress 1995*, ed. H. Robinson (Milwaukee: Marquette University Press, 1995), vol. 1, pp. 675-90.

The project of developing this second edition received special stimulation and encouragement from Dieter Sturma,

xxxviii   *Acknowledgements*

Manfred Frank, and Eric Watkins. I reiterate my thanks to those acknowledged in the first edition, and for the new Preface and Postscript I have added specific acknowledgements in the notes. I am very indebted to the many Kantians—and friends, colleagues, and students of all persuasions—with whom I have discussed these issues, especially since the international meetings of 1981 and 1990, where there was a first opportunity to express my basic views. Through all this time, as before, I have been very fortunate to enjoy the support of 'all in the family', and especially my wife Geraldine, and, since 1974 and 1978, our children Michael and Kevin. My work on this edition was completed on what would have been the eighty-fifth birthday of my mother; this volume is dedicated to her memory and, with gratitude, to my father for all.

Contents

I. Introduction   1

    1. Prefatory Remarks   1

    2. Major Problems in Approaching Kant's Theory
       of Mind   5

    3. The Major Stages in Kant's Theory   12

    4. Evaluation of the Major Claims of Kant's Theory   17

       Notes to Chapter I   23

II. Immateriality

    1. Historical Overview   27

    2. Kant's Lectures   32

    3. Appearance Immaterialism and Scientific
       Immaterialism   37

    4. Phenomenal Immaterialism and Noumenal
       Immaterialism   42

    5. The Structure of the Second Paralogism   47

    6. Other Evidence Against the Soul's Simplicity   52

    7. The Fallacy in the Unity Argument   55

    8. The First Paralogism   64

    9. Final Evaluation   73

       Notes to Chapter II   76

III. Interaction   84

  A. 1. Interaction in General: an Historical Overview   85

      2. Evaluation   87

      3. Mind-Body Interaction   89

      4. Evaluation   91

  B. 5. Embodiment: an Historical Overview   95

      6. Embodiment in Life   99

  C. 7. The Problem of the External World:
        an Historical Overview   108

      8. The First Edition Fourth Paralogism   111

      9. The Second Edition Fourth Paralogism   115

10. Evaluation 120
Notes to Chapter III 123

IV. Identity 128

A. 1. Personality: an Historical Overview 129
2. The Third Paralogism 130
3. Rationalist Interpretations 137
4. Empiricist Interpretations 143
B. 5. Contemporary Views on Person Identity
and their Historical Background 148
6. The Idea of Survivalism 152
7. Evaluation: Kant and Survivalism 156
8. The Non-Criterial View of Personal Identity 164
9. Final Evaluation 167
Notes to Chapter IV 171

V. Immortality 177

1. Historical Review 177
2. Immortality in the *Critique* 182
Notes to Chapter V 187

VI. Independence 189

1. Introduction 189
2. Historical Review 193
3. The Deduction of the *Foundations* 203
4. The Rejection of a Deduction of Freedom 209
5. How the Doctrine of the Second *Critique*
Developed 211
6. Contrary Interpretations 220
7. Conclusion 226
Notes to Chapter VI 227

VII. Ideality 234

A. 1. Introduction: Historical Review of Kant on
Rational Psychology 234
2. Introduction: the Critical Breakthrough 239
B. 3. Three Theories of Inner Sense 241
4. The Reflection Theory and the Independent
Stream Theory 243

		5. The Act Theory	250
		6. Affection	252
C.	7.	Interpretations of Transcendental Idealism: the Passivity Argument	255
		8. The Time Argument	260
		9. The Essence Theory	267
		10. The Relational Argument and the Flux Argument	272
		11. The Species Theory Supported	277
D.	12.	Radical Objections to our Transcendental Ideality	280
		13. Conclusion	290
		Notes to Chapter VII	294

Postscript: Kant and Mind: Mere Immaterialism   303

Bibliography   323

Index   343

Chapter I

Introduction

1. Prefatory Remarks

Until recently Kant's philosophy of mind received little attention. This is remarkable for a number of reasons. The nature of the mind obviously should be of central importance in an idealistic philosophy such as Kant's. Furthermore, Kant's major treatment of the topic, his chapter on the paralogisms in the *Critique of Pure Reason*,[1] is generally admired by contemporary philosophers and is one of the least challenged sections of the *Critique*. None the less, the relative lack of studies of Kant's treatment of the mind is also understandable. The general place of the mind in Kant's idealism is notoriously difficult to determine, and the Paralogisms has attracted support largely because of its popular critical tone, not because philosophers have been able to extract from it a clear theory of mind. On the whole, the chapter has generated the impression that Kant was uncommitted or had little to say directly concerning the classical problems of mind. Interpreters often have been taken in by the superficial structure of the chapter, the appearance of Kant simply dismissing a string of outdated Cartesian views.

In the late 1960s this pattern began to change when a number of major philosophers (e.g., Wilfrid Sellars, Peter Strawson, Jonathan Bennett, and Roderick Chisholm) began to make an effort to provide a closer analysis of Kant's discussion with an eye to bringing out its contemporary relevance. There also have been increasingly sophisticated historical studies of Kant's views here, for example Alfons Kalter's *Kants vierter Paralogismus: eine entwicklungsgeschichtliche Untersuchung zum Paralogismen-Kapitel der ersten Ausgabe der Kritik der reinen Vernunft*. Important as these interpretations were, they did not provide a detailed overview and evaluation of Kant's entire doctrine of mind. Moreover, although recent analyses of the text have become more fine-grained, they have not converged. A broad consensus may still hold to the effect that the Paralogisms provides an antidote to naïve Cartesianism, but beyond that there is surprisingly little agreement on the reconstruction of what Kant literally argued, let alone the evaluation of what he ultimately meant. The following chapters are meant to provide a remedy for this situation, and they aim not only to adjudicate between the different readings that have been offered of the Paralogisms, but also to demonstrate how even the general understanding of it as anti-Cartesian is often misleading.[2]

The guiding motivations of this study can be introduced by means of two recent remarks by Strawson. The first is that, 'to follow the exact course of Kant's thinking in the Paralogisms is surely a task equalled in difficulty only by that of following the exact course of his thinking in the Transcendental Deduction'.[3] I take it that in addition to the parallel in the level of difficulty of these two sections of the *Critique*, there is also some similarity in their structure and importance and even an interdependence in their arguments (see below, Ch. VII.8). A fully adequate study of the Paralogisms surely must be rooted in an understanding of the *Critique* as a whole, and the latter requires at its centre an interpretation of the transcendental deduction of the categories. I have elsewhere put forth a sketch of my interpretation of that deduction.[4] This interpretation will be alluded to at various points in the following analysis of the Paralogisms and obviously colours its nature, but on the whole I have tried to keep to a minimum discussions that go beyond a direct focus on the problems of mind. In particular, the goal has been not to elucidate all aspects of the self as a knowing subject, but rather primarily to clarify Kant's views on the traditional questions of its nature as a known object.

To explain that there should also be something in the way of a balance to this strategy of maintaining a focus on a set of specific arguments, I turn to the second guiding remark from Strawson. In a recent review of Bennett, Strawson warned that we ought not to keep 'turned away from the darker, the more mysterious side of the *Critique*. Kant was not just a good phenomenalist unfortunately liable to fits of inexplicable raving about the thing in itself. We must take the man whole and shan't fully appreciate the best in him unless we see it steadily in the context of the worst.'[5] The main feature of this comment that is relevant here is the emphasis on the need to see Kant 'whole' and in the light of his own peculiar metaphysical commitments. The comment can be understood as a corrective to analytic interpretations such as Bennett's, in so far as such interpretations tend to look so narrowly at the contemporary viability of specific assertions in the *Critique* that they ignore the full original meaning and historical context of Kant's discussion.

The moral of these remarks is that some way should be found of maintaining a focus on Kant's arguments about the nature of the mind without treating the pages of the Paralogisms on the level of a recent journal article. Above all, the more obscure passages of the *Critique* (which are concentrated in the discussion of mind) must receive attention, and Kant's allegiance to abstract and unfamiliar doctrines, such as the transcendental ideality of the self, should be recognized and patiently explained. For this reason, and to compensate for omissions in this regard to this day, I will devote much of this study to the exposition of Kant's early views and their development, especially as revealed in his recently edited lectures.[6] All of Kant's positions in the Paralogisms become more comprehensible when one is familiar with the extensive and surprisingly neglected discussions outside the *Critique*. In fact, I shall go so far as to argue that only in the light of these discussions are his positions here truly comprehensible.

In referring to these discussions, I will treat Kant's views on the mind as developing through four periods, which will be characterized as empiricist (roughly to 1755), rationalist (to 1763), sceptical (to 1768), and critical (this last period will be divided into a number of important subperiods). This periodization and the terms of characterization are meant primarily as heuristic tools. The claim is not that at any time Kant was, e.g., a strict empiricist, and then underwent a radical conversion to another *Weltanschauung*. The guiding idea is merely that Kant's remarks on the mind need not be treated in isolation, one publication at a time, for there are obvious continuities that reflect a general attitude which can be described as, e.g., more empiricist or critical than his views at other times. This attention to the genesis of Kant's views, and as a consequence to Kant's special indebtedness to the metaphysical orientation of his time, will be matched by a substantive claim. I argue that the theory of mind in the *Critique* is much more traditional and rationalistic than it at first appears, but that it is also more defensible than is generally recognized. To support this claim, due attention will be given to a number of recent analyses that severely criticize Kant or imply they have an evidently superior position on problems of mind.

In sum, I intend both to give a closer reading of the Paralogisms itself and to put it more in the context of Kant's metaphysical system and historical development than has been done before. This all will be done not merely for exegetical purposes but also to allow a fair critical evaluation of Kant's work, especially in the light of contemporary philosophical options. The comprehensive nature of such a study and the peculiar difficulties of its topic place considerable demands upon the reader. I have attempted to keep the analyses as concise as possible and to introduce no more Kantian and other technical terminology than necessary. None the less, I suspect that since even philosophers quite familiar with Kant will find many new or forgotten passages treated here, it may become difficult to sift the main points out from all of the detail. This difficulty is compounded by the fact that the Paralogisms does not lend itself well to a straightforward line-by-line commentary. One reason for this is that two versions of the text exist, since in the second edition of the *Critique* Kant considerably revised the Paralogisms and various sections closely related to it. Another reason is that the chapter has a position quite late in the *Critique* and presupposes an understanding of various doctrines expounded earlier. In order to alleviate this problem and to meet the goal of presenting a thorough but surveyable analysis of a set of very closely related issues, I have reorganized Kant's discussions as much as possible along thematic lines. In addition, since the systematic nature of Kant's philosophy requires that each part of it be understood in relation to many others, a large number of cross-references have been provided. As a further aid to the reader, the remainder of this Introduction will be devoted to (a) an elementary overview of major problems in Kant's theory of mind, (b) a brief review of the major stages in Kant's theory, and (c) a preview of our major findings about the theory.

2. Major Problems in Approaching Kant's Theory of Mind

The importance of the theory of mind for Kant's philosophy in general can be seen easily enough by considering its obvious relevance to the two main doctrines of that philosophy, namely the transcendental deduction and transcendental idealism. The transcendental deduction implies that we can prove certain *a priori* principles that structure all our experience. The doctrine of transcendental idealism implies that in some sense these principles, and so all our objective knowledge, have validity only for us. What I will call the Copernican image of Kant's philosophy adds to these doctrines by suggesting that the reason we can be certain of such principles is that we have legislated them ourselves, and it is because we have legislated them ourselves that we ought not expect them to apply to things in themselves.

Given these formulations, it is striking that Kant's main doctrines do not manifestly entail the central image of his philosophy. On the other hand, without something like that image, the meaning and justification of the doctrines remain mysterious. It is at this point that the concept of mind comes to play a key role. For example, there are those who hold that the obvious way to fill out the doctrines is to say that Kant meant to give a privilege to the study of our own mental operations. Yet if this privilege is exploited in a natural way, the Kantian doctrines are given content only at the cost of absurdity, and there is even a direct conflict with Kant's major treatment of the mind, the Paralogisms. That is, if we say the way to determine *a priori* principles is to see how one's mind works, then we would seem to be turning the transcendental deduction into an instance of psychologism. And if we read transcendental idealism as a thesis about being able to know only the workings of one's

mind, then we would seem to be left with not a transcendental but an empiricist and viciously relativistic doctrine.
Furthermore, all this would seem to go directly against the
point of the Paralogisms, which ostensibly is to remind us
that on Kant's view we cannot treat the mind as a privileged
object for philosophical scrutiny.

These considerations naturally lead us back to trying to
flesh out Kant's philosophy in some other way which would
not put so much emphasis on the mind as it is ordinarily
understood. One way this can be done is to take the project
of the transcendental deduction to be merely a Strawsonian
search for a minimal objective framework in our experience.[7]
Those who pursue this project prefer to discount transcendental idealism, for they see no good reason to suspect that
this framework isn't the framework of reality *simpliciter*.
Given this attenuation, the question arises of whether such
a project still has a significant relation to Kant's philosophy
and the emphasis on the mind suggested by its image. In so
far as such a relation can be found, it tends to be expressed
in the following way. We are reminded that Kant was an
opponent of Hume and scepticism, and that the natural way
to meet such opponents is on their own ground, their profes-
sion to be sure of nothing more than the ideas within their
mind. The project of the transcendental deduction then can
be tied to Kant and the mind by holding that the way to
establish the minimal principles of experience is to show that
they are necessary even if one is merely to be able to say
that one is sure one does have ideas within one's mind.

Although this approach has been very popular, it can no
longer be said to be intrinsically promising, and in any case
(for reasons reviewed in the material cited above in note 4)
its connection with Kant's own procedure in the *Critique* is
quite questionable. Because of these difficulties, we are led
to a third strategy for bringing together Kant's doctrines and
the concept of mind, namely to reverse Strawson's evaluation
of the two doctrines but to continue, like Strawson, to read
references to the mind in a non-psychologistic way. Such
a strategy has been pursued most recently by Ralph Walker,
who stresses difficulties in Strawson's conception of the
transcendental deduction while indicating support for a kind

of transcendental idealism.[8] This approach is surely appealing, for it should not be surprising that it is unlikely one will find *a priori* principles demonstrable from a basis that even a sceptic must concede, although there may be some significant principles which are derivable from a richer basis and which are such that we would be unjustified in assuming they have an absolute validity. Put another way, transcendental idealism can be expressed as not so much a metaphysical extravagance as rather a principle of modesty, as a reminder that things in their intrinsic character need not be the way that our specific modes of knowing must take them to be. Indeed, it seems only proper to distinguish in meaning between the way things are determinable by us and the way things are *simpliciter*, and to mark at least this difference I shall henceforth speak non-problematically of 'phenomena' and 'noumena' (or 'things in themselves').

Even if this much is accepted, there remains a need to explain how this third strategy ties in more specifically with Kant and the mentalistic image of his philosophy. Walker's tactic is to play up the notion of self-legislation while divorcing this from Kant's full understanding of transcendental idealism. That is, he rejects Kant's own claim that things not only could be other than as we know, but really must be, because in themselves things cannot be spatio-temporal. Walker replaces this claim with the mere idea that all our knowledge rests on projections 'we' have introduced, in that they are underdetermined by any given past experience or preformulated principles about things in themselves. Walker prefers this way of fleshing out the notion of self-legislation, for he thinks that taking Kant's own idealism literally leads only to an absurd and inconsistent understanding of mind. That is, since the mind has temporality, it would follow that it too would have to be only ideal, and this supposedly would conflict with not only good sense but also the central image of our knowing as being due, in an ascertainable way, to the constructions of the mind. At this point, however, the third approach appears to be committing itself and Kant to a privileged kind of knowledge of the self, and thus to an even clearer conflict with the project of the Paralogisms to restrict claims to know the mind in itself.

These difficulties lead us to seek a fourth approach, if we are to understand Kant's theory on his own terms. This approach would emphasize the full meaning of the doctrine of transcendental idealism, and yet it would refer to the mind not merely in terms of the weak notion of self-legislation that Walker employs, but rather in some other way that is closer to the spirit of Kant's philosophy and still within the restrictions that are stressed by the Paralogisms. This is to be done by arguing that, although the restraints of the Paralogisms are important, they may be meant primarily to restrict only fairly determinate (i.e., positive and specific) claims about noumenal individuals. Thus it still may be possible to allow some knowledge about mind, simply in the sense of truths that apply to one's intrinsic individual being, as long as this involves merely such indeterminate claims as that being is non-spatio-temporal. Similarly, it may be possible to allow some quite determinate knowledge about mind in another sense, as long as this involves merely the transcendental structures of our experience, for this need not (*contra* Walker) amount to illicit knowledge of an individual self in itself.

I believe this approach involves the most appropriate Kantian strategy for supplementing Kant's doctrines by providing them with some kind of mentalistic surroundings and yet not implying clear absurdities or conflicts with the Paralogisms. The strategy involves only a very modest reference to the mind and eschews any literal use of the Copernican image. None the less, it retains a kind of mentalistic character in committing Kant to a claim that we should not say that knowledge or reality in itself — including one's self — is to be understood materialistically. It is admittedly not so clear how this modest mentalism can help positively in the task of making Kant's own transcendental deduction very convincing (and it is not so clear how anything can do this), but I believe it at least helps us to avoid some tempting but inappropriate ways to construe the deduction (e.g. the first and second approaches). Most important, however, is the fact that this approach (unlike the third) appears to be forced on us if we want to be true to the Paralogisms and the full meaning of transcendental idealism.

The chapters that follow will have the primary aim of substantiating this last claim in detail. As indicated previously, this substantiation involves the first systematic study of the history of Kant's views on the mind, and the first thorough analysis of the text of the Paralogisms. Before briefly summarizing these projects, I would like to elaborate on a special reason for pursuing them. This reason is that Kant's doctrine of transcendental idealism takes on a particularly interesting form when it is applied to the self. The passages which express this aspect of the doctrine are probably the most challenging and least adequately deciphered in all of Kant's work. The doctrine has occasioned tremendous resistance here, for (as Kant himself noted) although there are many who would grant that the world may be really quite other than we think of it as being, the reason for granting this is often simply the idea that, in contrast, one's own self must be what it appears to be. At the very least, Kant here forces us to see that this resistance rests on a questionable doctrine, and that self-knowledge may well be parasitic on, and so suffer the same fate as, knowledge of the world at large.

It is at this point that transcendental idealism can take on an especially interesting meaning, for it is to be understood not as the narcissistic notion that intrinsically reality is like what seems most familiar to me, namely my empirical mind, but on the contrary, as the notion that even my own self may be intrinsically unlike what I know most about, namely the empirical realm. Idealism thus becomes interesting, for whereas in general it is not clear why we should care that there may be a real essence to things beyond our grasp, in our own case we cannot help but be concerned with whether the possible gap between what we know and what is should turn out to be a real gap. Traditionally, this concern has expressed itself in the hope that we are, in the most attractive way possible, intrinsically unlike what we are acquainted with throughout ordinary experience. That is, rationalists have committed themselves to the idea that we have a special kind of identity that can withstand all the kinds of change that ordinarily spell the end of ordinary objects. Kant can be seen as wanting, above all else, to put this commitment into a respectable form. On the one hand, he wanted to show

how unjustified it is to make specific claims about the noumenal powers and character of the self. On the other hand, he argued that the best theoretical philosophy shows that all empirical reality must be quite other than we at first believe, and so we need not expect that our ultimate being is vulnerable to oblivion because of the common process of empirical change.

This characterization of Kant's aim is not meant to be especially controversial, and yet it is remarkable how rarely it is fully accepted. Interpreters who stress the Paralogisms often suggest it means the death of any theoretical defence of the core of the rationalist commitment just described. Such interpreters rarely distinguish in a proper way the different implications Kant's discussion can have for phenomenal and noumenal claims, and they often forget that usually the central point of a Paralogism is merely an account of how a particular kind of philosopher might in some specific ways illegitimately go beyond the core commitment of rationalism. Thus it is forgotten that such an account need not commit Kant to saying that the conclusions of the specific paralogisms (or other related claims) are false, or even that there is no way they can be justified. An opposite kind of error is made by interpreters who minimize the Paralogisms, and in their analysis of Kant's general doctrines (e.g., in trying to reconstruct an ambitious transcendental deduction) implicitly commit him to claims that go far beyond the rationalist core. My hope is to avoid these extremes by showing, first, how an understanding of the history of Kant's views demonstrates that he definitely was committed to a basically rationalistic position, and then how a close reading of the Paralogisms, and especially of its revisions, demonstrates that he had a very sophisticated conception of how that position had to be restricted to some quite minimal, though all-important, claims. In this way I will try to show how an important meaning can be salvaged for even the most difficult of Kant's doctrines, the ideality of the self, although this will not entail that the doctrine is to be regarded as above suspicion.

3. The Major Stages in Kant's Theory

It should be evident by now that considerable emphasis is to be placed on the development of Kant's views. Although the overall structure of this study of Kant's theory of mind will be thematic, within that structure the approach will be at first historical. Thus the discussion of the Paralogisms' position on each major topic of mind will be prefaced by an account of the development of Kant's views on that topic. Only in this Introduction will an overview be given of the development of Kant's entire theory of mind, but the individual points of this brief overview will be returned to in more detail in the chapters that follow.

Although, as noted earlier, I will be working with the common distinction of four main stages in Kant's philosophy, my aim throughout will be to clarify not only the differences between these stages but also the deeper continuities. Here again an effort will be made to transcend common extremist tendencies in the interpretation of Kant. That is, some interpreters treat most of the *Critique* as if it were a mature work wholly intelligible by itself, whereas others have seen it as mostly a patchwork of inconsistent levels, with passages that are fully pre-critical next to others that are fully critical. Each of these approaches has its strong points, for surely there are arguments consisting of passages that are analysable in isolation, and surely there are also arguments with passages that are infected by views truly understandable only to those who know about the philosophy that preceded the *Critique*. The weakness of these approaches is that often they both assume that the line between critical and pre-critical passages is a line between light and darkness, and between what Kant really meant to say and what he simply forgot to leave out.[9] The two approaches then differ only on where this line falls (viz., throughout the *Critique*, or generally before it); an alternative approach (stressed long ago in the so-called metaphysical school of interpretation in Germany) would begin by questioning whether there is such a line.

It is this alternative that appears most justified by a historical perspective on Kant's theory of mind. Although there certainly is a contrast between Kant's espousal of rational psychology in his pre-critical works and his attack on it in his critical works, the fact is that there are ways in which that espousal was tempered from the beginning, and many important ways in which the form and content of that psychology colour the critical period as well. Here the writings outside the *Critique*, and above all the many sets of untranslated notes from Kant's lectures, become extremely significant. The other writings prepare us for the notes by revealing the over-all rationalist inclination of Kant's thought; the notes themselves convince us of that inclination by their evidence of Kant's similar treatment of issues of mind in the 1770s, 1780s, and after. Time and time again they show how deeply he was attached to various formulations in the *Critique* which otherwise might seem accidental and sheerly pre-critical. This attachment may appear bizarre, and it may appear that we are making matters only more mysterious by suggesting that the appearance of both pre-critical and critical views is a constant and deliberate matter, rather than simply the result of a pressure to ready a large book for publication. My view, however, is that there is nothing very mysterious here, for it should not be so surprising that Kant himself continually wanted to try to do justice to both sides in the theory of mind. That is, he wanted to bring out aspects of the mind that empiricists had covered over, while at the same time he wanted to be as critical as he could (within the bounds of his commitment to the core of rationalism) of what is to be made of these. Of course, this is not to deny that the *Critique* – and in particular its theory of mind – marks a kind of threshold in the development of the critical perspective. But it is important to realize that even when that threshold was crossed, it could be that there were many positions still held then, with sincerity and strength, which Kant later (sometimes properly, sometimes over-ambitiously) could deem worthy of further improvement by his own critical methods. For the theory of mind, at least, this need not be very difficult to see, as will be demonstrated in the later discussions of such topics as the proofs of the external world and freedom. Before I outline my evaluation of Kant's final treatment of such topics, however, a review should be given of the main stages Kant went through in developing that treatment.

The period in Kant's work which is no doubt the least typical is his first one. That in his first publications Kant can be described as (relatively speaking) an empiricist should not come as a surprise to anyone at all familiar with the main works of the period, e.g., *Thoughts on the True Estimation of Living Forces* and *Universal Natural History and Theory of the Heavens* (the *Nova Dilucidatio* also belongs here). What is surprising is that even these writings, which resulted from Kant's early focus on physics, are not lacking in discussions of mind. Each of the publications contains a treatment of the soul, and together they define a view of the mind which places it squarely within the cosmic order of the New Physics.

During this period the soul is regarded as located in the world and, like everything else, as interacting with material things and fully dependent upon them. It is characterized as having a capacity for representing the world, and as being self-determined in a way in which other beings are not, but no more sophisticated analysis or comparison of its powers is provided. No separate place is reserved for a field of rational psychology, and no deep appreciation is expressed for traditional philosophical difficulties with kindred topics such as causation and certainty about the external world. Although there is a reluctance to espouse materialism in a direct manner, there is hardly a development of idealism in this period. There is, however, a position on immortality which seems out of line with the other views: it is asserted as a matter of faith that the soul has an eternal status.

The last view shows that it would be inaccurate to label even the early Kant as at any point a sheer naturalist. To this extent there is some anticipation of the works of Kant's second period (e.g., the *Physical Monadology, The Mistaken Subtlety of the Four Syllogistic Figures*, the 'Metaphysik Herder' (1762)), which reveal a philosophy much more oriented towards non-empirical and rationalistic concerns. For example, rather than stressing the soul's causal position within the world, Kant now emphasizes that it can be assigned only a 'virtual' location and that it might be able to function without a body. Compatibilistic readings of human freedom are now sharply rejected, a move that coincides with the development of some of the main points of Kant's ultimate ethical theory. In this period Kant also speaks without qualms about the soul as a simple, immaterial, and spiritual substance. For the first time he attends to the distinctive capacities of the human mind and stresses that it has more than a mere faculty for representation. A distinct capacity for feelings and desires is discussed, and the uniqueness and irreducibility of our rational self-consciousness is asserted.

In its methodology Kant's analysis of mind is especially uncritical at this time. To establish *a priori* claims and to meet questions having to do with issues such as personal identity, Kant seems satisfied with the deliverances of 'immediate consciousness'. None the less, a certain sophistication is shown in Kant's turn from his earlier views. It was probably not any specific discovery or deep reflection on the mind that was responsible for this change, but rather merely a growing appreciation for idealism and for the rationalist topics and views that had been ignored or dismissed earlier (it is typical that in this period Kant's 'only possible proof' of God appears). This shift was not abrupt, for already in the *Nova Dilucidatio* (1755) Kant had noted difficulties with the doctrine of physical influx that he had accepted earlier. The *Physical Monadology* of 1756 reflects Kant's growing belief in the need for a metaphysical explanation of the physical. 'Material elements', which themselves are not extended, are now posited as the ultimate ground of the physical world. In accord with his rationalist doctrine of bodies (*Körperlehre*), Kant announced plans for a rational doctrine of the soul (*Seelenlehre*).[10] In its first draft he replaced his mere assertion of faith in immortality with a list and approval of various proofs of survival.

In his third or sceptical period (the *Essay Concerning the Clarity of the Principles of Natural Theology and Ethics*, the *Dreams of a Spirit-Seer*, the essay on 'negative magnitudes'), Kant's philosophy of mind takes a turn which is only natural in view of some obvious difficulties with the preceding rationalistic developments. After positing material elements which are simple, not literally spatial, and known not in themselves but only through the empirical mark of impenetrability, Kant had to face the problem of distinguishing such elements from immaterial ones. The difficulty is that the soul is also described as a simple being that is only 'virtually' spatial, i.e., that has spatial effects. At this point there is no clear *a priori* basis for saying the soul is not material, and also no way to rule out the possibility that material elements enjoy a rich spiritual life.

It is thus understandable that by this time Kant found rational psychology the 'hardest of all subjects'. His general questioning of metaphysics included pessimism about such problems as the existence of an external world. But while radicalizing his doubts about making certain existential assertions, Kant continued his discrimination of the concept of the human soul as opposed to other possible types of thinking beings. He also, almost incidentally, developed several ideas which were to play a major role in his later discussions, e.g., (a) the notion of a *'sensorium* of the soul' which mediates all representations, (b) the observation that the unity of a complex thought cannot be explained by the mere existence of individual thoughts in a number of separate substances, and (c) the argument that matter is 'lifeless' and cannot be essential to what has life. Ideas (a) and (b) are the seeds of the doctrines of ideality of space and time, the concept of the transcendental unity of apperception, and the central argument for the simplicity and immateriality of the soul. Ideas (b) and (c) figure in Kant's last attempts at a speculative rather than practical ground for immortality.

One can speak of a fourth or critical period in Kant's philosophy after approximately 1768. The term 'critical' is meant in a very broad way here to cover all of Kant's work after he had committed himself in effect to some version of transcendental idealism. The move to this commitment was prepared by Kant's argument in 1768 against the relational theory of space, that is, against regarding all of its features to be mere effects of 'material elements' or 'physical monads'. Kant did not wish to move to giving space an absolute metaphysical status, and instead he expanded the notion of a *sensorium* of the soul into the doctrine that space and time are mere forms of human sensibility. Of course, this doctrine by itself hardly entails the whole critical philosophy. Especially with respect to Kant's theory of mind it is important to distinguish between (a) the work of the first 'critical' years (the *Dissertation*, the Pölitz lectures), (b) the first *Critique* itself (1781), and (c) and the later development and revision of the doctrines of the first edition of this work (e.g., the lectures, the *Metaphysical Foundations of Natural Science*, the *Prolegomena* and the second *Critique*).

In view of Kant's critique of rationalism in his sceptical period, it may come as a surprise that Kant's lectures in the first subperiod of the critical stage continue to have a very extensive section on rational psychology, with sympathetic remarks on the soul's status as a simple immaterial substance. These remarks may be explained largely by the fact that at the phenomenal level Kant is inclined to follow common sense in distinguishing minds and bodies, and that at the noumenal level he can use his idealism to assert that whatever our being is in itself, it isn't material. During this period Kant also provides the analysis of souls with an elaborate systematic structure. Rational psychology is divided into: (a) the study of the soul in terms of its intrinsic categorial determinations, (b) the study of the soul's possible relation to other beings before, during, and after life, and (c) the comparison of various types of souls, especially with respect to epistemic capacities. In all these domains there is considerable continuity between the earlier and later lectures.

The precise relation between the *Critique* (the second critical subperiod) and the philosophy of mind presented in these lectures is a complicated matter to be elucidated in detail later. At this point only some of the main points of divergence and of agreement will be noted. Whether the *Critique* is taken as wholly rejecting our substantiality and/or immateriality, or only as bracketing its assertion in certain ways, there is no doubt that here, in contrast to his other work, Kant does not wish to encourage positive arguments about the categorial characterization of the mind, even as a phenomenon. Furthermore, in its over-all tone the *Critique's* view of the mind often seems closest to that of the sceptical period. Thus Kant implies that rational psychology is barren if one cannot (theoretically) prove, from the mere representation of the 'I', that the soul in itself is spiritual. None the less, in its remarks on the status of the soul in relation to other items, as well as in its comparative analysis of our cognitive powers, the first *Critique* clearly continues to give the self a special status. On the whole, the Paralogisms recapitulates not only much of the form but also some of the older content of the lectures.

The tensions implicit in the *Critique's* treatment of mind were not resolved all at once. The first direction in the last critical subperiod is a remarkable firming up of the rationalist line. A rational doctrine of the soul is promised to complement the treatment of physics, and indications are given of a more direct theoretical affirmation of our freedom and substantiality. Immediately thereafter, however, Kant reverses direction and makes some of his most sophisticated critical moves by imposing new restrictions on arguing for our freedom and substantiality. This reversal dominates several very important revisions that are made of the Paralogisms, as well as of his practical philosophy and of other parts of the first *Critique* that bear on the self. Kant now distinguishes more clearly between general transcendental structures and metaphysical features of the individual self. He does this largely by making much more use of a distinction between apperception and inner sense, and by stressing the limitations that it implies for our self-knowledge. He also tries to give a better account of the ideality of the self and of our knowledge of the external world, and in both cases he emphasizes how we need to refer to spatiality in order to have concrete self-knowledge. Despite all these developments, however, it can be argued that even in the final version of the *Critique* a commitment remains to many doctrines that are questionable even from a natural extension of Kant's own critical framework.

4. Evaluation of the Major Claims of Kant's Theory

Our brief historical review was meant to give some idea of the complex context in which the passages on the mind in the first *Critique* should be approached. It should now be expected that practically every topic handled in those passages involves issues on which Kant already had frequently reflected and expressed himself. This background cannot but be relevant to the full understanding and proper evaluation of his final views. We will turn now to a preview of the major conclusions that are arrived at in the following chapters by keeping this background in mind.

The next chapter (II) covers the characteristics of the soul that are discussed in the first two Paralogisms. These include four closely related claims: immateriality, simplicity, substantiality, and incorruptibility. Although traditionally Kant is hailed for his critique of these claims, I will argue that there is quite a range in his views here and that his very critical attitude on the last claim contrasts with a more tolerant view of the others, especially immateriality. Only in the second edition is a clear and direct challenge presented to the assertion of our substantiality, and even this challenge focuses on theoretical assertions specifically about a pure soul. In general, both Paralogisms attempt to impugn rational psychology because of difficulties in establishing our incorruptibility. This illustrates a very characteristic feature of Kant's discussion: he often strikes a critical pose with respect to an issue largely by coupling that issue with another more extreme claim about which he is critical, while with respect to the original issue he remains basically rationalistic.

In this chapter, as elsewhere, historical considerations are also brought in to demonstrate weaknesses in other major interpretations. Because interpreters of these Paralogisms have ascribed too much of a critical position to Kant, they often have either castigated or applauded him on a false basis. With regard to the first Paralogism, the most recent interpreters have taken the first path and have mistakenly held that Kant's critique of substantiality claims goes so far as to conflict with what common sense and his own system must say about the mind. With regard to the second Paralogism, some of the best recent work tends to the other extreme, that is, to endorsing various radical ways the claim of our simplicity can be criticized — without showing that Kant actually developed these ways, or even that he really would have been sympathetic with their over-all aim.

The next chapter (III) focuses on Kant's views on interaction and the major disputed relations between the mind and other items. Here again an adequate understanding of his theory of mind requires investigations that go far beyond the short passages of the Paralogisms. These investigations reveal that Kant's understanding of the general nature of interaction turns out to be so dependent on various traditional views that it hardly constitutes a clear improvement on its rationalist predecessors. On the other hand, his treatment of two specific relations appears to be relatively promising and of considerable contemporary significance.

First, the problem of the peculiar relation between a human self and its own body is shown to be illuminated by some neglected Kantian discussions. Here his distinction between phenomenal and noumenal claims is shown to be useful in challenging some popular views on our embodiment, although on the whole Kant's treatment of this topic still reveals a bias against taking our spatiality to be ultimate. Secondly, the *Critique* offers an important and original treatment of the epistemological problem of establishing the existence of beings outside the self. Here I defend Kant's fourth Paralogism, even in the first-edition version, as consistent with a coherent and genuinely Kantian version of transcendental idealism. I argue that the fourth Paralogism is hardly a solution to what is typically understood as the problem of the external world, but in combination with other points in the second edition of the *Critique*, it amounts to a strong challenge to many uncritical views naturally held by those for whom the external world is a severe problem. Thus once again the valid Kantian critique bears to a large extent only on such strong claims as that the self is independent of the world in the sense of being a spiritual eternal being.

The issue of personal identity, treated in Kant's third Paralogism (Ch. IV), turns out to be the most complex. Whereas elsewhere Kant usually is interpreted as being more critical than he truly is, here, in both rationalistic and empiricist ways, he is generally and improperly taken not to be ultimately critical of the assertion of personal identity. To deal with the overly rationalistic interpretations it becomes necessary to attend closely to passages in the transcendental deduction that have been taken to mean that personal identity is *a priori* certain. To deal with the overly empiricist interpretations a special emphasis has to be placed on the implications of transcendental idealism and Kant's concept of numerical identity. It then can be maintained that Kant has some serious suspicions about all claims that personal identity is certain. These suspicions reflect the general metaphysical doubt Kant must have about our claims to know the ultimate identity of anything, as well as his specific critical doctrine about the self as not being in an epistemically privileged position.

The sceptical consequences of Kant's view are then evaluated in the light of the fact that alternative contemporary analyses of personal identity do not appear satisfactory either. I argue that Kant's distinction between appearances, phenomena, and noumena provides a helpful framework for sorting out various criteria of personal identity and for rejecting some recent radical theories. In the end, though, Kant's view is taken to be vulnerable because of its close ties to the doctrine of transcendental idealism. Even if the doctrine is allowed to be meaningful and to apply truly to some things, it is hard to accept its implication that we have no certainty about merely having some identity over time. Again it appears that Kant's valid critical points generally bear on more specific assertions such as *a priori* claims about the self as a necessarily persistent being.

Kant's treatment of immortality is allotted a separate but brief chapter (V). Kant suggests this idea is central in the demonstration of the limits of rational psychology, but what his focus on the idea really serves to reveal is how limited his critique of that psychology is. Moreover, as far as his own beliefs go, Kant is clearly favourable to the doctrine of immortality, and he even presents a variety of arguments, which in the end are qualified as practical, in support of his belief. These arguments are explained as being, like Kant's other views, a continuation of long and relatively sympathetic reflections on the tradition, but they are not taken literally to have much weight in Kant's theory, let alone great intrinsic merit. Rather, they again reflect Kant's fundamental adherence to an immaterialistic position that he is unable, and in general properly unwilling, to specify further in a theoretical way.

Chapter VI is devoted to Kant's treatment of human freedom. Although this issue receives no direct coverage in the Paralogisms, I argue that it plays a central and un-acknowledged role in Kant's theory of mind. Confidence in absolute freedom is a hallmark of Kant's mature philo-sophy, and for a long time it was explicitly a central theme in his treatment of mind. His initial reticence about it in the Paralogisms is not so much a sign of a fundamental reversal as rather merely a tactic to avoid complicating the new more critical appearance of his philosophy as a whole.

By bringing out the way in which the issue of freedom is displaced in the first edition of the *Critique*, I try to make more understandable Kant's extra emphasis on it immediately thereafter. I propose that it is precisely because Kant then ran into difficulties in trying to develop his own rationalistic commitment to freedom, that he made his later writings and revisions focus on making stronger and clearer restrictions on theoretical claims about the self. In the process of substantiating this hypothesis, I offer new in-terpretations of the central arguments of the *Foundations of the Metaphysics of Morals* and the *Critique of Practical Reason*. By bringing out the different aims and weaknesses of these two works, my interpretation challenges both those who back the strategy of the *Foundations* and take it as a fair guide for the later work, as well as those who instead em-phasize the strategy of the second *Critique* and believe it to be an adequate model for the earlier work. Here an apprecia-tion of the development of Kant's theory of mind has per-haps the greatest consequences for the understanding of the rest of his philosophy.

The last chapter (VII) begins with a brief retrospective survey of all the major topics associated by Kant with rational psychology. This reveals that the only relevant topic not covered up to this point is the general claim of the tran-scendental ideality of the self. I explain how this claim is closely related to Kant's doctrine of self-knowledge as a synthesis of inner sense and apperception. An effort is made to obtain a precise definition of these components, and once this is done an account is given of the difficult passages in which Kant speaks of our being able to know ourselves only as phenomena because we are 'affected' by ourselves.

At this point an attempt is also made to give an account of the general meaning of Kant's transcendental idealism. Within the context of that account the special difficulties in the claim of the ideality of the self are explained. A number of strategies for establishing the claim are distinguished, and Kant's major argument is isolated and criticized. The coherence of his claim is defended, however, against several strong attacks to the effect that it is meaningless or inconsistent.

In sum, although few of Kant's specific arguments about the mind are held to be entirely convincing, his over-all orientation is taken to be more viable than is generally thought, and the details and ramifications of his doctrines are shown to have been seriously misunderstood. I conclude that at least three kinds of general lessons are to be learned from a close study of Kant's theory of mind.

First, for specialists in Kant, such a study can underscore in a new way how vital it is to place the *Critique* in the historical context of Kant's entire work, and to see how it relates to what he taught both before and after 1781. If for such topics as freedom and self-knowledge it is impossible otherwise to have a proper understanding of Kant's view, then this is likely to be true of other major topics in all branches of his philosophy. More specifically, the recognition of the pattern of tension, reversal, and growth that underlies Kant's theory of mind can lead to a new understanding of the relation between pre-critical and critical ideas throughout Kant's thought, that is, to an understanding that goes beyond the models of an inconsistent patchwork, an absolute break, or a constant linear progression.

Secondly, for those who take a broader interest in the history of philosophy, this study is meant to provide a trenchant illustration of the flaws in the tempting practice of reducing the theory of a well-known figure to a neat and simple doctrine. Although there is a common pattern to be found throughout Kant's theory, it is a very complex one, and it is a mistake to treat Kant as being caught in a refuted rationalist system or as being wedded to a single basic technique for exposing dogmatic fallacies. Many have been forced to treat Kant's theory of mind in just this way in order to get on either with their broader story of the history of philosophy or with the development of their own systematic views. Certainly such ambitious endeavours can be quite valuable, and in comparison it can be a dry business to take the opposite course of following out all the twists and turns of a thinker like Kant. None the less, it seems worthwhile to point out in a concrete instance that there is much to be done simply to set the record straight on what certain major philosophers have held on certain major issues, and that we ought not to be satisfied with the simple formulae that these philosophers themselves often suggest.

Thirdly, for philosophers of mind, this study can reveal how on many current issues Kant probably has more to offer than any of the other great modern philosophers. Although Kant's rationalist tendencies kept him from being as revolutionary as many of his contemporary admirers would like him to be, there is something to be learned from even these tendencies. The tradition of dualism is well served by his distinction between phenomena and noumena, his notion of the limits of a psychology modelled on physics, his analysis of the complexities in asserting personal identity, and his many advances over cruder versions of dualism. If this tradition is to be overcome, materialists can hardly find a more suitable basis to build on than Kant's own critique of spiritualism and his late doctrine of the primacy of spatial knowledge. We ought to take it as a sign not of inconsistency but of rare depth that Kant can still provide ammunition for both sides in current battles in the philosophy of mind.

Notes to Chapter I

[1] The capitalized term 'Paralogisms' will refer to the Chapter 'The Paralogisms of Pure Reason' in the *Critique of Pure Reason* and indirectly to the critical arguments therein; the uncapitalized term 'paralogisms' will refer to the four specific rationalist arguments mentioned by Kant in this chapter. Thus, 'Paralogisms' is a singular term referring to a whole chapter, whereas 'paralogisms' is a plural term referring to the rationalist arguments called 'the first paralogism', the 'second paralogism', etc. Similarly, a capitalized singular term such as 'the first Paralogism' will refer to the whole subsection of the text in which the first paralogism is discussed. (Similar conventions will be used for the Antinomies.) This is an

24   Introduction

important distinction because the philosophical attitude expressed in a particular paralogism can be quite different from that of the Paralogism in which it occurs. The terms 'the *Critique*' and the 'first *Critique*' will refer to Kant's *Critique of Pure Reason*. As is customary, all citations in the text will be to Norman Kemp Smith's translation of this work (Macmillan, 1929) and will be prefaced by 'A' and/or 'B', referring respectively to pages of the first and second German editions.

² It must be admitted, though, that I follow the Paralogisms in dealing primarily with the theory of mind only in the theoretical as opposed to practical branch of Kant's philosophy. I will not bother always to make explicit this restriction.

³ Peter Strawson, 'Review of Jonathan Bennett's *Kant's Dialectic*', *Philosophical Quarterly*, 25 (1975), 166.

⁴ 'Kant's Transcendental Deduction as a Regressive Argument', *Kant-Studien*, 69 (1978), 273–87. See also my 'Recent Work on Kant's Theoretical Philosophy', *American Philosophical Quarterly* (forthcoming).

⁵ Strawson, 'Review', p. 169.

⁶ These lectures are found in volume 28 (edited 1971) of *Kant's Gesammelte Schriften* (Königliche Preussische Akademie der Wissenschaften, Berlin). Citations in general will be to this *Akademische Ausgabe* (abbreviated hereafter as '*AA*'; otherwise complete bibliographical information will be given in each chapter with the first citation of each reference) of Kant's works, except where there is an easily available English translation. Where there is no such translation I sometimes offer my own, but then as in all citations it should be assumed that all emphases have been added by me. I make many references to the lectures of volume 28, and so the following data should be kept in mind: pp. 1–166 correspond to (approximately) 1762; pp. 167–350 correspond to the 1770s (the 'Pölitz' lectures); pp. 351–460 correspond to 1784–5; pp. 461–524 correspond to the late 1780s; pp. 525–610 correspond to 1790–1; pp. 611–704 correspond to 1792–3; pp. 705–816 correspond to 1791–4; pp. 817–38 correspond to 1794–5.

⁷ See P. F. Strawson, *The Bounds of Sense* (London, 1966), and Ross Harrison, *On What There Must Be* (Oxford, 1974), especially pp. 22–8.

⁸ R. C. S. Walker, *Kant* (London, 1978). Cf. below, Chs. II.8 and VII.12, and my review in *Teaching Philosophy*, 3 (1980), 358–63.

⁹ In these contexts the terms 'pre-critical' and 'critical' obviously have more of a systematic than historical significance. Here a view would be 'pre-critical' to the extent it involves any endorsement of traditional metaphysical and rationalist propositions, and it would be 'critical' to the extent that it rather shows how such propositions have an inadequate justification in our experience. In this sense, to the extent that Kant endorses *some* such propositions and criticizes *others*, my point is that he may be simultaneously, and sometimes even justifiably, pre-critical and critical.

¹⁰ *AA*, vol. 28, p. 175.

Chapter II

Immateriality

The organization of topics in philosophy of mind that usually is associated with Kant is no doubt the one that he gives near the very beginning of the Paralogisms section of the *Critique*:

> The topic of the rational doctrine of the soul, from which everything else that it contains must be derived, is accordingly as follows:
> 1. The soul is *substance*.
> 2. As regards its quality it is *simple*.
> 3. As regards the different times in which it exists, it is numerically identical, that is, *unity* (not plurality).
> 4. It is in relation to *possible* objects in space (A 344/ B 402).

Kant accordingly distinguishes a first Paralogism entitled 'Of Substance', a second entitled 'Of Simplicity', and so on. In devoting this chapter to the issues of Kant's first two Paralogisms, it would be natural to follow the exact order of topics Kant gives here, but I shall not do so. There are many reasons for this departure. The subject matter itself resists this architectonic, and Kant departed from it himself both before and after the first edition of the *Critique*.

Instead of rigidly distinguishing the first topics of the Paralogisms in the way Kant initially does, I think it is helpful to have in mind the complex question, 'Is the soul a simple immaterial substance?', and then to approach this question by focusing first on the issue of immateriality. Some hint of the appropriateness of this strategy is given by Kant when he continues:

> All the concepts of pure psychology arise from these elements, simply by way of combination, without admission of any other principle. This substance, merely as object of inner sense, gives the concept of *immateriality*; as simple substance, that of *incorruptibility* . . . (A 345/B 403)

The claim of the soul's immateriality is thus emphasized from the start, and the surprising fact (explained below at n. 94) that it is associated with the first rather than the second of Kant's topics signals the very close interrelation that exists between the first two Paralogisms. Another and more important reason for beginning with the claim of immateriality is that it is the one that most clearly connects Kant's many discussions of mind prior to the *Critique*, and it reveals what remains fundamentally traditional about his position. Hence, rather than proceeding directly with an analysis of the *Critique's* Paralogisms, I first will build a case that for a long time Kant developed a nuanced but basically rationalistic attitude towards the immateriality issue, and then I will explain how this attitude remains behind the overtly anti-rationalist tone of the *Critique*.

I also will show how Kant's attitude towards the immateriality issue is always closely linked to his views on the simplicity issue, and thus I will claim that a kind of rationalism remains even when this latter topic is taken up in the second Paralogism. As a close analysis of that Paralogism will demonstrate, this claim is complicated but not defeated by the fact that Kant indicated some especially incisive and frequently misunderstood points against certain fallacious ways of trying to establish our simplicity. On this point I will attempt to correct recent interpretations of the second Paralogism by Margaret Wilson, Wilfrid Sellars, and Jonathan Bennett.

In presenting an exegesis of the first Paralogism, I will argue that, in contrast, Kant eventually develops a fairly strong critique of claims about the soul's substantiality, and this fact may be largely responsible for the general but false impression that he wholly rejected the other rationalist claims. The first Paralogism thus will be approached only quite late, but appropriately so, for it will turn out that the concept of substantiality in general plays quite an anomalous role in Kant's system, and that attitudes toward the soul's substantiality in particular undergo the most dramatic and complex shifts in Kant's development. A full discussion of these shifts will have to be postponed until later in this study, where the issue of our substantiality will be put in the broader context of Kant's theory of freedom. At this point I will argue only that, contrary to the recent interpretations of Roderick Chisholm and Ralph Walker, there is no evident absurdity or inconsistency in Kant's critical position in the first Paralogism.

1. Historical Overview

The issue of the soul's immateriality arises at the very beginning of Kant's career, as a natural consequence of some undeveloped discussions of substance. In his first work Kant offers a general and traditional definition of substance as that which can exist without anything else.[1] Without reference to this definition, however, he speaks unproblematically about material substances and the soul's being in causal relation to such substances, and he implies that it can be regarded as a substance simply because in a very common-sense way it appears as a subject of action.[2] Precisely because its involvement with physical substance is taken as so unproblematic, the soul is not yet clearly differentiated from such substances, and so in this period Kant has to defend himself against the suspicion of materialism. Beyond a confession of faith in the soul's being beyond the physical world,[3] Kant offers only two weak defences against this suspicion. First, he identifies materialism with a view that the world proceeds by chance rather than by rational universal laws.[4] On this basis, Kant obviously can say he is not a materialist, but this hardly gives an answer to what most would understand by the question of the soul's immateriality. Equally unsatisfactory though more typical is Kant's second ground, his assurance that, unlike a crude materialist, he holds there definitely are beings (viz., at least human souls) who really do have representations, and so in that sense there are minds which are more than *mere* matter.[5]

In his early rationalist period Kant moves towards acceptance of the full traditional meaning of the claim that the soul is known to be a simple immaterial substance. He does not argue directly for this claim, but his acceptance of it is implicit in various formulations that occur in discussions of other topics. For example, in an essay on logic he mentions as apparently unproblematic the inference that the soul is immaterial because unlike matter it isn't composite.[6] Other remarks imply a belief that the soul is substantial (Kant says he does not see how the soul could be brought into being by another natural being),[7] and that it is simple (Kant repeats the claim that it is incorruptible because simple).[8] Kant also offers a new reason for the soul's immateriality, namely that it is directed by an inner principle whereas matter is 'lifeless', that is, it is subject to inertia and acts only in response to external forces. This argument has a longer tenure than the previous ones, but it is no more convincing a resolution of the traditional issue of immateriality. The argument is mentioned with reservations in the essay[9] on the *Dreams of a Spirit-Seer* (1766) and occurs again in Kant's lectures,[10] but it is never given priority although it is used often in saying that animals are immaterial.[11] This reveals the argument's limitations, for Kant himself remarks that it means that even the crudest fish is 'immaterial' simply because it is alive.[12] The tendency of Kant's thought here is revealing, however, in that from beginning to end he inclines toward understanding the assertion of immateriality as something which in at least some sense should not be taken as controversial, though at the same time as something which need not foreclose locating the soul (theoretically) within a naturalistic framework.

None the less, in his rationalist period Kant clearly seems to have believed the soul to be immaterial in a full traditional sense, for he became concerned when he saw that other aspects of his philosophy made it difficult to back that belief. Difficulties arose because he had presumed that the soul's immateriality followed closely upon its simplicity, while at the same time, in a quasi-Leibnizian way, he had argued that the physical world ultimately must be composed of simple elements. Kant had stressed that the simplicity of these elements was necessary to their being the ultimate metaphysical components of the physical world, and that this did not conflict with their having complex extended effects.[13] The extended structure of the physical world was to be understood as the product of unextended monads that 'dominate' spaces without themselves really 'filling' them. Thus, they are literally unextended and not merely very small — something which Kant felt was obscured by Leibniz's followers, though not Leibniz himself.[14] Kant differed from Leibniz, however, in designating these monads as physical, primarily because he felt they were involved in real interaction with the monads underlying other masses of matter.

Simultaneously, Kant had asserted that on evident phenomenological if not metaphysical grounds the soul is also simple,
and he had stressed that it too should be understood not
as a very small atom with a location merely at a particular
point, but rather as a being related to a spatial field (a body)
in which it is 'virtually' but not 'locally' present (see below,
Ch. III.6).

These views led to an inevitable question, which Kant set
in his lectures. He asks: 'The soul is a simple substance. But
is it present to space in the same way as a simple material
element, that is, according to laws of impenetrability?'[15] The
lecture notes list two replies to this question, but Kant seems
to have recognized that the problem was not satisfactorily
resolved, for he said these replies 'must' show the soul is
unlike matter simply because if they don't, nothing else can.
The first reply is the familiar idea that the soul is distinguished by freedom, that is, it is determined by inner grounds
whereas matter is determined from outside. This idea has
obvious weaknesses, and of course it was given up by Kant
himself in his later theoretical philosophy. Secondly, Kant
says that the concept of a soul is such that we don't say a
group of souls strung together amounts to a 'cubic soul',
whereas a group of material elements together can constitute
a cube.[16] Kant criticizes this argument later as well (see below
at n. 27). Clearly it does not itself establish that we really are
souls; rather, it merely points to some possible limitations in
the term 'soul' as we use it. The argument is significant, however, in that it introduces one of Kant's favourite ideas,
namely that a complex of extension is not a unity in the way
a complex of thoughts can be.

The idea of a special kind of unity in thought is mentioned
in Kant's early lectures,[17] and eventually it is developed into
an argument (discussed below as the 'unity argument') which
comes to dominate his discussion of the weaknesses of
materialism. The idea appears in a relatively undeveloped
form in the *Dreams* essay when Kant notes that we need not
believe a single mass of matter amounts to something which
by itself can have *a* (complex) thought.[18] Here Kant is not
using the idea to claim a fundamental difference between
mind and matter, which is just as well, for it has not been

shown that there could not be a *material element* which would have within itself a plurality of thoughts that would amount to *a* thought. The reason why a mass of matter wouldn't amount to a thought might be simply that the mass would be rooted in a plurality of substances (physical monads). But when there is a plurality of thinking sub-stances it is also the case (at least for Kant)[19] that a plurality of thoughts will not amount to a thought, and so it still isn't proven that there are distinct non-material beings that think or alone apperceive.

In the *Dreams* essay Kant accordingly professes scepticism about distinguishing between immaterial and material sub-stances. He says that because we cannot know (theoretically) that the simple substance which we are does not have the feature of impenetrability, we cannot assert that we are immaterial.[20] Yet the position of the *Dreams* period is much more complicated than it appears, and in fact it is more accurate to think of Kant as still holding the general position mentioned earlier, namely, that in a sense our souls obviously can be said to be immaterial, although this leaves open the possibility that in some sense (at another level) we may not differ from matter. Even in the sceptical *Dreams* essay Kant says, 'we are obviously persistent, non-bodily substances',[21] that is, we never *appear* to ourselves (*qua* soul) as spatial (this idea is discussed below as 'the inner sense argument'). At the same time, Kant was moving towards considerations that make idle the speculation that *intrinsically* we may be material. The speculation was kept alive, after all, not by any insight into the possibility of our thoughts being properties of matter as we ordinarily experience it, but rather merely by the possibility that we may be like simple material ele-ments. Now these elements are even called monads, and from a Leibnizian perspective they would be considered a kind of mental being. Therefore, the difficulties which Kant raised in the *Dreams* might well strike an immaterialist as not threatening his own position but rather as reaffirming that ordinary extended matter does not have metaphysical primacy. Moreover, not only is the 'material' status of the simple elements from which we supposedly cannot (with certainty) distinguish ourselves unclear, but the very existence of these elements becomes questionable when in 1768 Kant argues that space and time are not to be understood as the effects of physical monads.

It therefore should not surprise us so much that in his lectures Kant is reported by Pölitz to have asserted that the soul is a simple immaterial substance, and even that our general concepts of substantiality, simplicity, and immateriality stem from our representation of ourselves.[22] More surprising is one of the apparent grounds for this statement, namely a belief that in the case of the self we have what is achieved nowhere else, an intuitive insight into a substance in itself.[23] Kant retreats from this belief later when he distinguishes apperception from inner sense, for then genuine consciousness of the self is expressly characterized as also (like the consciousness of things) a mediated synthesis of data and not a direct cognitive intuition. This retreat does not take place all at once though, and only near the end of our study can we explain Kant's complex reaction to its implications.

For now we will note simply that the very first pages of the Pölitz notes appear to reflect an extremely rationalistic position, and one that may have been held prior to the 1770s, for in some cases it implies views that seem earlier than those of the position published in the *Dreams*.[24] Without getting further involved in issues of dating, we shall focus on the immateriality issue and shall treat Kant's position as revealed by the notes from his lectures as falling into three phases:

(i) an initial and most rationalistic phase, expressed in the first pages of the Pölitz notes;
(ii) a transitional stage, expressed in the latter part of these notes;
(iii) a final stage, reaffirmed throughout the many other sets of notes from lectures of the critical period proper.

The transitional stage still corresponds in some ways to the position of the *Dreams*, and just as that position has been argued to be ultimately not so different from its predecessor, so it also will be argued that the so-called final stage does not differ so much from its predecessor. That is, on the whole the lectures show Kant still committed to a project of showing both that there are many ways in which the immateriality of the soul can be supported, and also that in some sense the claim of immateriality needs to be restrained. In contrast, the writings of the rationalist period tend to overstress the first point, whereas the *Critique* itself overemphasizes the second point. To explain the latter phenomenon and to simplify the ultimate task of analysing the complex attitude toward immateriality in the Paralogisms, I shall dwell for a while on outlining the relatively consistent and balanced position of the lectures.

2. Kant's Lectures

We have already noted that in his initial stage Kant asserts the soul to be both simple and immaterial. The first claim is based mainly on the *unity argument*: I am aware of a unity of distinct thoughts; such a unity could not be had if the thoughts were grounded in distinct substances; therefore I am a simple being.[25] Although Kant eventually uses part of this argument in a proof of the soul's immateriality, it is originally only an argument for simplicity and so it will be evaluated later when that topic comes to be discussed directly in the analysis of the second paralogism. Kant initially offers a separate ground for the immateriality claim, a ground which shall be called the *inner sense argument*.[26] This argument simply says that I am immaterial because I am not and cannot be an object of outer sense. That is, although I may have a body, the components of my mind, my representings and feelings, cannot appear as extended and divisible. We can attend immediately to the difficulties with this argument, for it is undercut by a point made by Kant himself in the crucial text of the transitional stage. Kant there repeats the observation that the *Dreams* emphasized, namely that there may be simple material beings and hence that, notwithstanding our simplicity, our souls might be material if (like physical monads) they have the feature of impenetrability. In a rejection of one of his own earlier remarks, Kant now argues that we could even speak of a cube of souls — if it were the case, for example, that the presence of a number of souls in effect required that the equivalent of a cube of matter be displaced.[27] What is most important here is not this specific idea but simply the fact that Kant says that in such a case the soul should be said to be an object of outer sense. He admits that it would not be an 'actual' object of that sense, that is, we would not directly intuit the soul as outer (or feel its power of impenetrability). None the less, the soul could be outer in the same way that physical monads were thought to be, namely as being part of or at least intrinsically connected with the empirical world of spatial reality. What can belong to the realm of outer sense is thus ultimately to be determined by *theoretical* as opposed to *phenomenological* factors.

This is an important point which Kant did not appreciate enough himself (cf. below at n. 56). That he did not forget the point is clear from the energy with which he later emphasized one of its implications, namely that the mere impossibility of a clear image or direct intuition of an item does not make it part of an intellectual or supra-empirical realm.[28] It is just as clear that Kant did not emphasize adequately the implications of this point for the inner sense argument, namely that our not directly appearing material to ourselves does not mean that *qua* mind we are in no empirical way material. Properly speaking, the inner sense argument proves (at most) only what will be called *appearance immaterialism*, i.e., that our soul always directly appears non-material to us, but not *phenomenal immaterialism*, i.e., that the soul is in no constitutive empirical sense material.[29] That Kant did not attend enough to the difference between these two is shown by the fact that he continued to speak of the inner sense argument as showing the soul is clearly 'empirically' immaterial or immaterial 'as a phenomenon'.[30]

The above is but one example of Kant's failure to display weaknesses in grounds that he gave in favour of speaking of the soul as immaterial. Because of his interest in presenting a (supposedly) balanced position on immaterialism, this failure led him to develop bizarre senses in which the claim of immateriality might be restrained. Such at least is the hypothesis one is driven to, given the oddity of the considerations against immaterialism that Kant does offer, and the fact that he doesn't take the considerations he offers in favour of immaterialism as decisive, even though he does not directly attack the arguments they involve. Kant's over-riding interest in presenting such a balanced position can be demonstrated by noting the formal similarity in the three points that define the positions of his transitional and final stages. In each stage Kant presents two allegedly non-ultimate senses in which the soul's immateriality is suppo-sedly unproblematic, and then he notes that with respect to a third and supposedly more significant sense there is a reason, but only *a* reason, for saying the soul is immaterial.

In the transitional stage, the three points Kant makes are in effect these:[31]

(A_i) the inner sense argument shows that at least appearance immaterialism is unproblematic;

(A_{ii}) the unity argument shows at least that what will be called *scientific immaterialism* is unproblematic, i.e., that regardless of what kind of stuff constitutes the soul, there is no foreseeable scientific value in our seeking to use the structure and laws of matter to account for the mind as such;

(A_{iii}) there is (merely) *a* reason, namely a line of considera-tions to be discussed later under the title of the *divisibility argument*,[32] for asserting that the soul is also at least phenomenally immaterial.

The three points defining the position of Kant's final stage are these:

(B_i) because of the divisibility argument, which says there can be no empirical beings that are material and simple, it follows that the soul (which according to the unity argument is simple) is clearly at least phenomenally immaterial;[33]

(B_{ii}) the soul is clearly scientifically immaterial;

(B_{iii}) yet there is only *a* reason for saying the soul is *tran-scendentally immaterial*, that is, that even in its substrate it differs from (the substrate of) matter.[34]

The oddity of the restraints that Kant places on the assertion of immateriality should now be evident. The re-straint in point (A_{iii}) is odd because what Kant there calls only a ground for immaterialism would seem to be (as in

B_i) a conclusive argument. This restraint can be understood, I believe, only because at the earlier stage Kant did not have a more ultimate sense of immateriality in mind which he could contrast with the sense dealt with in the argument. But in later making a contrast with a new and supposedly more ultimate sense, Kant only replaced one oddity with another (viz., B_{iii}). That is, it is hard to see any genuine restraint against asserting the immateriality of the soul merely because of difficulty in completely excluding what Kant calls 'transcendental materialism' or 'materialism in an extended sense'.[35]

Kant is driven to holding up the possibility of such a materialism because he must presume not only that material-ism 'properly speaking' (i.e., phenomenal materialism) is clearly false, but also that the next natural possibility can be eliminated, namely that the soul might be material in itself. This possibility — which he does not designate separately and which we shall call *noumenal materialism* — is excluded because according to Kant nothing can be material in itself.[36] This exclusion might have been opposed as long as Kant entertained the possibility of physical monads, but it was unavoidable once he had decided that only what can be itself divisible (and not only divisible in its effects) can be called matter, and hence (given Kant's view of infinite divisibility) that all matter is merely phenomenal. He thus was forced into a position in which the soul could not be characterized as material either phenomenally or noumenally, and at this point it would seem nothing was left but a categorical accep-tance of the soul's immateriality. However — and this is typical of Kant's critical phase — Kant chose neither to express this conclusion directly nor to probe for weaknesses in his arguments against phenomenal and noumenal material-ism. Instead he chose time and time again to restrain the assertion of the immateriality of the soul on the ground that transcendental materialism had not been disproven.

As has been noted, this restraint is quite odd, for tran-scendental materialism is merely the possibility that the substrate of matter may not differ from what intrinsically characterizes us. This is not the suggestion that intrinsically we might be material or even that we might be like matter.

In fact one way — indeed *the* way, given what Kant suggests — in which such transcendental materialism would be true would be if the substrates of material things (as well as of us) were thinking beings! Of course, Kant was very critical of such an idea, and although he was quite familiar with it from Leibniz's monadology, he preferred to mock it and to note that it is wholly unsupported by evidence.[37] None the less, he does try to get theoretical mileage out of the idea, and yet if it were true in the way we have noted, surely most people would take it to show not that our immateriality is dubious but only that there are more immaterial beings than we might expect.

I think the best way to understand Kant's odd discussion of immateriality here is to admit that it is largely a tactic to keep up the appearances of his new critical philosophy, in order to distract attention from the fact that he can't avoid all his old commitments to general views about the nature of reality in itself. At the same time, it should also be admitted that there are a few specific ways in which Kant may be right in suggesting we should take care not to make too much of the claims of immateriality that in effect he does allow. It should not be thought, for example, that it has been proven that we are composed of spiritual stuff. Kant defines 'spirits' as thinking beings who are not only distinct from matter but also definitely can exist as such even when material beings do not.[38] Thus, even if immaterialism with respect to the intrinsic nature of the self is accepted, *spiritualism* is not thereby entailed.[39] Furthermore, it should not be thought that what can be called *pneumatism* is entailed either, that is, the doctrine that intrinsically we are thinking beings in the full sense in which we are now familiar with such beings, namely as beings with temporal thoughts and experiences.[40] Given Kant's view of time this doctrine is in the same boat as the idea that in ourselves we might be material, that is, it is not only unsupported but also definitely false. Finally, nothing in Kant's immaterialism commits him to *idealism* if that doctrine is understood in Leibnizian terms as a claim that bodies can be reduced to underlying immaterial monads.[41]

These considerations may help to make plausible the claim

that Kant thought he had a balanced position on the immateriality of the soul, even though in at least four major senses of the term (the appearance sense, the phenomenal sense, the noumenal sense, the scientific sense) he felt immaterialism was unproblematic. To balance this, Kant seems to have counted as anti-immaterialistic the following four points: the inexcludability of 'transcendental materialism', the falsity of pneumatism, the unproven status of spiritualism, and the rejection of (Leibnizian) idealism. It should be obvious that this is only a numerical balance. As long as we are concerned merely with the specific issue of immaterialism, the so-called anti-immaterialistic considerations bear not on it but on further positions, even though they are admittedly positions with which an immaterialist might naturally be associated.

3. Appearance Immaterialism and Scientific Immaterialism

Given that the ultimate direction of Kant's position appears to be so immaterialistic, it is only fitting to evaluate how well the various senses in which that immaterialism is approved are grounded in the major arguments Kant offers, namely the unity argument and the divisibility argument (the limits of the 'inner sense argument' having been exposed already).

We will begin by looking at what Kant would call the *non-constitutive* doctrines, appearance immaterialism and scientific immaterialism, and by considering first how the unity argument bears on these. Kant takes at least *appearance* immaterialism to be something we do not infer but just see.[42] This claim may rest on taking inference to be a quite explicit process; in any case, Kant surely must believe appearance immaterialism could also be reached by inference, and here the premiss of the unity argument would be a natural starting point. The relation of the unity argument to *scientific* immaterialism is more complicated. Kant eventually uses the unity argument as the ground for saying there can be no physical explanation of the mind, but he is extremely sketchy in his grounds for the claim, even though he seems to take it to be a major and definitely unproblematic aspect of the case for immaterialism. It is the only point he makes on the issue in the *Prolegomena* (where it is made three times, but without explanation),[43] and it seems to be what (i.e., all that) he means in saying the sole (presumably valid) object of the rational psychology is the 'refutation of materialism'.[44] Kant's most direct use of the argument is a late formulation which runs as follows:

That he [man] is not wholly and merely body (when the matter is considered on the level of appearances) can be strictly proven from the fact that unity of consciousness must be met with in all cognition (thus also in cognition of oneself), and it is impossible that many representations divided among various subjects could constitute a unified thought; therefore materialism can never be used as a principle for explaining the nature of the soul.[45]

Note that the claim here is not that materialism cannot explain anything about the soul, as if physical science couldn't predict the course of one's thoughts at all. Although Kant sees some difficulties here, his general view is that in principle the course of our mental life can be correlated with and therefore predicted via reference to fully determined physical phenomena. Kant's claim here is rather only that the 'nature' of the soul, presumably in its capacity for achieving a certain kind of unity, escapes materialism. Even so, his argument obviously depends on a fairly narrow conception of what can count as a materialist explanation. Here his dominant idea is not so much the old view that matter is sheerly inert as rather the belief, developed after the rejection of physical monads, that matter as such must be spoken of as consisting in and operating through extensive forces. Kant also appears to presume that materialist explanations in principle allow of being improved by explanations which posit a finer grain, a more divided set of physical substances, and that any such explanation would be inappropriate where the phenomenon to be explained is supposedly one which as such does not appear as a plurality of substances. The claim of scientific immaterialism thus does not rest simply on a reference to the unity of our thoughts but on a set of presumptions: first, that the unity argument shows our thought involves a simple phenomenon; second, that matter as such does not ever constitute anything simple — a point which must rest on Kant's divisibility argument — and, third, that whatever is simple cannot be explained as such by something that is not simple.[46] We will again postpone examining the first claim until we deal more specifically with simplicity (see below, Ch. II. 5), but it is appropriate now to go into the second claim and the exposition of the divisibility argument. The fact is that the unity argument will not get us very far here in the discussion of immateriality unless the divisibility argument can be made convincing.

As has been noted (see at n. 31), Kant first presents this argument quite tersely and implies it is not decisive:

But there is still *a* reason for immaterialism and it is this: everything that comprises a part of the whole of space is between two limits. The limits of space are parts; whatever is in space is divisible; therefore there are no simple points of matter. Rather, all matter is in space and divisible to infinity. Now if the soul were material it would at least be a simple point of matter, for it has already been shown that the soul is simple. But no part of matter is simple, for that is a contradiction; so the soul is immaterial not material.[47]

What is remarkable here is that Kant is simply rejecting out of hand one of the most basic ideas of his previous philosophy, namely that there may be items that are material and yet not *parts* (extended portions) of matter but rather simple founding elements. It is this rejection that the divisibility argument rests on and not merely the relatively uncontroversial notion that whatever is a part of matter must itself have parts. In the later lecture notes this rejection is not explained, and a number of times the divisibility argument is simply assumed as conclusive. The notes give only quite incomplete versions of the argument. For example, Kant is reported to have said, 'Material is not only what is matter [i.e., presumably what appears as such] but *also* what can be *part* of matter. So something simple cannot be a part of matter'.[48] For this to justify the relevant claim that nothing can be simple and material the first sentence should rather read: 'material is *only* what is matter (i.e., in appearance) *or* can be a part of matter' — and then support for this assertion should be offered.

The *Critique* could be expected to make up this inadequacy, but it does not, although the divisibility argument is Kant's only explicit route to completing his transcendental idealism, i.e., to showing that not only space and time but all of the empirical world is merely phenomenal.[49] Only after the *Critique* does Kant concentrate on the divisibility argument and get to the task of directly demonstrating that matter is merely phenomenal. Kant gives the argument an extensive formulation in the *Metaphysical Foundations of Natural Science*, and he admits a gap in his other discussions by pointing out that the infinite 'mathematical' divisibility of space and time cannot be presumed to establish by itself the infinite 'physical' divisibility of matter.[50] What he argues now is that between any two separate bits of matter there must be a further repulsive and hence material bit, for otherwise the bits would not remain separate. There are surely problems with this argument (as well as with the further inference Kant draws that anything infinitely divisible must be merely phenomenal),[51] but for our purposes the main point now is that even if these problems could be patched up, this need not save the specific thesis of scientific immaterialism. For, even if it is granted that there are no simple material items, or at least that there is no reason to think the mind is one, the further claim that materialism cannot explain the soul remains unclear. Even if matter is not mind, only a very narrow theory of explanation would entail that materialism could not explain mind. Such a theory seems inappropriate to adopt here, for Kant's claim of scientific immaterialism is interesting precisely because it can be meant as a thesis distinct from the judgement of the ultimate phenomenal or metaphysical relation of mind to matter (i.e., the thesis may be held even if, as Kant eventually seems to allow, our mind, like matter, ultimately may rest on a composite).

That such a scientific immaterialism could be given an interesting meaning if developed is shown by those recent positions which Donald Davidson describes as 'anomalous monism', that is, the view that the inherent complexity of the description of items of the psychological realm (broadly speaking) makes wholly implausible the expectation of our finding physical laws explaining regularities corresponding to the terms in which these items are ordinarily described.[52] This view fits nicely with the specific idea of a scientific immaterialism, for it states a regulative restriction on what is to be expected from reference to matter with respect to our explaining the mental as such, without making an onto-logical claim that the things that are mental are not consti-tuted by entities covered by physical laws. Another con-temporary development of scientific immaterialism closer to Kant's text could focus on his speaking of the limitations of the 'materialistic principle'.[53] Here his scientific immaterial-ism could be taken to mean just that the unity of thought cannot be *analysed* materialistically, for to have a group of items unified in thought means something other than to have a group of items unified in space. Kant then could be taken to be pointing to an idea that modern functionalists have emphasized, namely that reference to physical structures as such doesn't give the proper explanation of cognitive opera-tions even if the operations are embedded in physical mechanisms.

There is, of course, more to Kant's own position than whatever may be its parallels to views such as anomalous monism or functionalism, for Kant distinctly rests his view on the phenomenon of the unity of thought. Unfortunately, it is unclear how this phenomenon gives the additional support that is needed for Kant's own version of scientific immaterialism. If by this unity Kant means the basic capacity for synthesis which he ascribes to the understanding and claims no set of data or receptive faculties can ever explain, then evaluating it may involve a global judgement about the validity of Kant's epistemology (i.e., a claim that a materialist epistemology — even in an extended form — is impossible). But even if such a judgement were to come out positively for Kant, it would seem to have little to do with the immateri-ality of the soul in any relevant individual sense. Even if it were a fact that in judgement or logical operations there can be unities of content (e.g., abstract entities) which transcend naturalistic explanation, this still cannot be easily translated into a fact about our particular souls. On the other hand, if Kant's claim is understood in terms of unified acts achieved by particular individuals, it becomes open to a critique based on natural extensions of his own views.

One way to develop such a critique is to note that at one

point Kant suggests that to have a thought is to be able to express it.[54] On this basis a materialist could argue that the unity of thought any particular individual has is explained when his capacity for expressing propositions is materialistically explained (which is not to say such a language-user must be mere, i.e., disorganized, matter). The latter is no easy task and there may even be in principle Chomskian difficulties with it, but at least there is nothing in Kant's divisibility argument and its associated considerations to rule out the possibility of such an empirical theory of the acquisition and use of language.[55] One could also make the critique without committing Kant to a linguistic theory of mind, for Kant also speaks of the phenomenon of a subjective unity of mind that arises when various contents are associated. In such a case it appears the premiss of the unity argument is still satisfied, and yet Kant himself allows that such a unity is in effect capable of materialist explanation, though of course the unity (as conscious) isn't one that mere matter is said to have (but rather one that mere animals would have). All this leads to the conclusion that although Kant has hit upon a valuable idea in advancing the specific thesis of a scentific immaterialism, still — in the sense in which he understands that thesis — it is not adequately supported even within a Kantian framework.

4. Phenomenal Immaterialism and Noumenal Immaterialism

If we turn now to Kant's specific arguments that the mind is not *constituted* out of matter, and in particular first to his claim of *phenomenal* immaterialism, we find the divisibility argument and the unity argument employed again in conjunction. The divisibility argument concludes that the phenomena of matter are all to be considered divisible, and the unity argument would seem to show the soul is not to be considered divisible and therefore it cannot be identified with the phenomena of matter. Yet, even if we were again to agree with the conclusion of the divisibility argument, there would remain difficulties with the notion of a unity of thought. That such a unity does not appear material is sufficient for appearance immaterialism; that ultimately it cannot be grounded in distinct substances is a claim which, if true, would prevent its metaphysical or noumenal identification with matter; but nothing yet clearly rules out identification of the mind *qua* phenomenon with matter. The mind *qua* phenomenon is what it can be in principle empirically determined to be, not what it privately appears to be or what it may be intrinsically beyond the sensible realm of our knowledge. This is the relevant sense of mind for phenomenal immaterialism, and yet it is one to which Kant pays little specific attention.

In the *Critique* Kant says 'empirical dualism' is certainly true, but here he seems to be simply moving illegitimately from appearance immaterialism (A 379).[56] He might have been working on the assumption that the only way the mind could be material in a not directly evident but indirectly empirical way would be for it to be a physical monad (which would also not appear material), and that once this possibility had been discarded there was no obstacle to asserting phenomenal immaterialism. But surely there might be other indirect but empirical ways in which the mind could be said to be material. One need only develop the previously cited points that the linguistic and associative capacities of the mind might be given a materialist explanation which would leave no reason to posit, at least on the phenomenal level, anything other than material beings. One could also call upon the argument of Kant's own Refutation of Idealism that any knowledge of the mind is implicitly knowledge of its spatial location and general situation in a physical (though not necessarily material in the sense of involving impenetrable three-dimensional stuff) framework.

An additional way to attack phenomenal immaterialism by developing Kant's own thoughts is suggested by the Antinomies. In Kant's treatment of the antithesis of the second Antinomy, which concludes that 'there nowhere exists in the world anything simple', it is argued that, 'the existence of the absolutely simple cannot be established by any experience or perception, either outer or inner' (A 435/B 463; A 437/B 465). The point of the argument is that the characterization of the self cannot rest merely on data such as the 'non-consciousness of a manifold' which occurs when the 'bare representation "I" ' is 'only thought as object' (A 437/B 465; A443/B 471 — amended translation). Rather, it must consider 'every kind of intuition', or at least what happens 'when this subject is viewed outwardly [as it must be] if we wish to know whether or not there be in it a manifold [of elements] external to one another' (A 437/B 465; A 443/B 471). These considerations are presented as bearing on the issue of simplicity, but obviously they can be extended to an attack on immaterialism by showing that phenomenal immaterialism must rest on an intersubjective and not a mere subjective warrant, and that from such a perspective the characterization of the mind as a physical mechanism could be appropriate. All this can still be said without necessarily rejecting the unity argument, that is, without excluding the possibility that *in itself* the soul is simple and immaterial, for the objective here would be simply to establish the possibility of a materialistic concept of the soul in so far as it is an object within the realm of empirical knowledge. To say this should determine its phenomenal status is only to develop a point which Kant himself had suggested when he said that theoretical determinations decide what counts as belonging to outer sense (see above at n. 27).

Kant may have become insensitive to this possibility not only because at times he tended to slip over the distinction between appearances and phenomena, but also because at least for a while he apparently thought knowledge of the mental has to be a projection from what one is acquainted with merely through one's own inner sense (A 346/B 405). At that time Kant also made the misleading claim that 'observations concerning the play of our thoughts and the natural laws of the thinking self to be derived from these' can function only in an empirical and not in a rational psychology (A 347/B 405; cf. B 407). The claim is misleading because even if positive supra-empirical characterizations of the self may not be justified by mere empirical data, a convincing characterization of the mind in its phenomenal status might be derived by moving from some such data to a determination of the general conditions of the empirical knowledge of minds (see below at n. 71).

Here one might be tempted to try to save Kant's position

by using a tactic of contemporary dualists, by arguing that immaterialism says only that some mental properties are irreducibly immaterial, and hence that despite the previous points our feelings and sensations are enough to establish our immateriality. But there are a number of objections to such a move. It could be countered that contemporary materialists have said enough directly to refute this claim.[57] Or it could be argued, as Sellars has, that the material realm could be properly understood as being able to include in an extended sense the adequate counterparts of the mental properties in question.[58] Finally, and least controversially, it could be noted that this whole strategy of defending immaterialism is foreign to Kant, for he suggests (see below, Ch. VII.8) the designation of our feelings is wholly parasitic on our acquaintance with physical objects,[59] and that, to the extent that feelings cannot be understood through interaction with such objects, they do not belong to the phenomenal world,[60] that is, the realm of the empirically knowable. In sum, Kant's phenomenal immaterialism, like his scientific immaterialism earlier, can be shown to be quite weakly grounded even in the framework of his own philosophy.

Matters get more complicated if we turn now to Kant's attitude toward the soul's *noumenal* immateriality. Sometimes it appears as if Kant overlooked the difficulties of phenomenal immaterialism simply because he thought that in any case he could present a critical position *vis-à-vis* the soul's noumenal immateriality (see, e.g., B 409-10). But in fact Kant must accept immaterialism at the noumenal level, for the only specific criticisms he develops have to do with the familiar spurious difficulties of what was called transcendental immaterialism and spiritualism (A 358, A 360). Noumenal immaterialism proper remains quite defensible, for *given* the divisibility argument and the other strategies noted earlier, it follows that nothing, including the soul, can be in itself material. As long as this claim is not inflated into transcendental immaterialism, spiritualism, pneumatism, or (Leibnizian) idealism, there is nothing to be said against it from a Kantian perspective.[61]

Beyond the Kantian perspective, the defensibility of Kant's noumenal immaterialism hinges on the claim that things somehow can be more adequately perceived than merely as extended and with such relational properties as force. I think this idea can be evaluated in the same way as Kant's idealism in general, that is, as not evidently trivial, false, or absurd, but also as not clearly established by the arguments Kant presents (cf. below, Ch. VII). None the less, of the senses of immaterialism we have examined – the appearance, scientific, phenomenal, and noumenal senses ('transcendental immaterialism' not being considered a genuine form of immaterialism) – this last one has a special importance. We have taken the first of these positions to be adequately defended (or at least to point to an idea that is defensible; I do not mean to exclude the possibility of significant phenomenological objections here) but weak in significance, whereas the next positions are substantive but vulnerable on extended Kantian grounds. The last position, however, concerns the intrinsic characterization of the self and so ultimately must be most important from an orthodox Kantian view, and hence it is significant that there is no criticism of it from that view.

If we now turn directly to the *Critique* we can see in detail how Kant's discussion in the Paralogisms expresses the position already outlined: the approval of immaterialism in the appearance (A 357, A 358, A 379, B 427), phenomenal (ibid.), noumenal (A 359, A 260), and scientific (B 420) senses. This only increases the need to explain how the *Critique* could none the less be known for having a distinctly negative stance toward (theoretical) immaterialism. In what follows I shall argue that although the *Critique* presents what is prima facie not even a balanced stance on the immateriality of the soul but rather a negative one, Kant's position here still can be seen as fundamentally favourable to immaterialism. To show this we will underline again the ways in which Kant still accepts an assertion of immateriality, and we will argue that the negative considerations he does offer are not substantive or relevant to the specific issue of immateriality. In the end it will be shown there is no strong case made by Kant himself for restraining the assertion of immateriality, and this is just what should be expected given what we already know he asserted in lectures (and other

writings) during and after the period of the *Critique*. Moreover, this immaterialistic position will be shown to be consistent with Kant's similarly prima facie negative stances
in the *Critique* on such associated issues as the soul's simplicity and substantiality.

5. The Structure of the Second Paralogism

Kant's discussion of immateriality in the *Critique* is found
primarily in his treatment of what he calls the second paralogism, which supposedly invalidly argues for the simplicity
of the soul. In that discussion five types of points are made
that could be taken as evidence of an attitude critical of the
assertion of the soul's immateriality:

(A) remarks stressing that transcendental immaterialism
is not demonstrable;
(B) various implicit arguments and undeveloped remarks
which could be developed into proper challenges to the
assertion of immateriality;
(C) suggestions as to how the assertion could be made
because of various types of 'transcendental illusion' (three
types, C_i-C_{iii}, will be distinguished);
(D) claims that the assertion conflicts with the general
limits the *Critique* places on *a priori* knowledge (four
types, D_i-D_{iv}, will be distinguished);
(E) objections based on saying the assertion of immateriality is founded on the assertion of substantiality, and
the latter is unfounded.

If the nineteen paragraphs of the section on the second
paralogism in the first edition are numbered, they can be
aligned with the above points in the following way: (A) is
found in §§ 11, 13, 14, 16, 17, 18; (B) is found at least
later at A 402; (C) in §§ 6-9; (D) in §§ 4, 5, and 19; and
(E) in § 10. The remaining paragraphs (1-3, 12, 15) make
no critical arguments and even offer remarks that support
asserting immateriality in various senses. Even if we take
only a brief look at these points, the case offered against
immateriality appears weaker than it is generally thought
to be. It is clear that (A) is especially emphasized by Kant,

and yet it has been shown to yield no genuine restriction on claiming the soul's immateriality. Point (B), on the other hand, may yield genuine restrictions but ones precisely not developed by Kant himself. Point (C) is also stressed by Kant, though obviously it constitutes not an argument against asserting immateriality but only a set of hypotheses about ways such an assertion might be badly although naturally made. Thus, none of the text involving the first three points yields a proper direct challenge by Kant himself to the assertion of immateriality. By itself point (E) also cannot offer a sufficient challenge, for even though the possible lack of justification for asserting substantiality could embarrass someone arguing the soul is an immaterial substance, it does not by itself really undercut the mere assertion of the soul's immateriality. In fact, today one generally asks merely whether mental properties are immaterial without first trying to show the soul is a distinct substance.[62]

This leaves point (D) as the one we will have to focus on in defending the thesis that Kant himself does not have serious and well-founded reservations about asserting immateriality. Points C, B, A, and E will then be returned to in order. First, however, we should briefly survey the structure of the course of Kant's own discussion, which can be divided into four parts. In the first (three) paragraphs the unity argument is exposited and designated as formally invalid, although it appears formally valid and no explicit demonstration of a formal error is made. In the second part (§§ 4-5), the conclusion of the unity argument, the proposition that the soul is a simple substance is said to be unjustifiable in view of the *Critique*'s theory of the nature of analytic, synthetic *a posteriori*, and synthetic *a priori* claims. Thirdly, in §§ 6-10, hypotheses are made as to why the conclusion might appear justified. Finally, after § 10, reasons are given why even if the conclusion of the unity argument is allowed it must be 'empty' and 'useless'.

Kant's discussion here has an odd organization and it is easy to see reasons for revising it in the second edition, if only for the purpose of achieving a better presentation without any changes in essential content. At first, Kant seems to say the soul's simplicity can't be demonstrated, and yet he goes on to suggest that it may well be demonstrable although somehow this wouldn't matter. The whole introduction of the complicated syllogistic argument is thus made to appear unnecessary, and the second part of the discussion (§§ 4-5) is given an ambiguous status. Perhaps Kant could be understood here as reasoning merely that, given §§ 4-5, *he* can't see *how* simplicity could be proven, although this is not to say that it definitely can't be true or provable. Such an interpretation fits his statement at A 399, when after reviewing essentially the same points that are made in §§ 4-5, he says this merely 'throws suspicion' on the rationalist view. Moreover, the suggestion that there may be an argument for the soul's simplicity which gives a conclusion that seems out of line with Kant's general philosophy but none the less appears properly demonstrated, fits precisely the situation in which Kant has left the unity argument. He has said that it is invalid, but he hasn't demonstrated the invalidity in the argument itself (although in (C) he has pointed out some associated invalid inferences), and so it is understandable that he ends by trying only to show that even if it is allowed, the argument doesn't prove anything very damaging to his philosophy.

This explanation cannot be the whole story, though, because it leaves mysterious the general characterization of the paralogisms as invalid arguments. This problem also affects the first paralogism, although it is at least rewritten in the second edition in a form that clearly does contain an appropriate transcendentally motivated invalidity (see below at n. 106). No such reformulation of the second paralogism is given, however, although additional considerations of type (D) are provided (B 408). Many have held that Kant's position is simply incoherent, but I believe there is an appropriate implicit and invalid syllogism here that Kant can be taken to have ascribed to the rational psychologists concerned with the issues of the second paralogism.

The reconstruction of this paralogism was suggested to me by the analysis of Henry Sidgwick, who emphasizes a fact we have already confirmed, namely that the rational psychologists tended to approach the issue of the nature of the soul in terms of general ontological and cosmological doctrines about the elements of the world.[63] Accordingly (i.e., ideally, according to Kant), one can take them to have reasoned in this way: simple substances are permanent; the mind is a simple substance; therefore the mind is permanent and immaterial. This 'extended argument' is invalid because the major premiss needs to assert that all simple substances are permanent, whereas what the rationalists established was at most only that the monads which underlie the physical world are permanent.

It might be objected that from Kant's perspective this argument is not only invalid but rests on a false premiss, for by the time of the *Critique* Kant had rejected the idea that there are any physical monads (i.e., simple permanent substances that have physical effects). However, this rejection is not clearly expressed in the first edition, and Kant rather speaks of what could be said — viz., that the soul is permanent — if only it could be shown that the soul is a *'simple part of matter'* (A 401). This implies a willingness to countenance the possibility of physical monads, which is only fitting because, as we have already noted, his case against them was developed only in the divisibility argument of the *Metaphysical Foundations of Natural Science* of 1786.

One might also try to object to the last step of the extended argument, for it may seem odd to try to show the soul is immaterial by arguing it is like a 'simple part of matter'. But in fact in the first edition Kant does indicate that to be like a simple part of matter, in the sense of being permanent, would be in a way to be immaterial:

Everyone must admit that the assertion of the simple nature of the soul is of value only in so far as I can thereby distinguish this subject from all matter, *and so* can exempt it from the dissolution to which matter is always liable (A 356; my emphasis).[64]

This statement means that if the soul is proven to be permanent, then it at least can't be like matter *in the sense of* the particular material items that *appear* to us, all of which are as such corruptible. In this way the extended argument would be invalid because of the improper inference from simplicity to incorruptibility, and this in turn would be all there is to Kant's suggestion that in no sense that has 'value' have we distinguished the soul from matter.[65]

There is further textual evidence that at least in the first edition Kant preferred not to challenge the assertion of the simplicity (and hence immateriality) of the soul as such but rather only the extended argument we have reconstructed. In the second Antinomy Kant focuses on the question of whether there are simples or 'mere aggregates'. Kant eventually claims that in the first two antinomies both thesis and antithesis are false, and so he might be expected to claim the soul is neither simple nor a mere aggregate. Fortunately he does not say this. His real position is roughly that things, i.e., noumena or substances, are and must be simple (i.e., there can be complexes of substances but not complex substances), but phenomena (i.e., all empirically knowable entities) are complex, that is, in principle can be further divided (which is to say not that they are complex substances but that properly speaking they are not substances — see below at n. 100). Of course, Kant does not come out and say this, for this could give the impression that he is taking the antithesis to be true, and to do that, Kant believes, is to hold the incoherent idea that there is a 'real infinity' of parts in experience, i.e., that an infinite set can be given as such.[66] None the less, it would seem that Kant should say that at least for all practical purposes the soul *qua* phenomenon is complex. He avoids doing so by neatly stipulating that the thesis concerns only the question of whether things *given* as complex are ultimately simple (A 441/B 470). The soul is not given as complex and thus the topic of its nature is not settled by the discussion.[67] The overt warrant for this move is the fact that Kant sets up the antinomies to deal solely with 'cosmological' issues, but this warrant is limited, for surely the soul as phenomenon must also be considered a member of the cosmos.

On balance, the second Antinomy thus leaves Kant implicitly committed to our noumenal simplicity and immateriality (for Kant never says anything against the argument that all things must consist ultimately of simple elements) and to avoiding a resolution of the valid question of our phenomenal simplicity. This situation is hardly admitted by Kant, and it is only obscured when he concludes his second Paralogism discussion with the remark that 'even the fundamental concept of a simple nature is such that it can *never* be met with in any experience, and such, therefore, that there is no way of attaining to it, as an objectively valid concept' (A 361; my emphasis). This remark is not justified by the preceding discussion, and can only be understood as a hint of what he says later in the appendix (point (ii) below) to the Paralogisms, or as an anticipation of the second Antinomy, as if it showed that in general there can be no phenomenal simple natures — something which it does not do.

6. Other Evidence Against the Soul's Simplicity

We now can turn to the appendix and other places where point (D) arises, i.e., where Kant attacks the assertion of the soul's simplicity as incompatible with his general constraints on human knowledge. Kant formulates this point in at least four different ways:

> (i) by claiming the assertion 'the soul is simple' cannot be proven either as an analytic, or synthetic *a posteriori*, or synthetic *a priori* proposition (A 353, A 398–9, B 410);
> (ii) by claiming the assertion lacks the intuitive backing that any objectively valid proposition needs (A 399–400);
> (iii) by claiming the 'I' itself cannot be known objectively because it is the condition of all knowing (A 402, B 422);
> (iv) by claiming the assertion purports to being immediately known and yet there can be no such immediate *a priori* knowledge (B 408).

It has already been noted that Kant himself labels (i) as a mere 'suspicion' and not a conclusive consideration. Despite Kant's systematic consideration of the various types of propositions, it is not all that difficult to classify the assertion of the soul's simplicity as a synthetic proposition known *a priori* via an inference from the *a posteriori* fact that we have unified complex thoughts. This fact is of such a general nature, comparable to the fact that we are acquainted with change, that it need not invalidate characterizing the inference as *a priori*, for Kant similarly calls *a priori* the law that all change is causal. Moreover, Kant's implicit objection (A 353) that objective principles can be established *a priori* only as necessary conditions of experience hardly refutes the unity argument, for Kant himself treats the unity of thought as a necessary condition of our experience.[68] To do so is not explicitly to say that a characteristic of the soul itself, such as immateriality, is such a necessary condition but if immateriality follows from such unity then logically it is one of the conditions of experience. Kant might also have continued to resist the inference because it appears to be like the ontological argument in that it moves from a thought to the positing of something beyond. He similarly resisted allowing one to conclude from the *cogito* to the existence of a self, and proposed that '*cogito, ergo sum*, is really a tautology' (A 355). None the less, in the unity argument the inference is not from a thought in the sense of a mere concept to a being outside concepts, but rather from a particular effect in the phenomenal world (for, as Kant stresses in the second edition, 'I think' also expresses an empirical proposition) to a ground of that effect.

Given the weakness of point (i), it is understandable that Kant moves on to stress point (ii), the claim that the assertion of simplicity lacks intuitive backing. Now it is true that what Kant calls 'simple natures' (in the context of the second Antinomy) are not to be intuited, for even if there are minimal visibles, one cannot intuit that such items cannot in principle, as members of the world, be further divided. But Kant's argument against even physical simples ultimately cannot rest on such a narrow conception of the role of intuition and rather requires the theoretical considerations of the divisibility argument. Moreover, it is one thing to ask whether something given (such as extended body) as complex can be eventually determined to be simple, and something else to ask whether that is simple which is originally given as simple (such as mind) and such that it is unclear how otherwise it can be given. This observation also undercuts objection (iv), for in view of the given differences between mind and matter it need not be so 'surprising if what in other cases requires so much labour to determine — namely what of all that is presented in intuition, is substance, and further whether this substance can be simple (e.g., in the parts of matter) — should be thus given me directly' (B 408). Or more precisely, it need not be said that any more than apparent simplicity is 'given directly', and yet from this intuitive datum it might be inferred that the soul is ultimately simple. Kant tries to establish that propositions require a stronger grounding in intuition than this, but in so doing he only distorts his own philosophy by implying that in outer experience at least we do intuit substances and the permanent (A 399).[69] In fact the situation there is similar to that with the mind: a claim (in one case the permanence of matter, in the other the absolute simplicity of the soul) that transcends what is merely given in experience (in one case, changing items, in the other an apparent simplicity) is presented as a necessary condition of our experience having the form it is actually taken to have.

Kant's only remaining general objection to the unity argument and its consequences is (iii), viz., that 'the subject of the categories cannot by thinking the categories acquire a concept of itself as an object of the categories. For in order to think them, its pure self-consciousness, which is what was to be explained, must itself be presupposed' (B 422). This objection exploits the idea that rational psychology must use the 'I' as its 'sole text' (A 343/B 401; cf. A 346/B 404). This 'I' designates but a formal or logical consideration; it represents the fact that whatever (discursively) thinks must have a synthetic unity of thought.[70] As such a general condition the pure 'I' does not designate a particular object and *a fortiori* is not 'to be explained' or characterized objectively by the categories.

Now even if this formal 'subject of the categories' is not to be determined as an object, this does not show that any individual I that thinks is not *a priori* characterizable by categorial or derivative predicates. Point (iii) thus establishes only limits in treating as a knowable object certain aspects or conditions of the self. It does not show the self is wholly unknowable *a priori* as an object, for there are more alternatives than Kant expresses here. The 'I' can stand for not only the pure formal condition of being a subject, or the mere *a posteriori* and known details of the object of inner sense;

it could also designate the *a priori* nature of each particular thinking self. This ambiguity in the term 'I' is suggested by Kant's own introductory remarks to the Paralogisms when he alternates between discussing the 'I' as a pure form, a 'vehicle of all concepts', and as a 'given' item allowing us to distinguish soul from body (A 341/B 399).[71] As part of a plea for temporarily entertaining the possibility of a rational psychology, Kant points out that although we become aware of even the formal 'I' only on the occasion of experience, this empirical starting point does not taint the purity of the concept of the 'I' as related to 'inner experience in general and its possibility' (A 343/B 401; cf. A 346/B 404). Similarly, we can go a step beyond Kant's temporary plea and recognize that in the concept of 'inner experience in general and its possibility' there *may* lie not only structures characterizing a general formal 'I' but also data which allow us to infer something about the essence of our selves.

7. The Fallacy in the Unity Argument

This last observation anticipates limitations that need to be placed on the various considerations which fall under what was labelled point (C). In these considerations Kant suggests how one might be misled by features of the pure formal 'I', or 'I' of pure apperception, to make unjustified substantive inferences about the nature of the soul. Kant's diagnosis of these errors can still be endorsed, for even if we are defending the possibility of justifying within a Kantian framework some rationalistic characterization of the self, we do not have to withdraw from Kant the credit for unmasking, or at least pointing to, various ways in which the self is illegitimately but naturally given various kinds of epistemological primacy. Thus we can agree (in principle, if not in detail) that the concept of the 'I' can generate the various kinds of fallacies criticized by Kant:

(i) The fallacy of confusing subjective and objective conditions, of treating what may be necessary from our perspective as if it were universally necessary (A 354; cf. A 396). That is, just because I cannot help[72] but see myself as simple, it doesn't follow that I am simple. Kant also speaks of a version of this fallacy which involves misconstruing the 'absolute simplicity' of the 'I'. That is, because the representation of the 'I' is universally found in experience, it might be (badly) inferred that it is a representation universally required for experience, something Kant apparently thinks is dubious because of the possibility of an intelligence that would think without having to unify (distinctly given) representations (A 405).[73] (ii) The fallacy of inflating analytic into synthetic claims. Kant stresses this fallacy in the second edition exposition, which in this regard improves on an unsatisfactory formulation in the first edition. There his example is that the fact that our representation of the I may be simple does not mean that the I represented is simple.[74] Kant apparently characterizes this as an error about an analytic proposition because the premiss does not seem to be a proposition in the material mode, i.e., it is the proposition ' "I" is simple', not 'I am simple'. ' "I" is simple' is only about representations and it might seem to be analytic, because analytic propositions can be thought to be only about representations — though representations in the sense of concepts. But here the 'I' stands not for a representation *qua* concept but rather for a representation *qua* act of thinking, and so although one can understand why Kant might be led to call the proposition analytic, his terminology does not seem proper. In the second edition Kant has a better candidate for the analytic proposition that tends to be improperly inflated, though he still does not give it an explicit formulation (B 407–8). The analytic proposition he seems to have in mind is something like, 'a thought must have a subject', and the associated synthetic proposition would be, 'the subject of a thought must be simple'.

(iii) The fallacy of making a determinate claim from an indeterminate representation, of inferring, for example, that because the representation of the self is not the representation of a complex self, then it must be the representation of what is a non-complex self.[75] This fallacy is closely related to what Kant calls the error of moving from the 'abstracted' pure or logical aspect of the 'I' to making claims about a 'real' or particular I (see especially A 350 and B 427).

It is no doubt possible to combine these considerations, and also to note that in various senses they all manifest the general error of moving from 'mere concepts' within oneself to claims that would require some objective intuitability. Yet although Kant often speaks of 'the' fallacy of the paralogisms, it is helpful to note the different formulations he uses. They reveal that there are a variety of tendencies in the text, as well as various starting points for expansions of his criticisms and for different interpretations of what in general Kant really meant. Rather than explore these possibilities further, I will note only that as stated none of the formulations demonstrates either that there is a fallacy in the unity argument as such or even indicates precisely what the fallacy is in the argument that obviously is fallacious, viz., the extended argument.

This is not to say that the unity argument cannot be adequately criticized along lines at least indirectly suggested by Kant. As a starting point for such a criticism, consider Kant's reference to the 'illusion which leads us to regard the unity in the synthesis of thoughts as a perceived unity in the subject of the thoughts' (A 402).[76] By itself this remark, like the others we have examined, does not reveal precisely where the Achilles' heel of the unity argument is to be found. In fact, by continuing to suggest the argument involves a perceived rather than an inferred unity, Kant continues to do it injustice. But the remark does indicate that he is properly suspicious about believing a 'unity in synthesis' must entail a 'unity in the subject'. This scepticism could be seen as part of his general insistence that no presumption can be made about how the numerical differentiation of phenomenal entities or functions maps on to that of noumenal entities.[77] However, this still does not reveal precisely what is wrong with believing a unified, synthesized thought cannot rest in a diversity of subjects. Does not the unity argument still show that to allow such a diversity is precisely to destroy the unity of the thought, just as 'single words of a verse,

distributed among different beings, never make up a whole
. . . verse' (A 352)?

The answer to this central question is no, for all the unity
argument really does is remind us that the mere fact that
a set of thinkers each has a single word in mind is not enough
to entail that any thinker has a whole verse in mind. So, the
unity of a complex thought cannot be explained *as the mere
conjunction* of a complex of thinkings by different thinkers,
but this does not prove that 'the' thinker of a (complex)
thought cannot be a complex being (i.e., a complex of
beings). That is, although he may be complex and have a
thought, he wouldn't have it through being a complex of
thinkers.[78] All that is required for the unity argument to fail
is that a complex thought possibly be properly ascribable
to something which is a complex of substances, and it does
not require that the substances individually be thinkers (let
alone that their thinking distinct thoughts is what explains
the unity of a complex thought).

What may have misled the rationalist here is the belief
that the most understandable way for a property to attach
to a complex is for it to attach (in at least a partial way)
to each of the members of the complex. For, if it might
not be at all ascribable to any of the members, it may seem
mysterious how it could be ascribable to the whole. But this
is simply to fall prey to the fallacy of believing emergent
properties are wholly impossible. That this is a fallacy should
be clear from such facts as that we could say, e.g., that the
heat of a room is due to a complex of molecules although
it may not be sensible to speak of 'the' heat of any one
molecule. None the less, this example, like most physical
ones, differs somewhat from the situation with a thought
in that theoretically it still might be possible always to
assign each (physical) item partially responsible for an effect
a precise share of responsibility for that effect. Such a move
may not be so open in the case of thoughts. Whatever the
complexity of substances may be that underlies the thought
of a verse, it would be absurd to expect it to have to reflect
the structure of the verse, so that, for example, a seven
word verse would have to be rooted in a complex of seven
substances. None the less, all that is required is that there be

some possible metaphysical relation whereby a number of substances each would have some (possibly odd and unknowable) partial responsibility for the thought as a whole, and as long as the unity argument cannot exclude this possibility it fails to prove the soul's simplicity. The possibility does seem to be what is to be excluded in the longer presentation (in § 3 as opposed to § 1) that Kant gives of the unity argument, but only at the cost of the introduction of an obviously weak premiss. Here the argument goes, 'For suppose it be the composite that thinks: *then every part of it would be a part of the thought*, and only all of them taken together would contain the whole thought. But this cannot consistently be maintained' (A 352; my emphasis). The italicized phrase is just the absurdity discussed above, and if it is included in the formulation of the unity argument, that argument becomes no longer tempting though invalid but rather manifestly tainted by a material weakness.

It is remarkable that the precise weakness of the unity argument is not spelled out by Kant or by most commentators who presume Kant properly labelled the argument invalid. To illustrate this point I will digress for a while by considering three of the best recent interpretations. The first is by the one commentator who does take pains properly to exhibit the weakness of the unity argument, namely Margaret Wilson.[79] Unfortunately, she still does not accurately clarify Kant's position because she entirely misses the implications of his noumenal immaterialism. She says that as long as one 'lacks a distinct knowledge of the nature of the self or the referent of the "I" . . . one cannot confidently reason from propositions about the self to the falsity of materialism'.[80] This statement is not entirely applicable in a Kantian framework, for without knowing anything 'distinct' about one's self one can know the self isn't noumenally material, for nothing is noumenally material.[81] Not having seen this point, Wilson appears to take the discussion of the unity argument to be directed to the phenomenal status of the self. Wilson thus suggests this is what Kant means: 'We are, he [Kant] says, ignorant of its [the "I"'s] referent precisely in so far as we are ignorant of the true causal account or "ground" of thought',[82] and so, presumably, our thinking might be causally and materialistically explainable after all and our minds may be at least phenomenally material. But then Wilson adds in a footnote that Kant's 'rejection' of the unity argument 'is not conceived as opening the way for a naturalistic account of thought or subjectivity'.[83] That is, Wilson implicitly recognizes Kant's scientific immaterialism and the fact that he gives no reason to think our mind is rooted in matter as a phenomenon. But this means that for Wilson Kant's 'rejection' of the unity argument must after all be the suggestion that we might be noumenally material – a suggestion that we know Kant could not make.

Rather than directly address the issue at a noumenal level, Wilson finishes by developing some other ideas as to what Kant may have thought about the unity argument. She says, 'Kant suggests that the Leibnizian (or more exactly the "rational psychologist") somehow confuses the lack of any determinate content with the *datum* of a simple entity or something that can only be explained by reference to a simple substance'.[84] Kant does make this suggestion, but it is but one of the ideas discussed under point (C) above, and this point by no means amounts to a demonstration of a fallacy in the unity argument proper. Finally, Wilson says Kant's view on the 'true unity of consciousness' is that 'the "datum" itself is suspicious until the theoretical analyses (and related experimental results) are in'. But the only example she gives to back this up is Kant's suggestion that 'for all "I" know over time "my" consciousness is being passed along a series of material substances',[85] – a suggestion which bears on the third paralogism and not the unity argument. In the end, Wilson has no proof that Kant works out a proper 'rejection' of the unity argument, although she is certainly right in showing how the argument is suspicious and in noting that Kant did suspect it.

There are two other important recent interpreters of Kant who fail properly to represent his views on the unity argument: Jonathan Bennett and Wilfrid Sellars. One of Bennett's mistakes is the same as the last error noted above with respect to Wilson, namely that of confusing the second with the third paralogism. Bennett presents the possibility of mental fission as an objection to the unity argument, and says that here he agrees 'with Kant against Descartes'.[86] This is quite misleading, because for Kant the issue of the soul's simplicity is distinct from the issue of how it might persist or be subject to splitting over time. Of course, given the recent much discussed possibility of brain bisection, whereby two beings could develop from the brain hemispheres of a person to become creatures with a distinct mental life, it is tempting to believe this shows 'the' person prior to the bisection was really a complex. But when Kant himself discusses something like this possibility in his famous footnote to the second edition, he emphasizes he is speaking of the 'possibility of the division of a *simple substance* into several substances' and that 'although divisibility presupposes a composite it does not necessarily require a composite of substances' (B 416).[87]

Here it might be argued that Kant still would *allow* that such a case of fission could demonstrate a complex of substances in 'the' original person. But although he perhaps should do this, he does not, and this reveals another misleading aspect of Bennett's interpretation. For, as Bennett describes this possibility, it involves the idea that what we take to be a simple soul might all along have been an aggregate of 'half minds', so that where there seemed to be but one mind there were really (at least) two. But this is one idea that Kant clearly would not bring against the unity argument, for he accepts it as evident that a set of individual minds as such cannot come together and explain the appearance of *a* mind (see above, n. 19). Moreover, we have just shown that such an idea is not needed to refute the unity argument. All that is needed is that the apparently simple self possibly be grounded in a set of individuals who as such do not think. Thus equally irrelevant is the other 'Kantian' consideration Bennett offers against the unity argument, namely the supposed evidence of contemporary neurophysiology that even in non-bisected persons the two brain hemispheres can be thought to have such distinct capacities that what is taken to be *a* mind may really be a duality or team[88] of minds. Moreover, it should be clear that neither this possibility of simultaneous mental disunity nor that of mental fission presents an objection to the fundamental claim of the unity argument, namely that *mental* unity is ultimate, for the bisected or separately operating hemispheres would still each presumably be a mind.

The interpretation of Wilfrid Sellars is less developed and not open to such objections. In criticizing Wilson I made much of Kant's noumenal immaterialism, but it is also important that not too much be made of it. As Sellars notes, by itself this kind of immaterialism need not even exclude the possibility of characterizing the self noumenally as in a peculiar sense a person rather than a mere thinking thing. This is possible as long as 'person' is defined broadly as a 'single subject which has both mental and non-mental attributes',[89] and not narrowly as a being with immaterial and material attributes (note that not all that is non-mental need be material). Sellars goes on to say, 'the being which thinks might, as noumenon, be a Strawsonian person which, in addition to thinking, has the noumenal counterparts of physical attributes'.[90] Now this statement is already a bit misleading because the term 'Strawsonian' tends to connote the narrower definition of 'person', rather than the broad one which is alone defensible here. But where Sellars definitely goes wrong is in holding it is precisely this ('broad') possibility that Kant has in mind when he (Kant) says perhaps 'the thesis that only souls (as particular kinds of substances) think, would have to be given up; and we should have to fall back on the common expression that men think' (A 359–60).

This difficult passage occurs right after Kant discusses what is in effect a situation of transcendental materialism, that is, one in which 'the substance which in relation to our outer sense possesses extension is in itself the possessor of thoughts' (A 359; cf. A 365, A 373). Now in that situation the self *qua thinker* could be the being in itself underlying the self *qua* bodily appearance, and it need not (*contra* Sellars) have any extra non-mental 'counterparts of physical attributes'. Thus, when Kant says we should say 'men think', he doesn't mean to be referring to noumena which (as such, as noumena) would be complexes of mental and non-mental properties. And of course, given his phenomenal immaterialism, he here also doesn't mean our thought is ultimately to be ascribed to a complex appearance of inner and outer sense. What he does mean is that *not only* the substrates of souls *qua* inner appearances (this is what he means in speaking of the soul as a 'particular kind of substance' (A 342)) *but also* the substrates of outer appearances could be thinkers, and indeed they could be one and the same beings. It is admittedly odd for Kant to refer to this possibility as one in which we should say 'men' think, but it is no odder that his general suggestion that in a sense we can't deny matter can think (and hence can't assert that in a sense our thinking proves our immateriality) until we can say that the substrates of matter definitely don't think. Moreover, it is probable that Kant believed this possibility is actually realized, that is, that at least in the case of human bodies their substrates are one with the substrates of temporal and phenomenal thinking selves. To believe otherwise would be to encourage the idea that within one's own body there are many selves, each with its own rich inner life.

The difficulty in Sellars' interpretation can be seen as being only a more complicated instance of the general recent tendency to misread Kant here by imposing on him a more critical and less immaterialistic position than he really had developed.[91] The fact is that Kant himself fails to spell out the precise objection to the unity argument proper, and nothing he says in his discussion of simplicity elsewhere directly undercuts the conclusion of that argument.[92] His major attack elsewhere on asserting the soul's simplicity typically stresses only that such an assertion couldn't prove the soul's permanence (A 400-1), and so it is really a criticism of the extended argument and not the unity argument. Although this hardly shows Kant is assuming the soul's simplicity, it must be admitted in the end that such an assumption would fit most easily with his commitments to our necessary noumenal immateriality and to the doctrine that from at least a scientific or regulative standpoint the simplicity of the soul must be granted (A 672/B 700; A 682/B 710; A 771/B 789). Of course, such an assumption can be criticized, just as earlier we found extended Kantian grounds against scientific immaterialism, but this would not change the fact that as examined so far Kant's text offers no basis for directly rejecting the soul's simplicity.

The final challenge to consider against the thesis of an underlying positive attitude on Kant's part toward our simplicity and immateriality is what above was called point (E), namely the implications of Kant's critical attitude toward asserting the soul's substantiality. Here it can be replied that Kant goes on carefully to examine and implicitly to accept the possibility of the soul's being a simple but corruptible being, that is, something which would be phenomenal but, precisely because of its impermanence, a simple phenomenal accident (B 413). There is no reason why this point could not be extended to the issue of the soul's noumenal status, that is, no reason why the soul might not in a sense be called noumenally simple even if not substantial.

Furthermore, even if the assertion of our simplicity were taken to be unjustified in a Kantian framework, it would have to be remembered that this would not by itself undermine the assertion of the soul's immateriality. To believe otherwise is to confuse Kant's eventual claim that a material item must be complex with the unargued-for and not at all evident claim that a complex item must be material. Of course, given the unity argument it would be wrong to imagine the complex of substances that a thinker might be as a complex of thinkers. Yet the fact remains that without its being such a complex, it could still be non-material and mental as a whole, as well as at least non-material in its components. Thus one could assert the soul's immateriality even if its simplicity as well as its substantiality were given up, and this provides some confirmation of our earlier suggestion that here the notion of immateriality is at the base of Kant's rationalism. Hence, even if the elimination of grounds for asserting simplicity would no doubt eliminate the main ground traditionally offered for our immateriality,[93] it would not destroy Kant's ultimate grounds.

8. The First Paralogism

Having indicated that a critical attitude toward substantiality need not imperil our general interpretation, we can now approach Kant's first Paralogism directly. Kant did not always emphasize the distinction between the substantiality and immateriality issues, and in his earlier works he even tended to equate materialism with the view that the soul is a determination or accident as opposed to a substance. He did this in the course of remarking that ironically the rational psychologists played into the hands of the materialists by calling the soul a substance but equating substantiality with power. Kant believed that the physical powers of an entity reveal only its relational and merely phenomenal properties, and so these must be distinguished from the entity *qua* substance or thing in itself. Similarly, he believed the mind must be distinguished from its powers lest it be entirely identified with what is merely dispositional and thereby allowed to belong sheerly to the phenomenal and, in an extended sense, material (because of its thorough interaction with the physical) realm.[94]

What Kant's early beliefs show at most is not that non-substantiality entails materiality, but only that substantiality entails immateriality. Kant still does not bother carefully to distinguish these points when he begins his discussion of mind in the *Critique* by associating the concept of immateriality merely with substantiality rather than simplicity, which he associates with incorruptibility instead (A 345/B 403). This latter association is understandable now in view of the concern we have shown that Kant had with what was called the extended argument of the second Paralogism. The former association can now be explained in part by Kant's just noted earlier reflections on the nature of substance and power. It can also be explained by an idea that he tended to emphasize more later, namely that as appearances the immateriality and substantiality of the soul go together and are equally unproblematic. Kant takes it as evident that the mind is given to us as an item different in kind from extended matter, and therefore at least in that sense it is a distinct thing. He says, ' "I"', as thinking, am an object of inner sense, and am called "soul" ' (A 342/B 400), and this means 'the thinking "I", also as substance in the [field of] appearance, is given to inner sense' (A 379). This claim is also allowed in the *Prolegomena*[95] and the *Metaphysical Foundations of Natural Science*,[96] and many times in his later lectures Kant is reported to have called the soul a simple substance.[97]

These assertions must be put into context. Some interpreters have suggested that such assertions are mere residues of Kant's dogmatic period. However, these statements are not merely part of a patchwork *Critique*; they also occur in later works when it is clear that Kant was fully aware that the assertion of substantiality in his earlier dogmatic lectures was based on inadequate grounds, such as a supposed intuition or an argument from 'concepts alone'.[98] I believe that the best explanation of the statements is that Kant was approaching the issue here at the scientific (cf. A 721/B 700) or appearance, as opposed to the phenomenal or noumenal, levels. This interpretation saves Kant from inconsistency when he does challenge assertions of the soul's substantiality, for that challenge can be understood as meant to be relevant simply for the latter levels.

The challenge to the soul's noumenal substantiality is a complex matter, for even Kant believes that ultimately substance underlies the soul, for whatever ultimately exists is a substance, that is, there is something substantial in everything. However, even if there must be substance 'in' the soul, this does not mean that ultimately there is a *soul-substance*, for it may be that noumenally there is a complex of substances which make up what is one's soul, and even that no one of these has by itself any mental character. This is one thing Kant means when he says that I don't know that 'what is substantial in me is the transcendental subject' (B 427), that is, the substances which ultimately constitute me need not themselves be mental.

Rather than emphasize these points, Kant at first tends to use another and less satisfactory tactic against assertions of the soul's substantiality. He claims that the substantiality of the soul (as the rational psychologist argues for it) is a substantiality 'merely in idea', and that without permanence proven of it 'real' substantiality is undemonstrated (A 351). This contrast between the 'merely conceptual' and the 'real' can give a very misleading picture of Kant's ultimate views on substance. If the soul truly is a substance 'in idea' (in the sense Kant speaks of at A 350–1), that is, if it meets the pure definition of substance by being something 'whose representation cannot be employed as a determination of another thing', then ontologically this is a more basic thing to say of it than that its appearance is permanent. Although for Kant permanence gives 'substance' an empirical and in that sense a real definition, it defines not what is genuinely substantial but only what is material and phenomenal. In this case the items falling under the schematized category are not — as generally is the case — a subclass of the items falling under the pure category.[99] No matter how permanent something may be, for Kant it remains as such temporal and so phenomenal, i.e., not genuinely substantial but existent only relative to a limited sensibility. Ultimately, schematized or phenomenal substance can't be a kind of substance for Kant, because it is essentially relational whereas genuine substances are essentially non-relational.[100] So, if a being is a substance 'only in idea', that is, a being that meets the general necessary ('transcendental') conditions for being a substance, this hardly counts against its truly being substantial — any more than the fact that matter 'in its substrate' might also think really counts against our being mental and immaterial. *The supposedly critical points of Kant's first edition analysis of the first two paralogisms are thus similarly spurious.*

The first edition's lack of an adequate argument against the soul's noumenal substantiality is matched by the nature of its treatment of the relevant syllogism. That syllogism, like others in the Paralogisms, is quickly characterized as a formally invalid *sophisma figurae dictionis* (A 341/B 399; A 401-3). Yet there is nothing demonstrably invalid with the argument Kant cites, and he even says that its conclusion may 'quite well be allowed to stand' (A 350). This is the argument Kant cites:

That, the representation of which is the *absolute subject* of our judgments and cannot therefore be employed as determination of another thing, is *substance*. I, as a thinking being, am the *absolute subject* of all my possible judgments, and this representation of myself cannot be employed as predicate of any other thing.
Therefore I, as thinking being (soul), am *substance* (A 348).

Various interpreters, seeing the logical validity of the syllogism, have suggested that for Kant the argument's real weakness is a material one having to do with the premisses. For example, Kalter and Wood for quite different reasons object to the second premiss.[101] This premiss is admittedly odd, for the fact that I am in some sense the 'absolute subject' of all my possible judgements, namely as their executor,[102] does not clearly amount to the fact that 'this representation of myself cannot be employed as a predicate of any other thing'. But Kant himself does not object to the premisses, and their parts might be broken up into independent statements not meant to be derived (improperly) from each other. Given that Kant presents a quite different formulation in the second edition, it seems plausible that here, as in the second paralogism, the original rationalist argument that Kant explicitly presents is not the direct object of his critique. That is, I suspect that what Kant at first was really concerned with is again an associated *invalid extended argument* that deals with what he calls phenomenal substantiality or permanence. The extended argument would look like this: substance is whatever cannot be a determination of another thing; I cannot be a determination of another thing; therefore I am substance; therefore I am permanent. To the extended argument, but not the original one, one can apply Kant's charge of a subreption whereby a specific empirical claim is concluded from a premiss with only a general transcendental meaning (A 403). This interpretation also fits the end of Kant's discussion of the first paralogism, where he says the argument 'cannot yield us any of the usual deductions of the pseudo-rational doctrine of the soul, as for instance, the everlasting duration of the soul in all changes and even in death' (A 351). Here again Kant is defining the aims of rational psychology in terms of the prime practical-rational question of immortality, and so he simply does not attend to the claims of a more modestly conceived rational psychology.

In saying that Kant is originally not primarily concerned with noumenal substantiality and the argument of the first paralogism proper, I do not mean that Kant has attacks only on claims of phenomenal substantiality.[103] I also do not want to go so far as Bennett does in claiming that (presumably for himself and for Kant) the argument proper 'really does establish that I am a substance, this being understood as an empty or formal truth'.[104] To back this claim Bennett says, 'I cannot escape giving my concept of myself a substantival role, and so I must regard myself as substance'.[105] But even if *I* must *regard* myself in a substantival way, this does not prove that I *am* a substance. For something to be a substance it is required not only that it be represented as a subject in some contexts (e.g., all those in which I represent myself merely as thinking), but also that it must be so regarded in all contexts. Something either meets the requirements for constituting substance or it does not; there is no merely empty or formal middle way such as Bennett suggests.

There is, however, a fallacy implicit in the argument of the first paralogism, as originally set out, that might lead one (wrongly) to believe one is a substance because of certain complications having to do with the formal nature of the representation 'I'. These implications are not clearly brought out by Kant for they have to do with the odd part of the argument, later excised by him, which uses the phrase, I am the 'absolute subject' of my thoughts. The problem is this: 'I' as a formal representation really is the representation of an 'absolute subject' of all my thoughts merely in that whatever thoughts are had, they necessarily can be prefaced by the phrase, 'I think'. The representation 'I' is absolute here *in that* there is no proper way of representing these thoughts which *leaves no room* for the phrase 'I think'. Yet this does not mean that I am truly the absolute subject of my thoughts as a substantial mental being. Prima facie I am certainly such a being, but as long as it is metaphysically possible — and at this point nothing has been said to exclude such a possibility — that what I take to be a substantial soul is ultimately a set of (individually) non-mental beings, then the real subject could be these things (even if no one of these beings of *itself* would be a *thinking* subject). In such a case I (as the thinking personality that I take myself to be) would really be an accident or resultant of those beings, and so but a prima-facie or relative and not absolute subject, and yet the *representation* 'I' would retain its ultimacy in the specific sense indicated earlier.

This diagnosis is not developed in the original first Paralogism, but later Kant does effectively put into question the mere assertion of the substantiality of the soul by reformulating a relevant argument in the second edition which is shown to be invalid:

> That which cannot be thought otherwise than as subject does not exist otherwise than as subject, and is therefore substance.
> A thinking being, considered merely as such, cannot be thought otherwise than as subject.
> Therefore it exists also only as subject, that is, as substance (B 410-11).

Here it is clearly the case that a transcendentally motivated subreption occurs, although not one with an empirical conclusion. But there is in this fallacy a move in the premisses from a transcendental to an empirical meaning (and so a kind of *per sophisma figurae dictionis*), involving an ambiguity which Kant describes accurately: ' "Thought" is taken in the two premisses in totally different senses: in the major premiss, as relating to an object in general . and therefore to an object as it may be given in intuition; in the minor premiss, only as it consists in relation to self-consciousness' (B 411 n.). That is, in my self-consciousness whenever I consider myself merely as thinking, I can't help but represent myself as subject. Yet that doesn't mean I really am substance, for to be such I would have to be representable only as subject *no matter how* I am 'thought', i.e., represented (this is the transcendental major premiss), and thus no matter how *any* beings might intuit me.[106]

Here Kant's discussion has the obvious advantage of focusing directly on problems within the rationalist's explicit syllogism. It also first gives a genuine critical meaning to the charge that the soul is a substance merely 'in idea', for here 'idea' can mean not 'according to the pure category' but 'according to (merely) how I think', i.e., how I tend directly to represent myself. The fact that Kant has reformulated his syllogistic discussion to amount to a direct critique of noumenal rather than phenomenal claims can also explain why in the second edition he goes on to append

a clearly distinct challenge to the soul's phenomenal substantiality. Thus after noting there is no adequate basis for
claiming the soul's permanence (B 413), he adds a long discussion stressing that I may well be a phenomenal accident,
i.e., a temporary being, even if I have a kind of simplicity
(B 414-20).

Although Kant's final syllogistic representation of the
first paralogism is a great improvement, it is not an easy
argument to follow, and I believe important recent interpreters — Ralph Walker and Roderick Chisholm — have
seriously misunderstood it. Walker believes the first premiss
is something taken to be true simply at the phenomenal
level.[107] The fallacy supposedly begins when the rational
psychologist then takes

a second premise which Kant also accepts as true: 'As a thinking being
I cannot think of myself otherwise than as subject'. But when I think
about myself as subject it is not my observable, phenomenal self that
I am interested in, but the real or noumenal self which does the constructing. So the rational psychologist is not entitled to put the two
premises together and draw his conclusion, that I 'exist also only as
a subject, that is, as substance.'[108]

This interpretation cannot be correct because, as Kant's
own analysis indicates, the first premiss of the syllogism is
meant as a valid transcendental definition and is not restricted
to the merely phenomenal level. Walker believes that the
difficulty is that the 'self that I am interested in', which is
the noumenal self, can't be concluded about from the first
premiss because that premiss is merely about phenomena.
But the real reason the difficulty arises is just the opposite:
precisely because the first premiss is *not* restricted to phenomena, in order to apply it we need to know that *absolutely*
speaking the self can't 'be thought otherwise than as subject'.
So the real difficulty is not at all that subsumption under the
first premiss isn't sufficient to entail our noumenal substantiality; the difficulty is rather that, despite systematically
misleading appearances, we don't have sufficient evidence
to make any subsumption under the first premiss.

Chisholm's difficulty is of a different nature and rests
primarily in the fact that he overlooks that what the Paralogism challenges are assertions of the substantiality of the

soul, not beliefs that there is some substance underlying the
I. Chisholm believes that the point of the Paralogism is that
'according to Kant . . . the word "I" . . . doesn't refer to
anything'.[109] To back this belief Chisholm cites only Kant's
remark at A 350 that 'we do not and cannot have any knowledge whatsoever of any such subject'. Now even this statement does not deny that one could justifiably say the 'I' refers;
it simply states that one can't know what it ultimately
refers to. And of course Kant definitely does believe the 'I'
refers in that there is something substantial underlying it.
What he questions is only that we can say positively what
kind of thing that substance is, especially through the 'mere
thoughts' employed in the first paralogism. Kant is sure there
is an underlying reality here and he even asserts that we are
acquainted with its existence (B 429). Moreover, he hardly
denies all kinds of knowledge of the self, for he has a whole
theory about how we know the self in a phenomenal way.
The statement at A 350 thus contains crucial restrictions
that Chisholm ignores: it concerns restrictions not on the
existence of or our acquaintance with an underlying substance, but rather simply on knowledge of it; and it concerns
restricting not all knowledge of the self but merely knowledge of 'any *such* subject', i.e., specific noumenal knowledge
of the *nature* of what underlies us (see Kant's references to
the 'real subject' and 'subject in itself', ibid., and cf. B 427).

Ironically, Walker's interpretation happens to focus on
passages just like these (B 158, A 402). Walker says that
with such passages 'the flood-gates are opened' and that Kant
is drawn into a position inconsistent with his idealism.[110]
That is, Walker thinks that to allow there certainly is some
substance(s) underlying the self is to undercut Kant's restrictions on noumenal knowledge. Walker believes that here we
even have an important disproof of Kant's idealism, for he
thinks we must grant that absolutely speaking, 'without
the self as the active subject of synthesis neither knowledge
nor experience would be possible at all'.[111]

This kind of objection will be considered again later (see
below, Ch. VII.12) when we consider the more general
problems of Kant's idealism. For now it can be observed
simply that, just as we handled Chisholm's objection by

noting that Kant isn't wholly denying the 'I' refers but is merely blocking the assertion of knowledge of a noumenal soul-substance, so here we can handle Walker's objection by noting that precisely by blocking the assertion of a noumenal soul-substance Kant can prevent opening any dangerous 'flood-gates'. All Kant need allow is that there is some absolute reality underlying us, and that there is some absolute reality responsible for the synthesis that is our knowledge. These admissions do not amount to any specific knowledge of a noumenal soul or self. The admissions do not lead us back into rational psychology nor by themselves do they amount to any significant new exceptions to Kant's doctrine of the phenomenality of our knowledge. After all, there were always some indeterminate noumenal claims that Kant must have been making simultaneously with that doctrine, for example, claims that reality in itself is neither spatial nor temporal. The claims about an underlying substance and a transcendental subject (which need not be identical; see again B 427) are similarly indeterminate, and it is merely a relapse to dogmatism on our part if we think that thereby the I *as* a soul or self has been shown to be absolutely real.

9. Final Evaluation

We shall now attempt to summarize very briefly the results of this chapter in terms of the meaning, implications, and validity of Kant's doctrines. As for the implications with respect to the rest of his system, we have argued that Kant's treatment of the soul's immateriality is especially closely related to what he has to say on other topics such as immortality, and that at times the importance for him of these latter topics even obscures and distorts what he has to say about immateriality as such. Similarly, his concern with a unified and critical epistemological stance tends to lead him to much more restrictive claims than clearly necessary about the possibility of making some minimal *a priori* statements about the soul.

As for the meaning and validity of Kant's views here, the following table provides an overview of the results of our study of Kant's attitude with respect to the issues of the first two paralogisms. The most controversial attributions are followed by section numbers which indicate where their justification was presented. It should also be noted that the positions have been evaluated as positive or negative with respect to the mere justifiability of theoretically asserting the relevant doctrines, and thus a negative mark need not mean that there are any grounds against the mere truth of the doctrine.

	Kant's stance, the position Kant is commonly thought to have in view of the *Critique* and the overall superficial format of the Paralogisms.	*Kant's text,* the position that is left when arguments explicitly developed in the *Critique* are evaluated on the presumption of the general validity of Kant's system.	the *'Kantian'* view, the position that results when the most critical elements implicit in Kant's philosophy are developed.
appearance immaterialism	+	+	+
scientific immaterialism	+	+	− (II.3)
phenomenal immaterialism	−	+ (II.4)	− (II.4)
noumenal immaterialism	−	+ (II.4)	+
appearance simplicity	+	+	+
scientific simplicity	+	+	−
phenomenal simplicity	−	+ (II.5–II.7)	− (II.4, II.7)
noumenal simplicity	−	+ (II.5–II.7)	− (II.4, II.7)
appearance substantiality	+	+	+
scientific substantiality	+	−	−
phenomenal substantiality	−	− (but with many −	−
noumenal substantiality	−	− texts supporting the other position)	−

An obvious question generated by this table is why there should at all be differences between the attitudes designated as Kant's 'stance', his 'text', and his (in a very extended sense) 'view'. Without again going into the details of the differences of the three attitudes distinguished by the table, we can note that they follow a general pattern: the anti-rationalist stance that one expects from Kant's program fails to be adequately supported by what Kant actually says, but can be backed by developing and extending what is implicit in his philosophy. This should not be surprising, for philosophers often project a position which they do not adequately work out but for which they at least provide materials that others can appropriately develop. A more surprising point that I want to make here is that the middle attitude is the one with the best claim to be looked on as Kant's own real position.

This claim is not meant to rest on the fact that the middle attitude's positive evaluations of the various doctrines can fit the uncontroversial fact that Kant felt the doctrines are true and can be fully justified in a practical–rational way. Nor does my point rest simply on the claim that a philosopher is most appropriately identified with what his text justifies rather than with what he may promise to hold or with what others may make out of him. The prime reason for my claim is that it ascribes to Kant the attitude most consistent with what he said in his works as a whole and that, despite appearances, such an attitude is fully consistent with the basic critical impetus of his section on rational psychology, namely to block the theoretical road to its defining 'Idea', the idea of immortality (see B 395 n.). Of course, were Kant to prove that not even simplicity or immateriality can be ascribed to the self, this idea would be undercut from the start. But the general strategy Kant employs (in the lectures, in the extensive formulation of the arguments of the first paralogisms, and in the treatment of the topic in the second edition) is rather to stress that the justifiability of the idea requires support for a *series* of claims, such as the ones found for example in the 'extended arguments' we developed earlier, which are directly argued to be without foundation and yet necessary for the idea to be assertible. Moreover, if Kant were to sacrifice the weaker, earlier claims and allow, for example, that the soul is complex and material, he surely would have even more difficulty in holding to *his* view that human minds have a special epistemological and moral capacity. I think these considerations would outweigh for him the prima-facie tension between the minimal rationalist claims about the self and the general limits on knowledge set down by the Transcendental Analytic, and later I will argue further that ultimately there is no contradiction here. That there is tension and a set of considerable complications would explain why Kant is reluctant to emphasize the rationalist claims in the *Critique*. Finally, it is generally his favoured strategy to exaggerate the limits on theoretical philosophy so as to make the achievements of his pure practical philosophy appear more impressive, and this, along with his architectonic concerns, could also explain much of the negative tenor of the section on the Paralogisms.

In defending a generally rationalistic view of Kant in the first two Paralogisms, we only increase the desire for finding at least a genuinely balanced critical view in the third Paralogism and in the treatment of the associated topic of immortality. In fact, just as Kant's real position in the first Paralogisms is marked by an excess of dogmatism (e.g., in the rejection of scientific materialism), his position in the later Paralogisms is not fully balanced and at times even inclines to an excess of scepticism. This scepticism is primarily to be found not, as is generally thought, in the fourth Paralogism but rather in the complicated third Paralogism. Before analysing that Paralogism we shall devote a chapter to drawing together Kant's views on the various remaining issues of the mind–body relation.

Notes to Chapter II

[1] *AA*, vol. 1, pp. 21f.
[2] Ibid., pp. 20f.
[3] Ibid., p. 367.
[4] Ibid., p. 225.
[5] *AA*, vol. 1, p. 412. Cf. vol. 28, p. 681, and below, n. 44.
[6] *AA*, vol. 2, p. 52.
[7] *AA*, vol. 28, p. 283.
[8] *AA*, vol. 2, p. 51.
[9] *AA*, vol. 2, p. 327 n. Cf. below, n. 62 and Ch. V., nn. 10–12.
[10] *AA*, vol. 28, p. 115. Cf. also vol. 8, p. 392 and vol. 12, p. 32 n.
[11] *AA*, vol. 28, pp. 275, 680.
[12] Ibid., p. 115.
[13] *AA*, vol. 1, p. 480.
[14] 'On a Discovery According to Which Any New Critique of Pure Reason Has Been Made Superfluous by an Earlier One', in *The Kant–Eberhard Controversy*, tr. and ed. by H. E. Allison (Baltimore, 1973), p. 158 = *AA*, vol. 8, p. 248. Cf. J. Bennett, *Kant's Dialectic* (Cambridge, 1974), p. 45.
[15] *AA*, vol. 28, p. 145. This passage and many others must force one to agree

with M. J. Scott-Taggart that, 'if we cease looking for what is changing rather than for what is constant, the question of how the soul is present in the world is revealed as one of the questions most constantly in Kant's mind throughout his life' ('Recent Work on the Philosophy of Kant', *American Philosophical Quarterly*, 3 (1966), 177).

[16] *AA*, vol. 28, p. 144; cf. *Kant: Selected Pre-Critical Writings and Correspondence with Beck*, tr. by G. B. Kerferd and D. E. Walford (Manchester, 1968), p. 26 = *AA*, vol. 2, p. 293.

[17] *AA*, vol. 28, p. 44.

[18] *AA*, vol. 2, p. 327. Cf. C. D. Broad, 'Immanuel Kant and Psychical Research', in *Philosophy, Religion and Psychical Research* (London, 1953), p. 129.

[19] *AA*, vol. 2, p. 365. Cf. *Selected Pre-Critical Writings*, p. 26 = *AA*, vol. 2, p. 293, and vol. 28, p. 755.

[20] Kant may also mean here to attack Crusius, who spoke of impenetrable spiritual beings. See H. Heimsoeth, *Atom, Seele, Monade* (Mainz, 1960), p. 377.

[21] *AA*, vol. 2, p. 370.

[22] *AA*, vol. 28, p. 226. Cf. *AA*, vol. 17, p. 346 (R 3921), and G. Leibniz, *Selections*, ed. P. Wiener (New York, 1951), p. 539.

[23] *AA*, vol. 28, p. 226. Cf. *AA*, vol. 18, p. 145 (R 5295).

[24] Some very pre-critical views are found as far as *AA*, vol. 28, p. 296, where it is said that personal identity is proven by inner sense.

[25] *AA*, vol. 28, p. 226. Cf. ibid., pp. 266, 590, 682, 754, 759, 830, and vol. 20, p. 308.

[26] *AA*, vol. 28, p. 226. Cf. ibid., pp. 272, 590, 682, and A 345/B 403. In the latter cases only simplicity is explicitly argued for, but there Kant presumes what will be called the divisibility argument, and from this the immateriality of the soul can be inferred.

[27] *AA*, vol. 28, p. 272. Cf. above, n. 16.

[28] *The Kant-Eberhard Controversy*, pp. 117-23 = *AA*, vol. 8, pp. 199-207. Cf. A 226/B 273.

[29] This distinction may be behind what Kant says when he remarks that the soul's immateriality cannot be certainly assumed but is only likely given what we know: 'Dieses [immateriality] aber können wir auch nicht so fest und gewiss behaupten; sondern nur so weit als wir sie kennen' (*AA*, vol. 28, p. 272). On the difference between appearance and phenomenon in Kant, see Gerold Prauss, *Erscheinung bei Kant* (Berlin, 1971), pp. 1 ff.; G. Bird, *Kant's Theory of Knowledge* (London, 1962), pp. 54-7; A 20/B 34, A 249.

[30] E.g., A 379. Cf. *AA*, vol. 28, p. 756.

[31] The following is meant as an outline of *AA*, vol. 28, pp. 271-3. By 'scientific immaterialism' I mean not the view that there is a science of the immaterial but rather the view that there can be no science of the mind because of its immateriality.

[32] *AA*, vol. 28, p. 272. Cf. ibid., pp. 509, 754, 830, and below n. 50.

[33] These three points are all presented at *AA*, vol. 28, pp. 681-2. On the first point, cf. ibid., pp. 755, 830.

[34] *AA*, vol. 28, pp. 681-2. Cf. ibid., pp. 590, 755, 759.

[35] He also calls it 'virtual materialism'. See *AA*, vol. 28, pp. 682, 759.

[36] See A 385 and below, n. 100. Cf. *AA*, vol. 17, p. 679 (R 4699).

[37] *AA*, vol. 20, p. 285.

[38] See, e.g., *AA*, vol. 28, p. 273; vol. 2, p. 321.

[39] Cf. A 690/B 718, and *AA*, vol. 28, pp. 683, 755. At ibid., p. 591, Kant emphasizes that this holds even if scientific immaterialism is true; that is, even

if mind is unexplainable by a 'materialistic principle', it still may be corruptible like matter.

[40] The term occurs at A 379–80. Kant's use of such terms is not very consistent. In rejecting 'pneumatism' Kant at first says he is rejecting the claim that the 'transcendental object' which 'underlies inner intuition', i.e., the intrinsic nature of the soul, is 'a thinking being', but then he goes on to say 'thinking beings, (*that is*, beings with the [temporal] form of our inner sense)'. This last statement fits our definition. At A 380 Kant goes on to imply 'spiritualism' and 'pneumatism' are equivalent, and thus he passes over the distinct meanings we have singled out.

[41] *AA*, vol. 28, p. 680. At B 420 Kant also uses 'spiritualism' (in another deviant way) as apparently equivalent to this sense of idealism.

[42] *AA*, vol. 28, pp. 590–1. Actually what Kant says we 'see' here is our apparent simplicity, but at this point in Kant's philosophy that entails our immateriality. See above, n. 26.

[43] *Prolegomena to Any Future Metaphysics*, ed. by L. W. Beck (New York, 1950), pp. 82, 100, 111 = *AA*, vol. 4, pp. 334, 352, 363.

[44] *AA*, vol. 28, p. 768. Elsewhere Kant says the mere existence of thoughts, i.e. appearance immaterialism, refutes 'materialism', just as the (phenomenal) existence of bodies refutes 'idealism'. See ibid., p. 680 and above, n. 5.

[45] *AA*, vol. 20, p. 308. Cf. *Critique of Judgment*, tr. J. H. Bernard (New York, 1951), p. 312 = *AA*, vol. 5, p. 461, and B 419–20. In the passage from the third *Critique* it appears especially clear that Kant's resistance to materialism is primarily a resistance to saying the soul *must* be corruptible. This may explain why Kant himself was not very concerned with, and thus was vulnerable to, the criticisms developed below, to the effect that in many ways his own philosophy can be developed to encourage a kind of materialist explanation of the present operation of the mind.

[46] In the *Prolegomena* (pp. 100, 111 = *AA*, vol. 4, pp. 352, 363) Kant hints at another ground for scientific immaterialism, namely that there is a 'psychological idea', a notion of the soul as an 'absolute subject', that can never be done justice by the piecemeal and supposedly in principle incomplete explanations of the materialist type. Kant does not develop this idea adequately for it to be given much weight.

[47] *AA*, vol. 28, p. 273.

[48] *AA*, vol. 28, p. 754. Cf. ibid., pp. 591, 830.

[49] Kant does make a move toward the divisibility argument at A 439/B 467, but what he says in the *Metaphysical Foundations of Natural Science* concedes the inadequacy of this move. He also suggests that his transcendental idealism has made physical monads unnecessary. But even if such monads don't serve as the grounds of space and time, they still might exist. Ironically, Bennett (*Dialectic*, p. 172) and P. F. Strawson (*The Bounds of Sense*, p. 184), without any sign of familiarity with Kant's earlier views, attack this passage in the *Critique* by defending what is in effect the concept of a physical monad — as if Kant had never thought of it! Bennett also misconstrues Kant's picture of physical monads by saying they must be homogeneous, separated by void, and without relation to extension — all factors lacking in the physical monadology Kant had developed earlier (*Dialectic*, p. 173).

[50] *The Metaphysical Foundations of Natural Science*, tr. by J. Ellington (New York, 1970), pp. 49–56, 73–4 = *AA*, vol. 4, pp. 503–8 and 520–1. Cf. *The Kant-Eberhard Controversy*, p. 125 = *AA*, vol. 8, p. 209. A. C. Ewing draws attention to the importance of the *Metaphysical Foundations* here (*A Short Commentary on Kant's Critique of Pure Reason* [Chicago, 1938], p. 217).

[51] Cf. Bennett, *Dialiectic*, p. 173: 'If a region of space R is dominated by a "repulsive force" which prevents anything from entering R from the outside, then every sub-region r of R must be dominated by a force which protects r's borders from invasion. That sounds reasonable in itself; but Kant takes it to imply that the source of the repulsive force dominating r must lie within r itself and must be separable from the sources of such power which dominate other sub-regions.' Ironically, Bennett's objection appears to conflict with his own view that a thing is to be equated with its effects (ibid., p. 172) — a view that Kant thinks appropriate for phenomena but not things in themselves. Mary Hesse sweeps the difficulties of the argument under the rug by saying that what we have called the divisibility argument amounts to a 'regulative' position for Kant which does not assert the truth or falsity of the existence of material simples (*Forces and Fields* [New York, 1961], p. 175). Such an interpretation is unacceptable because it makes inexplicable Kant's categorical claim that matter is therefore (i.e., because of its divisibility) 'merely phenomenal'.

[52] See D. Davidson, 'Mental Events', in *Experience and Theory*, ed. by L. Foster and J. Swanson (Univ. of Massachusetts, 1970), and 'Psychology as Philosophy', in *Philosophy of Psychology*, ed. by S. C. Brown (London, 1974). Cf. T. Mischel, 'Kant and the Possibility of a Science of Psychology', *The Monist*, 51 (1967), 599-622.

[53] *AA*, vol. 28, p. 831. Cf. A 683/B 712.

[54] 'Wir haben nur dann etwas im Kopfe und haben es gefasst, wenn wir es aus uns selbst, wenigstens in uns, hervorbringen können. Man hat die Wörter nur im Kopf, wenn man sie in sich aussprechen kann'. *AA*, vol. 18, p. 84 (R 5090).

[55] See, e.g., H. Putnam, *Philosophical Papers*, vol. 2 (Cambridge, 1975), and Jerry Fodor, *Psychological Explanation* (New York, 1968).

[56] As Wilfrid Sellars notes, 'although this [commitment to dualism] conflicts with the flexibility of his [Kant's] concept of "matter", and his sensitivity to the possibilities of sophisticated physical theory, he never seriously questions it'. 'This I or He or It (the Thing) Which Thinks', *Proceedings of American Philosophical Association*, 44 (1970-1), 10.

[57] See, e.g., *The Mind/Brain Identity Theory*, ed. by C. V. Borst (London, 1970).

[58] See W. Sellars, *Science, Perception and Reality* (London, 1963).

[59] See Prauss, *Erscheinung*, p. 318.

[60] Cf. Sellars: 'But the deeper thrust of Kant's transcendental idealism is the thesis that the core of the knowable self is the self as *perceiver of material things and events*' ('Kant's Transcendental Idealism', in *Proceedings of the Ottawa Congress on Kant in the Anglo-American and Continental Traditions*, ed. by P. Laberge, F. Duchesneau, and B. Morrissey (Ottawa, 1976), p. 181. Sellars moves too quickly, however, in saying ('The I Which Thinks', pp. 15-18) the first Analogy should force Kant to treat the phenomenal self as a complex of matter because it speaks of all changes as a modification of permanent matter (B 225). Sellars overlooks the fact that Kant modifies this statement in the *Metaphysical Foundations of Natural Science* (p. 103 = *AA*, vol. 4, p. 542).

[61] Thus it is misleading for Bennett (*Dialectic*, p. 91) to say that for Kant 'transcendentally', i.e., noumenally, anything goes.

[62] See, however, *AA*, vol. 28, pp. 283, 680, 754, where Kant suggests that because we are 'alive' we operate from a different principle than matter and so are a distinct thing.

[63] H. Sidgwick, *Lectures on the Philosophy of Kant and Other Philosophical Essays and Lectures* (London, 1905), pp. 141-6. Sidgwick's analysis provides

a rebuttal of Bennett's claim that here 'Kant has presented a jumble of points which no philosopher would string together on a line' (*Dialectic*, p. 72).

[64] Corresponding to the ambiguity about 'matter' is an ambiguity about 'substance'. Cf. Kant's odd remarks in the first Analogy about substances, although his eventual theory of permanent empirical substance implies there may be ultimately no plurality of empirical substances (A 118, B 231).

[65] See also A 400, A 401, and B 413 for more support of the claim that corruptibility is Kant's prime concern here.

[66] For a good analysis of Kant's problems with infinity, see Bennett, *Dialectic*, pp. 114 ff., especially p. 133.

[67] At A 466/B 494, however, Kant treats the soul as the topic of the second Antinomy. Perhaps this passage is the sign of an earlier plan for the Dialectic that wasn't realized.

[68] I thus believe N. Kemp Smith moves too quickly in claiming that 'being a synthetic *a priori* judgment, it can be established only by means of a transcendental deduction. But in that form it will define only a condition required for the possibility of consciousness; it can tell us nothing in regard to the noumenal nature of the thinking being'. *A Commentary to Kant's 'Critique of Pure Reason'* (London, 1923, second edition), p. 459.

[69] It is also inadequate here to object that inner experience is a mere flux, for the unity argument can apply to the unity of a complex thought had at a moment, and is not affected by the fact that from moment to moment our experience is in flux.

[70] Cf. W. Sellars, 'The I Which Thinks', p. 7: the 'I' is 'an *unrestricted* principle in the philosophy of mind, which transcends the distinction between the noumenal and the phenomenal self, to the effect that "an I thinks of a manifold" is not to be confused with "an I has a manifold of thoughts".' For this reason Kant can say the '*pure*' I is empty. I do not believe his argument is (as Sidgwick suggests, *Lectures*, p. 149) that it is empty because the 'I' is in 'sheer flux', for what Kant stresses is that the flux attaches to the 'I' *qua empirical* representation.

[71] Kalter contends — quite unnecessarily I believe — this ambiguity is but a residue of different times of composition and that only the first meaning is relevant for Kant's mature philosophy (*Kants vierter Paralogismus* [Meisenheim am Glan, 1975], pp. 111-19). H. Heimsoeth, on the other hand, goes too far in asserting that Kant himself in his mature work developed extensive knowledge of the I as noumenon (*Studien zur Philosophie Immanuel Kants* [Cologne, 1956], pp. 236 ff.).

[72] This fallacy can have two forms. If the 'can't help' refers to what can't help but *appear* to me, then the fallacy involves referring even to a merely phenomenal claim; but if it refers to what can't help but be determined *phenomenally*, then the fallacy involves referring to a noumenal claim (as at B 421). In either case, Kant here may have gone too far in presuming what we 'can't help' but think (cf. Bennett, *Dialectic*, p. 86).

[73] I cannot find a separate point in Kant's extra assertion that, 'Since it is at the same time in all respects unitary, it carries with it the illusion of an absolute unity of the conditions of thought in general, and so extends itself further than possible experience can reach' (A 340/N 398) — unless Kant is trying to get at the two points distinguished in the above note. Cf. also A 323, A 335.

[74] 'But the simplicity of the representation of a subject is not *eo ipso* knowledge of the simplicity of the subject itself' (A 355; cf. A 402). Strawson appears to use this text as his model for understanding the paralogisms in general as a

fallacy of a type that infers from a 'unity of experience' to an 'experience of unity' (*Bounds of Sense*, p. 162).

[75] 'The representation . . . must no doubt be simple if only for the reason that there is nothing determinate in it' (A 355). Formulations like this are used by Sellars to characterize all the paralogisms. See 'The I Which Thinks', p. 14; and 'Metaphysics and the Concept of a Person', in *Essays in Philosophy and its History* (Dordrecht, 1974), pp. 236-8.

[76] The argument that follows can be compared with the 'extended' Kantian points made above (at n. 54) against scientific immaterialism.

[77] *The Kant-Eberhard Controversy*, p. 125 n. = *AA*, vol. 8, p. 209 n. Cf. A 358. Kant must say this, for the doctrine of the unknowability of things in themselves is in trouble if the differentiation of noumenal things is *known* to be identical with that of phenomena. It is primarily because of this point that I must disagree with H. E. Allison's otherwise convincing 'Things in Themselves, Noumena, and the Transcendental Object', *Dialectica*, 32 (1978), 48-76. Cf. N. Rescher, *Conceptual Idealism* (Oxford, 1973), p. 118.

[78] This point (i.e., that ' "the subject of thoughts, the 'I', is a plurality" is not the same as "the subject of thoughts is a plurality of 'I''s" ') is made by Sellars, who implies that Kant appreciated this is all the unity argument establishes ('Metaphysics and the Concept of a Person', p. 239). However, Sellars does not discuss the unity argument precisely as Kant formulated it and neither does he give any evidence that Kant saw its precise weakness.

[79] M. Wilson, 'Leibniz and Materialism', *Canadian Journal of Philosophy*, 4 (1974), 510-11.

[80] Ibid., p. 512.

[81] Ironically, Wilson sees this is Leibniz's position: 'If there must be "something real" underlying physical phenomena, and if this something real must be unextended, then (assuming the traditional mind-matter dichotomy) it may well seem to follow on this basis alone that there are mental substances – or at least "mind-like" substances' (ibid., p. 507). Kant can accept these premisses and conclude at least that what ultimately is, is immaterial, and so we too are ultimately immaterial.

[82] Ibid., p. 512.

[83] Ibid., p. 512, n. 45.

[84] Ibid., pp. 513-4. Sellars similarly offers only this point as his justification for saying 'Kant's analysis of the Paralogisms opens the way for him to hold' the self is an attribute of a complex physical system ('The I Which Thinks', p. 14). And he surely goes too far when he expresses this claim elsewhere as meaning Kant 'has kept the way clear for the view that other thoughts and representations are in reality complex states of a system, and in particular, of a neurophysiological system' ('Metaphysics and the Concept of a Person', p. 240).

[85] Wilson, 'Leibniz', p. 513. Cf. A 363-4.

[86] Bennett, *Dialectic*, p. 86.

[87] Kant does complicate matters when he goes on to speak of 'the extinguished half as preserved' in the bisection, but then he says clearly that when the mind 'has been halved, *another* separate substance would then come into existence outside it' (B 415 n.). At *AA*, vol. 28, p. 761, Kant calls the notion of mental fission 'idle fancy'.

[88] Bennett, *Dialectic*, p. 87. Cf. T. Nagel, 'Brain Bisection and the Unity of Consciousness', *Synthese*, 22 (1971), 396-413.

[89] Sellars, 'The I Which Thinks', p. 10.

[90] Ibid., p. 12. A clearer explanation of the relation of Kant's text to Strawson's view is given by Bennett (*Dialectic*, p. 92).

82   *Immateriality*

[91] I omit discussion here of a very different kind of interpretation which would attack Kant by suggesting he is being *too* critical about the unity argument. In particular, R. Chisholm tries to show it is absurd to suggest 'I might be "annexed to" or "placed in" a thinking being or individual substance' (*Person and Object* [London, 1976], p. 107). I have argued elsewhere that this kind of response involves a misreading of the point of the unity argument ('Chisholm's Paralogisms', *Idealistic Studies*, 11 (1981)).

[92] Affirmations of our simplicity, combined with criticisms of the 'extended argument', occur at *AA*, vol. 28, pp. 590, 753-5, 831.

[93] This tradition is treated at length in B. Mijuskovic, *The Achilles of Rationalist Arguments* (The Hague, 1974). Mijuskovic's reading of Kant, however, must be approached very carefully. For example, elsewhere Mijuskovic fails to see the difference between the unity argument and what we called the extended argument, for he says, 'if the [unity] argument is sufficient to "explain" (in however broad a sense we allow the term) the unity of apperception, then on what possible grounds could Kant continue to deny that it is also a perfectly adequate demonstrative proof of the immortality of the soul?' ('The Premise of the Transcendental Analytic', *Philosophical Quarterly*, 23 (1973), 160, n. 12).

[94] 'He who says, *"anima est vis"*, maintains that the soul is not a distinct substance but only a power, and thus a phenomenon and accident' (*AA*, vol. 28, p. 261; cf. ibid., pp. 24, 671 and vol. 8, p. 181).

[95] *Prolegomena*, § 47 = *AA*, vol. 4, p. 334.

[96] *Metaphysical Foundations of Natural Science*, p. 103.

[97] *AA*, vol. 28, pp. 590, 684, 691, 755, 830. Cf. vol. 20, p. 308.

[98] *AA*, vol. 28, pp. 226, 266. Cf. A 379.

[99] Some (e.g., Kalter, *Kants vierter Paralogismus*, p. 109: 'alle Kategorien beziehen sich auf Erscheinungen. Die Differenzierung in eine *substantia phaenomenon* und eine *substantia noumenon* ist ein Relikt der vorkritischen Phase Kants') have avoided this problem by saying that for Kant only the schematized categories have meaning, but this move has problems of its own and is demonstrably contrary to Kant's own views. See J. Nolan, 'Kant on Meaning: Two Studies', *Kant-Studien*, 70 (1979), 118. Kant often says items are without 'meaning' when what he means is what we would express by 'demonstrable reference' or 'application'. See e.g., A 239/B 298, B 308, A 248/B 305, A 696/B 724. See also below, Ch. VII, n. 111.

[100] Bennett rightly chides Kant for not coming clean on this point in the *Critique* (*Dialectic*, pp. 166, 176). (See, however, A 525/B 553: 'that which we entitle substance in the appearance is not an absolute subject'. See also above n. 94, and below, Ch. VII, n. 79, and *AA*, vol. 28, p. 759: '*Phaenomenon substantiatum* ist eine zur Substanz gemachte Erscheinung, die an sich keine Substanz ist'.) Bennett is wrong, though, to say (*Dialectic*, p. 170) that Kant even argues against the noumenal definition of substance (at B 467-9). What he is trying to do there is rather to say only that we cannot *apply* the concept as noumenally defined to the empirical world because we can't determine anything simple in it. Bennett remarks that 'a proof that there must be simple things is not embarrassed by the claim that we couldn't discover any empirically' (ibid., p. 166). But such a proof is at least disqualified from being relevant if the issue is what Kant restricts it to being in the second Antinomy, namely whether there are simples *within* the items in the world that are given as complex. Sellars tries to get around this problem by saying that for Kant matter is first matter in Aristotle's sense, and as this functions only as a subject it meets the pure definition of a substance ('The I Which Thinks', p. 17). The problem with this interpretation

is that by 'matter' Kant clearly means a set of determinate relational properties, in the sense of modern physics, and not in the sense of Aristotle's prime matter. And if Kant were to use such a concept, he would have all the more difficulty calling matter merely phenomenal.

[101] A. Wood, 'Kant's Dialectic', *Canadian Journal of Philosophy*, 5 (1975), 603; A. Kalter, *Kants vierter Paralogismus*, p. 121.

[102] Here I am opposing Bennett's view that in the second premiss Kant means I am the subject of all my possible judgments in that they are all implicitly *about* me (*Dialectic*, pp. 73-5).

[103] I thus oppose both those who treat the Paralogisms as if they were challenging only noumenal claims (e.g., Sellars, 'Metaphysics and the Concept of a Person', pp. 236-8; and R. C. S. Walker, *Kant*, p. 114) and those who treat him as if he were challenging only phenomenal claims (e.g., Bennett, *Dialectic*, pp. 69, 76; and C. D. Broad, *Kant: An Introduction* [Cambridge, 1978], p. 255).

[104] Bennett, *Dialectic*, p. 72.

[105] Ibid., p. 73.

[106] I thus believe Kant's point does not rest, as Bird thinks it does (*Kant's Theory*, p. 182), on the fact that the thinking subject is not 'intuited generally' (rather each intuits only his own) and so 'does not contain that possibility of agreement which is required for the objective use of the concept "substance" '. For the issue is ultimately not whether we can use the concept in a way others can directly verify but rather simply whether assertion of the applicability of the concept is itself adequately justified.

[107] Walker, *Kant*, p. 132.

[108] Ibid., pp. 132-3.

[109] Chisholm, *Person and Object*, p. 42. For more detail, see again my 'Chisholm's Paralogisms'.

[110] Walker, *Kant*, p. 134.

[111] Ibid., p. 134. See below, Ch. VII.12.

Chapter III

Interaction

In the previous chapter it was argued that Kant's first two Paralogisms are best approached in terms of a complex over-riding question that can be broken down into three sub-problems (immateriality, simplicity, substantiality). In this chapter I will approach Kant's fourth Paralogism by focusing again on a complex overriding issue, namely the nature of mind-matter interaction, and I will also break this down into three subproblems:

(A) the general problem of the interaction of the physical and the mental,
(B) the specific problem of the relation of a human mind to its own body, and
(C) the epistemological problem of demonstrating the existence of items external to the mind.

With respect to the first problems, I argue that Kant's views on mind-body interaction are embedded in his under-standing of the nature of interaction in general, and this understanding does not depart adequately from traditional views on the subject. None the less, there are subtle and unappreciated aspects to Kant's treatment of human embodi-ment that are worth bringing out, especially in the light of contemporary discussions. I conclude that even when this is done, however, Kant's view must be said to be still funda-mentally in line with the immaterialism charted in the last chapter, although it can be defended from charges that it amounts to an evidently absurd idealistic position. The same general line of interpretation is applied to the last problem, the existence of the external world. Here I argue that once Kant's discussions are read closely with attention to the developments and terms that have been analysed so far, he remains safe from the common objection of a lapse into subjective idealism. While in this way I defend both versions of Kant's fourth Paralogism, I also conclude that Kant's arguments do not amount to as radical or successful a response to scepticism as many interpreters have thought.

A.1. Interaction in General: An Historical Overview

In his empiricist period, Kant addresses arguments directed to the issues of the soul's causal and spatial relation to the physical world, and he even develops these into a proof of the external world. His first work, an essay on 'living forces', begins with an argument that there is nothing mysterious about mind-body interaction. Kant suggests a problem has been generated here simply because of the influence of a too narrow concept of the possible effects of force. If it is assumed that the only possible effect of force is movement, then of course the actions of the mind can appear mysterious. But Kant points out that it is not clear that this assumption has to be made, and he believes it can easily be shown that an adequate theory of even the ordinary physical world requires a broader notion of the possible effects of physical forces. It is the exposition of this theory that occupies the bulk of his essay, but Kant also emphasizes his belief that it can resolve the mind-body problem. His early view is that as long as we allow a force to be whatever in general is responsible for a change, then given that there are obvious changes of mind consequent upon changes in body and vice versa,[1] it follows that mind and body can be understood to be in a normal relation of interaction of forces.[2] This position is surprisingly close to what Kant says in the end, although with time he not only becomes aware of genuine complications in the issue, but also moves away from the liberality he exhibits here about the range of intelligible relations.

The second work of Kant's empiricist period, the *Universal Natural History*, continues to treat mind-body interaction as unproblematic. Here Kant discusses the external world not only as the source of all the material for our empirical knowledge but also as the sufficient determination of human character. It is probable that he could remain comfortable with this position because he then held to a version of compatibilism. Later Kant rejected this compatibilism, but first he went to considerable lengths to defend it against the objection that it might impugn not only our sense of freedom but also God's character.[3] At that time he seems not to have appreciated the conflict inherent in saying, on the one hand, that freedom is merely determination via an inner principle, and in arguing on the other hand that all our inner changes must have external causes.[4] What Kant wanted to hold is that the human mind is universally subject to physical causality, and yet that it may be spontaneous in a special way because of capacities which transcend those of other animals and relatively self-directed machines (or animals). But the theory of mind presented in the *Universal Natural History* remains much too simple to defend this position. Typical of the work is the fact that from the idea that character depends on external influence, Kant moves to the suggestion that the less material the influence, that is, the less rough the atmosphere and gravitational force on a planet, the better chance one has for a proper moral life.[5]

By the end of his empiricist period, Kant began to criticize the common theory of interaction as occurring through a kind of 'physical influx', and he in effect conceded he had not resolved the philosophical problem of the interaction of mind and body. His immediate solution, typical of his rationalist period, was to say that mind and body, like all substances, are ultimately connected via a common ground in God.[6] This view had the consequence of preventing mind-body interaction from becoming a special problem, because it made all interaction ultimately require a basis in a mind. What Kant was most attached to was this last doctrine, and not any specific reference to the divine. In his sceptical period he acknowledged the weakness of using God as a solution to theoretical philosophical problems, but he was forced to employ such a tactic in the *Dissertation* of 1770.[7] He then explicitly connected his general theory of interaction to the mind-body problem by saying that only through God can we assert the mind is affected by external things.[8] But he confessed that he still had not really given an explanation of either body-body or mind-body interaction.[9]

In his critical period, Kant eventually rejected all reliance on references to God in theoretical demonstrations, and thus he undermined his previous account of the connection of substances. He then presented a position on the issue of interaction which he contrasted with all traditional approaches and which also can be contrasted with his own earlier views. Previous positions on the subject can be divided into what can be called influx theories and harmony theories. The first kind of theory appears in various guises in Locke,[10] the opponents of Leibniz, and in Kant's own earliest work. It traditionally involves what Jonathan Bennett has recently called the 'balance principle', i.e., that causal influence requires a literal transfer of an accident from one substance to another, so that one gains exactly what the other loses.[11] Kant denied this principle in the *Prolegomena*[12] and the *Metaphysical Foundations of Natural Science*,[13] but in the *Critique* he rested his objection to the influx theory on the mere claim that it is tied to a belief in transcendental realism. That is, he argued interaction is an insuperable problem only when one fails to accept his doctrine of transcendental idealism (A 384). Therefore, the harmony theory, which in effect can be found in Malebranche, Leibniz, and Kant's rationalist period, is also to be rejected, for it supposedly arises when the influx theory is denied not on the basis of the above critical objection but simply because it takes real interaction (between finite substances) to be unintelligible (namely by denying that precisely what the balance principle calls for can occur).

2. Evaluation

In now evaluating the influx, harmony, and Kantian theories, we will consider first how they are relevant to the topic of interaction in general and then how they bear on mind-body interaction in particular. The general topic is not one Kant has much to say about (nor one that can be adequately handled in a mere study of the philosophy of mind), but it is obviously inextricably related to the more specific one. For example, the harmony position that there is no special problem to mind-body interaction follows directly from its view that in general there cannot be real substantial interaction. The liability of the harmony theory is then that it holds one of our most basic beliefs (substantial interaction) cannot be true, and it leaves no purely philosophical ground (assuming there is difficulty in antecedently establishing that God exists and acts) for asserting there is more than one monad.[14] Kant, on the other hand, always believed philosophy must leave room for the truth of substantial interaction, even if it cannot explain how it takes place (A 393). He thus agrees with the influx theorist that there is real interaction, while he also sides with the harmony theorist's point that the influx theorist has an unacceptable understanding of interaction. Yet Kant does not go so far as he might here, given his early liberal view on force, for he is not willing to say that real substantial interaction might be mere lawful regularity.

At this point it can become difficult to see the advantages of Kant's theory, for he does not make much of an effort to convince the harmony theorist that there is real interaction. According to Kant, his view is superior simply because it is at least 'critical' rather than 'dogmatic' (A 388). There is something to this, for although there are also some presuppositions in Kant's own position, he does not hold to such a strong claim as that ultimately there cannot be real interaction. Rather, he notes that there is no evident contradiction in substantial interaction, and so we might as well go along with common sense in believing in it – as long as we do not in turn make any 'dogmatic' presuppositions about the specific nature of the interacting items (e.g., that ultimately they have the same character as spatial phenomena). Kant appears to share the common-sense belief that our receptivity shows there are substances beyond us. His idea here is that to be receptive is to be acted upon, and since what acts is substantial, it follows that there is a substance acting upon us. Unfortunately, this argument doesn't prove that the substance is distinct from one's self,[15] nor does it establish its premiss that our experience really is receptive (and not simply finite) instead of merely appearing so. Moreover, although Kant gives a theory of (merely) phenomenal interaction in his Principles, there is no way a Kantian can move from this to saying how many substances there really are or how they can be numerically differentiated. These difficulties reinforce the observation of the previous chapter that Kant's concept of substance is strained by conflicting meanings at the phenomenal and noumenal levels. If what is phenomenally substantial, namely matter, cannot be noumenally so, then it should not be surprising that where there is phenomenal interaction there might not, noumenally speaking, be *inter*action.

Despite these difficulties in establishing Kant's position, there is as yet no reason to presume that from the very start his view on the mind-body relation must be disqualified by a peculiar dogmatic presupposition. And although Kant hardly gives a satisfying explanation of interaction in general, he can fairly reply that we ought not to expect a full account of how noumena relate (B 428), or at least that here we cannot demand a complete resolution of all metaphysical problems. Moreover, the mind-body problem involves a particular feature, namely the apparent heterogeneity of the items, which Kant believes his philosophy can accomodate especially easily. Kant's claim that his philosophy provides a better perspective on the particular problem of mind-body interaction thus deserves a special hearing, although we should be forewarned that there still may be difficulties arising from unresolved more general issues.

3. Mind-Body Interaction

We can reconstruct Kant's contrast of his own views here with those of the influx and harmony schools in terms of the following three points:

(1) mind and body are heterogeneous things in themselves;
(2) mind and body really (substantially) interact;
(3) heterogeneous things in themselves cannot interact with each other.

Both Kant and the harmony theorists see the influx theorist as simultaneously and inconsistently holding (1), (2), and (3). The harmony theorist avoids inconsistency here by giving up (2). Kant surrenders (1), agreeing that mind and body are heterogeneous, but only as phenomena (here again

Kant may not be adequately distinguishing between what we called appearance and phenomenal immaterialism) and not as things in themselves, for bodies cannot at all be things in themselves. It is remarkable that none of these theories pursues the final option, the one perhaps most attractive to contemporary philosophy, namely the surrender of (3).[16] Kant emphasizes instead that if matter were transcendentally real, then the difference in the nature of spatial and mental items would make the effect of the one on the other un-intelligible, for 'we altogether lose the thread of the causes in the effects' (A 387).[17]

With respect to his immediate opponents, it still might seem that Kant has a superior position because he alone can consistently affirm (2). But in fact, although all Kant draws attention to is denying (1), he in effect also denies (2) (for if a body ultimately is not a substance, it cannot substantially interact), and he replaces it with an account of mind and body in phenomenal interaction. Here it becomes difficult to see how he differs from harmony theorists, for they too say that phenomenally speaking there can be a kind of mind-body interaction; that is, mind-body 'interaction' is just the lawful co-ordination of different types of representations. All that Kant says fundamentally separates harmony theorists from him is commitment to point (1), and that is, the dogmatic claim to know that matter in its substrate differs in kind from our mind (A 390–1). Unfortunately, it is hardly clear that traditional theorists really were attached to this claim. Moreover, the claim appears irrelevant to the specific issue of mind-body interaction, for Kant agrees with the only conclusion that is drawn from it here, namely that there is no substantial interaction of mind and body (for he says, 'the question is no longer of the communion of the soul with other known substances of a different kind outside us' (A 386)). The difference between him and the harmony theorists on this specific issue is merely that Kant rests this conclusion on what was earlier called noumenal immaterialism. This leaves him with only a trivially distinct position, for although the harmony theorists may not have Kant's exact reasons for claiming nothing can be ultimately material, they do agree with the claim.

Major disagreement arises only when we go back to the issue of interaction in general, for then the harmony theorists preclude interaction even of immaterial things in themselves, whereas Kant believes such interaction must be left open as a possibility, and that in fact it is a realized possibility even if its truth can't be explained. Yet Kant never fully considers why the harmony theorists don't leave this open as a possibility, and instead he unfairly suggests (A 392) that they are forced to their position because of the contradiction that arises in simultaneously asserting (1), (2), and (3). But as none of these points bears on the exclusion of real immaterial interaction, it must be concluded that here Kant has not adequately spelled out the virtues of his system over Leibniz's. Thus, Kant's position on mind-body interaction in particular is not only laden by some presuppositions (viz., (3)) questionable from a contemporary perspective, but moreover, as was suspected earlier, its supposed superiority over its traditional opponents remains questionable because of difficulties hanging over from the problem of interaction in general.

4. Evaluation

Whatever difficulties there may be in maintaining the superiority of Kant's theory, there is no escaping the fact that it is at least strikingly harmonious with what the previous chapter revealed about his concept of mind alone, that is, it is fundamentally immaterialist. However, just as we have noted that there are some qualifications to Kant's immaterialism, so we should note that there are also some qualifications to his quite rationalistic theory of interaction. Thus, it should be stressed that although Kant reaffirmed principle (3), he still was not saying that all real interaction must be between substances consisting in the specific kind of stuff that we recognize as mental. This is because he believed that what we know as mental is also merely phenomenal, for it is dependent on inner sense and the form of temporality (thus Kant's position remains 'anti-pneumatic', as defined above at Ch. II, n. 40).

Kant's general position is best expressed in a late lecture

note which in some ways is also like what he said in his earliest work. To those who say that if the body doesn't work on the soul through a literal physical influx, or flowing out of power, then it can't be in real interaction with it, Kant counters that even among bodies we require a broader notion of causation.[18] But what Kant now believes is not merely that regular co-ordination is enough for us to speak of a kind of interaction ('connectibility' rather than 'communion'), but also that ultimately only noumena (and not bodies as such) substantially interact. Similarly, for mind and body in particular Kant holds that although they can't substantially interact *as such*, the non-material substrates of these phenomena can and presumably do.[19] This point is recorded a number of times in his lectures. There Kant asserts that bodies as such could not be understood to operate on one's mind,[20] for he still requires that ultimately whatever affects the mind must be of the same kind as the non-material substrate of mind: 'It is impossible to consider the influx between soul and body as material, and such that both are distinct and exist in themselves. . . . Thus there must be an immaterial interaction of the noumena of each, which means only that something directly influences [*einfliesst*] the soul, and then there is no heterogeneity'.[21] All this is consistent with what can be found in the *Critique* as well:

Neither bodies nor motions are anything outside us; both alike are mere representations in us; and it is not, therefore, the motion of matter that produces representations in us; the motion itself is representation only, as also is the matter which makes itself known in this way (A 387).

Seen from the perspective of our interpretation so far, this passage is hardly surprising, and yet often it has been taken to indicate a basic weakness in Kant's system. Like many in the first edition, the passage admittedly is formulated in terms that initially appear all too close to an individualistic form of idealism. Strawson, for example, takes this passage, along with the first edition version of the fourth Paralogism, as his major basis for saying there is a strong and immature subjectivist strand of phenomenalism in Kant.[22] None the less, we have just noted the passage is quite consistent with

Kant's mature work, and it can be explained easily enough in a non-subjectivist way. Contrary to what Strawson suggests, Kant here is not saying that there is no problem to the relation of mind and body because bodies too are merely items literally within individual minds. Rather, in saying matter does not ultimately interact with us and that mind-body interaction is merely a relation of representations, Kant is saying only that in a specific metaphysical sense bodies are not external to us. This is merely his noumenal immaterialism, and it is consistent with holding both that, phenomenally, bodies are external (i.e., part of a common empirical world, and not mere figments of individual minds), and also that there is *something* underlying these bodies that is completely external to us.

More specifically, in saying matter doesn't produce representations in us, Kant surely doesn't mean to say that particular representations of bodies in one's experience can't be correlated with, and in this way explained by, individual bodies that transcend anyone's particular representings. As mere 'representations', bodies are 'in us' for Kant not as ideas may be in an individual's mind, but as the constant perspective of a species or kind of knower may be 'in' or define that species (see below, Ch. VII.8). Once it is recognized — as Kant believes he can independently establish — that matter is 'mere representation', i.e., that it's something that we all do experience, but absolutely speaking would not have to experience in order to be in the best contact with what ultimately is, then the only question is why we all do happen to have this kind of experience. Given the general position of his philosophy, Kant can fairly say that the question 'comes then simply to this: *how in a thinking subject outer intuition . . . is possible*. And this is a question which no man can possibly answer' (A 393). Precisely in precluding an answer Kant properly distinguishes his idealism from any picture of particular selves imposing or choosing the framework of outer intuition itself. As long as he does this, it is unwarranted for Strawson and others to insist that Kant's idealism, and therefore his theory of mind-body interaction, demonstrably lacks 'coherence and intelligibility'.[23] Once again, the problem with Kant's theory so far is not that it's absurd, trivial, or evidently false, let alone incoherent, but rather that it may be insufficiently warranted.

I believe a similar evaluation can be given of a related common objection to Kant (also recently formulated by Strawson[24]), namely that although Kant need not be caught in violating (3) in the way an influx theorist does, still he seems to be committed to the unintelligibly heterogeneous interaction of immaterial noumena and material phenomena. In reply it can be pointed out that it seems quite proper and Kantian to be uncommitted to any determinable mapping between phenomena and noumena, and so individual phenomenal relations may be seen not as resultants or effects of noumenal ones but as a contingent and coherent distinct system (see below, Ch. VII.12). Thus even if there is great heterogeneity between phenomena and noumena, this is not an objectionable heterogeneity of ordinary causes and effects. It is true that here Kant approaches something like a double affection theory, in that the mind is seen as subject to certain phenomenal regularities as well as noumenal immaterial influence. But only the latter is thought as a genuine 'affection', and only the former requires determinate laws. There is no reason to presume that for *each* phenomenal regularity there is a distinct noumenal affection, or vice versa. That there is some substantial affection is simply something Kant must hold so that he can say there is something absolutely beyond oneself.

Strawson tries to trap Kant here by saying either Kant must accept that, contrary to his own general principles, we are familiar with the ultimate and known grounds of some of our representations, or he must dogmatically assert 'a pre-established harmony' between the phenomenal affection of spatial items and the underlying things in themselves.[25] But Kant can avoid the latter horn of the dilemma even while admitting that in some cases there is something distinct from us that affects us in some way other than mere phenomenal regularity. Such an admission is so indeterminate it is hard to see how it is any breach of Kant's general principles, for it still could leave quite strict limits on knowing specific individuals beyond experience.

This objection to Kant's theory of interaction thus does

not succeed without at the same time being a rejection of his general doctrine of our having irreducible and merely phenomenal forms of sensibility. This result would hardly bother Kant, for he does not hide the relation of his theory to that doctrine but rather emphasizes it. None the less, there might be still other grounds for objecting to Kant's theory which need not take us directly to evaluating this general doctrine. In particular, Kant needs to offer some explanation of the peculiar relation to one's own body that we do seem to experience, as well as some strategy for supporting the belief that there is something external to the mind. Without being filled out in these ways, Kant's immaterialist theory would verge upon a solipsism that doesn't even try to save the phenomena.

B.5. Embodiment: An Historical Overview

What Kant has to say about an individual's relationship to his own body is connected very closely to his doctrine about mind-body interaction in general. At first Kant held that the mind has a normal location within the world, a doctrine that was in accord with his view then about the soul's being in normal interaction with physical things.[26] In fact, it is because the mind is said to have effects at various places that it is said to be spatially located, and not vice versa.[27] This statement has a radical implication, namely that the mind's place is derivative and not essential. That is, although the soul is now definitely in the world, we can imagine that it need not have been, for to imagine this (at this point in Kant's philosophy) is simply to imagine its not being in interaction with bodies. Along this line Kant went into some detail about the general possibility of non-spatial substances and even of whole 'worlds' that are 'outside' the spatial one.[28]

Near the end of his first period, Kant shifted to the opposite extreme of completely rejecting such possibilities. He asserted that finite souls cannot be without bodies and external causes,[29] an assertion that in many ways is in keeping with both his original empiricist orientation and his later critical argument for the dependence of human beings on spatial intuition. Even the support for this assertion is an anticipation of later views — namely that changes within a substance require spatial grounds. At this point, however, Kant does not yet back up his claims with a detailed argument or relevant epistemological considerations.

The thought experiment of multiple wholly disassociated 'worlds' does not receive a serious counterargument until Kant later reflects on the ambiguity of 'world'. He then suggests that in *a* sense being in a 'different world' may be simply having a basically different perspective on or interaction with things,[30] but that in a more fundamental sense there is only one world or set of things, which can be seen in different ways.[31] According to his later philosophy, to be able to perceive non-spatial beings is to be in some sense non-spatial oneself, but this involves only having access to another or better view of things; it does not mean that one can wander into a second, metaphysically distinct world. So even if we were wholly to dispense with our spatial sensibility, according to Kant we would remain ultimately within the one world of things that there is, which we happen to have intuited spatially.

Kant further believes that ultimately our spatial sensibility can be dispensed with, and that we must acknowledge that a non-spatial perspective on our metaphysical situation is not only logically possible but necessary. It took him a while to reach this position, and even then he qualified it in many ways, as should be expected given all the qualifications already encountered with respect to his immaterialism. For a while Kant was even almost forced to reject this position, because after he denied that space is grounded in physical monads, it seemed to follow that space is an absolute being, something everything is always located in, no matter what its interactions. But Kant did not accept such implications. He feared that taking space as absolute would lead to saying God is within or at least directly present to space, and he felt it was just as absurd to insist that the soul would have to be located somewhere even if all physical things disappeared.[32] Once Kant added the Antinomies to back these views, he could say we must exist in some possible world without any spatial or bodily characteristics.

By making space but a form of human intuition, Kant eliminated the danger of an absolute space compelling us to be spatial, but he did not mean thereby to prove that the *soul* necessarily will exist independently of space. He insisted that we can know the soul (theoretically) only in conjunction with a body, and therefore that theories about how it can be independent of a body must be unfounded.[33] Here Kant was questioning not the mere idea that noumenally we are non-embodied, but rather the claim that we will be non-embodied *minds*, especially in the long run of the *temporal* phenomenal realm of existence. Once again the main targets of Kant's criticism turn out to be pneumatism, the theoretical claim that our mind, as it appears to us now, is our ultimate reality, and spiritualism, the theoretical claim that we can exist in worlds where the substance underlying our body doesn't exist. Here Kant's position also closely parallels his doctrine that we cannot rule out what he called 'transcendental materialism'. That doctrine implied we don't know that we *are* noumenally different in kind from what underlies matter, whereas now Kant is implying that we don't know whether, noumenally, we *depend* upon what underlies our specific body.[34]

Despite all these precautions about what can be proven, Kant's positive views still tended to be quite rationalistic. In his late lectures he treats the specific questions of our existence before and after life, and he indicates that *if* such existence is granted, then there are grounds leading us to conceive it in non-spatial terms. In particular, in discussing the origin of the soul Kant points to severe difficulties with any hypothesis other than pre-existence,[35] and he indicates that such pre-existence should be thought of as barren of worldly experience and presumably without a body and location.[36] Kant is critical of believing the soul comes into existence at birth, for to believe this is to believe the soul is the result of either the souls or the bodies of its human parents.[37] The former theory is said to be unacceptable because a substance, such as the soul appears to be, cannot be naturally created.[38] The other alternative, that the soul is produced by bodies, is questioned because Kant does not see how a simple being, such as the soul appears to be, can result from an extended cause.[39] As for existence after life, Kant emphasizes that there is no evident need for an individual to maintain a body, and that it is most appropriate to believe in a bodiless existence.[40] He even gives the perjorative label 'materialistic' to the resurrectionist view that the same body is to be had in the afterlife.[41]

Of course, these speculations about bodiless pre- and post-existence are not meant to be theoretically decisive. Yet they surely reveal considerable sympathy for the belief in some form of bodiless existence for our soul within the temporal span of the phenomenal realm. They also suggest sympathy for the distinct idea that our souls have some non-spatial form of existence outside that realm. Unfortunately, Kant does not bring out the difference between these two ideas here, and he does not adequately clarify the possibility that space and time might be both phenomenal and yet not co-extensive. For example, at one point he says we *cannot* know whether 'the condition of all outer intuition, or the thinking subject itself, will cease with this state (in death)' (A 394 f.). At another point he says we *are* definitely 'freed from the fear that on the removal of matter all thought, and even the very existence of thinking beings, would be destroyed' (A 383). At first sight these passages present a bewildering inconsistency. However, in the phrase 'the thinking subject' there is an important ambiguity, for it can mean either the noumenal underlying subject (as substance) or the phenomenal temporal subject. Consistency can be saved if we say that only the former sense is meant in the second passage, and only the latter sense is meant in the first passage. That is, as the second passage says, we can be sure something noumenal in us exists even 'on the removal of matter'; but, as the first passage indicates, this doesn't mean that we can know the thinking subject *qua temporal* being exists in those states. However, even if we don't know this, it still is a real possibility, and so for us a temporal and phenomenal but non-spatial form of existence (existence 'pre' and 'post' the life of one's body) is a matter distinct from that of having a non-spatial *and* non-temporal noumenal being.

All these possibilities must in turn be distinguished from the specific claim of our having, as *active* minds, a noumenal immaterial and non-bodily being. That is, even if there is a better and non-spatio-temporal way that we could be seen, this need not mean we would really be (metaphysically) able to see ourselves in such a way. Although, *qua* object, we are definitely non-spatio-temporal in that ultimately we, like all else, must be non-spatio-temporally perceivable by something, still we might not as an actual epistemic subject be able (metaphysically) to realize and enjoy that perspective.

In sum, the problem of Kant's attitude toward our non-bodily existence outside life needs to be broken down into at least three issues:

(i) the general question of our phenomenal existence outside our ordinary life;
(ii) the general question of our noumenal existence;
(iii) the question of our existence in either case as self-cognizant subjects.

With respect to (i), Kant seems to be positive, but he thinks our non-bodily status there is to be believed in, not proven. With respect to (ii), Kant is more clearly positive, but he must remain sceptical about (iii) and definitely negative about asserting that noumenally we could be *temporal* self-cognizant subjects. His grounds for his view on (i) are hardly compelling, but he himself puts little weight on them. His position on (iii) is refreshingly contemporary though hardly complete; fortunately it is filled out some more by what he has to say on personal identity and immortality. His position on (ii) follows simply from the general tenets of his philosophy. Typically, then, these doctrines of Kant's philosophy of mind must be evaluated as neither clearly to be rejected nor by themselves convincing.

6. Embodiment in Life

However positive Kant may be about the possibility of our being in some sense independent of a body, he definitely recognizes that within life our embodiment is an indisputable and peculiar fact. He describes this fact in a fairly consistent way throughout his philosophy by saying that in life the soul has a virtual and not a local spatial presence, that is, it has focused spatial effects but does not inhabit a spatial point. Eventually for Kant this doctrine is tied up with a rejection of materialism,[42] but its original target was the quasi-Cartesian idea (which had not been completely shaken off even by such later rationalists as Crusius[43]) that the presumably immaterial soul exists at one spot or at least has a very circumscribed *Sitz* or location within the body. Kant had no qualms about speaking about the soul in life in some spatial terms, for he took it as evident that each soul senses itself as having a body that in some way puts it in the world of extension. What he felt inappropriate was to ask where *within* the body the soul is located. If there is any response to this question on his view, it must be that the soul is wherever it feels,[44] or, in more contemporary terms, its place should be determined more by the proximate object than the ultimate cause of its feelings.

This is a complex issue because Kant also held that one determines the soul's virtual location by its interaction and not vice versa.[45] That is, we do not know where we are in space and time and then find out where we act (and are acted upon); rather we feel virtually present in our body because that is where we identify ourselves with various spatial happenings which appear as proximate causes or effects of our mental events. The issue is complicated even further by the fact that the effects and objects that Kant takes to be essential to our thus determining our own spatial presence may be other than those which *others* use in locating us, or even those which we *ultimately* accept as determining where, from an objective standpoint, we should be said to be in the world.

In this way Kant raises but hardly resolves the difficult problem of finding a concept of human embodiment that is both subjectively and objectively satisfying. It is worthwhile to digress on this issue for a while, for in emphasizing the experience of feeling or 'intending' to be at a certain place Kant strikingly anticipates some contemporary views on embodiment.[46] Jonathan Harrison has given the most interesting recent overview of this problem. He makes the suggestion that there are 'five different things which make us want to say that a given body is my body [and these] might not go together but get separated. In this case I might [1] feel pain when things were stuck in one thing, [2] feel the inside of another, [3] directly control a third, [4] look out on this world from a fourth, and [5] my thoughts, feelings, and decisions be determined by a fifth.'[47]

The problem Harrison has hit upon here is that what might be called the intentional or Kantian definition of a person's place seems to have no guarantee of uniqueness. It appears one could be present (*qua* feeling) in many quite disparate bodies, or many minds could be present in one ordinary looking human body. The latter possibility ('multiple inhabitation') is left open by Kant, and it appears that neither he nor anyone else has much to say against it except that it is a mere possibility whose realization it is hard to imagine we could ever see conclusively established. On the former problem ('multiple embodiment'), however, Kant does have, as was noted, a sensitivity to causal factors,[48] and this points to, or at least is compatible with, some moves that can be made to counter Harrison's suggestions and to save the principle that no person should be said to have more than one body. I shall now sketch some of these moves and indicate ways that Kantian distinctions can help to challenge the popular view that Harrison formulates.

The five factors that Harrison cites are surely all relevant to locating one's body, but it not so clear that they are distinct and can 'get separated'. For example, the first factor can be said to be but an instance of the second, for to feel a pain somewhere is simply intensively and negatively to feel the 'inside' of something. Harrison offers only two ideas as to how such feelings might be had in another body: the experiences of Siamese twins, and the possibility of referred sensation, e.g., feeling 'in' an amputated leg.[49] But the first idea can be taken to show at most not that one person has two bodies, but rather that the body one has may in some sense be shared by another individual. The second idea can be met by an obviously necessary qualification of the intentional theory. Anyone holding to such a theory still must recognize that the determination of one's place ultimately depends upon what one can in some way *properly* feel are objects of one's sensations. That is, to avoid absurdity some distinction must be made between immediate or 'apparent' objects of feelings and corrected or 'phenomenal' objects. The first has to do simply with where one originally and confusedly feels one's pains to be, and the second with where one eventually locates them in order to have a coherent picture of the empirical world. Thus, although an amputated leg might well be the apparent object of one's feelings, the genuine phenomenal object would be some actually present part of one's body.

This distinction can lead to the initially disturbing consequence that the ultimate object of one's feelings, and so the location of one's body, might be nothing more than a small part of the brain or something else one understands little about. But this is merely a possible consequence, and modern science indicates that for human beings feelings must involve a relatively spread-out nervous system, what some philosophers have called a live neural skeleton or 'core body'.[50] In rejecting the pineal gland and related theories of the soul, Kant in a way anticipated this result, but it is significant that his arguments here were also empirical and not purely philosophical. That is, given the biological nature of our experience it seems that (despite some contrary indications) there is no point or small set of points that is causally sufficient for one's ordinary bodily feelings. Kant did not argue that it is impossible that there be such a point, and so although he no doubt would have preferred locating feelings at the edge of rather than inside one's skin, his philosophy still doesn't rule out this latter possibility.

There is, moreover, surely something to the popular and Kantian desire to say one feels things at one's toes or finger tips, for example, and not in some hidden place between these and the brain. One explanation of this desire is the fact that there can be a considerable difference between the body image we need for operating smoothly in a practical way (given our environment and training), and the body location most defensible from the standpoint of an ultimate determination of what is really necessary for our experience to be as it is. Thus even within the phenomenal perspective one could distinguish at least two layers of the body, as for the world in general: the stratum of coherent attributes and descriptions most handy for our common sense and everyday concerns, and, secondly, the ones most appropriate for explanatory and theoretical purposes. In this way colours and other sensible qualities can have an intersubjective and so more than merely apparent status without being ultimate even with respect to the phenomenal world. (Kant unfortunately was not so clear about this. See, e.g., B 69 n.) Furthermore, even if it were granted to the causal theorists that it is the second (or 'scientific') layer which ultimately determines which qualities things have and what place we have in the empirical world, the concerns of the intentional theorist could still be given their due by allowing that the first phenomenal layer, e.g., the ordinary body image of the common man, may have a significant and perhaps even indispensable heuristic role. That is, without one's feeling oneself at first, and for the most part, to be *at* the perimeter rather than the core of one's flesh, it might not ever be possible to achieve the more complicated but correct view that one is really not as extended as it may seem, and that much of what is taken to be literally a part of oneself is merely attached. While the causal theorist may have to concede this much, the intentional theorist may have to admit that even the supposedly immediate knowledge of the place and object of feelings that he emphasizes must rest on some inferences and considerable implicit comprehension of one's situation, and thus of one's general causal situation in the world.

Just as the real embodiment of a person might thus turn out to be much smaller than is generally thought, so too it could turn out to be much more extended than it is generally thought of as being. In discussing his third criterion of embodiment, Harrison speaks of our possibly being able to move distant objects immediately and so in this way supposedly being located in many places. But as he implicitly concedes, in that event one could also regard such places as merely spread out parts of one person's one body.[51] In a similar way it might be true that what one ordinarily takes to be one solid human body is really riddled by thousands of gaps and in that way consists in many distinct parts. Now just as in that case it could (and surely should) be said that the person none the less has but one body, so in the case Harrison suggests it could be said that the person has but one body, although its gaps are a bit more spread out. Moreover, this third criterion hardly amounts to a distinct one that might easily 'get separated' from all the others. For, no matter what objects Harrison supposes that one could move 'immediately', unless one had some feeling in those objects, it would still seem more plausible to regard such items as coincidentally mobile rather than as parts of one's self. (And even if such coincidences regularly followed up changes in one's brain, this alone wouldn't make the items parts of one's self, for surely the same thing happens to such things as the air immediately surrounding one.[52])

The fourth factor that Harrison discusses, the perspective from which one visually perceives the world, can be developed into a more serious threat to our resistance to allowing multiply-embodied minds (that is, simultaneous minds; the diachronic nature of the self will be discussed in the next chapter). If one were to have a constant and coherent picture of events as they would be seen, for example, from a certain tree in. Australia, why not say one has another body there, even if, for example, one still feels one is sitting in a chair in America? Here, as before, the response to Harrison's challenge can make use of causal considerations. It would not be enough, after all, simply to have an image of the Australian locale which in no physical way was an effect of it, for in such a case we could say simply that a person located in America had a remarkable gift for imagining himself to be in Australia. On the other hand, if there were causal connections between the Australian locale and the person's vision, then it still would be open to say either that (a) if there is a suitable distinct viewing instrument in Australia (e.g., an eye felt to be in contact with the lounging American), then the person is also there, that is, his one spread out and gapped body has a part there; or (b) if there is no such instrument, but only an odd chain of influences, then the Australian place is merely an incidental attachment to the body (just as one's firmly attached glasses are not a part of one's body, although a confused person with bad eyesight might think he is right at the edge of his lenses).[53]

There is a last and more extreme challenge, also suggested by Harrison (corresponding partially to his attempt to separate the fifth of the factors listed above), that can be mounted against the one man-one body (at most) rule. It is simply the thought experiment of having a number of very distinct and yet coherent perspectives of the world 'from the inside', as might happen, for example, if each sense were tuned in to a spot on a different continent. Now even in such a case it is possible to say again that the person has a very odd and spread out but still single body, for all the experiences do belong to one experiencer, who is somehow in immediate contact with all the locales. To support his argument for multiple embodiment Harrison here again employs the device of choosing not merely different perspectives, but ones that happen to seem to be occupied by other persons too.[54] But although in such cases we might want to drop the claim that a body, or portion of it, is inhabitable by only one person, there is nothing forcing us to yield the doctrine that each person has at most one body.

None the less, if a person's experience really were tied up simultaneously with what would appear to be the distinct courses of a number of evidently (spatially) separated human bodies acting in various similar ways, then it does seem a temptation would arise to say there is one person in many bodies. However, this temptation is quite theoretical, and it is not so easy to see precisely for whom it could become pressing. The person with the peculiar experiences himself would not necessarily feel multiply-embodied. Many things that he felt would have little direct relation to other things that he felt, but this is to some extent true of everyone's experience. Harrison's thought experiment becomes a serious challenge only when it approaches a point which (perhaps not coincidentally) boggles our imagination, namely one at which a person can feel himself to be at once here, and yet distinctly also there, without the slightest asymmetry or pre-ponderent inclination to feel merely especially broadminded in a sensual way. (It is revealing that at this point Harrison shifts to a description of diachronous items in his attempt to flesh out an experience of multiple embodiment.)[55]

On the other hand, if we consider how Harrison's experiment might be confirmed from outside, equal difficulties arise. One and the same personality manifested simultaneously in different places would not be a proof of one person being multiply-present unless adequate causal connections were also establishable. Yet whatever could support such amazing connections could also be used to support the amazing – but no *more* remarkable – claim that a person has managed to manifest himself not only in one enclosed and spread-out space, but in a number of them, and so has an especially large and gapped, but still single, body. We would gain nothing theoretically by rather saying there is but one person in many bodies, for that there are many parts to a person's embodiment no one need dispute. As long as those parts are especially related in a unity of feeling, we have all that is necessary to say there is one mind and one body, and as usual we would do best not to multiply entities. It is true that there remains the logical possibility of a special immaterial relation whereby one and the same essentially bodiless spirit could contact and animate distinct physical masses which had no connection as such between them, and so metaphysically there might really be but one mind in many bodies. But this would no longer be a multiple *phenomenal* embodiment, for the immaterial relations are posited precisely as ones inaccessible to intersubjective empirical access and confirmation. Multiple embodiment thus remains an open possibility only as an in principle unsupportable hypothesis about things in themselves. It is no weakness in Kant's theory that he has no sympathy for this idea, but it is a significant characteristic of his system that he has a place to locate it, namely as possibly consistent but outside the realm of what is empirically determinable.

All this is not to deny that, were very strange things to occur, we might feel constrained by *practical* concerns to speak in certain contexts of multiple embodiment. The phenomenal theoretical dispensibility of the notion of multiple embodiment is not endangered by hesitancy to banish the notion totally from sheerly metaphysical or merely practical realms.[56] The notion of single embodiment is thus very much like Kant's schematized principles: they too – for example, the principle that all objective succession is causal — cannot be asserted to be valid outside the realm of our cognitive powers, nor can they be dismissed simply because in certain practices it might be easier temporarily to deny the principle (we can, for example, obviously regard a succession as objective before we *know* any causal law it falls under).

Although Kant's theory of embodiment is hardly developed enough to resolve the problem of multiple embodiment, in the end this problem may be taken to present not so much a refutation as a challenge for Kant's philosophy, namely a challenge to develop the notion of schematic principles ('criteria' for central concepts) of experience which are neither merely pragmatic nor sheerly metaphysical. Unfortunately, Kant did not meet this challenge very directly himself. On this particular issue he seems generally to have been too satisfied with the quick claims that the soul is intuited only via inner sense, and that since something can have a local presence only if it is intuited via outer sense, the soul cannot have a precise location as physical things do.[57] Here (possibly because of his immaterialism) Kant fails to attend adequately to his own recognition that what belongs to the realm of outer sense should be determined by theoretical considerations (see above, at Ch. II, n. 27), and hence that a precise physical location (in the human body) for the mind need not be absurd. So, although Kant was surely right to chide those who presumed a kind of pineal gland location is needed and proper for the soul, he cannot be said to have offered conclusive arguments against placing the soul within the brain or whatever makes up the core of the human nervous system. He only offered hypotheses accounting for some tendencies to give the brain an undue primacy here,[58] and these are not decisive given the fact that at least on the phenomenal level he has no strong case in principle against a mind-brain identity theory.

Even if such a contemporary theory is to be preferred, it should not be forgotten that by itself it does not explain the peculiar nature of our embodiment to which Kant is at least sensitive. On the other hand, Kant does not go on to explain precisely how, phenomenologically speaking, we do come to locate outselves in a world of outer sense, nor does he detail the special epistemological significance of the body that is called for by his own philosophy, especially with the second edition of the *Critique*.[59] Instead, in accord with his general immaterialism, the space allowed by Kant for the topic of the body is devoted primarily to outlining very specific senses in which the embodiment or spatiality of the soul can be qualified. Kant's position can be summed up in terms of three senses in which something can be said to be less than fully spatial: (1) its spatiality may be said to be not logically necessary and in that sense unessential; (2) its spatiality may be said to be derivative, that is, dependent on something else (e.g., interacting forces), though still perhaps essential to it (if, e.g., those forces are essential to it); (3) its spatiality may be said not to take the form of the occupation of a single point or fixed set of points, and so may be a virtual presence throughout a field of activity. In Kant's view, the soul in life has spatiality, but one which is unessential, derivative, and virtual in the above senses. This position is undeveloped but it does point to a provocative and consistent alternative to familiar options, in particular to the mind-brain identity theory and traditional dualism. It contrasts with the former in so far as the form of the theory which is now generally recognized as the most defensible (viz., that which takes such identities to be necessary identities) requires a denial of (1). It contrasts with the latter in so far as that position involves a total denial that the self is spatial. Thus Kant has introduced an option which is not merely interesting, but also appealing, for intuitively it does seem that our spatiality is central but not essential to our being. In sum, Kant has hardly eliminated his opponents, but he has made a start towards what could be the most defensible theory of human embodiment compatible with common sense.

C.7. The Problem of the External World: An Historical Overview

The last issue to be focused on concerning the mind-body relation is the so-called problem of the external world, which is traditionally the problem of proving, from what is given to a mind, that there exist bodies outside that mind. Until his first *Critique*, Kant did not give this problem much attention, and he commented on it only in the course of elaborating more general points. In his first period, he argued that the external world can be demonstrated as a consequence of the general principle that all changes within substances require external causes.[60] Since our minds obviously change, it would follow that we can thereby be certain there is an external cause of that change. Kant's presentation of the argument is unconvincing because it is extremely sketchy, especially with respect to the general causal principle.

As Kant moved beyond his empiricist starting point, he came to realize the philosophical difficulties in justifying causal claims in general, and this led him to an admission in his lectures that philosophically the external world is indemonstrable. He expressed this point by remarking that 'logically' Berkeley can't be refuted.[61] Kant was impressed by the evidence that many representations are only subjective, and by the fact that there is no way the vivacity or even the connectedness of representations is inconsistent with their being merely implanted in us. He even adds that such implantation would have been the simpler thing for God.

By the time of the *Dissertation* of 1770, there is still no solution offered to this problem, and it is not discussed in the lectures of the years immediately following. Suddenly in the first *Critique* Kant changed and even distorted the structure of his treatment of the soul in order to raise (under the heading of 'modality') the question of the soul's 'possible' relation to an external world. The urgency that the issue took on is evident from the manner in which Kant forced it into his categorial psychological discussion. Later he admitted the topic did not belong on a list of categorial determinations, and by the end of his career he did not even discuss it within the rubric of rational psychology as such.[62] Kant's discussion of the issue was not, however, a mere response to external pressures, for it occurs before the charges that his philosophy is largely indistinguishable from Berkeley's. It is probable that although Kant was quite aware of Berkeley,[63] he was mainly motivated to take on this issue because of his own constant desire to distinguish his philosophy from the rationalist tradition around him.[64] Kant had always held that a monadology offers only theological and inadequate grounds for asserting the existence of an external world, for if a monad can represent a whole world within itself, it seems unnecessary for there actually to be such a distinct world (or other monads), and impossible to prove there is such.[65] If Kant could improve upon Leibniz here it obviously would be a major advance.

Kant's eventual solution was a critical and epistemological argument to the effect that an external world, in the sense of spatial phenomena distinct from our representings, is necessary for us to have any determinate empirical knowledge, and so even knowledge of our own self.[66] This is not a proof that metaphysically there are things distinct from us, nor that the mere existence of consciousness (even with temporal characteristics) entails that there are spatial things.[67] It is merely an argument that for us knowledge of one kind of object (the temporally determinable self) requires knowledge about another kind of object. In this way, it is meant to refute not the complete sceptic but the traditional 'material idealist', who believes he can know specific things at least about himself without reference to the spatial world. As Kant points out, all this is compatible with still granting that no particular empirical claim about spatial objects is apodictic, and that on any specific occasion the mere claim that I seem to be experiencing spatial objects can be more certain than the assertion that there really are these objects.[68]

Before examining the validity of Kant's argument, certain problems in its interpretation must be acknowledged. The first and severest problem has to do with Kant's first edition treatment of idealism, a treatment that completes and dominates the original version of the Paralogisms. This discussion has been taken by many interpreters to give a quite subjective meaning to Kant's idealistic theory as a whole, a meaning that would contrast strikingly with the interpretation we have been offering. We will counter these interpretations immediately by a brief exegesis of Kant's first edition refutation of idealism. The exegesis will aim to show that Kant's discussion here is basically in accord with what has already been seen in respect to the other paralogisms, and that this text cannot be used either as a special ground for rejecting Kant's philosophy in general or as a justification for bracketing this part of the *Critique* as a mere residue of an earlier period.[69] This provokes the question, however, of why Kant later so extensively revised his treatment of the problem of the external world. By looking at what he says in the second edition version, we will answer this question by noting how Kant there attempts to improve on two aspects of his earlier discussions: the sketchiness of his positive argument for knowledge of an external world, and the unclarified status of the connection between this issue and the field of rational psychology proper.

8. The First Edition Fourth Paralogism

The fourth paralogism, as originally conceived, can be formulated in these terms:

(1) What can be only causally inferred is never certain;
(2) outer objects can be only causally inferred, not immediately perceived by us;
(3) therefore, we can never be certain of outer objects.

Once again, despite Kant's general claim, the paralogism which he formulates seems acceptable as at least a valid argument. Its soundness, however, is questionable, and Kant himself begins his discussion by inviting us to 'test' (I think this term has a more accurate connotation now than Kemp Smith's 'examine') the premises (A 367). From a contemporary perspective, (1) invites criticism, and there may be grounds for saying even Kant should put it in question. The main point of his discussion, however, is to challenge (2). The challenge rests entirely on the invocation of his doctrine of transcendental idealism (that is, it rests on the possibility of this doctrine, not on its truth). The claim that 'outer' objects can't be immediately known is fundamentally ambiguous given the transcendental idealist's distinction between what is 'intellectually' or transcendentally external, and what is merely phenomenally or empirically external (A 373). That is, there may be items which are distinguishable from me as a mental individual, and hence are empirically external, without being external to me *qua* my species of sensibility. Such items are then, transcendentally speaking, not external to me. On the other hand, that which, transcendentally speaking, is external to me, i.e., is in itself apart from whatever contingent forms of sensibility human subjectivity may have, can turn out to be not external in the empirical and spatial sense, for in itself nothing can be spatial.

Now Kant is willing to grant that transcendentally 'outer' objects can't be perceived immediately, and so it can be allowed that, as he says, the rational psychologist 'is justified' in some sense in saying that we can't be certain of outer objects (A 367).[70] But the rational psychologist errs if he makes the flat claim that we cannot be at all sure that there are outer objects, and it may be the case that in some *other* sense (namely the empirical one) 'outer' objects can be even immediately perceived. Thus, as long as the term 'outer' is used without equivocation, the argument from (1) to (3) may be valid, but it still could be unsound, given the possible falsity of (2) on an empirical reading. On the other hand, the argument can also be understood (as Kant's general diagnosis of 'paralogism' requires) as an invalid one (with perhaps true premisses), namely if 'outer' is understood in a transcendental sense in (2) but in an empirical sense in (3). It is not clear which of the readings Kant wanted to assign the rational psychologist, for his syllogistic presentation explicitly follows the valid formulation (in using the phrase 'outer appearance'), whereas the informal exposition he gives in the next paragraphs (A 367) understands (2) in terms of the invalid argument we have just described. There should, however, be no doubt that Kant has an understanding of these possibilities, for he devotes a long section precisely to elucidating the distinction between phenomenal and transcendental externality. Moreover, right at the beginning of his exposition he indicates that this distinction should be kept in mind, for he says that the existence of an object 'outside me (*if* this word "me" be taken in the *intellectual* [i.e., transcendental versus empirical] sense) is never given directly' (A 367; my emphasis). This shows that already in the first edition Kant is quite clear that, unlike Berkeley, we are not to say that objects *empirically* outside us can't be given; that is, Kant clearly refuses to express the problem of knowledge in terms of an individual consciousness trying to get beyond ideas literally within it.[71]

None the less, it is precisely this section that most often has been singled out to indicate a subjectivist position on Kant's part. To show how questionable this interpretation is, we need only consider the main text to which it appeals. At A 370 Kant says, 'external objects (bodies), however, are mere appearances, and are therefore nothing but a species of my representations, the objects of which are something only through these representations'. Admittedly, there is a subjectivist tone in any talk about bodies being 'mere representation', but Kant has gone to some length to warn us about the special way his talk must be understood, and even this passage contains clear reminders of that warning. In relating bodies to 'my' representations, for example, Kant surely should be taken to mean, as he said in the beginning, the me in an 'intellectual' sense, not a merely empirical and individual me. Moreover, Kant distinguishes here between a mere appearance and the object which is achieved 'through' representations. This clearly requires us to take the bodies that are spoken of as 'representations' to be items represented and not mere representings. That the objects are spoken of as relative to a process of representation that they go 'through' also indicates that here we should bring into play Kant's whole theory of how objects (*qua* knowable) are constituted via a conceptual apparatus. This means that bodies as objects are not mere bundles of sense data or collections of sensations. It is therefore unjustified to say – as even recent interpreters have[72] – that by calling something 'mere representation' Kant means it is a 'collection of sensations'. Such an interpretation wholly ignores the valuable distinction Kant has made between the ideas of an individual subject and a species of subjectivity, and the contrast he has established between a mere sensing as opposed to an objective representation. These distinctions are further clearly reinforced when Kant goes on to emphasize that for us the 'actual' realm of representations includes all that is connectible to our experience via empirical laws (A 376). Again he is reminding us that what he means here by 'representation' cannot be restricted either to things occurring *sensibly* within minds or even to whatever is merely *occurrent* within minds, let alone within *a* mind.

If Kant's first edition discussion of the fourth paralogism is, as we have just claimed, already so well in accord with the most defensible form of Kant's idealism, it may appear all the more mysterious that Kant dropped this text in his second edition. One explanation of this is that in fact the fine distinctions Kant made were not comprehended, and so it was only natural for him to make another effort to prevent a misunderstanding of his idealism. However, it is also true that there are some formulations in the first edition which plainly invite, even if they do not justify, a subjectivist interpretation. In particular, Kant's 'solution' here, his claim that we do 'immediately perceive' the outer and that it is 'sensation . . . that indicates a reality' (A 374), threatens to wipe out the distinctions we have just observed, and can encourage taking the immediately perceived to be what is merely sensory and extant within one's own mind. This encouragement arises in another way when Kant suggests (though here he is probably not speaking in his own voice) that if there aren't provable *transcendentally* external objects, then all may be a 'mere play of our inner sense' (A 368). If Kant's 'solution' to the problem of the external world were simply that bodies are real because they are immediately perceived in that they are as close to us as mere inner sense, then of course he would not appear to have a very attractive form of idealism. But in fact it is possible for bodies, like all else in the realm of representation, to belong in some sense to the realm of inner sense without being merely items of that sense (cf. A 371). It is also surely possible – given the various meanings of 'immediate' – that in some way an item can be 'immediately perceived' without being a mere Berkeleyian or Cartesian component of the mind. All the same, it must be admitted that Kant hardly develops these possibilities adequately when he only says, 'objects are nothing but representations, the immediate perception (consciousness) of which is at the same time a sufficient proof of their reality' (A 371).

9. The Second Edition Fourth Paralogism

The prime weakness of Kant's discussion in the first edition is that it simply doesn't explain in what sense the 'immediate' perception of something amounts to a 'sufficient proof' of its reality. It is important to recognize that this is still merely a weakness and not a devastating objection to Kant's text, for here what he primarily needs to do is merely show that the rational psychologist's claim that an external world can't be proven isn't compelling. Thus he can succeed in his main aim even if his own proof of that world is too sketchy or appears too related to obviously unsatisfactory strategies. It is therefore in a way quite appropriate that in the second edition the Refutation of Idealism (i.e., the proof of the external world) is not located in the discussion of the fourth Paralogism proper. None the less, Kant must still indicate in some systematic way how the inclinations toward material idealism that rational psychology fosters can be met. It is not sufficient for him merely to exhibit some bad ways such inclinations can arise.

In the second edition of the *Critique* Kant faces up to this problem better, but he addresses it in a rather radical way. He claims that if and only if knowledge of the external world can be shown to be a condition of all self-knowledge, the sceptic can be defeated (B 418).[73] Although this is certainly an interesting strategy for meeting scepticism, it isn't proven to be the only one, for even if we could adequately know some things about ourselves without reference to an external world, there might be particular experiences or evidence that we could have which still would be sufficient evidence for an external world. After all, that such a world is demonstrable would seem to be a matter quite contingent upon the sort of basis one happens to have to argue from, and there is no *a priori* reason to think the basis must be tied to the crudest experience we might have.

All the same, the strong claim Kant makes in the second edition is an improvement, at least in clarity, on the stronger sounding claim of the first edition. Instead of suggesting sheer immediate perception is a proof of the external world, Kant now emphasizes that it is experience, that is, knowledge of one's self, that provides the premiss of the argument.[74] Outer sense and its objects are now said to be a necessary condition not of mere sensation, perception, or inner sense, but of inner *experience* (i.e., determinate empirical knowledge): 'only by means of it [outer experience] is inner experience — *not* indeed the [mere] *consciousness* of my own existence, but the *determination* of it in time — possible' (B 227; cf., B x1 n. and B 429). Kant still speaks of knowledge of the external as 'immediate', but now that statement can be given a clear relative sense. The knowledge is 'immediate' in that not only is it not a matter of (causal) inference to something transcendently external, but, moreover, this knowledge is not cognitively mediated by self-knowledge, but on the contrary self-knowledge is mediated by it. That is, even though, logically, mere 'inner consciousness' might take place without outer objects or even their appearance, and even though in some sense such consciousness is 'immediate' in that it is an empirical part of us in a way that outer objects can't be, none the less knowledge of the outer may be, as Kant says, at least 'just as' (B x1i n.) certain as *knowledge* of something concrete about oneself.

Unfortunately there is another, and less satisfactory, sense in which Kant still speaks of the immediacy of outer knowledge. In the first edition he puts considerable emphasis on the fact that the mere sensory, i.e., passive and material, aspect of our perception proves that there is something real, 'for if it were not real, that is, immediately given through empirical intuition, it could not be pictured in imagination, since what is real in intuition cannot be invented *a priori*' (A 374). He goes on to say, 'all outer perception, therefore, yields immediate perception of something real in space . . . the real, that is, the material of outer objects of outer intuition, is actually given in this space, independently of all imaginative invention' (A 375). This argument suffers from an ambiguity in the term 'real'. Obviously sensation does reveal elements that are real and immediate in the sense of not being fabricated by imagination, even in a subliminal way, for clearly all our fabrication requires something to begin with. But the fact that such elements are required and are in this sense independent of us, viz., independent of our imaginative whim, does not prove that there is anything even empirically external to the mind, for these elements could be taken to be simply original mental qualities and not distinct items which might be truly (for example) spatial. In the second edition, Kant wisely no longer gives this argument a central position, but he does refer to it in a footnote in which he clarifies what he calls the 'possibility' of 'outer consciousness' (B 277 n.; cf. B 308). He says that it proves that we really have an 'outer sense' as opposed to a mere 'outer imagination', but he still does not explain that such a sense is by itself no guarantee of objects distinct from the mind; it may be merely a sign of limits to the soul's spontaneity and an indication of the diversity of our mental life. Only in a remark added even later in another footnote did Kant remedy this difficulty somewhat by saying, 'the reality of outer sense, in its distinction from imagination, rests simply on . . . its being inseparably bound up with inner *experience*' (B xl n.).

Despite this last complication, it can be granted that in general the second edition Refutation of Idealism employs a concept of immediacy that at least avoids even the suggestion of an individualistic idealism. In addition to providing a clearer response to material idealism, the second edition also provides a general theory about how rationalists get involved in doubts about an external world. Supposedly this error, like all the others of rational psychology, can be understood as an inflation of an analytic into a synthetic statement, and in particular as a move from the justified assertion that I can distinguish myself from what is distinct in idea from me, to the claim that I can exist separately (B 409, B 427). This last claim is familiar enough, for it is simply what was earlier called the doctrine of spiritualism (see above, Ch. II, at n. 40). It thus turns out that *this doctrine, which was shown to be the ultimate object of attack in the first two Paralogisms, is also the target of the fourth.*

Kant hardly emphasizes this connection, and in fact the concern with spiritualism is peculiar here, for as a metaphysical hypothesis it seems all too plainly separate from the epistemological level at which the fourth paralogism operates. That is, even if we were to start with the notion that an external world is not only separate in idea from us, but moreover is not at all demonstrable, it still would not follow that it is even likely that we are independent of that world (or its substratum). The fact that something's existence is unprovable by us is simply no sign that its being is not necessary for us. Despite Kant's account of philosophical illusion, it is not so clear why a rationalist should jump to the metaphysical level of such a doctrine as spiritualism. Ironically, though, if the discussion is pursued at that level the rationalist could remind Kant that on his own view the mind (at least *qua* substrate) is really independent of spatial phenomena and may even be independent of their substrata. Hence, even if spiritualism isn't an assertible doctrine, it is not a refutable one either, and this is enough for it to be successful as what Kant calls a 'problematic' thesis. Thus neither the problematic status of claiming the existence of transcendentally external items nor that of claiming our independence from them is to be denied. The same can be said for the relevant independence claim (about us as noumena) *vis-à-vis* spatially external items; only their existence is non-problematic in Kant's system.

In sum, the second edition treatment of the fourth paralogism tries to impugn rational psychology by tying it to (i) the claim of spiritualism and, (ii) the claim that the self can be known in a determinate way independently (i.e., not via the mediation) of knowledge of anything external. The first claim is in a way surely paralogistic and rationalistic, although, as has been noted, it is not directly related to the traditional problem of the external world. The second claim also seems typically rationalistic, and it is more clearly related to the problem of the external world. Still, there could be those who are committed to it who are not rationalists and/or who believe there is a way to demonstrate the existence of the external world. (Conversely, one could deny the claim and still be a rationalist, or at least believe that the existence of an external world is indemonstrable — on the grounds that nothing objective is demonstrable, even if knowing the self *would* require knowing outer objects.) Thus, to reconstruct a rationalist position here that would escape Kant's critique we need only to do what has been proposed already in the preceding analyses, namely to trim that position down by omitting any assertion of spiritualism or self-transparency. Then, just as a belief in one's simplicity and immateriality remains defensible from a Kantian perspective (despite the relative certainty of spatial items), so also one could hold to a kind of theoretical scepticism about our depending on or even having anything to do with transcendentally distinct items.

However, as usual with respect to claims about the noumenal, Kant's view is not all that clear, and he probably would be reluctant to profess scepticism about the existence of objects fully transcendent to us. It is true that as he states the sceptical problem, especially in the first edition, he emphasizes only that we need not *worry* about not proving there is something transcendent, for we can show there is something at least phenomenally external and that is supposedly the main issue. Kant thus seems to allow that we can't *prove* things in themselves beyond us (A 372, A 378), although we also of course should not deny them. On the other hand, Kant definitely believes there surely are things in themselves that need to be in some way contrasted with phenomena, and he holds that even if we can't specifically determine them we can be sure they exist and do not have a spatio-temporal character (A 537/B 566; A 696/B 724). These points can be reconciled with one another by saying merely that for Kant there definitely is something in itself beyond the phenomenal self, although it is not evident that this must be anything distinct or different in kind from one's substratum.

This is a rather significant result, for it seems to grant as much as any sophisticated sceptic would want. That is, it *could* (on the theoretical level) turn out that even given a non-subjectivist interpretation of the meaning of Kant's idealism, the phenomena that are known may be in fact phenomena for only one individual (though still not reducible to his mental acts).[75] None the less, this result is not much of a point against Kant's philosophy unless it can be shown that someone else can provide a better solution. It may be that Kant is simply right in leaving room for us to grant that, absolutely speaking, i.e., as a mere logical possibility, scepticism is unassailable,[76] but as such it doesn't provide us with any reason to give up any particular beliefs about the world or to claim that the self is an especially privileged item of knowledge. Or, more precisely, from a Kantian (theoretical) perspective its privilege amounts to little more than the mere possibility (which, to be sure, is supposedly not had by the spatial forms that seem distinct from us) that ultimately, in some form unlike that by which even we know it, our mind is all there is. This position is left open by Kant's careful reluctance to characterize the thing in itself (e.g., A 380), and it again gives a motivation to his discussion of closely related but rejectable doctrines such as pneumatism (which would positively characterize a thing in itself, namely by saying the temporal mind is one).

10. Evaluation

Having clarified the general nature and ultimate consistency of Kant's position, as well as having evaluated his view on what is transcendentally external, we need finally to evaluate his argument for phenomenally external items. Here we will focus on his second edition Refutation of Idealism, and its argument that we can know our temporal determinations only via reference to spatial items. We shall pursue objections in the argument by considering whether they can be met even when Kant's claim is given its most defensible form, that is, when it is weakened by trimming down its more extreme components. For example, although Kant himself appears to be resting his case here on the broad claims of the first Analogy, a Kantian need not; for the main claim of the Refutation of Idealism would follow even if not all temporal determinations of the self required reference to the *completely* permanent items of which the first Analogy speaks. Similarly the argument could be more modestly phrased to concern not what is necessary for any but rather merely for *some* permanent features of our experience. In particular, it might bear not on what is required for *any* objective temporal claims, such as a mere ordering of some experiences, but for the specific claim that certain experiences occurred at a particular objective time. Finally, a Kantian might be better advised to claim not that something specifically *spatial* but merely something somehow phenomenally external is required.

Kant himself phrases the Refutation of Idealism in these terms: the determination of one's temporal position 'depends upon something permanent which is not in me, and consequently can be only in something outside me, to which I must regard myself as standing in relation. The reality of outer sense is thus [necessary]' (B xl-xli n.). In light of our above proposals we can see Kant's project here as coming down to showing that (given self-knowledge of the relevant kind) sometimes we need something *beyond our representings* which is *in some sense permanent*. The last emphasized phrase may in turn come down to meaning little more than the first. For although Kant believes there is in fact nothing permanent in our representings, that inner sense as such is mere flux, he goes on to add that even if there were a 'permanent intuition', this would not provide the 'intuition of a permanent' needed for time determination (B xli n.). That is, if one were in the strange position of never changing one's state of mind (or at least some aspect of it), there still seems to be no way one could thereby determine the time of one's experience. Not only would a constant image be obviously inadequate, but even if the image appeared to change in some constant way, there is no clear ground for saying its apparent changes would be enough to determine empirical temporal position — even if it were also the case that these changes just happened to reflect that position (i.e., its objective duration) precisely.

Let us concede that a mere representing, whether or not it is even relatively permanent in content, is insufficient for time determination and so we need something in some sense beyond it. Whatever the nature of that item might be, it is understandable that one might speak of it as 'permanent' to contrast it with the evident flux character of our representations considered as mere inner items, as representings. Kant surely means at least this much when he says we need something 'permanent' and 'perception of the permanent is possible only through a thing outside me and not through the mere representation of a thing outside me' (B 275; in formulating his thesis, Kant makes it clear that by 'thing' here he means 'object in space' and so 'mere representation' must be given an empirical and not a transcendental meaning). The reason why we need such an item here is epistemic, for what we are after are the conditions of objectively and temporally determining something, namely ourselves. Since knowledge in general requires more than mere appearance, it is natural to take Kant, as Myron Gochnauer has, to be arguing 'we need something permanent in the sense that it does not depend on the appearances we are trying to check'.[77] Gochnauer goes on to say Kant's point is that

representations may be *determined* as changing only if there is something independent to which they can be related or by which they can be checked. Now, since this is said of representations in general and not any specific group of them, it must be the case that the permanent is something other than a representation.[78]

Even if we again leave aside any claims about the permanent as absolute and spatial and as needed for all aspects of self-knowledge, there is still a very strong and not clearly justified claim being made here by Gochnauer and apparently Kant as well. It is the claim that we need to get beyond not merely a representation and the flux character of representations as mere acts, but that we need to get beyond our representations, empirically speaking at least, altogether. But this is simply not evident from Kant's general statement that we need something 'independent' of our inner representations, for this statement can be understood distributively rather than collectively. That is, all that is clearly established is that we need something independent from any particular inner representations, not that we need something independent of all (empirically) inner representations. Similarly, it is not clear why Kant's call for something 'not in me' in order to determine myself could not be answered by reference to a *set* of my inner experiences, which together might provide a system for ordering experiences without reference to space or something similarly non-mental.[79]

There is a possible explanation of why Kant himself did not go to too much trouble to clarify these distinctions. The reason is that he simply believed that no matter how many representations are considered, and no matter how complexly their contents may be related, still unless they have some spatial or quasi-spatial content, they are too bare to provide a complete determination of time. Here it seems Kant's view rests on beliefs about the limits of our imaginative powers (see A 34/B 50, B 154-6). With this move Kant enters a considerably less than apodictic realm, for although I may need some contents whereby I can organize and so date my thoughts, and although in fact the contents I use may always involve spatial references, there is still no evident necessity here.[80]

To this extent, that is to the extent that the possibility of determining the time of one's experiences by reference to their systematically related intrinsic features as thoughts (as opposed to spatial items) isn't in principle excluded, the Kantian Refutation of Idealism, even in its most modest form, is less than convincing. We cannot conclude then that on either the phenomenal or noumenal levels Kant has established the existence of non-mental items, although he surely was committed to them. The fourth Paralogism thus presents an ultimately unsuccessful, though certainly notable, effort by Kant to supplement his general immaterialistic theory of mind with a positive theoretical doctrine about our being in some sort of certain interactive relation with something beyond our mind.

Notes to Chapter III

[1] Even later Kant thought there was a perfect correspondence here: 'so kann in der Seele nichts stattfinden, wo der Körper nicht ins Spiel kommen sollte'. *AA*, vol. 28, p. 259; cf. ibid., pp. 286, 757, but also vol. 2, p. 191.

[2] *AA*, vol. 1, p. 20.

[3] Ibid., p. 399.

[4] Ibid., p. 394, 402. Cf. below, Ch. VI.1.

[5] Ibid., p. 357; 365.

[6] Ibid., p. 413.

[7] *Kant: Selected Pre-Critical Writings and Correspondence with Beck*, p. 76 = AA, vol. 2, p. 408.

[8] Ibid., p. 78 = *AA*, vol. 2, p. 409.

[9] Ibid., p. 84 = *AA*, vol. 2, p. 414. Cf. AA, vol. 2, p. 371; vol. 28, p. 280.

[10] John Locke, *An Essay Concerning Human Understanding*, Bk. II, Ch. xxi, § 4.

[11] J. Bennett, *Kant's Dialectic*, p. 59. Cf. C. D. Broad, *Leibniz: An Introduction* (Cambridge, 1975), pp. 47–8.

[12] *Prolegomena to Any Future Metaphysics*, p. 29 = *AA*, vol. 4, p. 282.

[13] *Metaphysical Foundations of Natural Science*, p. 113 = *AA*, vol. 4, p. 550. Cf. *AA*, vol. 1, p. 415.

[14] 'On a Discovery According to Which Any New Critique of Pure Reason Has Been Made Superfluous by an Earlier One', in *The Kant-Eberhard Controversy*, p. 158 = *AA*, vol. 8, p. 249.

[15] Although Kant defines causality as a special conditional relation among substances, it is not clear why states of *a* substance couldn't be all there really is in anything like that relation. The general objection that he has to this idea is that ultimately, if understood in a Spinozistic way, it could make our thoughts attributes of a being that is not us; but this objection clearly is irrelevant if the possibility is that we may be the only substance.

[16] This is the option, for example, that Schlick emphasizes at first after reviewing Kant's discussion. See M. Schlick, *General Theory of Knowledge*, translated by A. Blumberg from the second German edition (New York, 1974), p. 301.

[17] There are texts, however, where Kant backs off from this principle by saying that since causality is, after all, a 'dynamic' relation between substances, we ought to expect them to differ (*AA*, vol. 28, p. 685). But more often Kant argues that homogeneity should and can be noumenally preserved (see, e.g., *AA*, vol. 28, p. 831).

[18] 'Wenn wir sagen, das Intelligible des Körpers wirkt auf die Seele, so heisst dies, dieses äusseren Körpers noumenen bestimmt die Seele, es heisst aber nicht: ein Theil des Körpers (als Noumenen) gehe als Bestimmungsgrund in die Seele über, er ergiesst sich nicht als Kraft in die Seele, sondern er bestimmt blos die Kraft, die in der Seele ist, wo also die Seele aktiv ist. Diese Bestimmung nennt der Autor [Baumgarten] *influxum idealem*, aber dies ist ein *influxus realis*; denn ich kann mir unter Körper auch nur einen solchen Einfluss denken' (*AA*, vol. 28, pp. 758-9).

[19] 'Der Körper als Phänomen ist nicht mit der Seele in Gemeinschaft. sondern die von der Seele verschiedene Substanz, deren Erscheinung Körper heisst' (*AA*, vol. 28, p. 758).

[20] 'Die Körper als Körper können nicht auf die Seele wirken' (*AA*, vol. 28, p. 758). Cf. ibid., p. 146, and vol. 2, p. 327.

[21] *AA*, vol. 28, p. 832.

[22] Strawson, *The Bounds of Sense*, p. 258.

[23] Ibid., p. 260.

[24] 'Was it not disingenuous to represent the supposed heterogeneity of outer causes and inner effects as constituting even the appearance of a problem when his own thesis commits him to no smaller a degree of heterogeneity of causes and effects ∴ .' Ibid., p. 261.

[25] Ibid., p. 263.

[26] *AA*, vol. 1, p. 20.

[27] Ibid., p. 21. Cf. *Selected Pre-Critical Writings*, pp. 91-2= *AA*, vol. 2, p. 419.

[28] *AA*, vol. 1, p. 22.

[29] Ibid., p. 412.

[30] *AA*, vol. 28, pp. 113, 446; vol. 2, p. 338.

[31] A 394; Cf. *AA*, vol. 28, pp. 445, 592. 'Man bleibt in dieser Welt; hat aber eine geistige Anschauung von Allem' (*AA*, vol. 28, p. 298). This is perhaps meant to counter his own earlier suggestion (at the end of *Universal Natural History*) that in an afterlife we may inhabit other planets.

[32] See the attack on Crusius in the *Selected Pre-Critical Writings*, p. 84. Cf. ibid., p. 30 = *AA*, vol. 2, pp. 413-14, 297.

[33] *AA*, vol. 20, p. 309; vol. 28, p. 261. Cf. A. 394.

[34] At one point (*AA*, vol. 28, p. 114) Kant suggests we may also be dependent upon some sort of schema of the body – which apparently would be less determinately physical than our phenomenal body but more related to the physical than our noumenal being – if genuine continuity of personality is to be maintained.

[35] *AA*, vol. 28, p. 761: 'Es bleibt daher weiter nichts übrig also die Seele präformiert anzusehen'. Cf. vol. 17, p. 417 (R 4107), and A 683/B 711.

[36] *AA*, vol. 28, p. 284. Kant also rejects the Leibnizian alternative that we might exist in a tiny corpuscle (ibid., pp. 445, 760).

[37] See, e.g., *AA*, vol. 28, p. 105. At ibid., p. 760, Kant excludes as sheerly theological the idea that God creates souls at birth.

[38] *AA*, vol. 28, pp. 283, 684, 761. Elsewhere, however, Kant suggests souls need not follow the principle of conservation. Unlike matter, they may go out of existence in time, and so they presumably could come into existence too (ibid., p. 764; *Metaphysical Foundations of Natural Science*, p. 103 = *AA*, vol. 4, p. 542).

[39] *AA*, vol. 28, pp. 685, 761.

[40] Ibid., pp. 278, 296, 299; *Religion Within the Bounds of Reason Alone*, tr. by T. M. Greene and H. H. Hudson (New York, 1960), p. 119 n. = *AA*, vol. 6, p. 128 n.

[41] *AA*, vol. 28, pp. 767, 769.

[42] Ibid., p. 282; Cf. ibid., pp. 144-9 and C. D. Broad, 'Immanuel Kant and Psychical Research', in *Philosophy, Religion and Psychical Research*, p. 132.

[43] Here Kant is influenced by Euler. See H. Heimsoeth, *Atom, Seele Monade*.

[44] *AA*, vol. 28, p. 281; vol. 2, p. 324. Kant goes on to note that something's being present or effective throughout a space does not by itself show that it consists in a set of parts composing that space, so the soul can have a kind of extension and still remain simple. Cf. Broad, 'Kant and Psychical Research', p. 132.

[45] *AA*, vol. 2, p. 419, and vol. 28, pp. 756 ff. Cf. D. Armstrong, *Bodily Sensations* (London, 1962), p. 110.

[46] The term 'intention' here is used in the sense derived from Brentano. For more recent discussions of feelings as intentional, see, e.g., G. E. M. Anscombe, 'The Intentionality of Sensation: A Grammatical Feature', in *Analytical Philosophy*, second series, ed. R. J. Butler (New York, 1968).

[47] J. Harrison, 'The Embodiment of Mind, or What Use is Having a Body?' *Proceedings of the Aristotelian Society*, 74 (1973-4), 41. Criteria of embodiment similar to Harrison's are found in A. J. Ayer, 'Privacy', in *The Concept of a Person* (London, 1963), and S. Shoemaker, 'Embodiment and Behavior', in *The Identities of Persons*, ed. by A. O. Rorty (Berkeley, 1976), p. 112. Shoemaker's discussion contrasts with the others and is much closer to Kant's view, for he argues that for embodiment the intentional criterion of the body is prior to the 'biological' or sheerly causal one. In the end, though, unlike Kant, Shoemaker suggests the fittingness of a mind to have a particular kind of body may imply that ultimately its embodiment is not contingent. (Of course, Kant's views here should also be compared with those of Schopenhauer, who was the major follower of Kant focusing on this issue.).

[48] Thus, Kant speaks of the notion of a 'ghost body' as a mere subterfuge. For him, to have a spatial appearance and effects is to be (phenomenally) spatially located (*AA*, vol. 28, pp. 685, 769). Contrast Harrison, 'Embodiment', p. 53.

[49] Harrison, 'Embodiment', pp. 37-8.

[50] See D. Long, 'The Bodies of Persons', *Journal of Philosophy*, 71 (1974),

291–301; and W. Sellars, 'The Identity Approach to the Mind-Body Problem', *Review of Metaphysics*, 18 (1965), 430–51.

[51] Harrison, 'Embodiment', pp. 38–9.

[52] I believe this point can be extended to meet Harrison's objection that one's hair is really part of one's body (ibid., p. 39).

[53] Other arguments against the idea of vision without a single body, i.e., of multiple embodiment, are to be found in V. Balowitz, 'More on Persons and Their Bodies', *Philosophical Studies*, 27 (1975), 63–4; and S. Shoemaker, *Self-Knowledge and Self-Identity* (Ithaca, 1963), pp. 174–83.

[54] Harrison, 'Embodiment', p. 46.

[55] Ibid., pp. 47 f.

[56] Arguments similar to those behind his attitude to multiple embodiment also appear to underlie Kant's treatment of telepathy. See *AA*, vol. 2, pp. 327 ff.; vol. 28, p. 593; A 770/B 798.

[57] *AA*, vol. 28, pp. 225, 756. Typical is his statement at ibid., p. 282: 'Die Seele hat im Körper keinen besonderen Ort; ihr Ort ist aber in der Welt durch den Körper determiniert, und sie ist mit dem Körper unmittelbar verbunden. Die Möglichkeit dieses *commercii* sehen wir nicht ein; die Bedingungen dieses *commercii* müssen wir aber nicht allein setzen, wie sie bei den Körpern unter einander sind, nämlich durch Undringlichkeit, denn sonst wird sie materiell. Einen Ort und Platz im Körper fur sie anzuweisen, ist widersinnig und materialistisch.'

[58] *AA*, vol. 2, p. 325; vol. 28, p. 757.

[59] Cf. W. Sellars, 'Kant's Transcendental Idealism', *Proceedings of the Ottawa Congress on Kant in the Anglo-American and Continental Traditions*, pp. 165–81; and K. Hübner, 'Leib und Erfahrung in Kants Opus Postumum', *Zeitschrift für philosophische Forschung*, 7 (1953), 204–9.

[60] *AA*, vol. 2, p. 286.

[61] *AA*, vol. 28, p. 43; it is not clear how seriously Kant meant the idea that Berkeley can be refuted only by 'the agreement of others and one's own conviction'.

[62] *AA*, vol. 20, p. 286. For an explanation of what is behind this change see also below, Ch. VI.

[63] *AA*, vol. 28, pp. 680, 770. See especially H. Allison, 'Kant's Critique of Berkeley', *Journal of the History of Philosophy*, 11 (1973), 43–63; and M. Wilson, 'Kant and the "Dogmatic Idealism of Berkeley"', *Journal of the History of Philosophy*, 9 (1971), pp. 459–75.

[64] See Alfons Kalter, *Kants vierter Paralogismus*, p. 207.

[65] *The Kant-Eberhard Controversy*, p. 158 = *AA*, vol. 8, p. 249.

[66] Note that this is compatible with Kant's allowing that other types of creatures might only require some other (non-spatial) kind of 'external' phenomena. This point is forgotten in Onora O'Neill's 'Space and Objects', *Journal of Philosophy*, 73 (1976), 30; and J. Bennett, *Dialectic*, p. 54.

[67] This point is made by M. Gochnauer ('Kant's Refutation of Idealism', *Journal of the History of Philosophy*, 12 (1974), 198) and M. Wilson ('On Kant and the Refutation of Subjectivism', in *Kant's Theory of Knowledge*, ed. by. L. W. Beck [Dordrecht, 1974], p. 214). The point is missed by T. E. Wilkerson (*Kant's Critique of Pure Reason* [Oxford, 1976], p. 82) and P. Strawson (*The Bounds of Sense*, p. 257).

[68] See again Wilson, 'On Kant and the Refutation of Subjectivism', p. 214, and J. Bennett, *Kant's Analytic*, (Cambridge, 1966) p. 217.

[69] The former view is advocated by Wilkerson and Strawson, the latter by Kalter and Kemp Smith.

⁷⁰ I think Kalter (*Kants vierter Paralogismus*, p. 141) is right in criticizing Smith here for interjecting the phrase 'it is argued' in the text, as if Kant were reciting a thoroughly problematic position. But although Kalter goes on nicely to demonstrate how the over-all argument of the rational psychologist here closely parallels views Kant had held earlier, I think he goes too far (see, e.g., ibid., pp. 133, 141 f., 188 f.) in claiming that at the time of the first writings of the *Critique* itself Kant was committed to this argument, and so the text represents a view which he really endorsed when he wrote it. Such a conclusion is not at all forced on us, and we can simply hold, as G. Bird does, that 'Kant regards the premises, and their elaboration, as ambiguous, so that he might accept them in some constructions, but not in others, while the central point of the following discussion is to list these important ambiguities' (*Kant's Theory of Knowledge*, p. 21).

⁷¹ This point is well elaborated in H. Allison, 'Kant's Critique of Berkeley'.

⁷² 'Objects thus become as immediate to me as any of my experiences, and I can no more doubt the existence of the external world than I can doubt the occurrence of my sensations' (Wilkerson, *Kant's Critique*, p. 183). Cf. ibid., pp. 117, 180; N. Kemp Smith, *A Commentary to Kant's 'Critique of Pure Reason'*, p. 305.

⁷³ Bennett notes the peculiarity of this claim (*Kant's Analytic*, pp. 216-7).

⁷⁴ It is therefore hard to understand W. H. Walsh's view that the second edition provides a 'more radical' argument (*Kant's Criticism of Metaphysics* [Chicago, 1975], p. 190).

⁷⁵ A. C. Ewing (*A Short Commentary on Kant's Critique of Pure Reason*, p. 193) points this out, but then claims that Kant dogmatically denies it. This goes too far I believe, for it rather seems that, as usual, Kant is merely hesitant to parade his lack of a complete rejection of rationalism.

⁷⁶ Cf. my 'Husserl's Realism', *Philosophical Review*, 86 (1977), 498-519.

⁷⁷ Gochnauer, 'Kant's Refutation', p. 200.

⁷⁸ Ibid., p. 201.

⁷⁹ Gochnauer fails to see this and goes on to applaud Kant's argument, comparing it to Wittgenstein's attack on 'private language' and mere ostensive definition. The weakness in Gochnauer's interpretation reveals a questionable (though common) understanding of Wittgenstein that is related to the error about the validity of Kant's argument. The main point of Wittgenstein's attack on 'private language' may be simply the general inadequacy for cognition of any mere ostensive act, whether or not the act is focused on a mental content. (Gochnauer goes on to make another common and related error here by saying that for Wittgenstein 'inner states simply drop out of the picture'. See my 'Recent Work on Wittgenstein and the Philosophy of Mind', *New Scholasticism*, 43 (1975), 108-112.) Similarly, Kant's well taken point that for knowledge we need something independent or beyond a mere representational act does not *mean* by itself that we must have something beyond the mental contents of our acts. However, a strong argument − that goes beyond Kant − that objectivity does require spatiality is found in O'Neill, 'Space and Objects'. A strong claim to the contrary is found in R. C. S. Walker, *Kant*, pp. 30 f.

⁸⁰ Cf. Strawson, *The Bounds of Sense*, p. 127.

Chapter IV

Identity

The problem of personal identity is the topic of what is perhaps Kant's most difficult and misunderstood Paralogism, the third. The problem of this Paralogism will be approached in two ways, exegetically and then systematically. First, after a short review of Kant's earlier treatment of personality, the text of the third Paralogism will be analysed. I will argue that here Kant's position is more sceptical than is generally realized, and that he wants directly to challenge a positive rationalist conclusion about the self, namely that its ultimate identity over time is (theoretically) known with paradigmatic certainty. I will show this is consistent with Kant's claims in the transcendental deduction, and also that it does not amount to a mere forsaking of inner for outer or empirical criteria of identity. In this way I will be arguing against both overly rationalistic (e.g., Dieter Henrich) and overly empiricistic (e.g., Strawson and Bennett) construals of Kant, for such construals imply Kant was certain about our personal identity.

In the second part of the chapter, I argue that Kant's position on personal identity fares relatively well when it is systematically compared with other alternatives, including those appearing in current discussions. These discussions have often lacked a clear distinction between phenomenal or epistemological contexts and noumenal or metaphysical ones, and consequently there have arisen a number of questionable extreme positions (e.g., in Parfit, Perry, and Shoemaker). Here I defend the value of Kant's discussion, although I conclude that his position is still not entirely acceptable because it is tied to especially questionable idealistic views about time.

A.1. Personality: An Historical Overview

Kant entitles his third Paralogism 'Of Personality', and he immediately takes this to be the question of whether one has an appropriate numerical identity over time (A 361). In some of his other writings Kant uses a slightly different terminology which tends to equate the question of whether one is a person with the issue of whether one is an intelligence. This latter issue — which occupied the place of the identity question in Kant's first categorial characterizations of the soul[1] — has to do simply with whether one has certain appropriate complex powers (at any time).

In his earliest period Kant thought these powers could be understood naturalistically. Spontaneity, in the sense of governance by rational principles, is said to be the characteristic feature of persons and to be compatible with a throughly deterministic world.[2] Later Kant often still tied personality to spontaneity, but eventually he decided that 'spontaneity' should be understood to refer primarily to an absolute and noumenal moral freedom that is only 'practically' establishable. He also came to emphasize that in theoretical contexts it is not enough to characterize persons merely as rational beings, and that other features, in particular reference to operations of memory, need to be introduced.[3] Unfortunately, sometimes he still said this has to do only with whether one is the *same* person over time, and that simply being a person is established merely by having the ability to say 'I'.[4] This terminology cannot be accepted for the *Critique*, for it would collapse the third Paralogism into the second and would wholly obscure Kant's critical arguments. We must rather take as our standard Kant's remarks elsewhere that the ability to say 'I' (i.e., in some way to have a sense of a unity of representing as opposed to a multiplicity of representeds) may show one is an intelligence, but this, and even its persistence, is not the same as being a person in the sense of an intelligence that is genuinely conscious of its identity over time.[5]

The prime reason for Kant's introduction of temporal features into the definition of personality was probably not merely a desire to find an adequate theoretical way to distinguish man but rather a wish to do justice to certain basic human interests. Kant noted early and often in his lectures that man is interested in more than the mere continuance of the soul.[6] According to Kant an eternal but sleeping soul would be as good as nothing, even though he also believes that sleep does not rule out the possibility of some clear thought.[7] His point is that even if the mental substrate of man persists in some form, a certain amount of continuity and connectedness of thought seems necessary before one can take a well-founded interest in a (past or future) soul as one's own. Yet although Kant was familiar with the Lockean tradition of seeing this idea as essential to what constitutes a person as opposed to a mere soul-substance, it was a while before he emphasized it and the specific problem of personal identity.[8]

This may be partially because even in the period of the Pölitz lectures Kant believed that recollected data, like all the givens of inner sense, automatically convey knowledge and so can guarantee personal identity.[9] Personal identity can become a problem, however, when this belief is rejected, as it is with Kant's critical distinction between inner sense and apperception. Because it is now understood as a mere conveyor of data, inner sense alone is obviously incapable of justifying any claims to self-knowledge. The alternative of claiming personal identity *a priori* on the basis of the mere idea of apperception may still be tempting, however, and it is primarily with this target in mind that Kant developed his critical discussion in the third Paralogism.

2. The Third Paralogism

Kant initially formulates the third Paralogism in this way:

That which is conscious of the numerical identity of itself at different times is in so far a *person*. Now the soul is conscious, etc. Therefore it is a person (A 361).

Obviously this argument is at least valid. Furthermore, the first premiss of the argument is clearly accepted by Kant here, although as was just noted it contrasts with his usage in some other texts. The critique of the paralogism must therefore be directed against the second premiss, an assertion which from a modern perspective surely seems much safer than parallel claims about the soul's simplicity or substantiality.[10] In his first paragraph of discussion even Kant seems to support rather than suspect the assertion, for he says, 'the personality of the soul has to be regarded . . . as a completely identical proposition . . . valid *a priori*' (A 362). But of course Kant cannot mean this literally, for then he would be left without any critique. He must mean not that the personality of the soul, *as* defined in the first premiss, is 'valid *a priori*', but rather that there is some *related* proposition, seeming to bear on the personality of the soul, which a rational psychologist would be inclined to assert and which is valid *a priori*. (Thus the third paralogism needs to be extended beyond its explicit formulation, just as we argued that the first and second paralogisms also need to be extended.)

Kant immediately tells us what this valid proposition is, namely the 'identical' or analytic proposition that 'in the whole time I am conscious of myself, I am conscious of this time as belonging to the unity of myself' (A 362). Given that here by 'conscious' Kant means implicit and possible consciousness, and not necessarily explicit consciousness (cf. A 365), this proposition is obviously valid, for it merely expresses the thought that whenever I *am* conscious of myself, then *I* am conscious of myself. This proposition reflects what might be called an indisputable hypothetical identity. That is, if it is granted that I am really conscious of myself over time, then it follows that it is really I who am conscious over time, and so that there is one and the same I over time. This proposition is hardly a step to a proof of identity over time but simply asserts what trivially follows if that idea is granted. Kant surely must have in mind those who are attached to this proposition when he later says that with respect to the question of an 'unbroken continuance' of the subject, rationalists revolve 'perpetually in a circle' and 'give none but tautological answers' (A 366).[11] This analysis also fits what Kant says in the second edition about the third paralogism, namely that it involves the mere analytic proposition that 'in all the manifold of which I am conscious, I am identical with myself' (B 408). As Kant says, this hardly proves 'identity of the person in all [or any, for that matter] change of states' (ibid.). (Smith translates this as 'its states', but this goes beyond the text and transforms the synthetic proposition Kant wants to introduce here back into an analytic one.)

Given this interpretation there still remains the question of how anyone could ever think that such a clearly analytic proposition can lead to a valid material claim about the self. Here it is necessary to understand some more of the peculiar confusions of the rational psychologist who is Kant's primary target. Kant begins his analysis by talking about those who move from the belief that 'time is in me' to the notion that 'I am to be found as numerically identical in . . . time' (A 362). This whole paragraph, in which Kant alludes to the notion of time as merely the form of inner sense, generally has baffled interpreters.[12] It appears that here Kant is trying to impute to someone the odd idea that since time, supposedly, is only in him, he must be one throughout it. Although this idea may seem quite odd, I think it can be shown that there is some sense in Kant's associating it with rational psychology.

It must be admitted that the idea may seem not entirely appropriate for a pure rational psychology, for unlike the claims of the other paralogisms it must involve a statement about man as a temporal being. None the less, it bears on the most general feature of that temporality, although under the further presumption that the rational psychologist is willing to speak about temporality as but an inner form. However, if there were a rationalist who accepted these presumptions and insisted on asserting something *a priori* about the aspect of man they involve, then he might well fall for the odd idea Kant introduces. What makes the idea so odd, after all, is simply that it so blatantly involves the basic non-Kantian mistake of confusing the empirical and transcendental levels (here the mistake is made with respect to time; in the fourth paralogism it is made with respect to externality). That is, it mistakes the genuine transcendental claim that time is a mere form for us (i.e., only to be experienced from the human perspective in general) with the quite different and incorrect empirical claim that it is but a form of the individual.[13] If time were such an individual form, it would follow that the self is continuous and a person in it. In fact, as Kant notes, it would follow that one is a permanent person (A 365), *and so here, as with the other Paralogisms, it would follow that a central target of Kant's critique is the rationalistic doctrine of spiritualism.* (Cf. above, Ch. II at n. 40, and A 682/B 710, where Kant speaks of the idea of a 'self-subsisting intelligence', 'unchangeable in itself'.)

In the second paragraph of his discussion Kant encourages understanding this paralogism also in terms of the other basic fallacies common to rational psychology — fallacies which need not be expressed in terms of a formal syllogistic error, but which do reflect general confusions of a quasi-formal nature. We have already seen that these involve the conflation of not merely the analytic with the synthetic, and the transcendental with the empirical, but also of the *subjective* with the *objective*, and the *indeterminate* with the *determinate* (cf. above, Ch. II.7). Thus Kant remarks here that 'in my own consciousness identity of person . . . is unfailingly met with' (A 362). Once again, he cannot be taking 'person' literally, and what he must mean is rather that when one reflects on experiences at various times it always seems that the being who had those (now inwardly recollected) experiences is (numerically) the same as the present being. Obviously what is so *subjectively* convincing can still be *objectively* unfounded, and, as Kant points out, others may judge differently and say experiences that I take to be mine might have been had by others or by no one. This error is only trivial if instead there are still other experiences I had at those times that could be properly recalled. What Kant must rather be getting at is the possibility that I might be wrong in concluding that I existed at all as a person at those times. Similarly, one might be misled by the indisputable but *indeterminate* claim that one is not, and indeed cannot be, aware of being a plurality of beings over time (cf. A 364).[14] That is, one cannot be inwardly and recollectively aware of experiences at different times *as* belonging to someone else, and this might improperly lead one to make the *determinate* claim that one is hence numerically identical over time.

As Kant immediately suggests, this confusion might be specifically encouraged by misunderstanding the transcendental nature of the representation of the 'I', which is indeterminate in that it is a mere form and stands for the unity of thought required for any awareness directed to a multiplicity of contents. Kant expresses this point by saying that even if an 'outside observer' admits 'the "I" which accompanies, and indeed with complete identity, all representations at all times in my consciousness, he will draw no inference from this to the objective permanence [or persistence, for that matter] of myself' (A 363). This point may at first be difficult to see, for if it is true that there are various times in which my consciousness is accompanied by an I, then some 'objective permanence' of the self would follow. However, Kant's premiss is not that my consciousness really *is* in these various times but only that there are various times 'in my consciousness'. My consciousness is 'identical' then not in any numerical-persistent sense, but only in the sense of being a unified awareness directed to a plurality of times. Thus the fallacy might also be expressed as an inference from the idea that time is 'in me', in the sense that any intentional object is, to the claim that I am really one in time.

This point is not so clearly expressed in Kant's next paragraph:

The identity of the consciousness of myself at different times is therefore only a formal condition of my thoughts and their coherence, and in no way proves the numerical identity of my subject. Despite the logical identity of the 'I', such a change may have occurred in it as does not allow of the retention of its identity, and yet we may ascribe to it the same-sounding 'I' ... (A 363)

Here we must be careful to read the premiss ('at different times') not as an identity of individual consciousness *in* different times but as an identity or unity of consciousness *directed* to different times. Furthermore, if this consciousness arises as a result of changes, such as Kant suggests may occur, these should not be described as literally changes 'in it'. Rather, they can involve merely the fact that the intentional content of various experiences concerning different times has become the object of concern of a particular subject who previously did not exist.

Another way to appreciate the complex temptations to error here is to consider that although it is not true that, for all x and y, a y-type representation of x entails the representation of a y-type x, there might appear to be an entailment for some readings of 'representation' when y is the feature of persistence and x is allowed to range over appropriate objects. For example, a persistent representation of a pain might be a representation of a persistent pain. Moreover, the latter representation can be not only intentionally and truly of the pain but also of it in the sense that a representation belonging to or caused by something may be of it. Matters change, however, when we focus on the self as such rather than on particular states. That is, the persistent representation of an 'I' need not be the representation of a persistent I, at least if the phrase 'representation of' is meant in the latter case in the 'belonging to' sense.

This can explain why in the last quoted passage Kant speaks of the 'same-sounding "I"': he means that personal identity is unproven not only if there is (merely) a present unity of consciousness directed toward a thought of a consciousness existent at different times, but also not even if, by some odd mechanism (see, e.g., Kant's suggestions at A 363 n.), it were possible to 'transmit' consciousness so that it continually would be the case that a set of thoughts were accompanied by a 'same-sounding' representation of (i.e., about, in a broad sense) an 'I'. This representation could be merely the representation of the transcendental I, but it is also possible that *qua* content there may be a 'same-sounding' empirical representation. This is what Kant means in his next paragraph when he says that even the 'permanent appearance' of an 'I' does not mean that the I 'may not be in the same state of flux' as other thoughts (A 364). By 'flux' Kant here must mean not the Humean idea that representations of (i.e., about) an I may be rare and fleeting (for then he wouldn't have spoken of a 'permanent appearance'), and so not intentionally persistent, but rather that even a constant representation of (i.e., about) an I (viz., the transcendental 'I', or perhaps a 'same-sounding' set of thoughts) may *belong* to various beings and in this sense be 'in flux'.[15] At one time it may truly involve one subject, and at another time another — a possibility which then would have a Humean flavor in that there would be not one real and changing subject but rather a radical flux with new subjects (but common thought-contents or forms) every moment.[16]

This is a radical idea, but it is important to see Kant only wants to draw our attention to its being a logical possibility, and he doesn't mean to suggest we have any reason to suspect it is a realized possibility. Yet it is a coherent possibility, and it is not to be treated, as some have, as tantamount to the odd suggestion that there could be a literal 'transfer of a self from one substance or individual thing to another'.[17] That is, the suggestion is not that *my* consciousness inhabits one being and then another, but rather that all the contents of consciousness to which I now direct myself, under the impression that they were previously had by me, might have been had by another self.

Kant's other statements in this paragraph must also be read very carefully. He says, 'we must necessarily judge that we are one and the same throughout the whole time of which we are conscious. We cannot, however, claim that this judgment would be valid from the standpoint of an outside observer' (A 364). In speaking about the time 'of which' rather than 'in which' we are conscious, Kant reaffirms his point about how little can be inferred from a mere intentional unity of time. However, he confuses matters a bit by speaking simply about 'this judgment', as if it were one and the same proposition that would be certain to us and questionable for an outside observer. In fact, as Kant said earlier himself, judgements of the 'of which' type can be 'admitted' (A 362) by outside observers too, for it is only the claim that a consciousness exists *in* various times that needs to be challenged. It is also best slightly to amend or put in a definite context Kant's remarks that 'we must necessarily judge that we are one and the same', and his immediately prior claim that 'we are unable from our own consciousness to determine whether, as souls, we are permanent' (A 364). These texts are most easily understood as speaking only about limitations and necessities for someone focusing, as a rational psychologist would, simply upon consciousness in a pure sense. Bennett takes them rather to mean that Kant does 'not allow me to correct my judgments of self-identity in the light of evidence which the observer has'.[18] Such an interpretation goes directly against Kant's own introduction, here and in his Refutation of Idealism, of the relevance of data beyond the self for the determination of all temporal matters, including one's own states. Bennett fails to see that Kant's statement here can be directed simply against someone limited to the perspective of the rational psychologist, for in general he fails to see how well Kant's attack is organized against that perspective. Thus Bennett must confess, 'Are we to suppose that the rational psychologist claims to have proved that the soul "maintains a memory of itself", and that Kant denies his right to claim this? I can make no sense of the Paralogism along those lines.'[19]

Having made some sense of the Paralogism 'along those lines', we can give a more harmless reading to A 364, although from this it cannot be concluded that Kant can only have strictly limited challenges to claims of personal identity. Granted that Kant has charted a number of improper inferences that might tempt some rational psychologists, it is only natural to consider whether he also means to and/or can in principle challenge the conclusion of the paralogism. To answer this question it is obviously necessary first to determine more specifically Kant's positive doctrine of personal identity.

3. Rationalist Interpretations

There are a number of indications that Kant expects someone who is identical over time not merely to have true ideas of past experiences but also to have some sort of persistent constituents. In a lecture note that asks whether man retains his 'psychological identity' the answer is given that, 'theoretically this is not to be assumed, just as water in a river does not stay the same'.[20] Here Kant takes personal identity to involve more than mere functional continuity, although this does not make it necessary to impute to him the odd general principle that identity over time requires the maintenance of all constituents. Surely he would allow that identity can be preserved even when some constituents are lost, as long as some material is maintained in all (or perhaps only in each) change.[21] This requirement of something persistent appears in the third Paralogism when Kant ties the issues of personality and substantiality (A 365), for he clearly believes substantiality requires some maintenance of constituents. The first sentence of his analysis of the paralogism also suggests that in general to determine identity over time we 'pay heed to that [*sic*] permanent element in the appearance' (A 362).

Kant of course denies that we can find such an element by a mere rational inspection of the soul, but there are many ways in which this denial could be interpreted. Some, notably Strawsonians, have held that this element can be merely a relatively permanent phenomenon, such as a human body, and so there are means — albeit non-rationalist — to determine personal identity, and this is what Kant ultimately wants to emphasize.[22] Others, notably Bennett, have suggested that the element must be an absolutely continuous substratum, and there is no way such an element can be found. This is then said not to disturb Kant because he supposedly means that even the need for such an element is but a relic of rational psychology.[23] Thus, although they are quite critical of each other's views on the third Paralogism, Strawson and Bennett ultimately both affirm a basically empiricist view that Kant can and does assert personal identity merely by reference to ordinary phenomenal criteria. There is an obvious alternative position here, namely that Kant himself accepts the requirement of an element in a stricter sense than Strawson's. It is possible to believe this and then to argue in a strong rationalist way that somehow for Kant there is *a priori* knowledge of personal identity. On the other hand, it could be held that precisely because of this requirement Kant himself may be unable to call anyone's claim to personal identity completely justified. This last possibility has been least developed, although Allen Wood has remarked recently (in a critique of Bennett) that 'it seems quite evident that Kant believed (1) that the numerical identity of my person through time would have to consist in the existence of a permanent substratum underlying all my thoughts and, (2) that self-awareness . . . affords me no acquaintance with such'.[24] With the proviso that 'consist in' be replaced by 'require', this is the interpretation that we shall develop.

Assuming that our view is the one that prima facie is supported by the texts just cited, we shall defend it against the others by first handling a number of ways in which it might appear a rationalist Kantian could regard personality as (theoretically) non-problematic. Rationalists could begin by stressing that the issue is, after all, not the strong claim that all assertions of identity with previous (inwardly recollected) experiences are correct, but is rather only the claim that there are some 'recalled' events — which one may not even be able to determine by oneself — that one really did experience. Kant's own reference to time as a form of inner sense might appear to support the claim, for to deny it is in effect to assert that at least in one's own case that sense is wholly an illusion, that it merely seems to be the case that one has a past.[25] None the less, Kant seems to be willing to leave this open as a logical possibility, and he does not argue, as he does sometimes with respect to space, that here our data are such that they simply cannot be all imaginary. And although it may seem that any creature capable of raising the question of identity must, despite however otherwise confused he may be, still have had some experiences at other times, this idea is precisely what is challenged by Kant's suggestion of a wholly transmitted consciousness (A 363 n.), for in that case a complete impression of the past would be generated in a new being.

Despite these difficulties, rationalists might argue that Kant's own transcendental deduction of the categories involves a proof of personal identity. For example, he says 'the original and necessary consciousness of the identity of the self is thus at the same time a consciousness of an equally necessary unity of the synthesis of all appearances according to concepts' (A 108). However, this passage could also be translated as referring merely to a 'consciousness of the identity of itself'. That is, any cognitive consciousness must as such, i.e., as a unitary awareness, be identical —

but this is not to say that the subjects of the experiential contents it refers to must be identical over time. Unfortunately, there are other passages like this one, and they all have to be read quite carefully lest Kant be taken to be making precisely the paralogistic fallacy he clearly criticizes elsewhere in the *Critique*. The main thing to keep in mind here, although Kant's own exposition at times makes this difficult, is that the 'identity' of consciousness he frequently speaks of can be simply the idea of the transcendental representation of the 'I'.

For example, after remarking that 'no fixed and abiding self can present itself in [the] flux of inner appearances', i.e., in mere inner sense, Kant goes on to say that 'what has necessarily to be represented as numerically identical cannot be thought as such through empirical data' (A 107). The context indicates that he is not speaking merely of what would have to be the case if there were something numerically identical, but rather he means to be unpacking the fact that there is (in so far as there is experience) something 'numerically identical' that contrasts with the data of inner sense. Here it can appear that Kant is claiming we do have a pure representation of what is really a 'fixed and abiding self'. Focusing on such passages, Dieter Henrich has claimed that although Kant criticizes arguing from the soul's simplicity to its identity over time, he does not always reject the idea ('diesen Unterschied . . . nicht durchgängig geltend macht').[26] Moreover, Henrich himself seems to believe that the idea is not to be rejected, for 'the subject has knowledge of himself with Cartesian certainty, and in this certainty is included knowledge of its [persistent] numerical identity'.[27] This view, however, takes inadequate heed of Kant's own anti-Cartesian arguments, and fortunately it can be rejected because there is another way to interpret the texts in question.

A closer look at the context of the passage from A 107 shows that the 'identical' item here need not be a thing but can be merely a formal condition or its representation. Kant begins his paragraph by saying 'this original and transcendental condition [namely for knowledge of objects] is no other than *transcendental apperception*'; and right after his remark about 'what has necessarily to be represented as numerically identical', he talks about what we must do 'to render such a transcendental presupposition valid' (A 107). The 'identity of consciousness' spoken of can mean not a persistent self but rather simply the requirement that any cognition must be represented in a unity, no matter how multiple its objects. In the very next paragraph Kant himself speaks more properly only of the 'numerical unity of this apperception', which 'precedes all data of intuition, and by relation to which representation of objects is alone possible' (A 107).

There are also various harmless explanations of Kant's use of the term 'identical'. For example, even when he is not all concerned with temporal identity, he likes to point out that the idea of the transcendental unity of apperception can be expressed in an 'identical', i.e., analytic, proposition (B 135). He also likes to use the term 'identity' even when he easily can be taken to refer merely to immediate self-identity and the unity of an act, and not the persistent identity of a thing. Thus he says, 'the mind could never think its identity in the manifoldness of its representations, and indeed think this identity *a priori*, if it did not have before its eyes the identity of its act' (A 108), and, 'but as self-consciousness [in the sense of a 'totality of a possible self-consciousness'] is a transcendental representation, numerical identity is inseparable from it, and is *a priori* certain' (A 113, cf. B 135). Typical of Kant's style here is the fact that even when speaking directly about 'transcendental apperception', which surely must be a condition of knowledge and not a temporal item itself, Kant uses terms that misleadingly can seem to have to do with temporal identity. Thus he speaks of an 'original unchangeable consciousness' (A 107), when all he means is what he means when he also says that the 'pure concept of [the] transcendental object is always one and the same' (A 109), namely that in all knowledge (i.e., each cognition) there is a 'constant' unity despite the temporal plurality of its referents or contents.

Kant eventually makes this relatively clear himself when he states that to say 'all objects with which we can occupy ourselves are one and all in me, that is, are determinations of my identical self, is only another way of saying that there must be a complete unity of them in one and the same apperception' (A 129). Surely he should be read here as saying all his talk about an 'identical self' is really only a reference to the unity of apperception — and not as meaning that having unity of apperception already means having a self numerically identical over time. (Smith's translation is not literal here, for what Kant says is that the former phrase 'expresses' the latter, which can mean not that it is 'another way of saying it', in that it is equivalent to it, but rather that it may mean no more than the latter, i.e., may entail but perhaps not be entailed by it.) The identity of the self as a person is related to this unity, but only by having it as at most a necessary condition: without the general unity of apperception, the particular unity involved in self-cognition, and thus the unity of one's experiences over time, would be impossible.[28] Thus Kant can say representations 'belong' to one only if I 'can unite them' (B 134),[29] and without the 'necessary unity of apperception', 'thoroughgoing identity of self-consciousness cannot be thought' (B 135).

In sum, the complex texts of the transcendental deduction do not require us to assert a relation of mutual entailment for Kant between personal identity and apperception, and it remains obviously against his Paralogisms to do so. Both of these points have also been missed in other recent commentaries. Graham Bird claims, 'Kant wishes to say . . . identity of self-consciousness is a condition of our having any knowledge whatever'.[30] He takes this to mean 'consciousness of personal identity is equated to consciousness of a certain conceptual unity',[31] and that 'to be aware of any physical object, or any particular mental condition, is to presuppose a personality'.[32] R. P. Wolff also says that Kant denies 'perceptions or concepts may stand in associative relations *without being part of the same consciousness*'.[33] As he also believes all associated representations are subject to the transcendental unity of apperception, it appears that he too in effect falsely attributes to Kant an entailment relation between regular experiences of an event and identity of an experiencer over time.

4. Empiricist Interpretations

Just as there are texts that may appear to support a rationalistic Kantian route to affirming personal identity, so there are also Kantian texts that appear to support this affirmation on empirical grounds, namely through reference to the persistence of the body. Here the textual basis is even stronger, for Kant remarks:

the permanence of the soul, regarded merely as object of inner sense, remains undemonstrated, and indeed indemonstrable. Its permanence during life is, of course, evident *per se*, since the thinking being (as man) is itself likewise an object of the outer sense (B 415).

Similarly, in the *Prolegomena* Kant says, 'the permanence of the soul can therefore only be proved (and no one cares to do that) during the life of man'.[34] On the assumption that such permanence is tantamount to personality (cf. A 365, but see also below, n. 39), it would appear to follow that, given the persistence of an ordinary human body, there is nothing problematic about asserting it is a person. The considerable emphasis that Kant gives in the Paralogism to the perspective of an outside observer, and his example of a possible transmitted consciousness, can also be seen as supporting this Strawsonian idea, for all this draws attention to the procedure of determining identity by the intuition of bodies.[35] Such intuition might correct specific thoughts we have about our identity, or even refute all of them via reference to some kind of bizarre brain operation, but in most cases it would seem they could rather fully confirm our belief that we are persons. And although it may seem odd that in one context Kant says no one would 'care' to argue for persistence in life, whereas elsewhere he devotes a whole section to the complexities and fallacies that can be involved in so arguing, that section could be seen as merely an exposure of the difficulties that arise when empirical criteria are overlooked by rationalists. This view is also in harmony with Kant's Refutation of Idealism. That argument would be undone if without reference to something spatial (albeit not necessarily a human body) we could determine a temporal fact about ourselves, namely our persistence. Conversely, the argument that in general we know temporal things only by reference to spatial items nicely fits (although it still does not entail) the idea that we can know ourselves over time via reference to our spatial form.

Despite its advantages, there are some difficulties with this interpretation. Not only is it likely that in general personal identity need not be tied down to bodily identity, but there are also grounds for supposing that Kant in particular would have to regard bodily identity as ultimately not the central aspect of personal identity. It is true that Kant says features of the soul can be determined by reference to outer sense, because a 'thinking being can also be regarded as a man', but this statement is best taken as a casual formulation of a belief rather than as a summary of any proof. Given Kant's phenomenal or empirical dualism the statement can be explained merely in terms of a belief in a perfect phenomenal correspondence for now between mind and body (see above Ch. III., n. 1). Such beliefs aside, and given that it may well be that mental events ultimately are not identical with physical ones, a Kantian must allow that we cannot always — or, indeed ever — be theoretically positive that a disruption (or maintenance) of physical continuity would amount to a cessation (or maintenance) of personality.

There are independent reasons for accepting this point, for as Richard Swinburne has argued at length, we ought not to confuse the criteria for personal identity with what constitutes personal identity.[36] More generally, we ought to distinguish between (1) 'public phenomena, the occurrence of which makes it probable that the object in question is', and would justify our believing a particular concept applies to the object, and (2) logically necessary and sufficient conditions for the object's falling under the concept.[37] This point about the difference between being a person and being publicly determinable as one[38] is easily accepted from a Kantian perspective, and in fact it must be accepted given Kant's view (see above, Ch. III.5) that in an 'afterlife' we can and probably would be non-embodied persons. Thus, although Strawson's interpretation makes sense in so far as Kant happens to believe souls and bodies are presently perfectly coordinated, ultimately for Kant the concept of a person — and hence its identity — is still not bound to the concept of a sophisticated body and its identity.[39]

This does not mean that Kant would have to go so far as Swinburne suggests at one point,[40] however, and believe that a claim to *personal* identity can be sensible even when it involves no phenomenal evidence. What Kant says is rather that a future being 'would have to be *aware* it is the same soul, for otherwise I couldn't say that it is the same soul that exists in the future, but there would rather be another rational being'.[41] I understand this to mean that although Kant would grant that the maintained identity of one's *soul-substance* doesn't require satisfaction of any phenomenal criteria, e.g., physical continuity or any explicit recall of that substance's past, still personality is something else. It not only involves a mental substance that persists in ways that may be indeterminable from a phenomenal perspective (though not something in principle beyond the intuition of an outside observer such as God), but it also requires some appropriate mental events directed to specific past and phenomenal occurrences. At the same time, a Kantian can grant to Strawson that *phenomenally* speaking personal identity is adequately determined by appropriate complex and continuous bodily appearances. Yet what may be properly assertible in a phenomenal context may ultimately speaking be false. In particular, just as 'phenomenal substance' may turn out to be noumenally non-substantial, so too whatever is called numerically identical on a phenomenal level may be rooted in a multiplicity of noumenal beings. So much at least must be held by Kant if his transcendental idealism is to be maintained, for if we could determine the precise identity of noumena then they would no longer be individually unknowable to us. (The point made here with respect to the mind's relation to time has it analogue with respect to space when Kant phenomenally rejects but noumenally accepts the possibility of multiple embodiment. See above, Ch. III.6, and below at n. 71.) Therefore, only in a loose way of speaking is personal identity theoretically unproblematic for Kant. Its problematic nature arises from its tie to the noumenal realm, although strictly speaking it is not a sheerly noumenal characteristic but involves the satisfaction of both noumenal and phenomenal conditions; that is, as Kant indicates, it is dependent on but not reducible to the maintenance of one's substance and intelligence.[42]

The complexity of the characteristic of personality can also account for the fact that the ultimate general direction of the third Paralogism appears to go against the tendency of the other Paralogisms. That is, in general we have found that Kant ultimately accepts various (indeterminate) *noumenal* characterizations of one's being (e.g., simplicity and immateriality) while criticizing strong *phenomenal* claims about it, such as permanence and independence from bodies. In the Paralogism about personal identity, however, Kant seems to be *accepting* a specific and major claim phenomenally speaking, while *denying* it noumenally. But this should not be surprising, for the phenomenal affirmation here is one 'no one cares' to prove, and the reason why Kant has no noumenal affirmation here is simply that the characteristic of personality cannot be given a sheerly indeterminate noumenal meaning, for it refers explicitly to temporal experiences and specific individuals. Thus it is only proper for Kant to be ultimately critical here, for, as has been noted repeatedly, he generally rejects similar relatively specific claims such as spiritualism and pneumatism.

The emphasis we have placed on the noumenal also contrasts with the last major interpretation to be countered, namely Bennett's, for Bennett argues that although Kant distinguishes phenomenal and noumenal identity the latter is introduced only for 'ironic' purposes. Bennett takes Kant's passage about the possibility of a transmitted consciousness to be written *ad hominem*:

In it, 'substance' means 'substratum-substance', and Kant is saying to the substratum theorist: 'This is the sort of pseudo-problem that you have committed yourself to taking seriously, and that shows that your positio· is untenable.'[43]

More specifically:

Kant could be saying that although I truly judge that it was I who was *F* at *t*, this does not imply that between myself-now, and myself-at-*t* there stretches a substratum manifesting that special sort of unbroken continuity which lies so deep that there couldn't be empirical evidence for it.[44]

Thus, although Kant would be allowing that we might fail to have 'substratum identity', his point would supposedly be that this is quite irrelevant.

Contrary to Bennett, it would seem that rather than indicating an absurd pseudo-problem, Kant's reference to a possible substratum with a wholly transmitted consciousness has a clear and literal point. Precisely by speaking carefully about a wholesale transmission, Kant refutes in principle the rationalist belief that an assertion of personality can be grounded merely by reference to a unity of apperception, even when that unity is focused on continuously represented contents that range over time (that is precisely the context of A 363, to which the footnote about a possible wholesale transmission is appended). In introducing this point, quite without irony, Kant himself is not committed to any claim that personality consists in some entirely inaccessible entity. His point is simply that for beings who are not identical with us, it is logically possible to receive an intentional complex of thoughts equivalent to (and directly causally connected to) what we have. This point is a nice corrective to the tempting belief that if such a whole set of thoughts were transmitted, especially by some kind of physically traceable mechanism, the person would *have* to follow too.[45]

That such a consequence is not entailed is also recognized by recent discussions of the possibility of a mind's splitting — a possibility which Kant also mentioned (B 416) — and of its information being multiply-encoded.[46] In such cases the presence of contenders would show that one cannot immediately and non-arbitrarily claim identity with previous beings to whose past one would seem to have a direct and inner contact. Bennett also discusses such a possibility, and he analyses *other* aspects of Kant's third Paralogism as helping us to see the interesting fact that thoughts of the form 'I was *F*' might be false in their subject component even though, sheerly from one's own inner perspective, one would never suspect this.[47] None the less, Bennett's treatment of this fact differs considerably from Kant's precisely because he fails to see how the fact ties in with Kant's systematic objectives. What Bennett emphasizes is that the fact indicates the fallibility of particular 'I was *F*' claims, and he does not see that what Kant can and does mean to use it for is rather to show that in principle such claims can be wrong. That is, whereas Bennett sees this fact as interesting only in contrast to the psychological pressure to believe that inner data must be truly about their ostensible subject, Kant can see it as interesting in contrast to the rationalist dogma that a properly focused unity of consciousness can probe a concrete fact about the mind. Bennett's interpretation of the third Paralogism thus can be criticized for giving a misleading trivialization of Kant's views, for focusing improperly, as Strawson has said, on 'errors of detail which we may make about our phenomenal selves'.[48]

B.5. Contemporary Views on Personal Identity and their Historical Background

In now evaluating Kant's position on personal identity we shall contrast it with not only the traditional views already discussed (and rejected) as possible interpretations of Kant's texts but also with the major contemporary alternatives. Here we shall argue that Kant has a consistent and especially significant option to offer, although it is one whose idealistic commitments make it less than fully acceptable when taken literally. The main positions on the question of whether a being's personal identity (in cases where there is an apparently ordinary mental history) is knowable can be divided into five groups:

(A) those (e.g., rational psychologists, Locke, Leibniz) who say it is certain because *a priori* knowable or at least evident from ordinary self-reflection;
(B) those (e.g., Bennett, Strawson) who say it is certain but ultimately because of empirical and primarily behavioural evidence;
(c) those (e.g., S. Shoemaker and other Wittgensteinians) who say it is certain but neither *a priori* nor empirically

knowable (by the person himself) in any ordinary way, that is, it is not to be justified by criteria of inner or outer observation, and yet it is especially indubitable;

(D) those (e.g., D. Parfit, J. Perry) who say that although in some contexts strictly speaking it may not be assertible, there is then at least a 'psychological survival' relation which is logically less rigid than identity but is certain and in general is what 'matters' about personality;

(E) the Kantian view that (vs. A) such identity is not *a priori* or merely inwardly knowable, but that (vs. C) ordinarily speaking it is in a sense empirically determinable (even by the person himself), although (vs. B) ultimately speaking it is not thus certainly knowable, and (vs. D) it is this unknown identity (or non-identity) that matters most.

Although positions (A) and (B) have in effect already been dealt with, (A) especially deserves some further examination because of its central historical role. For Kant the paradigmatic version of (A) is the rational psychologists's argument that is dismantled in the third Paralogism, but in fact the position was presented in a more sophisticated form. Perhaps a naïve rational psychologist would be oblivious to the possibility of a series of mental events being had by what is an underlying multiplicity of substances. Locke, however, drew attention to precisely this possibility, though of course only to discount it by saying that it affects merely the identity of the substrate and not the person.[49] Although Kant can agree with Locke against a position like Swinburne's by insisting that personality isn't simply to be equated with the constancy of just any kind of mental substratum,[50] he still would reject Locke's notion that personality is a mere forensic term and that we can be satisfied with detaching it from debatable issues of substance.

Locke thought it was worthwhile to distinguish personal from substantial identity because (roughly speaking) he felt the former merely involves one's memory and is clearly more easily establishable. His view here is not as naïve as is sometimes thought, but it does have some striking peculiarities. In tying personal identity to memory Locke was hardly oblivious to such matters as the weakness of memory, for he clearly stated that he saw the whole problem of personal identity as beginning with the fact that we are constantly losing sight of the past and we can't bring it all into view at any one time.[51] But although he wasn't blind to the lack of direct recollections at our disposal, Locke overvalued the ones that we do have and apparently presumed that any given clear recollection shows that one is identical with the subject of the past experience. As long as this presumption is not made trivially true by definition, it can be countered by not only physical evidence (a possibility that Locke was willing to handle by allowing persons can change bodies) but also adverse evidence of a mental nature. There is simply nothing to guarantee that any set of given 'recollections' must amount to a coherent acceptable revelation of a single mental history. Given direct 'memories' that appear to me of various past experienced times, Locke appears to presume that I can automatically construct or infer a continuous personality between those times (so that each 'recollection' doesn't connect us with a different person). Yet it is clearly logically possible for one to have a set of seemingly direct memory data that do not allow any such construction. It is revealing here that Locke is quite willing to let a person's own judgements of identity be overruled by others when that person's claims rest merely on a lack of data: if a drunk can't recall what he did last night, he still has no right to reject his neighbours' charges.[52] On the other hand, Locke does not immediately discuss what to say if a drunk does seem directly to recall something that conflicts with what his neighbours claim. If there is any memory datum at all, Locke appears to presume it must be basically right, and so he is also oblivious to the possibility of a conflict among even one's own data.

When Leibniz reviewed Locke's discussion he made some helpful improvements but still held to the basic claim of (A) that mere self-observation can easily reveal personal identity. In particular, Leibniz left more room for outside observers to correct claims made by the person himself, even on the basis of seemingly direct data, and he also put more emphasis on the role of subconscious factors in identity, such as the mere influence or trace of childhood experiences. Leibniz also had a new way of drawing the distinction that Locke made in differentiating personal and substantial identity. Leibniz called the former the 'appearance', sign, or proof of the latter, which (latter) consists in the 'continuity of perception'.[53] 'Personal identity' then simply designates the self-reflective apprehension of the 'real identity' of the monad, an apprehension available only to an especially complicated kind of monad. Kant phrases his position largely in Leibnizian terms (see above, n. 20) but applies to it Locke's scepticism, for Leibniz has no basis other than his general presumptions of harmony for saying that on the whole (i.e., given some allowance for the 'confused' nature of appearances) the identity we feel we have on introspection must reflect an identity of the self in itself.

Once this problem is seen, the Lockean position becomes at least understandable, for if our real identity consists in a continuity of perception, some sort of underlying mental and unique connectedness from instant to instant, there seems to be no way for us to establish that with any specificity, except via construction from the limited particular points in the past that we can seem to remember. (As Hume noted, we can never directly compare the past experience and our present data to see if they match.) But it is a familiar story that even this 'only way' fails properly to guarantee certainty. If we take directly seeming to have the same consciousness as a past experiencer to be sufficient for being the same experiencer, then we make Locke's position clearly false (unless 'same experiencer' is read in such a way that it would be true by stipulation that the condition is sufficient). On the other hand, if we take him instead to require literally having the same consciousness, then we gain an admittedly sufficient and substantive criterion, but at that point genuine personal identity becomes as inaccessible as the substantial identity Locke rejected as irrelevant because inaccessible.

These difficulties in turn make somewhat understandable Leibniz's resort to a divinely guaranteed harmony. This harmony seems to have been a special matter of faith for Leibniz here, for unlike Kant he repeatedly and simply dogmatically rejected (somewhat as in his attachment to the unity argument) the possibility that a 'same-sounding' consciousness might be rooted in a plurality of substances. In contrast, he was at least willing to offer arguments, which emphasized the importance of causality, against the converse Lockean suggestion that one mental substance could underlie a plurality of persons.[54] Independently of Leibniz, recent theorists have attempted to block the remaining troublesome possibility of many beings in one 'person' by also emphasizing the importance of causality, that is, by applying the test of an appropriate causal background, so as to pare down the class of phenomenologically adequate but otherwise spurious 'memories'. This strategy still doesn't clearly eliminate Kant's counterexample of a wholly transmitted consciousness, and in any case the project of determining the meaning and actuality of 'appropriate' causal chains threatens to leave personal identity on the basis of memory still practically as difficult to know as underlying substantial identity. Those who move on to position (B) and to the adequacy of bodily criteria here may eventually make it possible to hold that assertions of personal identity are in some cases well justified phenomenally, but even in ordinary cases they still cannot give us certainty unless they are granted the implausible premiss of a known exact identity or correlation of psychological and bodily factors. On anything other than an extreme reductionistic theory, the public criteria for minds remain (as Swinburne has reminded us) logically distinct from what constitutes them and so from what we believe ultimately matters in them.

6. The Idea of Survivalism

Given these and other difficulties it should not be surprising that the major recent theory of personality, namely (D), has backed away, as Locke did, from claiming decisive criteria for the identity of minds over time. The following section will be devoted primarily to analysing that theory, and as this will be rather complicated it may help to outline its structure briefly beforehand. The first step will be to offer some further explanation for the motivation of (D)'s distinctive proposal to distinguish a relatively non-problematic concept of 'psychological survival' from that of our numerical identity and to say that the former is what matters most. (Advocates of (D) will hence be called 'survivalists'.) Various versions of survivalism are then distinguished and problems with the most promising are presented. In view of these problems it is contended that a special concept of survival is dispensable and that it is best to return to a notion of continuity that can be equated with identity over time and with what ultimately matters in personality. This notion leads to a position that is close to but distinguishable from views (C) and (E). In particular, it differs from Kant's view by implying that both temporality and personality may be asserted to be in some sense transcendentally real, an implication that need not seriously conflict with transcendental idealism in so far as it still does not yield any very determinate noumenal knowledge.

The basic motivation for survivalism rests in the apparent implications of an extraordinary possibility and an ordinary fact, namely the possibility that mind might undergo a perfect fission (e.g., in a brain operation providing a causally continuous duplication of one's psychological characteristics; processes such as cloning or information transfusion might also be cited), and the fact that as one ages psychological 'connections' (e.g., the seemingly direct relation between one's recollection and one's past) can vary considerably in number and intensity. The implication of the first phenomenon is supposedly that what could matter in fission is not a one-one relation. If only one part of the result of the fission operation persisted, personal identity could surely seem to be maintained, and yet there seems to be no reason why there could not be two or more exactly similar persisting parts, in which case the original being would seem to survive in each. The implication of the second phenomenon is that what matters in fact in our concern with our personality as we age is a matter of degree and is not all or nothing. Now if in fission what can matter is not a one-one relation, and if in ageing what does matter is not all or nothing, then it is concluded that since personal identity is one-one and all or nothing, there is something else, to be called 'survival' and distinguished in concept from identity, which is what matters in our concern for being a person.[55]

This survivalist argument is complicated a bit by the fact that there are at least two views on how to define survival. The first requires of survival from moments t_i to t_n only that there be *some* psychological 'continuity', that is, a chain of connections such that, for any time between t_i and t_n, there is some t_x and t_y such that x and y are greater than i and less than n and occur at the end points of a direct psychological connection. The second view requires not only such continuity but also lays down a specific minimum degree (in intensity or number) that each connection or set of connections must have. I take John Perry[56] and Derek Parfit[57] to have best formulated the first view, and David Lewis[58] to have best formulated the second. In evaluating these views I will argue that ultimately they do not serve to distinguish survival from personal identity on the issue of degree, and that where they may be able to effect a distinction with respect to the issue of being a one-one relation, this is not done in a way that requires saying that survival is what matters.

Consider first the fact of survival's having a degree, a fact to which the second view obviously draws special attention but which is also clearly emphasized by advocates of the first view. Parfit, for example, suggests the fact would justify survivalism even if such odd notions as fission were wholly dismissed.[59] It is not clear why this is so, why those who reject survivalism cannot just as well acknowledge the feature of degree. Parfit himself says that personal identity too is a matter of degree in 'its nature' if not in 'its logic'.[60] That is, either someone at t_i is identical with someone at t_n or he is not, but if he is, then there can be a degree in the intensity and number of significant shared characteristics. Yet it would seem that no more can be said of survival: whether we take the first or the second view, it is still an all or nothing matter as to whether the being at t_i survives or not at t_n. Degree enters in only once there is survival, and then of course, if the first view is accepted, the connections that constitute the necessary continuity can have any degree above zero, and if the second view is taken they can have any degree above some set number higher than zero. The same difficulty arises when Parfit also suggests that the feature of degree attaches directly to connectedness *as opposed to* continuity.[61] Surely the fact that two experiences are connected (in the survivalist's sense) is also an all or nothing matter, although if there is a connection the features that constitute it obviously can have degree. But the fact that two experiences are continuous would also seem to be an all or nothing matter, although again if there is continuity (which here is just a chain of connections) there obviously can be a degree to the features that constitute it.

There is another way one might try to make sense of what Parfit means in saying the survivalist view gives a distinctive place to degree. Parfit points out that one might have an identity view of personality such that this is something not constituted by any fact representing a set of properties and relations, let alone the psychological relations that may constitute survival, but is rather in principle a 'further fact'.[62] In that sense personal identity itself could be held to be not even indirectly a matter of degree, since then there would be no characteristics at all constituting it, which then might be had with various intensities and in various numbers. Unfortunately, even this interpretation fails, for it is inconsistent with other things Parfit says. Parfit rejects the 'further fact' view of our identity, although he still believes that in its logic, identity is all or nothing.[63] Hence he can't mean that something's being all or nothing *means* it is a 'further fact'. This interpretation also could not make sense of Parfit's idea that mere continuity too (as opposed to connectedness) is an all or nothing matter, for he clearly takes that continuity to be fully constituted by an appropriate relation and not to be a 'further fact'.

I conclude that survivalism is in trouble if it tries to rest its case on simply drawing attention to personal phenomena that involve degree. Despite first appearances, the survivalist also needs to emphasize the all or nothing aspect of continuity. In so far as survivalism moves beyond the requirement of sheer continuity toward an insistence on some specific degree of connections, as on the second view, it becomes a distinctive theory only at the cost of being more implausible. Thus it is a possible consequence of that view that human lives would have to be divided into any number of overlapping persons, and that children could not look forward to surviving into old age.[64]

Although he doesn't go quite this far, Perry at one point expresses an opinion close to that of the second view here when he remarks that one ought not, and probably would not, identify with any future being that would exist after the onset of (factually) incurable amnesia and sudden changes in desires.[65] Here the non-survivalist would counter that the fact that we would of course have a very strained emotional and moral attitude toward that future self hardly establishes any metaphysical doubts. And even at the emotional level, it seems that when we worry about senility what we have is concern for the self we will become and not the pity or sorrow appropriate for a merely closely related being.[66] Of course, as Parfit emphasizes, there is a sense in which we all become different selves as life goes on — but as he concedes himself, this hardly proves our identity has been lost.[67] Such new selves may involve (to use a distinction Perry himself introduced) losing 'what is important in survival' (i.e., intense continuity) but not 'what makes survival survival' (i.e., sheer continuity).[68] So, just as he can handle the feature of degree, the non-survivalist can also accept talk about 'new selves', as long as this is understood to reflect derivative though deep changes in one continuous person.

7. Evaluation: Kant and Survivalism

All that remains to distinguish the survivalist view is its specific definition of personal continuity as a chain of psychological connections and its belief that it does not matter if such a chain is duplicated. In both these respects survivalism is closely related to quite an old theory of the self, namely Hume's bundle theory — a fact that has not escaped advocates such as Perry.[69] Mentalist theories such as Locke's and Hume's long appeared vulnerable because of the logical possibility of duplication, but they have been regenerated by emphasis on two points: first, that the alternative theories of personal identity that rather insist on a bodily criterion (as a sufficient condition) seem to be just as open to difficulties with duplication; and, second, that various causal considerations can be made intrinsic to ascribing some psychological relations, and so countless odd cases of seeming duplication can be rejected. While these points may understandably make survivalism seem more attractive to many today, I believe they also could be taken to undercut the need for survivalism.

First I will consider how a Kantian would respond to a survivalism tied closely to a bundle theory. Despite what Hume may have suggested, in order to reject the bundle theory one need not be forced into the oddity of positing a distinct pure ego or an inaccessible empirical one. One may have to believe that there is an essence to individual perceptions[70] such that logically they cannot be shared by other subjects, but this need not involve any belief that there could never be a sharing in the knowledge of the contents of the perceptions. In this way a Kantian can believe that the I is more than a mere bundle and still not take it to be a distinct particular, in principle independent of *all* experience. What one believes then is at least that one could have been the same I without some of the experiences one has actually had (or with more than one has had), and thus that the I is more fundamental than any perception, since for any perception the I is necessary for it but not vice versa.

This is *not* to argue that the bundle theory is wrong because there is some kind of intellectual intuition of an ego as the source of apperception. Were a Kantian to argue this way, he would fall prey to the paralogisms, for however special the act of apperception may be, it is compatible, as Kant himself indicates, with a basis in a being that is a mere complex at any moment and over time. What Kantians could rather stress against the bundle theory is the problem of duplication. For that theory, I am simply the sum content of a certain set of appropriately related perceptions. But suppose another such set of perceptions were generated. On the one hand, the theory would have to say there is one and the same I there; yet by hypothesis there are two sets. Bundle theorists of a Leibnizian inclination might try to avoid this problem by saying that we only think the sets of perceptions would be distinct because we implicitly place them within a spatio-temporal manifold, and we forget that this manifold itself is a mere resultant of perceptions. That is, thinking beings with distinct spatio-temporal locations would already have to be different *qua* perceptions. Yet this rejoinder is clearly *ad hoc*, and there seems to be nothing within the mere concept of a set of perceptions which in principle excludes the possibility that there could be another set, exactly the same in perceptual content, which in some sense is otherwise located. The having of an experiential content seems always distinguishable from the content had, and so two similar bundles should always be possible.

Another weakness of the bundle theory is that it makes sheerly impossible the occurrence of multiple inhabitation (the presence of many minds in one body; cf. above, Ch. III.6), the converse of the earlier discussed idea of multiple embodiment (the presence of one mind in many bodies). It seems better to say that, just as we may not (from a first or third person perspective) ever have adequate reason for asserting two bodies to belong to one mind, but should leave noumenal room for this possibility, so too we should allow the logical possibility that two or more minds may be in one body, even if we can never expect to present evidence of this.[71] (The principle of the identity of indiscernibles need not be challenged here, for even beings who have equivalent sets of perceptions could differ in non-perceptual properties.)

In criticizing the bundle theory we have not yet directly refuted survivalism, for a survivalist could grant what has been said and simply remark that he emphasizes precisely that duplicated beings can be distinct *qua* identity and yet each be survivors of the original. A questionable bundle theory of personal identity could then be traded in for a safer bundle theory of survival, and to challenge the survivalist it would have to be shown that even the latter kind of bundle is not what matters in questions of personality. This challenge can be met by dividing the question in a threefold Kantian way into, first, what matters when strictly from one's own perspective it is to be decided whether one ought to identify with a past or future being (this may be called the appearance context); second, what matters when this should be decided from a third person or phenomenal perspective; and, third, what matters when this is considered noumenally, i.e., independent of any epistemological perspective. The appeal of survivalism rests, I believe, in a conflation of these contexts. We can agree with the survivalist that strict identity isn't what matters in all of them, and yet we need not introduce a distinct notion of survival.

It turns out that in the first two contexts survivalism, despite its appearance of tolerance, has too rigid criteria for identification. Contemporary survivalists all require that for a future bundle of perceptions to be called mine there should be a fully appropriate kind of causal link to my present state. Lewis, for example, says the causal chain should not have an 'unlawful' (i.e., accidental rather than regular) form or involve a 'sudden' change.[72] Perry says similarly that the change should not be 'accidental' or 'unsure'.[73] Parfit suggests the survivalists perhaps could allow sudden change (and maybe even 'unlawful' change; Parfit does not discuss this separately) so long as it is known that a 'reliable' (e.g., divine) ground is responsible.[74] Now from a strict first person perspective these restrictions seem irrelevant. They still leave an infinite range of possible similar bundles, and they appeal to factors that are interesting only when one is willing to suppress the pull of immediate experience in favour of identifications that can be justified from an interpersonal and theoretical perspective.

These difficulties point to a kind of duplicity in the survivalist position. On the one hand, the survivalist wants to dismiss the strict identity view of personality as too detached from what 'matters' to us, and so he uses terms such as 'concern' and 'importance', as if to indicate that what counts is how things appear from an individual's own purely mental perspective. On the other hand, the survivalist does not stay with that perspective, i.e., with such facts as that if I seem to remember clearly a certain doing as my doing, my identification with it will be automatic and will not involve theoretical considerations about how the impression came to me. Rather, it is said that 'what concerns us about our memory experiences, particularly in their bearing upon survival, is not merely the quality of the experience; but, additionally, *that* the experience has been produced in a very particular sort of way'.[75] The criterion for survival thus involves fully impartial considerations that transcend the first person perspective not only emotionally but also epistemically. This is in contrast to some earlier twentieth-century bundle theorists, such as Grice,[76] who were attracted to a psychological criterion precisely because they felt this would offer a way (indeed the only way) to make personal identity certain as a logical construction in the sense of being something in principle immediately evident (i.e., directly constructed rather than inferred) from one's own present experience. As Perry admits, the contemporary survivalist departs from this view when he includes in his analysis of memory a strong causal component that cannot be ascertained from immediate experience.[77]

Thus, despite its apparent appeal to what we feel is important in our own case, survivalism clearly goes beyond the emotional and individual nature of identification to the level of demanding an empirically well grounded criterion of re-identification. But at that point the distinctly psychological criterion it promotes becomes dispensable, for even if we were to grant the disputable claim that in some sense the continuity the survivalist speaks of is sufficient for an identification, it can hardly be necessary. Among the survivalists Parfit[78] and Perry[79] admit this point in passing, and recently Georges Rey[80] and David Wiggins[81] have discussed it further. They have argued that a survivor must be seen as having his psychological properties embedded in a material stuff, which can persist over periods when individual psychological capacities may not be realized or may have been wiped out by amnesia. In this way periods of deep sleep still may be said to belong to the person who has experiences in the sleeping body before and after. In effect, this makes bodily continuity central, as long as this is not understood naïvely as sheer physical continuity or preservation of one's ordinary physique and appearance. So understood, a bodily criterion can incorporate many of the psychological features of the original survivalist theory. This approach is not only possible but is evidently called for from a third person perspective, for there what counts is behavioural evidence and manifestations of inferred psychic activity. On this level it becomes irrational to assert identity on the basis of one's own 'memories', even given many vivid impressions, when these are contradicted by others' reports and relevant physiological data.[82] The contemporary survivalist thus ends up little better than Locke. He has conceded he can't handle the issue of noumenal identity, and his epistemological conscience has put even the concept of survival out of the realm of mere appearance so that it becomes necessary to determine one's persistence (albeit without certainty) by physical criteria that the survivalist originally wanted to play down.

The survivalist still might argue that even if his position needs to be reformulated, it points to a kind of bundle notion of the self that is significantly distinct from the traditional identity view of the person in that it has room for a sense in which one person could be said to survive in many beings, as after a fission operation. Here it can be granted that there really is a contrast. Yet as survivalists themselves have noted, they have not proven the traditional identity view to be wrong,[83] and it is no longer so clear what the backing is for the claim that the traditional view doesn't have 'what matters'. The traditionalist can agree that an operation could occur in such a way that from a phenomenal perspective we could not say which (if any) of the 'survivors' was the original, and even such that the person himself could be at a loss as to what he should identify with. All this does not mean that he or we should feel or say he survives as both. On the appearance and phenomenal levels it can be granted that our situation is one of not really knowing what to believe — and there is no reason why on these levels the matter couldn't simply be left at that. Furthermore, in so far as the notion of survival is introduced as not equivalent to identity, it is admitted that not both of the survivors are identical with the original being.[84] Thus on the noumenal level, where the issue is simply the ultimate metaphysical fact of our future existence, it is irrelevant to say identity isn't what matters simply because we can't determine which of the beings we are.[85]

Some survivalists go so far as to suggest that even if identity could be determined, it still need not be what matters. Instead of a fission case in which ultimate identity may be indeterminable, Perry speaks of a perfect 'benign imposter' case in which it is granted that the survivor is not the original person, for that person is by hypothesis struck by an 'incurable disease' and is 'painlessly disposed of'.[86] Perry says, 'On my account I would have the very same legitimate reasons to act now so as to secure for him future benefits as I would if he were me'.[87] Here the traditionalist may counter that it is only natural that I would want to secure the very same benefits for this person, given that he is going to be trying to accomplish all in the world that I wanted accomplished. The traditionalist then might add that the reasons behind securing these benefits are still different, for one might feel that the imposter doesn't really deserve the help even if it is understandable that he gets it.

To this difficulty Perry probably would reply that he was speaking about having the 'very same *legitimate* reasons' for helping the person, and so this last attitude of reluctant assistance doesn't count. It is, he suggests, not 'incoherent or self-contradictory', but 'it *need* be of no interest to us'.[88] None the less, if Perry's case carries any weight I believe it does so only because he has written into it the proviso that the original person would soon die anyway. In such a case it is no wonder that we ought to secure benefits for those who carry on, and especially those who carry on all our good projects. But if the original person were not struck by a disease, surely he could sensibly refuse painless replacement by a perfect benign imposter (even if, in living on, he wouldn't get more of the things accomplished that he wanted). If this is granted, it can be held that even in the case in which the original person faces a quick and inevitable demise, his concern for the 'survivor' would be properly different than for himself, even if quite deep. His feeling would be 'I'm glad the other fellow can carry on all my work, now that, sadly, I can't', and not, 'I might as well help this fellow, for since he's really my survivor I could just as well have let him take my place even if I weren't about to go'.

Other survivalists probably wouldn't go so far as Perry and, rather than admit a 'benign imposter' is in fact not identical with the original person, they may be tempted to say there is no fact here at all because personal identity is ultimately conventional. But survivalists hesitate making this move very openly, and there is no reason to believe the move is justified. If there is anything we have an overwhelmingly strong and unfalsified intuitive inclination to believe, it is that it is simply a fact whether we will exist in the future or not. Parfit tries to shake this belief by comparing the issue to the future existence of nations.[89] But the reason why it is possible to say that it may not be simply a fact whether England will exist in the next century (or existed in the tenth) is simply that it is not clearly a fact that it (as distinct from a set of clearly existent subjects) exists now. On the other hand, it seems quite clear that we exist now, and so unless the survivalist develops a radical version of the already rejected classical bundle theory of the self, he has no defence at all.

I conclude that ultimately speaking it is nothing less than sheer identity that matters, and that this is overlooked only because of too much influence by questionable reductionism, or conventionalism, or the fact that we may be generous to imposters, or that we may not be able to determine this identity. Survivalism cannot establish itself either in appearance, phenomenal, or noumenal contexts. It is not psychological continuity as the survivalists define it that is important to us here but rather sheer felt similarity, or complex bodily continuity (which we may have to admit we are simply uncertain about), or absolute and unique identity. And if before a fission operation I take steps that would benefit both 'survivors',[90] this is not because I somehow feel or understand they will each be me ('carrying on'), but rather simply because I don't know what will happen to me, and it's only prudent to cover all bets when possible.[91]

All this is compatible with Kant's belief that ultimately we can't justify certain belief in personal identity, although phenomenally speaking, we naturally and quite properly expect we will persist when (and only when) the ordinary signs of our experience do. Thus, even though survivalists are quite right to note that 'the possibility of distinguishing the issue of survival from identity was perhaps anticipated in a way by Kant when [he attempted] to block the move from the transcendental unity of apperception to the identity of the person',[92] the most important fact here is that for Kant the distinction had the *anti*-survivalist point of reminding us that a mere 'same-sounding' consciousness is not enough to *secure* us what matters for ourselves.

8. The Non-Criterial View of Personal Identity

In approaching the Kantian position that what ultimately matters is the noumenal and numerically identical persistence of one's being, we have left behind not only survivalism (position D above) but also those positions (A and B) that held that by some ordinary internal or external observations identity is certainly determinable. This still does not distinguish Kant from position (C) and its prime advocate, Sydney Shoemaker; for although Shoemaker appreciates the value of bodily criteria in a phenomenal context, he does not take these to be ultimate, and he emphasizes that personal identity is originally sensed by the person himself independently of any reference to internal or external criteria. This naturally raises the question of how it is that one can say one is identical with a previous experiencer. Shoemaker suggests a remarkable view here, namely that it is improper to ask how this is known, for the person 'simply remembers' his identity.[93] Since supposedly the only way directly to answer the question, 'How do you know *you* did *x*?' is 'I simply remember doing it', Shoemaker believes it is improper to suggest that a way of knowing is being used at all.

Shoemaker's view appears to rest on the principle that *A* properly knows *x* by certain procedures or criteria only if he could know them by others.[94] Shoemaker's position is a peculiar transformation of positivism, for it appears to rest on the theory that nothing that is not directly falsifiable-by-me can count as genuine empirical knowledge on my part. Thus he says it is senseless to identify an actual I with its sensory field *because* I can't observe the boundary of that field, i.e., can't directly observe anything beyond it.[95] Similarly Shoemaker calls Locke's idea, that I might be many substances but one person, meaningless because *I* could not determine the change of substance if it occurred.[96] More generally, Shoemaker takes the property of being perceived by me, or the mineness of a perception, not to be a genuine empirical feature because it is not 'something I could conceivably observe something to lack'.[97] Shoemaker takes experience to be necessarily tied to a subject and person, but in such a way that this tie is too certain to deny and yet such that (from the person's own ordinary perspective) it cannot without absurdity be justified by reference to any grounds. (This view has obvious similarities to a once popular view about avowals as being indubitable and yet not a form of knowledge.)

A Kantian can appreciate much of the motivation for Shoemaker's position on personal identity without tying himself to its odd theory of meaning and its foreclosure of the language of justification and doubt in first person contexts. Shoemaker's idea that we 'simply remember' ourselves obscures the fact, properly emphasized by Kant and the survivalists,[98] that in principle we could always be wrong and that strictly speaking we might not be identical with the experiencer whose past it seems we directly recall. Moreover, even in ordinary cases in which our recollection is right (about the subject component), this is not so sheerly because we simply remember, but rather also because we are sophisticated enough to have some concept of an 'I', some notion of the justification for the introduction of a subject term.[99]

This last claim is simply an application of a classical Kantian point, namely that some appropriate conceptual capacity is necessary for one to be right about anything. Shoemaker, on the other hand, says that, 'what [fully] entitles one to assert this [viz., '*I* see *P*'] is . . . the fact that I observe that *P*'.[100] He says this because he rightfully believes that there is no special intuition of a distinct I that we have to wait on; the sense of personality doesn't come, as a rationalist or Humean would think, by simply adding a peculiar intuition of ourself to our ordinary intuitions. Shoemaker holds his view also because he rightfully believes many philosophers were misled into an immaterialist theory of mind precisely because, even if they didn't experience a special self-intuition, they felt bound to posit an appropriate sheerly immaterial subject in order to account for the seeming certainty of their own sense of substantiality and personal identity independent of any reference to physical criteria. Kant can grant all this without accepting Shoemaker's general view. As our examination of the Paralogisms has shown, Kant's immaterialist theory of mind is quite free of any foundation in the bewilderment about personal identity that worries Shoemaker. Kant's view that there is an I that can be sensibly believed in, i.e., with some reference to observational justification and also some room for ultimate doubt,[101] is free from claims about pure self-intuition and about the subject as a bare particular. Kant can stress these points in common with Shoemaker, but he can add that beliefs in personal identity depend on conceptual capacities and in particular on the capacity to appreciate the value of distinguishing a subject term from the bundle of predicate terms that exhaust the content of one's actual perceptions. To have this ability is to have the beliefs discussed earlier, namely that *I* could be even without some of my actual perceptions, and that even if the *contents* of all my perceptions were duplicated, this need not bring about my existence.

This ability is tied to but not limited by the observations that we do make. It appeals not to any peculiar transcendent impression but simply to the notion of a kind of counter-factual, e.g., that a moment ago it could have been me without that pain (or even if a pain 'just like' mine occurred, it need not be mine). Once we leave room for such counter-factuals we can give sense to statements which flunk Shoemaker's too rigid falsifiable-by-me test. We could say the I, *qua* immediate experience, is its sensory field, for even though it is true that the I doesn't experience anything beyond that field, and in that sense doesn't experience a boundary, none the less, it can realize that the field could have been larger or smaller than it actually is, and so it is meaningful to speak of the I as bounded and of our perceptions constituting (as on the Kantian theory of embodiment) a field. Once this is granted, it need not be absurd to say that we do observe the field that we happen to have, for, *contra* Shoemaker, it is wrong to think that *A*'s observing or empirically knowing *x* requires that *A* be able actually to observe non-*x*'s, and not simply the possibility that *A* might not have observed *x*. More generally, Kant can agree that our own belief in personal identity is peculiarly immediate though not a pure metaphysical intuition, and yet in contrast to Shoemaker he can stress that it is in part an empirical matter that is epistemically grounded in, although not necessarily made certain by, ordinary self-observation and some rudimentary conceptual capacities.

9. Final Evaluation

To distinguish Kant's position from the main alternatives in the literature, especially with respect to how personal identity can be known, is still not to prove his is the best view, especially with respect to what that identity is. In now making a final evaluation of Kant's position we shall argue that despite its comparative advantages it is most acceptable only when slightly modified.

It will be recalled that Kant took personal identity to require more than the mere persistence of just any sort of inaccessible mental substance (see above, n. 42). In this way he was responding to the same sort of pressures that motivate survivalists to seek a notion of personality that accommodates the concepts of mind and continuity in some familiar psychological way. To this extent he was attracted to the traditional idea that our identity consists in a 'flow' of perception. (Compare a remark by Lewis that what we want is that 'my mental life shall flow on'.[102])

The metaphor of a 'flow' here is meant to indicate the harmony with which an ordinary person moves from intentional contents to intentional contents, understanding these all implicitly and properly as contents for one and the same process of consciousness. According to this view, it is because (and only if) my mind 'really flows' in this way from instant to instant that it *can* happen that at a later time I may reflect on and even come to know an earlier moment of that flow as my own. But even if such reflection or knowledge does not or in fact cannot occur (as with young children), there in some sense could be one and the same person. Thus, just as in general one can distinguish mere reflection from properly judgemental awareness, so in particular one can distinguish various levels or intensities of personal identity, i.e., between:

a) merely flowing as the same mind from moment to moment (as explained above);

b) being reflectively aware of some moments at other times *as* one's own;

c) knowing other times as one's own.

Of course, even finer distinctions can be made. For example, (a) could be divided into (a_1) a minimal kind of personal persistence and (a_2) persistence that involves some notable degree of similar characteristics, so that there can be some point in saying that that which is the same in process is also to some significant extent the same in content. Similarly, (b) could be divided into (b_1) levels with single explicit thoughts of identity, and (b_2) levels backed by some complexity of inferences and beliefs (e.g., the belief in counterfactuals discussed above). Finally, (c) could be divided between levels adequate for (c_1) phenomenal and (c_2) noumenal knowledge claims. These claims could also all be distinguished according to whether they involve merely the idea of identity, or rather richer assertions about one's position in the world (e.g., being a person located at a specific objective time).

While Kant does not allow an absolute divorce between being the same person and sensing that one is, his position is still quite liberal. He would seem to allow that to be truly aware of an experience as one's own it is not even required that one have in hand a definite description of oneself[103] or an explicit concept of oneself as distinct and unique. There are advantages to this position, but it also creates problems. It is not so clear, for example, how Kant could exclude (as he presumably wants to) subhuman creatures from personhood. Perhaps Kant does not worry much about this because even in the human case he does not allow that one can be entirely sure of personal identity — even when we have maximal objective evidence and the appearance of a 'same-sounding' consciousness. Here it becomes hard to accept Kant's radical belief that even if we can affirm our personality at level (b_1), this personality still is 'merely phenomenal', i.e., noumenally we remain non-temporal even when truly related to a phenomenal plurality of times.

Precisely because we are dealing here with such a minimal sense of identity over time, and not any determinate judgment of objective temporal position, it becomes quite difficult to see how Kant can restrain claims that one's ordinary primitive sense of personality can be a justified insight, albeit relatively indeterminate, into a transcendentally valid fact. As will be explained later (Ch. VII.10), Kant's arguments for the ideality of time in general are especially vulnerable, and when the temporal matter at issue isn't asserted to have any very specific form, Kant cannot even use the strategy employed in the Refutation of Idealism (namely of making specific self-knowledge rest on spatial and hence phenomenal knowledge) for defending the phenomenality of self-knowledge. The best Kant can do here, I suspect, is to fall back on the crucial claim of the transcendental deduction (B 160 n.; cf. A 107) that the whole temporal realm, and so all inner sense, must be ideal because it is subject to the unity of pure intuition and this unity can be accounted for only by transcendental idealism. If we fail to see this argument as convincing, Kant's position is not completely defeated, but the basis is gone for asserting that at least in normal (i.e., non-fission) contexts a phenomenal/noumenal distinction should be maintained with respect to one's sheer temporal persistence. To say this is still not to agree with those who criticize Kant's idealism as absurd, for we could allow that an appearance of temporality in a being in itself non-temporal may be possible (see below, Ch. VII., n. 92); all that is being questioned is that there are adequate grounds for thinking this is happening in our own case.

If one were to modify the orthodox Kantian position here, one still wouldn't have to depart very far from our general interpretation of the Paralogisms as compatible with a theoretically modest rationalist view of the mind, a view that is uncommitted to any traditional rationalist excesses and determinate claims about the destiny of the soul. The modification would be an extension of Kant's own belief that in some way we are surely in contact with the 'matter' of reality in itself. This 'matter' could now be said to have at least some temporally extended nature; it would be not a sheer unknown but rather a kind of perduring flow.[104] The specious present, the immediate sense of time within oneself, would be accepted as valid beyond all suggestions of our here seeing something merely from a perspective. Accepting this modification could also make things easier for Kant's moral philosophy. Temporality as such would no longer bring with it mere phenomenality, and so the issues of greatest significance for Kant, namely moral acts and states, could be allowed – as Kant is driven to allow implicitly in any case[105] – some kind of temporal character.

Despite all these welcome consequences it cannot be said that they coincide with the intentions of the *Critique* itself, for the Transcendental Deduction and the Antinomies, whatever their weaknesses, simply cannot be overruled as the prime indicators of Kant's intentions. But going against some of these intentions is a small price to pay, I believe, for a contemporary Kantian who can thereby achieve a comparatively attractive position on personal identity that differs from Kant's simply by a limited weakening of his transcendental idealism.

Our final view thus comes close to one recently defended by Chisholm, according to which the idea 'that we undergo change and persist through time' is one of the basic 'data' with which philosophy should begin, that hence it ought to be treated as epistemically innocent until we have found some reason to find it guilty, and that therefore we can accept it because no philosopher has presented a 'positive reason' for thinking it guilty.[106] We can also agree with Chisholm that even Kant has not produced any such reason, although we should not think, as Chisholm unfortunately does, that Kant means to present any such reason in the third Paralogism. There Kant is not trying to deny in principle any theoretical assertion of our persistence but is rather properly exposing an intriguing and wrong way to try to make that assertion. None the less, given his transcendental idealism, and in particular the parts of the *Critique* just cited (not mentioned by Chisholm), Kant eventually is committed to denying that any theoretical assertion of personality can be certain (for us). That is, we can neither lean toward (nor away from) any positive mapping of our apparent phenomenal identity onto a genuine and noumenal

one, nor say that purely *noumenally* we have any temporality
(see above, n. 25). In the end the problem with Kant's view
is not any one weak (let alone incoherent) sceptical argument
but rather the fact that here it is especially unlikely that he
can convincingly stretch the complex apparatus of his arguments far enough. That is, it is unclear how he can stretch
the argument for the mere phenomenality of our knowledge
far enough to cover such relatively unspecific but absolute
claims as that one certainly does have some past.

Notes

[1] *AA*, vol. 28, p. 265.

[2] *AA*, vol. 1, p. 402.

[3] *AA*, vol. 2, pp. 48, 326; vol. 28, p. 296.

[4] *AA*, vol. 28, p. 277; vol. 7, p. 127.

[5] See, e.g., *AA*, vol. 28, pp. 296 and 440 f.

[6] *AA*, vol. 28, pp. 107, 296, 441, 445, 593, 688, 764; vol. 17, pp. 471-3
(R 4237-9); vol. 18, p. 192 (R 5473).

[7] *AA*, vol. 2, p. 338.

[8] Cf. Kant's relatively naïve remarks that one might be two persons, one sensible and one intelligible, at *AA*, vol. 2, p. 337 f. But see also vol. 7, p. 142 and
vol. 20, p. 269.

[9] *AA*, vol. 28, pp. 277, 296. Locke expresses the same view, *An Essay Concerning Human Understanding*, Bk. II, Ch. 27, § 9.

[10] Thus Sidgwick, for example, happens to skip over the third Paralogism in
his statement of agreement with Kant's critique of the conclusions of rational
psychology, and he simply expresses the belief that we know we are 'one' and
'perduring' in life (*Lectures on the Philosophy of Kant and Other Philosophical
Essays and Lectures*, pp. 143, 151).

[11] These passages are said to be 'opaque', in J. Bennett, *Kant's Dialectic*, p. 102.

[12] See, e.g., ibid., p. 102.

[13] The idea here that the error is one of giving phenomenal significance to
what is merely 'transcendentally valid' contrasts with Kemp Smith's interpretation
that 'the fallacy involved is traced to a confusion between the [given] numerical
identity of the self in representation and the [falsely inferred] numerical identity
of the subject *in itself*' (*A Commentary to Kant's 'Critique of Pure Reason'*,
p. 461).

[14] Cf. Bennett, *Dialectic*, p. 95, and P. Strawson, *The Bounds of Sense*, p. 165.

[15] Thus, Kant's view contrasts with Locke's idea that our identity would be
unproblematic if 'perceptions, with their consciousness, always remained present
in the mind'. *Essay*, Bk. II, Ch. 27, § 9.

[16] This point can be seen as a corrective to Strawson's contrast of Hume and
Kant on the self (*The Bounds of Sense*, p. 170).

[17] R. Chisholm, *Person and Object*, p. 108.

[18] Bennett, *Dialectic*, p. 101.

[19] Ibid., p. 93. Similarly, we can take exception to Strawson's critique of Kant
for treating the 'delusive use of "I" ' not primarily as arising from an 'abstraction'
from 'its ordinary setting' (with bodily criteria) but as tied to the notion of

transcendental apperception (*The Bounds of Sense*, p. 166). On the contrary, precisely this notion is the proper focus for Kant given the target and nature of his attack.

[20] *AA*, vol. 28, p. 683. Cf. Leibniz, *New Essays Concerning Human Understanding*, Bk. II, Ch. 27, § 14.

[21] See B 319 f. and D. Henrich, *Identität and Subjektivität* (Sitzungsberichte der Heidelberger Akademie der Wissenschaften, philosophische-historische Klasse, 1976, Abhandlung 1), pp. 77, 82.

[22] See especially Strawson, *The Bounds of Sense*, p. 168, and J. C. Anderson, 'Kant's Paralogism of Personhood', *Grazer Philosophische Studien*, 10 (1980), 73–86. A similar view appears to be held by W. Sellars in '. . .This I or He or It (the Thing) Which Thinks', p. 13.

[23] Bennett, *Dialectic*, p. 109.

[24] Allen Wood, 'Kant's Dialectic', p. 604.

[25] The idea here that 'it merely seems to be the case that one has a past' is not to be confused with transcendental idealism. The latter says that in itself we are not temporal, although phenomenally we may well be, whereas the former says that we might not even have the derivative temporality of being noumenally one substance correlated with a plurality of phenomenally distinct temporal experiences.

[26] Henrich, *Identität*, p. 58.

[27] Ibid., p. 86. It is no coincidence that Henrich's interpretation of the transcendental deduction here is based primarily on the idea of self-consciousness and contrasts with the 'regressive' interpretation offered below (Ch. VII, at n. 65). Conversely, an appreciation of the critical structure of the Paralogisms helps promote a regressive reading of the Transcendental Analytic.

[28] Here we can agree with G. Bird that 'Kant is claiming that such a set of rules most govern also our recognition of personality' (*Kant's Theory of Knowledge*, p. 137).

[29] Kant here uses the phrase 'heisst demnach soviel', but although Kemp Smith translates this as 'equivalent', it could also mean merely 'entails', that is, 'only if' rather than 'if and only if'.

[30] Bird, *Kant's Theory*, p. 121.

[31] Ibid., p. 122.

[32] Ibid., p. 136. A similar view (despite disclaimers) can be found in H. J. Paton, 'Self-Identity', *The Defence of Reason* (London, 1953), pp. 99–116.

[33] R. P. Wolff, *Kant's Theory of Mental Activity* (Cambridge, Mass., 1963), p. 107. For a critique of Wolff here, cf. B. Mijuscovic, 'The Premise of the Transcendental Analytic', p. 83.

[34] *Prolegomena to any Future Metaphysics*, p. 83 = *AA*, vol. 4, p. 335.

[35] Cf. especially Anderson, 'Kant's Paralogism'.

[36] See R. Swinburne, 'Personal Identity', *Proceedings of the Aristotelian Society*, 74 (1973–4), 231–47; and 'Persons and Personal Identity', in *Contemporary British Philosophy*, fourth series, ed. H. D. Lewis (London, 1976), p. 221. Cf. Chisholm, *Person and Object*, p. 112.

[37] Swinburne, 'Persons and Personal Identity', p. 221.

[38] For an argument that on this latter level bodily criteria do have a priority, see below, n. 87.

[39] See G. Bird: 'Kant . . . held that a person is essentially that to which inner characteristics belong' (*Kant's Theory*, p. 181). Cf. ibid., p. 187: 'from the claim that it would be impossible to speak of persons only as Cartesian egos it does not follow that it is impossible to speak of them as Cartesian egos'.

[40] Swinburne, 'Personal Identity', p. 232.

[41] *AA*, vol. 28, p. 441; my emphasis.

[42] *AA*, vol. 28, p. 440 f.

[43] Bennett, *Dialectic*, p. 109.

[44] Ibid., pp. 108–9; cf. p. 105.

[45] See, e.g., N. Wiener, *The Human Use of Human Beings* (New York, 1971), pp. 129–41.

[46] See, e.g., B. Williams, *Problems of the Self* (Cambridge, 1973), p. 79.

[47] Bennett, *Dialectic*, pp. 97 f.

[48] Strawson, 'Review of Jonathan Bennett's *Kant's Dialectic*, p. 167.

[49] Locke, *Essay*, Bk. II. ch. 27, §§ 10–13. For a comparison of Kant and Locke, cf. H. Allison, 'Locke's Theory of Personal Identity: A Re-examination', *Journal of the History of Ideas*, 27 (1966), 58; and P. S. Madigan, 'Time in Locke and Kant', *Kant-Studien*, 67 (1976), 45.

[50] Kant's view here also differs from Sydney Shoemaker's. As Swinburne suggests, all we may need to be a person is to be a mental substance, so Shoemaker says being a mental substance is already being a person: 'The terms "subject", "substance", and "pure ego" . . . are either synonyms of the word "person" or without meaning' (*Self-Knowledge and Self-Identity*, p. 57). See above, n. 42.

[51] This admittedly would imply that to be consistent Locke should have thought a 'full vision' of the self (i.e., a perfect memory) would be adequate for knowing substantial identity — something which he perhaps didn't believe (but see above n. 15).

[52] Locke, *Essay*, Bk. II, ch. 27, § 22.

[53] Leibniz, *New Essays*, Bk. II, ch. 27, §§ 9 and 14. Because of this distinction, Leibniz should be sensitive to the fact that the permanence of one's soul-substance doesn't of itself guarantee one's continuing personal identity or immortality. See M. Wilson, 'Leibniz on Self-Consciousness and Immortality in the Paris Notes and After', *Archiv für Geschichte der Philosophie*, 58 (1976), 335–52.

[54] Ibid., Bk. II, ch. 27, § 14.

[55] This argument, and the term 'what matters', is taken from Derek Parfit's revised version of 'Personal Identity', in *The Philosophy of Mind*, ed. by Jonathan Glover (Oxford, 1976), p. 148.

[56] See especially J. Perry, 'The Importance of Being Identical', in *the Identities of Persons*, ed. by A. O. Rorty (Berkeley, 1976), pp. 67–90.

[57] Parfit, who is responsible for the notions of 'connection' and 'continuity' used here, originally said that the intensity of connectedness matters more than continuity. This, and his general emphasis on the feature of degree, could be taken to justify classifying him as an advocate of the second view. But more recently he has said that sheer continuity is equally important, ('Personal Identity', p. 162, n. 37, added 1976) and even that continuity rather than any degree of connectedness is what is decisive for being the same person ('Lewis, Perry, and What Matters', in A. O. Rorty, *Identities*, p. 106, n. 25). Thus, I have ascribed the first view above to Parfit, but as he himself admits, it is understandable that some, notably Perry, have in effect classified him under the second view: 'Perry thinks that on my proposal we should take the "special relations" — i.e., a sufficient degree of connectedness — as our "unity relation for persons" ' (ibid.)

[58] D. Lewis, 'Survival and Identity', in A. O. Rorty, *Identities*, p. 35. I am abstracting here from the complications of Lewis's discussion, namely his suggestion that rather than fixing on any one particular degree of connectedness or 'delineation' we can see 'what is common to all or most' choices of a degree; and that in the end the survival that matters can be shown to be logically not significantly distinguishable from an identity relation. This last claim depends on various logical manœuvres that, as Lewis himself admits (ibid., p. 38), appear

rather *ad hoc*, and in any case they seem to have been shown to be inadequate by Parfit ('Lewis, Perry, and What Matters', pp. 91-6; see also Penelope Maddy, 'Is the Importance of Identity Derivative?' *Philosophical Studies*, 39 (1979), 151-70). These abstractions may fail to do justice to Lewis, but they help to give a brief general characterization of what survivalism can be and has been taken to mean.

[59] Parfit, 'Lewis, Perry, and What Matters', p. 98.

[60] Parfit, 'Later Selves and Moral Principles', in *Philosophy and Personal Relations*, ed. by A. Montefiore (Montreal, 1973), p. 140.

[61] Parfit doesn't explicitly say that connectedness can't be regarded as an all or nothing matter, but he twice stresses the fact that continuity can be taken to be all or nothing, as if that were a distinguishing feature for it (ibid., p. 140, and 'Lewis, Perry, and What Matters', p. 98).

[62] Parfit, 'Later Selves and Moral Principles', p. 137. Cf. Parfit, 'Lewis, Perry, and What Matters', p. 100.

[63] Parfit, 'Lewis, Perry, and What Matters', p. 101. Cf. Parfit, 'Personal Identity', p. 162, n. 37 (added 1976).

[64] D. Lewis, 'Survival and Identity', pp. 30-1.

[65] Perry, 'The Importance of Being Identical', p. 84. For a critique see below, at n. 88, and the material cited in R. Pucetti, 'Memory and the Self: A Neuro-Pathological Approach', *Philosophy*, 52 (1977), 147-53.

[66] Perry is of course willing to allow that this is in fact how many people feel, but he claims this can be explained as a mere carry-over from the habit of generally caring especially about the mind in one's (ordinary) body. While I agree such an explanation may in some way account for the *force* of the habit, this need not undercut the habit's being correct in this case and not a mere carry-over Cf. Brian Smart's suggestion that a person could sensibly request an amnesia operation for *himself* (but not, so I would add against what Perry implies, an operation that replaces him with a 'survivor'). 'Diachronous and Synchronous Selves', *Canadian Journal of Philosophy*, 6 (1976), 24.

[67] Parfit, 'Lewis, Perry, and What Matters', p. 103, n. 10.

[68] Perry, 'The Importance of Being Identical', p. 86.

[69] Perry, 'The Problem of Personal Identity', in *Personal Identity*, ed. by J. Perry (Berkeley, 1975), p. 30.

[70] See Chisholm, *Person and Object*, pp. 29, 33, 39-41, 47-51; and cf. Perry, 'The Problem of Personal Identity', p. 25. For other discussions of the bundle theory, especially in its no-ownership version, see M. Schlick, 'Meaning and Verification', in *Readings in Philosophical Analysis*, ed. by H. Feigl and W. Sellars (New York, 1949), pp. 146-70; P. F. Strawson, *Individuals* (London, 1959), p. 97 (from Ch. 3, 'Persons'); T. Penelhum, *Survival and Disembodied Existence* (London, 1970), Ch. 6; G. Maddell, 'Ayer on Personal Identity', *Philosophy*, 51 (1976), 47-55; and D. Coder, 'Strawson, Particulars, "No-Subject" and "No-Ownership" ', *Philosophical Studies*, 23 (1972), 335-42.

[71] Cf. B. Russell, *Logic and Knowledge*, ed. by R. C. Marsh (London, 1956), p. 120. Note that such multiple inhabitation is to be distinguished from 'co-consciousness'. The latter claims not a complete overlap of two spheres of contents (about the same body) among minds but rather the existence of strictly separated distinct spheres within a mind. This latter idea may well be even noumenally excludable, and I think Kant properly rejects it and that Daniel Robinson ('What Sort of Persons are Hemispheres? Another Look at "Split-Brain" Man', *British Journal of the Philosophy of Science*, 27 (1976), 73-9) has dealt adequately with recent attempts to support the concept, attempts which make too much of the fact that we are capable of setting into motion habits and projects that can

take on a relatively autonomous status. See also K. Wilkes, 'Consciousness and Commissurotomy', *Philosophy*, 53 (1978).

[72] D. Lewis, 'Survival and Identity', p. 17.

[73] Perry, 'The Importance of Being Identical', p. 83.

[74] Parfit, 'On "The Importance of Self-Identity" ', *Journal of Philosophy*, 68 (1971), 689.

[75] Georges Rey, 'Survival', in A. O. Rorty, *Identities*, p. 55.

[76] H. R. Grice, 'Personal Identity', *Mind*, 50 (1941), 334.

[77] Perry, 'Personal Identity, Memory, and the Problem of Circularity', in *Personal Identity*, pp. 152 f.

[78] Parfit, 'Personal Identity', p. 151, n. 17.

[79] Perry, 'The Importance of Being Identical', p. 88.

[80] Rey, 'Survival', p. 58.

[81] David Wiggins, 'Locke, Butler and the Stream of Consciousness and Men as a Natural Kind', in A. O. Rorty, *Identities*, pp. 149, 164.

[82] This claim, and thus the phenomenal superiority of the bodily criterion of personal identity, is argued for in my 'Criteria of Personal Identity', *Canadian Journal of Philosophy*, 7 (1977), 47-69. Since developing the arguments of that article I have become acquainted with additional texts that in effect directly challenge them, but I believe these challenges can be met. Robert Young has argued that a person could be properly asserted to exist over a time-gap in which he would have no bodily manifestation, in the same way that we say a play continues to exist despite intermissions ('The Resurrection of the Body', *Sophia*, 9 (1970)). This argument is most peculiar in that it appeals to examples of entities which philosophically speaking are generally taken as paradigms of items that do not exist, and largely because they lack continuity. Charles Daniels has argued in a more complicated way that we should leave room for asserting the existence of time-gap bodily discontinuous individuals, but he has admitted this would in effect lead us to sacrifice our physical laws ('Personal Identity', in *Philosophers in Wonderland*, ed. by P. French [St. Paul, 1975], p. 212). Such a sacrifice is tantamount to what I mean by saying the assertion would be phenomenally irrational. Carl Ginet has also argued like Daniels, saying that in such a case we should posit identity over a time gap as an 'explanation' of the remarkable memory claims of the individual (*Knowledge, Belief and Memory* [Dordrecht, 1976], p. 171). But it is hard to see how positing identity explains anything here. Ginet is reluctant to allow us to leave such a situation as a mere coincidence, but as the identity claim by hypothesis can't fit in with, and even conflicts with, our ordinary phenomenal explanations, it is hard to see what is lost here by accepting the notion of coincidence.

[83] See, e.g., Rey, 'Survival', p. 62, n. 4.

[84] Parfit, 'Personal Identity', p. 146.

[85] A similar view, without an explicit phenomenal/noumenal distinction, is held by R. Chisholm, 'The Loose and Popular and the Strict and Philosophical Senses of Identity', in *Perception and Personal Identity*, ed. by N. Care and R. Grimm (Cleveland, 1969). Critics of Chisholm have returned to the bundle theory. See, e.g., T. W. Smythe: 'Chisholm says nothing that rules out the view that people are logical constructions out of evolving composita in whatever way physical things are' ('Chisholm on Personal Identity', *Philosophical Studies*, 26 (1974), 357).

[86] Perry, 'The Importance of Being Identical', p. 83.

[87] loc. cit.

[88] Ibid., pp. 80-1; my emphasis.

[89] Parfit, 'Later Selves and Moral Principles', pp. 140-2.

[90] Bernard Williams has tried to depict a similar situation in which we are forced to make a choice. As I have argued elsewhere ('Personal Identity and Memory Transfer', *Southern Journal of philosophy*, 14 (1976), 387), his specific recommendation on the choice to make is not convincing, but his final comment is most instructive: 'that there is room for the notion of a *risk* here is itself a major feature of the problem'. ('The Self and the Future', *Philosophical Review*, 79 (1970), 180.)

[91] Cf. a remark (in a different context) by D. Dennett ('Conditions of Personhood', in A. O. Rorty, *Identities*, p. 194): 'And if it is asked what could *settle* our doubts, the answer is: nothing. When such problems arise we cannot even tell in our own cases if we are persons'.

[92] Rey, 'Survival', p. 62, n. 4. Cf. Wiggins, 'Stream of Consciousness', p. 140.

[93] Shoemaker, *Self-Knowledge and Self-Identity*, p. 143.

[94] Ibid., pp. 135-6.

[95] Ibid., p. 115.

[96] Ibid., p. 147. Shoemaker also says, 'the idea that the subject of my present actions, thoughts, and so on may not be the subject of my actions and thoughts yesterday seems either self-contradictory or unintelligible' (ibid., p. 72). That may be, but it would be paralogistic to conclude from this that a 'same-sounding' consciousness can't rest in many substances. That I must be the same as the subject of *my* past actions is obvious, but it does not follow that I must be identical with the subject of the past experience I seem to recall.

[97] Shoemaker, ibid., p. 95.

[98] This point has also been seen by Shoemaker, who has changed his position considerably in 'Persons and Their Pasts', *American Philosophical Quarterly*, 7 (1970).

[99] For similar critiques of Shoemaker, cf. M. Woods, 'Reference and Self-Identification', *Journal of Philosophy*, 65 (1968), 568-78; and B. Williams, 'Knowledge and Meaning in the Philosophy of Mind', *Philosophical Review*, 77 (1968), 216-28.

[100] Shoemaker, *Self-Knowledge and Self-Identity*, p. 119.

[101] When Strawson concludes by saying it is 'needlessly paradoxical to deny that Jones can *confirm that* he has a pain' (*Individuals*, p. 134), he is surely speaking against Schlick and others influenced by Wittgenstein, but he is also in effect anticipating our critique of Shoemaker (cf. *Self-Knowledge and Self-Identity*, pp. 222-3).

[102] D. Lewis, 'Survival and Identity', p. 17.

[103] In contrast Wiggins appears to believe that to remember an experience of *x* as *my* doing it I must know a definite description of myself then ('Stream of Consciousness', p. 142). Here, as in general, the old theory that we must have descriptions in hand to make references seem questionable.

[104] In this way a Kantian eventually could come close to agreeing with such analyses of temporal experience as those offered by Husserl and by W. Sellars (*Science and Metaphysics* (London, 1968), 'Appendix').

[105] See 'The End of all Things', in *Kant on History*, ed. by L. W. Beck (New York, 1963), p. 78 = *AA*, vol. 7, p. 334; and *AA*, vol. 18, p. 413 (R 6427).

[106] Chisholm, *Person and Object*, pp. 104-5.

Chapter V

Immortality

The last specific topic listed in the Paralogisms (A 345/B 403) is the problem of immortality, a topic which Kant speaks of as providing the defining 'Idea' for the whole field of rational psychology (B 395 n.). This chapter will be devoted to Kant's brief analyses of specific arguments concerning immortality. Despite the importance of this issue and the critical nature of Kant's handling of the traditional proofs here, there is reason to distrust his suggestion that this criticism completely dominates his philosophy of mind. There is in fact not all that much attention given directly to immortality, and what there is can be handled fairly quickly. It is true, as has been stressed repeatedly, that Kant's criticism of immortality claims does have a kind of special importance in so far as here more than anywhere else he truly distances himself from the rationalist tradition. None the less, there is more to this tradition than the claim of immortality or the other particular claims we have examined so far, and so we will have to devote some further chapters to determining whether there are any remaining Kantian doctrines that can lead to a significant rational psychology of either a phenomenal or noumenal sort.

1. Historical Review

Kant's treatment of the question of immortality in the *Critique* is not very clearly organized, and, as usual, it helps to see how Kant's discussion fits in with his other writings, especially the more systematic approach of the lectures. Although Kant's first mention of immortality is without reference to its proof,[1] his discussions thereafter focus on the various arguments for immortality. Here what he is interested in is always whether man is necessarily immortal and not whether as a matter of fact man will live forever, for example as the consequence of biological developments or special divine action.[2]

The lectures of the 1760s present a position typical of Kant's early rationalist period. They claim an afterlife is 'very likely' because (i) 'the status of the world, without (enduring) rational beings is nothingness', and otherwise (ii) 'rational beings who die would be as if they had never been'.[3] (This comment contrasts directly with Kant's later statement that we can't even use expressions of probability with respect to transcendent theoretical questions such as immortality.)[4] These claims are not very well grounded. The first argument is obviously weak, and even if we admit the Leibnizian idea that there would be no 'true unity' without rational beings, it hardly follows that all or even any human beings must be immortal. (Kant also sees this later.)[5] The second argument appears to rest on the feeling of absurdity that a rational man is likely to experience upon recognition that his existence has a definite end. But such a feeling hardly proves that one's life cannot end, and Kant himself seems to have acknowledged that it is not even clear that such a feeling must arise.[6]

Fortunately, Kant's discussion generally is dominated not by these peculiar arguments but by four main types of proofs, which he distinguishes as (1) 'empirical' or 'rational', the latter including proofs based on either (2) 'metaphysical-theoretical' grounds or 'metaphysical-practical' grounds, and the latter in turn involving either (3) 'practical-theological' or (4) 'practical-teleological' arguments.

In the lecture notes from the 1760s there are specific comments on only the last two types. The last kind of argument is presented in this form: all species are given the chance to develop their peculiar talents; man has essential and unique talents that cannot be fulfilled in this life; hence he can expect an afterlife. Here, as at the end of his career, Kant is most sympathetic to this analogical argument, and he calls it the best because it (supposedly) could guarantee immortality to man on the basis of features natural to the entire species.[7] Kant implies that all the other proofs are inadequate, but the only specific criticism in the lecture notes is an odd objection to the practical-theological argument. The argument is that the distribution of rewards and punishments in this world is inequitable and therefore an existence in another world is required to even things out. The argument presumes the existence of an omnipotent just God and concludes that He will provide an afterlife. The objection raised here is that we don't know if there really is inequity in this world; perhaps we are wrong in our judgements of the good and the bad, and perhaps there are already imperceptible rewards and punishments which bring about a moral balance.[8] Fortunately, other objections to the argument are provided later.

The lectures of the 1770s are marked by the development of a special attachment to a metaphysical-theoretical proof from the mere representation of the self. Whereas previously Kant had said there is no sure proof from the consideration of the human soul alone,[9] he now expresses confidence in what might be called the 'principle of life' argument for immortality. Kant calls this 'the only possible *a priori* proof from the nature of the soul' (a phrase that nicely corresponds to a similar belief he had at one time about a proof of God), and he formulates it in this way:

The mere consciousness of the 'I' proves that life lies not in the body but in a special principle which is different from the body; that consequently this principle can also persist without the body, and thereby its life will be increased rather than diminished.[10]

Kant appears to ground this claim on the idea that simplicity distinguishes mental as opposed to material substance,[11] and that matter is 'lifeless', its inertia leaving it dependent on animation by some external and superior force in order for the organized phenomena of life to take place.[12] From a modern perspective, the whole notion of a principle of life is dubious (though it has a noble history, going back at least to Plato), and the argument from it appears to depend on a primitive notion that some qualitites or beings are nobler than others and that they can't be conditioned by lower ones. Moreover, even if the argument were valid, it would not show that man has an immortality different from that of the simplest animals, who are also said to have a 'principle of life'. These weaknesses are not noted here, but elsewhere Kant did come to stress the basic point that even if the soul were distinct from matter in its simplicity, this would not prove it must exist beyond life, let alone forever.[13] Were it not for what we have already seen of Kant's earlier arguments for our immateriality, it would be very hard to believe he was even temporarily taken in by the principle of life argument.[14]

During the rationalist period the teleological argument is also approved, and we now get details as to what Kant understands by the unique capacities of man that require fulfilment in an afterlife. They are man's scientific and moral pursuits, and Kant surprisingly emphasizes the former as most vividly showing man's supra-prudential interests. He now also formulates an objection to the argument, namely that it is hard to maintain the soul has a special destiny when its origin appears entirely conditional. Since birth is a matter of contingency, it is unclear how individuals can be taken to have a necessary persistence. Kant's answer at this point is simply to insist that although physical birth is contingent, it need not represent the beginning of the soul's existence, because the soul can exist before the individual's physical life.[15] This response is hardly compelling, as Kant admits, but perhaps he is right to say it neutralizes the objection, for it may be that it can't be asserted that man's origin is entirely contingent without in effect also presupposing the contingency of his end.

The practical-theological argument receives a more critical treatment. Kant calls it 'practically' adequate in that it supports the view of one who is already a believer,[16] but now he points out some good reasons why it won't stand as theoretically adequate. The need for another life to redress the injustices of this one can hardly justify a hope for an afterlife for all humans. It would not apply to beings such as children, who have not enjoyed much of a moral life, and in any case it would not prove an eternal afterlife is needed.[17] Kant held to these objections to the end and never directly questioned the premiss that God must bring about a state of absolute moral justice, although eventually he did observe that the premiss of inequity in this life could also be taken as an argument against God (which could then threaten the theoretical validity of the immortality argument).

By the time of his lectures in the 1780s Kant had clearly

changed his attitude, and he characterized the metaphysical-theoretical proof as 'very beautiful' but not convincing. Yet there is no evidence from the lectures that he traced the specific shortcomings of the argument (just as there is also no specific analysis of the closely related 'unity argument'). There is only the odd but typical remark that for all we know the substratum of matter may be just as permanent as that which in us has life. The empirical arguments are treated in more detail, but although specific examples are shown to be weak there is no proof that in principle such arguments could not be made appealing.[18] Kant merely notes that such facts as the transformation of animals or reports of ghosts hardly prove an afterlife. He balances this observation by noting that similarly reference to our actual dependence on a body in this life does not in itself prove we must always be so dependent. A man tied to a cart may depend on it for his movements, but this hardly shows he can't move when released from the cart.[19] (Kant's use of this comparison here is at least much less rationalistic than his earlier statement that the soul would surely be better if not 'tied down' to a body.)[20] Kant also points out the already noted weaknesses in the theological argument, and he continues to express a kind of sympathy with the teleological argument, although now he shifts its emphasis from man's scientific to his moral capacities.

By the time of Kant's last period of metaphysical lectures the principle of life argument is explicitly rejected as leading to *Schwärmerei*.[21] The teleological argument is still labelled as the best, but the lack of any criticism of it in the notes surely must be taken as a sign of the inadequacy of the notes and not as evidence of any full acceptance of the argument.[22] There is in these lectures also no mention of the important moral argument for immortality that Kant had developed in the meantime, but perhaps this is because he felt it belonged to practical philosophy and not to the discussion of rational psychology as such. The only specific remarks of interest in the last lectures concern the virtues and defects of the principle of life argument. Kant says this argument, which points to the simplicity of the mind, is valuable in providing a refutation of materialism, a claim that must be understood in the narrow sense of the term discussed earlier.[23] Another appreciation of the weakness of the argument is implied when Kant stresses that a proof of immortality should establish not only continued existence but also persistence of personal identity,[24] something the argument in question fails to do. Kant also points out that even if the principle of life in man is inextinguishable, this would not mean that the capacities of life we are familiar with need be preserved.[25] These views simply complement what has already been revealed about Kant's scepticism about establishing personal identity and a pneumatic or spiritualistic position (see above, Ch. II, n. 40, and Ch. IV, at n. 13).

On the whole, Kant's lectures reveal a clear but slow development towards rejecting all traditional proofs of immortality. Empirical proofs are rejected from the start. The metaphysical-theoretical approach is initially suspected, then temporarily given primacy, only to suffer a definite rejection later. Practical-theological arguments are criticized throughout and more actuely in the course of time. Their core idea, however, that man ought to have the chance to trace a full moral course, is in a way preserved in the moral argument for immortality which is developed in the second *Critique*. Finally, the practical-teleological arguments are eventually rejected as philosophically unsatisfactory, although they are given more of a moral formulation and are always treated with a special respect.

2. Immortality in the *Critique*

Kant's pronouncements on immortality in the main published works of the critical period do not conflict with what one would expect from his lectures, but his writings are considerably less perspicuous. The first edition of the first *Critique* nowhere gives a systematic rundown of the main proofs. Implicitly, empirical arguments are rejected by Kant's focus on rational psychology (see A 848/B 876) and his general theory of the limits of empiricism. Similarly, the metaphysical-theoretical approach is implicitly rejected by the negative judgement in the Paralogisms about all speculative proofs from the nature of the soul.[26] Yet in the first edition no specific weakness in the argument Kant had approved earlier is discussed, although Kant clearly still had it in mind, for he says that to think of the soul as an 'intellectual immaterial substance' is to think of it as the 'principle of life' in matter — a comment which is practically unintelligible without reference to the lectures (A 345/B 403).

The metaphysical-practical arguments are dealt with very briefly at the end of the *Critique* in sections that probably were drafted very early. Thus the practical-teleological argument is only referred to in one sentence, which states that man's scientific capacities justify a (mere) 'doctrinal' belief in immortality (A 827/B 855). The practical-theological argument does not appear in a clear form. Kant remarks that our moral status requires us to think of ourselves as members of an 'intellectual' order, and to do this is to think of ourselves as beyond space and time, existing in a realm governed by an absolute and just supreme being (A 811/B 839). Belief in membership in such a realm apparently amounts to belief in a 'future life'. Kant does not work out the details of the argument or consider how it relates to what is generally understood by a future life. He tends to lump the issues of God and a future life together throughout his discussion, and it seems he was primarily interested in the first issue.[27] Kant never repeats this particular argument, but it is very interesting in that it represents a transition from the basic theological argument to the moral argument for immortality that Kant was soon to develop. The argument is unlike what Kant had understood earlier by a practical-theological argument because strictly speaking it cannot be termed a metaphysical proof. That is, its basic premiss is a claim about our moral status, a claim based for Kant not on any cognitive insight but on the implications of our sensitivity to the categorical imperative. The proof is also not yet a complete moral argument for immortality, because no direct connection is made between our moral life and the need for an afterlife; it is merely vaguely suggested that being moral and related to God is in effect to go beyond this life.

Elsewhere in the *Critique* Kant expresses another understanding of the issue of a future life. He implies that if the soul were a simple part of matter, then its permanence could be assumed, given the proof in the Transcendental Analytic of the eternity of material substance (A 401). This remark is consistent with what he says elsewhere,[28] and it indicates a view that the question of immortality is to be understood as being about a continued temporal existence of the mind. The question then is not whether we belong to a realm beyond time but whether we will persist through all time. From a Kantian perspective such immortality would be a strange sort of existence, belonging neither to the phenomenal realm of universally accessible and scientifically determinable experience which the Transcendental Analytic describes, nor to the noumenal and timeless realm to which Kant's moral discussion generally refers (see, e.g., A 553/B 581). (Here again Kant's position would be made easier if it were not taken to require temporality as such to entail mere phenomenality.) Kant also requires this state to involve personal identity, and so his doubts about establishing this would count directly against asserting this kind of immortality.

In the second edition of the first *Critique* there is more evidence that at least in speculative philosophy Kant understood the question of immortality to be the question of the continuing temporal existence of the soul as a kind of inner phenomenon or 'object of inner sense' (B 415). It is in this context that he adds an argument against the metaphysical-theoretical proof developed by Mendelssohn. The objection is that even if the soul were shown to be a simple substance, its existence (presumably as an inner temporal phenomenon) need not be permanent because they could be a process of 'elanguescence' or gradual total diminution of the intensity of consciousness.[29] The second edition also gives more attention to the practical-teleological argument (B 424-6). The argument is given a lengthy exposition (with the emphasis now on moral capacities), but in his evaluation Kant is very curt. He simply calls it both 'incontrovertible' and 'theoretically inadequate'. The first comment should probably be taken as an indication of his general belief that this is the best of the traditional arguments and the one that responds most directly to the beliefs of the ordinary man. Unfortunately, Kant still does not express precisely what he finds philosophically inadequate in the argument. Presumably, he feels it suffers from the general weaknesses of such analogical arguments, which he outlines elsewhere (A 626/B 654).

All other discussions of immortality in the critical period are dominated by the moral argument that Kant sets out in the second *Critique*. The argument is that morality obligates us to seek holiness (perfect virtue), which therefore must be possible, and can be so only if God grants us an endless afterlife in which we can continually progress.[30] The argument has the advantage of applying to all humans and of giving some ground for the requirement of an eternal and personal afterlife. As a finite creature man is incapable of every achieving holiness, but in — and only in — an endless time we could supposedly approximate to it (in the eyes of God) as fully as could be expected. (Here it is assumed that, as Wood has argued,[31] Kant is saying not that real holiness is ever a human objective but rather that complete striving for it can be, and this could constitute for man a state of 'perfect virtue'.) The last phrase, of course, contains an ambiguity that reveals a notorious problem with the argument. It would seem that we still could have only a finite life and do all that can be expected of us if we seek virtue in that time; it is unclear why now we should be expected to aim at or have the chance for the maximal human virtue which is to be expected of beings who are clearly immortal. Moreover, even if we were immortal, it is not clear that we would ever be under obligation even to seek holiness; that may well be regarded as supererogatory virtue.

Just as questionable as the validity of Kant's proof is the meaning of the conclusion it involves. The afterlife he speaks of must be thought of, on the one hand, as a state of 'constant progress' (or regress — Kant suggests that immortality will be lived out in line with the general character one has developed in empirical existence, an idea that is close to that of the practical-teleological argument), and, on the other hand, as a noumenal, non-temporal form of existence. Kant eventually dedicated a separate work to the problem of making this 'afterlife' more intelligible,[32] but in doing so he seems either to have given up understanding the noumenal self as non-temporal, or to have severed the connection between the immortality he takes himself to have proven and the traditional issue of immortality that he discusses elsewhere. At most he succeeded in making clear that the 'continual progress' he speaks of can ultimately have a 'non-temporal' nature in that it is neither momentary nor of definite duration nor actually endless. But even then it still seems temporal in some sense, or it remains nothing to which we can literally look forward.

It could be that when Kant's moral argument for immortality is put in the full context of the pure practical branch of his philosophy, it takes on considerably more value (and a different meaning) than it has at first sight. From a sheerly theoretical perspective, however, the traditional objections to Kant seem sufficient to justify the considerable scepticism with which it has been generally regarded. This fact is not particularly disconcerting for our interpretation, for we have held it is precisely the theoretical unassertability of the spiritualistic doctrine of immortality that in a way is the target of each of Kant's criticisms of rationalist conclusions about the mind — so much so, in fact, that aside from this target it generally is hard to find an adequate explicit critique of the particular paralogisms. Yet it would be a mistake to conclude from this that Kant should be thought of simply as meaning to transform traditional theoretical doctrines such as immortality into mere objects of a narrow ethical stance, backed by special pragmatic or theological concerns. Kant has a very specific reason for calling his moral arguments 'practical' rather than theoretical, namely that they employ as an essential premiss a statement about what is taken to be an obligation, i.e., an ought rather than an is (A 633/B 661). But apart from this premiss the arguments are to be as straightforward as any mere theoretical ones, and even the moral premiss is to be taken not as a mere option but rather as something any self-respecting person can be presumed to regard as properly irresistible. Thus from a modern perspective (according to which Kant could be classified as having an objectivist morality) it could be said that the moral argument for immortality is in effect an objective one, although it still differs in certain ways from the dogmatic proofs that Kant and others advanced earlier.

The weakness of the argument is thus significant, for were it adequate it clearly would have provided Kant with a strong balance to his critique of other arguments for immortality. But Kant can hardly be said to demonstrate an exceptional interest in shoring up the argument,[33] and in any case it is obvious that the argument did not have any place in the original conception of Kant's critical philosophy. At first sight this is peculiar, but ultimately it is understandable given that, as we have argued, Kant always confidently holds some kind of immaterialist view of the self while also properly seeing enormous difficulties in making more positive and specific claims. Moreover, whether or not Kant's moral argument is an objectively valid or helpfully suggestive supplement to his pure practical philosophy, it is very hard to see it as essential even there. The responsive and fair moral attitude that Kant is generally trying to justify is surely most easily thought of quite apart from such long range and individualistic concerns as immortality. Thus, in all important respects the argument itself can be said to have an incidental role that fairly corresponds to the lack of strength and energy with which it is presented.

Notes

[1] *AA*, vol. 1, p. 367.

[2] *AA*, vol. 28, p. 284.

[3] *AA*, vol. 28, p. 108. Cf. *Critique of Judgment*, p. 293 = *AA*, vol. 5, p. 442; 'Without men the whole creation would be a mere waste . . .'

[4] *AA*, vol. 8, p. 396 n.; cf. *Critique of Judgment*, p. 312 = *AA*, vol. 5, p. 461.

[5] *AA*, vol. 28, p. 443.

[6] Allen Wood, *Kant's Moral Religion* (Ithaca, 1970), p. 182 n.

[7] *AA*, vol. 28, p. 109; cf. ibid., p. 766.

[8] Ibid., p. 110.

[9] Ibid., p. 109.

[10] Ibid., p. 287, but cf. ibid., pp. 443, 592, 687.

[11] Ibid., p. 283. This is perhaps a surprising claim in view of what is said in the *Dreams* essay, but it does support what was suggested earlier (Ch. II.2), namely that the suspicions raised in that essay are not ultimately tenable in a Kantian framework.

[12] Ibid., p. 285.

[13] See B 41 and *AA*, vol. 28, pp. 755, 763-4.

[14] Therefore, given what was shown earlier (Ch. II), I must disagree with L. W. Beck (*A Commentary on Kant's Critique of Practical Reason* [Chicago 1968], p. 265), who says that Kant *never* had much faith in theoretical arguments for immortality. See n. 10 above.

[15] *AA*, vol. 28, p. 295.

[16] Ibid., p. 289.

[17] Ibid., p. 290; cf. ibid., pp. 443, 767.

[18] Ibid., p. 443.

[19] Ibid., pp. 441, 444.

[20] Ibid., pp. 286-7.

[21] Ibid., p. 592.

[22] Ibid., pp. 592, 686, 766.

[23] Ibid., p. 687. See above Ch. II.3.

[24] Ibid., p. 763.

[25] Ibid., pp. 764-5.

[26] We have already shown how Kant's specific criticisms of the paralogisms are generally most effective if read as critiques of 'extended arguments' for immortality, although their success in even this regard does not prove all theoretical arguments must be doomed. Therefore I believe it is misleading to say (as Beck has, *Commentary*, p. 265) that Kant 'discovered' such a proof, and in particular that he did this by arguing the soul 'is not given under the only condition whereby a substance can be known, viz., in time'.

[27] For this reason I hesitate to say Kant's remark at A 813/B 841, about our having to presume 'God and a future life' as necessary to maintain our moral motivation, is meant as a distinct proof of immortality (*pace* Beck, *Commentary*, p. 266). The comment could rather be taken primarily to summarize a distinct and interesting moral argument for God. See R. M. Adams, 'Moral Arguments for Theistic Belief', in *Rationality and Religious Belief*, ed. by C. F. Delaney (Notre Dame, 1979).

[28] *Critique of Practical Reason*, translated by L. W. Beck (New York, 1956), p. 137 = *AA*, vol. 5, p. 133.

[29] B 414; cf. *Metaphysical Foundations of Natural Science*, p. 103 = *AA*, vol. 4, p. 542; and *AA*, vol. 28, p. 764.

[30] *Critique of Practical Reason*, pp. 126 ff. = *AA*, vol. 5, pp. 122 ff.; *Critique of Judgment*, pp. 312, 321 ff. = *AA*, vol. 5, pp. 461, 469 f.; *AA*, vol. 8, p. 418.

[31] Wood, *Kant's Moral Religion*, pp. 119-21.

[32] See 'The End of All Things', in *Kant on History*; cf. Wood, *Kant's Moral Religion*, p. 123.

[33] See the typical, short and cursory summations in the *Critique of Judgment*, p. 312 = *AA*, vol. 5, p. 312, and *AA*, vol. 20, p. 309. At A 798/B 826 f. Kant remarks that even if he could establish immortality in a traditional way, this would not of itself provide 'insight in explaining either the appearances of this present life or the specific nature of a future state'.

Chapter VI

Independence

The discussion in the previous chapters of Kant's critical remarks on immortality and personal identity should not lead one to assume that even in the *Critique* he has fully distanced himself from rationalism. In particular, it should be recalled that immortality is not the only Kantian idea that can be associated with the self. In this chapter I will argue that Kant's views on a second 'Idea of reason', namely our independence or 'transcendental freedom', betray very strong and important rationalist sympathies well into the 1780s. This argument will complement the interpretation in the earlier chapters of this study, and it will help to complete the account of the strange role of the concept of substance in the Paralogisms. The argument will also force us into the texts of Kant's practical philosophy, and in so doing it will lead to a new and more detailed theory about the precise nature of the basic changes between the first and second editions of the Paralogisms and related sections of the *Critique of Pure Reason*. In this way the issue of independence, which is not one of the explicit topics of the Paralogisms, will prove to be a crucial key to understanding the real meaning of that text and of Kant's critical period in general.

1. Introduction

Although Kant eventually tried to locate the idea of freedom under the rubrics of cosmology and practical philosophy, there is an obvious sense in which it is treated most naturally within the domain of rational psychology. It thus should not be surprising that the topic occurs prominently (under the categorial heading of relation) in what is perhaps the first indication of the emergence in Kant's philosophy of a separate doctrine of mental beings. In Reflection 4849, which probably stems from Kant's early rationalist period, God is characterized as a being who is (a) unique, (b) simple,

(c) free and (d) necessary; and man in contrast as a being (a) within the universe, who is (b) simple and (c) free but (d) exists contingently.[1] Although there are a number of ways this list of topics differs from the one given later in the Paralogisms (A 344/B 402), the most striking difference is surely Kant's later omission of any categorial treatment of the soul's freedom. This is especially striking because in the Pölitz lectures man's freedom is still asserted as part of the rational doctrine of the soul. There freedom is treated under the first and the fourth categorial heading. Kant says:

I am a substance . . . I can only say, 'I am, I think, I act' . . . Now the 'I' proves that I myself act.
I am conscious in myself of determinations [*Bestimmungen*] and actions, and a subject who is aware of such actions and determinations has *libertatem absolutam* . . .
When I say, 'I think, I act, etc.' either the word 'I' is employed improperly or I am free. . . . But I am conscious in myself that I can say, 'I act'. Hence I am not aware of being determined [*Determination*], and so I must be *absolutely free*.[2]

For complex reasons that we can only now begin to clarify, Kant dropped this line of thought in composing the Paralogisms chapter. If he had wanted to attack rationalist arguments along this line, he surely could have, but at first he did not clearly mount a direct attack on the soul's mere substantiality (see above, Ch. II.8), and he hardly discussed human freedom at all in the *Critique*. When he did approach the issue he was often not very critical, as in this peculiar statement which comes near the end of the *Critique* and sounds very much like the lectures:

Man . . . knows himself also through pure apperception; and this, indeed, in acts and inner determinations [*Bestimmungen*] which he cannot regard as impression of the senses. He is thus to himself, on the one hand phenomenon, and on the other hand, in respect of certain faculties the action of which cannot be ascribed to the receptivity of sensibility, a purely intelligible object. We entitle these faculties understanding and reason. (A 546f./B 574f.; this is from a part of the *Critique* that Kant never got around to revising at all.)

It is tempting to take such statements as mere careless relics from Kant's earlier views, and so to say that any sympathy in the *Critique* for asserting that the soul is transcendentally free must be due simply to the patchwork nature of the book's composition. What I shall argue instead is that even *after* the *Critique*'s publication there are very strong signs of sympathy for working out a theoretical proof of freedom, and that *only* shortly *thereafter* is there a clear break away from the idea of such a proof. What this means is that even after the *Critique* was written, Kant was in his own mind not fully critical about asserting the soul's independence, and so it is no accident that the *Critique* contains rationalist passages on freedom or at least a relative dearth of anti-rationalist ones. More specifically, it can be shown that while Kant maintained an ambiguous and restrained attitude on the topic in the original version of the first *Critique* (1781), he felt compelled in his next major work (*The Foundations of the Metaphysics of Morals*, 1785) to go further and to attempt a very strong rationalist argument for freedom. I will argue that once that attempt was worked out as far as it could be, it suffered shipwreck, for it conflicted with the critical strains that were being developed simultaneously in Kant's theory of mind and self-knowledge (e.g., in the efforts to meet criticisms and to complete his *Metaphysical Foundations of Natural Science* (1786) with an account of psychology). As a result, in the second *Critique* (1788) Kant had to recast his treatment of freedom radically so as to be in line with the more severe limits on self-knowledge that he had come to stress in the second edition revisions of the first *Critique* (1787).

It is impossible to develop these claims without getting entangled in some of the intricacies of Kant's moral philosophy. In particular, it will be necessary to get involved in an important dispute among Kant scholars about the validity and meaning of Kant's treatment of the deduction of freedom and the moral law in the *Foundations of the Metaphysics of Morals* and the *Critique of Practical Reason*.

There has been a notable lack of agreement about how to explain what at first sight appears to be a very striking difference between these two texts. In the first work Kant seems to desire and develop a theoretical argument for freedom in a sense which is absolute and from which the objective validity of the moral law is to be deduced. In the second work, however, Kant appears directly to reverse himself and to replace this project of a strict deduction[3] with the idea that the moral law (i.e., its validity, not its entire exact formulation and implications) is simply given as an '*a priori* fact of reason' (from which alone freedom can then be inferred).

Most commentators have admitted the appearance of a troublesome conflict here, but in effect they have argued that there is a deeper reconciliationist interpretation which shows Kant has a position that is both consistent and defensible. Thus some (e.g., H. J. Paton and Dieter Henrich) have said that in fact the *Foundations* properly anticipates the second *Critique* by *not* genuinely meaning to offer a strict deduction. Others (notably Lewis White Beck) have accepted that there *is* something like a strict deduction in the *Foundations*, but they have taken it to be continued and in effect better expressed in the second *Critique*. These lines of interpretation are obviously in conflict with one another, and I believe they are both unsatisfactory. I will argue that Kant truly does change his position just as he appears to at first sight, and that the key to this change is the elimination of some of the persistent rationalist sympathies that can be found underlying even part of the Paralogisms. I will also argue that this change still does not bring Kant to a fully acceptable critical position, although I will attempt to vindicate Kant somewhat by showing that his views undergo what is at least an understandable development, and that often the weaknesses of these views are best appreciated on the basis of considerations suggested by Kant himself.

The analysis that follows will begin with a brief study of the history of Kant's views on freedom (section 2). This will show how for a long time Kant had a very peculiar way of expressing himself which could leave the impression of a much less confident attitude than he really had then toward the possibility of our establishing human freedom. The implications of this study and of further information about Kant's development will then be applied directly to an interpretation of key passages from the *Foundations* and the second *Critique* (sections 3 and 5). This interpretation in turn will be used as a basis for countering the alternative reconciliationist readings of Kant (sections 4 and 6).

2. Historical Review

In the metaphysics lectures of the 1770s Kant appears to make nine basic points about freedom and morality which are then picked up in his later discussions. It is *usually* not the points themselves but only the specific support for them that is modified in the course of the discussions in the 'Reflections', the *Critique of Pure Reason* (1781, 1787), the *Prolegomena* (1783), the 'Review of Schulz' (1783), the *Foundations* (1785), the *Critique of Practical Reason* (1788) and other later writings.

The nine points are these:

1. Practical (or comparative) freedom, that is, independence from mere sensual impulses, is to be distinguished from transcendental (or absolute) freedom, that is, independence from anything predetermining a being's action.[4]
2. Man can justifiably assert he has practical freedom.[5]
3. The assertion of practical freedom is sufficient for the needs of morality, i.e., the acceptance of the categorical imperative.[6]
4. Compatibilism is unacceptable.[7]
5. Prima facie there are strong theoretical threats (God, science) to the possibility of our transcendental freedom.[8]
6. These threats can be dealt with.[9]
7. Man can justifiably assert he has transcendental freedom.[10]
8. None the less, theoretical philosophy remains in some sense incomplete with respect to the issue of freedom.[11]
9. However, this incompleteness involves only a human 'subjective' difficulty and not the objective validity of practical philosophy.[12]

The most important matters here are the first points and in particular the difficulty that would develop from the simultaneous assertion of (1), (3), and (4). A compatibilist can easily accept that lack of, or uncertainty about, transcendental freedom is no problem for morality. However, in sharp contrast to his own early writings, in these lectures Kant already characterizes compatibilism as giving us nothing more than the freedom of a 'turnspit',[13] and therefore it is hard to believe he would say anything like (3). What we would expect him to do is rather to say clearly that comparative freedom is precisely not sufficient for morality, that practical philosophy must also have a guarantee of our absolute freedom. Yet instead of doing this Kant seems to repeat (3) in his lectures and in a number of his mature publications.[14]

To make sense of Kant here I think we must introduce some hypotheses to correct the impression that his published work may at first leave. First of all, Kant simply can't have meant that comparative freedom in the absence of absolute freedom is *logically* sufficient for one to be able to accept the categorical imperative. Rather, I will suggest that a large part of what he meant is simply that practical freedom is sufficient *in the sense that* any man committed to (3) (and not himself already in possession of a proof of (7)) would not be making any *material* error; for given point (6) and other considerations, absolute freedom (i.e., its proof) is (supposedly) always clearly *within reach*, and so the foundation of morality is not really problematic. Thus, we should not understand Kant's statements at various points that it has been proven only that we are 'practically free' to mean that we don't at all need or can't also have a proof of our absolute freedom. Secondly, I will argue not only that Kant couldn't and didn't literally mean practical freedom is sufficient for morality, but also that what he meant primarily was that the *proof* of absolute freedom, which we do need and have, has certain peculiarities that make *it* in *a* sense 'merely practically sufficient'. That is, Kant's main concern here was generally with the fact that we don't and can't have a theoretical proof of absolute freedom *in the sense* of an explanation of *how* such freedom works, that is, a speculative deduction or clarification of its noumenal operation (here points (8) and (9) become important). Thus, we may have to settle with something less than a full theoretical account of freedom and so may be limited to a proof that in this sense is merely practically sufficient. I shall stress, however, that otherwise such a proof could be taken to be a straightforward theoretical deduction of our absolute freedom, and that this has great consequences for the interpretations of Kant's later and better known texts.[15]

To justify these interpretive hypotheses some details need to be given about how the points listed earlier are developed in Kant's works. In the lectures the distinction between absolute and comparative freedom is associated with a distinction between what rational and empirical psychology prove.[16] Our independence from mere sensory stimuli is taken to be an evident psychological fact but one without the universal and absolute meaning that Kant thinks can be drawn out of the pure concept of the *cogito*. As has been noted, in the lectures he argues that one can't say 'I think' without implying one is an ultimate subject or substance, and to be such a thing is just to be independent of external determination, i.e., absolutely free.[17] Arguments like this one are favoured by Kant for a number of years, and I believe they are often what explain his loose talk about practical freedom as sufficient for morality: although our lack of awareness of external determination doesn't by itself prove the lack of such determination, this need not cause any worry since a proof (though not an explanation) of the latter lack is always (supposedly) as close to us as our own thoughts.

This confidence can also explain Kant's attitude to points (5) and (6). The prima-facie threat to freedom that first concerns him is the omnipotence of God. To this question and the problem of fatalism the notes give no direct solution but only the observation that the fatalist case is not proven. However, given his concept of the *cogito* here,[18] Kant could (and later explicitly did) say that that case could not be proven, although this of course does not of itself tell us how we are to understand God's relation to us.[19] That is, to give a proof of our absolute spontaneity is not necessarily to give an explanation of how it operates. This fact constitutes point (8), which is emphasized not only in the lectures but also in nearly all of Kant's later discussions. The lectures also already give the main ground for (9), namely that it is only a natural and 'subjective' fact that we can't 'explain' our freedom, for we happen to be beings who must always explain events by laws of experience, and these obviously are not to be found here.

Kant's use of points (8) and (9) in the lectures is very important becuase it helps explain why *even when he clearly felt himself in possession of what we would consider to be a straightforward theoretical proof of human freedom, he inclined toward seeing it as inadequate in some sense and hence to calling such a proof merely practical.* What contrasts with 'merely practical' here is not proof that in fact we are free but rather simply a complete theoretical explanation of how such an absolutely free causality works in relation to nature and God. The most revealing passage here is the statement that, 'Our concept of freedom is practically but not speculatively sufficient. If by reason we could explain our original free actions it would be sufficient.'[20] Kant also says that we 'go beyond the practical' when we ask *how* freedom is possible.[21]

All this confirms our earlier hypothesis that we need not take at face value Kant's suggestions that practical freedom (as in (1)) is sufficient for morality. We can avoid attributing a blatant inconsistency to him by saying that what he really believes is that transcendental freedom is needed (and provable), but (for the reasons just given) our proof of this freedom is to be called 'merely practically' sufficient. (This belief may be called (3') and could be used to replace (3) in a more accurate formulation of Kant's position.) Another reason for Kant's terminology may be that the proof involves a claim about man as a practical being (i.e., one with a will) and in that sense it isn't what Kant would call a strictly speculative proof from 'pure transcendental predicates'.[22] In these ways we can understand why the proof might be called merely practical even though what it would establish is the existence of our absolute freedom, and its manner of proof is a set of straightforward factual (as opposed to deontological) propositions.

In the 'Reflections' there are no great shifts in Kant's position. R 4220, R 4336, R 4723, R 7440, and R 7441 all support strong claims about proving freedom. If one turns to the *Critique of Pure Reason*, it is easy to find the same general pattern of points that characterized the lectures. In the first *Critique*'s Canon Kant again distinguishes the transcendental and practical meaning of freedom (A 801/B 829), point (1)). It is even said that practical freedom can be proven by experience (A 802/B 830, A 803/B 831). (This constitutes point (2) and also fits our explanation of the first part of R 4724.) Kant also says that although this doesn't establish transcendental freedom, this 'does not concern us' in 'the practical field' (A 803/B 831, point (3)). Here it may be tempting to try to minimize this statement by ascribing it and the Canon in general to an earlier period than the rest of the first *Critique*, for in the Antinomies Kant clearly says that transcendental freedom is required (A 534/B 563, point (4)).[23] However, the Canon also refers back to the Antinomies (A 804/B 832), and its formulations are similar to those found in other later texts. Once again, it seems best to assume that when Kant suggested practical freedom was sufficient he meant that in a peculiar way, and he still felt confident there was no bar to asserting transcendental freedom.

This confidence is admittedly not as clear in the first *Critique* as it is in Kant's other works closest in time to it. Whether we not only may but also should (on theoretical grounds) assert such freedom is difficult to determine from the section of the first *Critique* that gives the longest treatment of this issue, namely the Antinomies. Kant concludes his discussion there by saying he has not even argued for the possibility[24] of freedom (A 558/B 586; this page in effect offers points (8) and (9)) but has tried only to show that it need not contradict the laws of nature (which now replace God — who is no longer a given in theoretical philosophy — as the backing for point (5)). But there are stronger threads in Kant's discussion that can be taken to approach a repetition of (7) and not merely an allowance that there may be transcendental freedom somewhere. Kant states that if transcendental idealism is accepted, then transcendental freedom is not only a possibility but also a necessity: there must be some ground for appearances which is itself unconditional (e.g., A 537/B 565). He also obviously believes independent arguments for the premiss of transcendental idealism are available. He even suggests that otherwise nature itself would have to be rejected (A 543/B 571); that is, without his idealism the only objection to our freedom, namely the universal laws of nature and our apparent complete subjection to them, could not be justified (thus points (5) and (6) are covered; cf. R 3855). Thus the very item that raises the threat to the assertion of transcendental freedom ultimately points to the existence of things in themselves and so the presence of transcendental freedom. This is consistent with the argument of the thesis in the third antinomy, in which it is claimed that without transcendental idealism we are led to a self-contradictory concept of nature (A 446/B 474). The argument is very questionable, but Kant never directly questioned it and rather seemed convinced by it.[25]

Thus, although at first sight it can appear that Kant's solution to the third antinomy is to say that both theses can be right, in that there may be transcendental freedom although there is no such freedom *in* the world, his real position seems to be the stronger claim that there *must* be transcendental freedom outside the world although there can be no such freedom in the world.[26] It is true that the dogmatic Observation on the antithesis claims that this latter position is untenable (A 451/B 479), but the rest of Kant's discussion is aimed precisely at disproving this claim, at showing that transcendental freedom can act on the world without interfering with it (A 538/B 566 ff.; this supports point (6), but see n. 67 below).

There is still an important gap in the argument here, because even if for the first *Critique* there must be some transcendental freedom, it is not clear that we must be transcendentally free. In the Antinomies Kant begins to bridge this gap by saying that in various contexts we all regard humans as transcendentally free (A 547/B 575). He hardly builds his remarks into a philosophical proof, but all he needs are grounds for asserting we are genuinely substances, i.e., that the substrate which we already (supposedly) know must lie behind the phenomenal self is itself a (not numerically distinct) self. A belief in such grounds may seem entirely pre-critical, but it goes along with the long passage from A 546/B 574, cited at the beginning of this chapter as well as with our earlier observation that the first edition discussion of the issue in the Paralogisms presents no direct argument against our mere substantiality. The main point of that discussion is simply that noumenal substantiality is of little use in that it does not prove a phenomenally substantial, i.e., eternal, existence for our personality (A 349-51, see above Ch. II.8). In this way there is a *sophisma figurae dictionis* in the original first paralogism that corresponds to the one Kant attributes to the antinomies in general: from the transcendental premiss that the conditioned requires the unconditioned (as our representations require an ultimate subject), and the minor premiss that we are given something empirically conditioned (e.g., the predications of thought), it is falsely concluded that we are given something *empirically* unconditioned (e.g., a first mover, or absolute, i.e., eternal, empirical substance) (A 500/B 520). Kant here does not directly question the material validity of the premisses, i.e., the claim that there must be some unconditional transcendental items, including an ultimate subject that underlies our thoughts and is transcendentally free.

It is true that Kant later revised his first paralogism, but it is important to know that in the meantime he first consolidated rather than altered his position. In the *Prolegomena*, for example, the only positive addition to the topic of morality and freedom is a clear attempt to show we do have a special reason to say the transcendental freedom we know must exist somewhere in fact exists (at least) in ourselves. Kant stresses that we feel a need to posit our transcendental freedom, and that when we do then the natural way to conceive its influence, namely according to moral laws, is such that it is particularly well adapted to give us a form of transcendental freedom that meets the difficulties presented by laws of nature. This is 'because [moral] grounds of reason give the rule universally to actions according to principles, without influence of the circumstances of either time or place'.[27] It is not clear whether here Kant means this to justify claiming that moral beings like us and only such beings are demonstrably free, but it is clear that he thinks at least a strong prima-facie case has been built for this claim.

Kant was drawn to strengthen his case by the publication in 1783 of Johann Schulz's *Sittenlehre*, which tries to find a place for morality within a fatalistic metaphysics. In his brief 'Review of Schulz' Kant runs through the now familiar main points of his position: the distinction between transcendental and practical freedom, the rejection of compatibilism, and the perplexing suggestion that our practical freedom is evident and sufficient for morality.[28] These claims can be understood as usual if Kant has in the background a ready argument for asserting transcendental freedom, and in particular one which he understands to locate such freedom directly in us. In fact, Kant appears to present just the kind of argument that could be expected from the lectures, the 'Reflections', and the passage at A 546/B 574. He says the mere claim to judge, i.e., think objectively rather than simply submit to the mere casual 'play' of subjective data, implies a 'freedom to think', and that similarly when we undertake to act objectively this involves a freedom to act.[29]

Kant's argument here is not only brief and suspicious (conflating 'subjective' with 'merely subjective') but also ambiguous and especially difficult to evaluate. At first Kant seems to be making an extremely strong claim, in the old style, about our (transcendental) freedom as derivable from features that are found in (or closely analogous to those found in) the self's mere existence as a *cogito*. But Kant ends his review with a touch of hesitation: he says only that one must presuppose freedom if one will have morality and do one's duty. That man is absolutely free to act is not said to be directly proven. Rather, it is simply concluded that if we can't ever bring this 'practical presupposition' into harmony with speculative principles 'not much is lost'.[30] It is possible to take this last phrase as but another way of making points (8) and (9), i.e., as a signal that we can never explain how our absolute freedom operates, especially in relation to God, even if we can be sure about its existence. But it is also possible rather to be struck by the lack of a distinct claim backing (7), and by the introduction of a new hypothetical formulation: Kant says that 'as soon as' he is to 'do his duty', 'even the most hardened fatalist' must act 'as if' he were free.[31] This formulation is troublesome, for if we cannot have grounds for saying we are really absolutely free, then there is something odd (given Kant's anti-compatibilism) about acting as if we are; and if we could have such grounds, then there is something odd about not appealing to or seeking them, but rather resting content with an 'as if' attitude.[32]

The troublesome formulations in the 'Review of Schulz' have an influence on Kant's next work, the *Foundations*, which also adds several new complications. It would be nice to be able simply to assert that the *Foundations* attempts to improve upon the 'Review' by offering a clearer case against fatalism and for a categorical deduction of freedom. Unfortunately, although I believe this is the way the *Foundations* is ultimately to be understood, some complex exposition is needed here, especially in view of the famous contrast Kant makes in the *Foundations* between our being known to be free 'in a practical respect', i.e., having to act 'under the idea of freedom', and our not being able to know we're free in a 'theoretical respect'.[33] I will now breifly suggest how this passage can be handled and explain what the general difficulties of the *Foundations* are, and then in the next section I will give a detailed analysis of the text to clarify these difficulties and confirm the hypothesis that it culminates long-standing efforts on Kant's part categorically to establish our transcendental freedom.

In the passage just cited we now can see the importance of the previous examination of what Kant means when saying that it is 'only' being shown that we're 'free in a practical respect'. It is tempting to understand this as meaning only that we are merely 'practically free' (as defined in (1) above), or, as some have thought (see n. 116 below), as meaning 'only' that we can't help but act as if we are free but can't say we are really free. However, although Kant does use the phrase 'as if' here, he does not mean thereby to question our transcendental freedom. What he says is that to know we are 'really free in a practical respect' *is* to know the *validity* of the law of a free will just 'as if its will were explained to be [*erklärt*] free by theoretical philosophy'.[34] This means that what a proof of our freedom 'in a theoretical respect' would add would be nothing about the truth of our freedom or its relevant practical consequences. We can presume that all it would add would be the 'theoretically sufficient' or 'strictly speculative' explanation [*Erklärung*] about *how* freedom operates that Kant spoke of earlier. Precisely this point is allowed by Kant at the end of the *Foundations* when he juxtaposes the claim that our freedom can be said to be 'unconditionally necessary', with the claim that 'how' this freedom is possible 'can never be discerned by any human reason'.[35] The problem in the latter case involves the opacity to us of noumenal mechanics, e.g., the difficulty of explaining how 'pure reason by mere Ideas' is able to 'instil a feeling of pleasure or satisfaction in the fulfilment of duty', i.e., 'an effect which does lie in experience'.[36]

What makes matters especially complicated here is that although Kant's ultimate statement on human freedom in the *Foundations* is categorical, when he originally speaks about showing our freedom 'in a practical respect' his discussion is not a proof but rather, as he says, a preparatory elucidation.[37] He means at first only to explain that *if* it can be shown that because of some *a priori* quality beings must act 'under the Idea of freedom', then it can be asserted they are free. Obviously, much still hinges on finding such a quality and determining that we have it, and it is in this context that the notorious problem arises of a vicious circle in Kant's discussion of freedom and morality. If the necessity that we act under the idea of freedom is simply one placed on us in so far as we feel bound by morality, then we do not have the categorical foundation for freedom needed here if morality is to be strictly deduced. A circle can be escaped only if independent reasons (i.e., reasons which do not themselves appeal to the validity of the moral law) can be given for our having to act under the idea of freedom.

Matters would be much simpler if it could be assumed that this is the only circle that can threaten the *Foundations*. However, when Kant says he is presenting a 'deduction' in the third section of the *Foundations* he makes clear that it has two parts, namely to show (i) that we are transcendentally free (and so a necessary condition of Kantian morality is established) and (ii) that the validity of the categorical imperative follows from what we are 'directed to' by this fact (and so sufficient conditions are also established).[38] Circles could thus arise with respect to either of these two parts. A circle can arise directly for the second part (the argument 'from freedom') if one argues for morality on the basis of freedom and then is able to defend freedom only by appealing to morality. But there may also be a circle threatening the first part (the argument 'to freedom') of Kant's deduction, namely if one tried to establish this freedom by appealing to morality and then could justify the latter only by claiming one's freedom. We shall proceed now with analysing Kant's text in terms of this distinction between the part of the deduction which is an argument *to* freedom and the part which is an argument *from* freedom. Only in the full course of the analysis will the significance of the distinction and the consequences for other interpretations that have failed to pay adequate heed to it become clear.

3. The Deduction of the *Foundations*

It was just noted that if the *Foundations* is to make a strict deduction, it should show in some non-question-begging fashion that we are beings who are under the necessity of acting under the idea of freedom. Yet instead of attending directly to this specific issue Kant first argues that *any* rational being with a will stands under such a necessity. Kant's argument here is no surprise after what was said in his earlier writings:

in such a being . . . we think of a reason which is practical, i.e., a reason which has causality with respect to its objects. Now, we cannot conceive of a reason which consciously responds to a bidding from the outside with respect to its judgments, for then the subject would attribute the determination of its power of judgment not to reason but to impulse. . . . the will of a rational being can be a will of its own only under the idea of freedom.[39]

This argument brings thinking and willing even closer together than in Kant's earlier lectures, but at this point it remains as unclear and hypothetical. If a being, *qua* thinking, is to have a 'will of its own', then this can be taken to mean that its judging acts (like all others) must have their absolute source in him. But this still doesn't show that the idea of such a rational will is anything more than a 'mere phantom'. Kant may be right that if there were such a will then it would truly have to regard itself as having a 'will of its own', but it does not follow that anyone who regards himself as having a will of his own has such a will. *A fortiori*, it doesn't follow that we have such a will, even if we happen to regard ourselves as having one, for it is not clear that we have to regard ourselves in such a way.[40] This may be why Kant characterizes the discussion as a 'mere preparation' and immediately goes on to say, 'we could not prove freedom to be real in ourselves and in human nature. We saw only that we must presuppose it if we would think of a being as rational and conscious of his causality with respect to actions, that is, as endowed with a will'.[41]

Obviously what still must be shown is an independent necessity for asserting we have a rationality that requires absolute and not mere comparative freedom. Rather than turn directly to this problem, however, Kant goes on to the argument *from* freedom to morality. Here for the first time he suggests the problem of a circle, and he says it has to do with the difficulty of 'proving the reality and objective necessity' of the moral law 'by itself'.[42] This is rather striking, for it means that Kant sees the primary difficulty of his deduction as lying in its second part, the argument from rather than to freedom. Although, as Kant has just admitted, that first part has not yet been categorically established, what he wishes to discuss is rather 'what follows' from our freedom once it is posited. What Kant says 'follows' is 'the consciousness of a law of action', i.e., that the maxims we choose should be able to serve as universal laws. What he focuses on then is the fact that this step is not yet clearly established; it is not evident why one should have to subject oneself to such a law. It is true that if we *define* a rational will as a will of its own in the sense that it is to obey only self-legislated principles, principles which according to Kant can be only of a universalizable type, the subjection to morality can follow from freedom of the will. But the entailment involves a kind of circle, for the free rational will that is the premiss leads to morality only if its freedom is understood not as mere (negative) transcendental freedom but as autonomy. Thus Kant says:

... there is a kind of circle here from which it seems that there is no escape. We assume that we are free in the order of efficient causes so that we can conceive of ourselves as subject to moral laws in the order of ends. And then we think of ourselves as subject to these laws because we have ascribed freedom of the will to ourselves. This is circular because freedom and self-legislation of the will are both autonomy and thus are reciprocal concepts.[43]

Kant's self-analysis here is not easy to follow. Paton, for example, says, 'In plain fact the objection [of the above vicious circle] totally misrepresents his [Kant's] argument. He never argued from the categorical imperative to freedom'.[44] On the face of it, this diagnosis seems correct although perplexing, for it is odd that Kant should be so unclear about his own argument. Here I believe it is helpful to keep in mind the two-part structure of the deduction. It is true that with respect to the first part, the argument to freedom, Kant here did not argue explicitly from the categorical imperative but rather observed simply that if we are rational in a specific sense then freedom follows. However, the main problem with this argument for Kant is not, as one might expect, that we have not yet established that we should ascribe rationality (in the appropriate sense) to ourselves. Rather, the problem seems to lie in finding a ground for saying that our rationality must be regarded as independent of 'foreign influences' not only in the sense of not being sufficiently determined by 'impulses' but also in the sense of not being guided by any other than its own principles. That is, for the second part of the deduction we need (as a starting point) not mere transcendental or negative freedom but rather freedom in the positive sense that Kant calls autonomy (for it would seem one could be negatively free and yet evil or indifferent and so not positively free), and the argument presented by Kant from the nature of judging does not by itself have any good promise of getting us that far. To get that far we need a stronger premiss, and the only one Kant mentions in his discussion here is 'the already assumed importance of moral laws'.[45]

We now can give some sense to Kant's diagnosis that in the first part of his deduction 'we assume that we are free in the order of efficient causes so that we can conceive of ourselves as subject to moral laws'. Although he did not explicitly argue first from a subjection to morality and then to our freedom (only later to argue to the validity of the moral law — which would make for a very small circle and not a 'hidden' one), it still seems that in effect this is the only way he could get to the positive and not merely negative kind of freedom that the second part of his argument needs. What disturbs Kant is thus the nature of the freedom argued for (so the argument from freedom can get going) and not a fear that no kind of transcendental freedom can be established (such that the argument to freedom cannot be concluded). However, if Kant could find a proof of an adequately strong freedom without antecedently appealing to morality, then he not only would have a chance for a non-circular argument from freedom but also could have a more effective one to freedom. This fact is quite relevant to the discussion that follows[46] in which Kant claims to remove the suspicion of a 'hidden circle'. In particular, it can explain the odd fact that at the beginning and end of the discussion Kant speaks only of what follows when we think of ourselves as free, whereas in between what he discusses are new grounds for claiming we are free in the first place. If, as we have suggested, what Kant was drawing attention to earlier was in effect the need for a better way of arguing to freedom, so that his argument from freedom would have a chance, then it is only natural that now Kant would go into the details of the former while emphasizing the latter in his preview and review.

Kant's new discussion depends heavily on the development of a concept that previously had been mysteriously alluded to only as the 'third term' that would be needed to complete the deduction.[47] This third term is the concept of membership in an 'intelligible world', a phrase which recalls Kant's remark of A 546/B 574 about our being a 'purely intelligible object'. The argument now is not simply that if we are members of the intelligible world we are free, but rather that at one and the same time we can see we are free and have such membership, and from such membership we finally can find the (supposedly non-circular) conditions for our subjection to the moral law. This argument can be persuasive only if what supposedly allows one to see all this is something more than Kant's earlier brief reference to the nature of judging. In fact, Kant's argument here becomes only much more complicated rather than convincing. At first Kant seems to concede that judging as such need not prove even mere transcendental freedom, for he says the understanding is in a way bound to sensibility.[48] He therefore shifts to another aspect of rationality and also for the first time categorically asserts that man does find rationality in himself.[49] Although everything would appear to hinge on this newly emphasized aspect of rationality, it is only briefly characterized as the 'pure spontaneity' exhibited in our having 'ideas' (a term which is apparently to be understood as designating the special concepts discussed in the Dialectic of the first *Critique*).[50] Moreover, in later summarizing his argument to freedom Kant makes no direct reference to ideas and seems rather to be saying little more than he did in his first formulations:

> The title to freedom of the will claimed by common reason is based on the consciousness and the conceded presupposition of the independence of reason from merely subjectively determining causes . . . the consciousness of itself as intelligence, i.e., as independent of sensuous impressions.[51]

In the end, although Kant feels this 'presupposition' must be conceded and he categorically affirms it himself, he does not clarify his grounds and rather says only that otherwise we would have to deny man is a 'rational and rationally acting cause, i.e., a cause acting in freedom'.[52] Here Kant never gives compatibilism a chance, never notes that although what we intend when we use our understanding and reason may appear transcendently *intended*, our *intending* it none the less might be sufficiently explained by a natural process that involves nothing transcendent in *us*.

Instead of firmly shoring up the first part of his deduction, Kant seems to take it for granted and to be fascinated by the belief, expressed clearly only in a later section, that now he has formulated its conclusion (viz., that we are free *intelligences*) in such a way that 'this thought certainly implies the idea of an order and legislation different from that of natural mechanism'.[53] This emphasis on an intelligible order is one half of Kant's new strategy for completing his deduction. To know we are 'intelligible' in the sense of not determined by sensuality is still not to know what our nature is; but if we know our being intelligible makes us part of a distinct 'order', then that order must be positively defined and, presumably, by laws of autonomy. The second part of Kant's strategy is also elaborated only in another later section of his discussion,[54] in which an argument is presented for saying that, given that we belong to an intelligible as well as sensible (natural) order, we should feel bound to serve the former. This argument rests on the claim that in general the intelligible world is the ground of the sensible one, and thus its rules should be preferred, and so in particular the rules of one's 'proper self' (as a member of the intelligible world legislating autonomous rules of conduct) should be given dominance over the rules of one's mere natural and apparent self.[55]

In the original discussion that supposedly removes the suspicion of a hidden circle in Kant's argument neither of these vital points are clearly set out. Instead, Kant emphasizes a peculiar argument (to be called the 'passivity argument') that the mere passivity of our sensible representations entails there is something in itself distinct from them and hence that even our own self, which we know through sensibility, has a distinct non-sensible nature in itself.[56] How Kant could still suggest an argument such as this is a mystery that eventually will have to be faced; first it should be noted simply that by itself the argument is quite inadequate to do any real work in the deduction and that hence it is only fair to appeal as we have to the later remarks. Even if we granted the argument shows all things known by us have a sensible and an intelligible (noumenal) side, this by itself doesn't show our transcendental freedom, let alone our autonomy or subjection to morality. It needs to be shown that the intelligible side constitutes a realm of laws and that they relate to our will and should be given precedence by us – and whatever can show all this would seem to make the passivity argument dispensable. The real needs of the deduction are addressed (even if perhaps not met) not be the passivity argument but by the points later in Kant's discussion that were referred to above. Only they respond to the crucial need recognized by Kant in the end when he stresses it is not enough to show, as he did in the first *Critique*, that transcendental freedom need not contradict nature:

> It must show not only that they [natural causality and transcendental freedom] can very well coexist but also that they must be thought of as necessarily united in one and the same subject; for otherwise no ground could be given why we should burden reason with an idea which, though it may without contradiction be united with another that is sufficiently established, never the less involves us in a perplexity which sorely embarrasses reason in its speculative use.[57]

4. The Rejection of a Deduction of Freedom

However one may judge its success, it is most significant that the *Foundations* at least sees what Kant's philosophy needs with respect to freedom and that it tries to meet that need. It does not rest content with the mere logical possibility of transcendental freedom nor does it rest with saying we can act as if we're free or as if there is some basis, but not a strong theoretical one, for saying we're free. Kant sees that nothing less than transcendental as opposed to practical (in the sense of mere comparative) freedom will do *for him*, and also that *mere* transcendental freedom is not enough, that what must be shown is that this freedom is *in us*, and in such a way that it points to our subjection to morality. In Kant's later works these views are repeated except for one very important difference: he *expressly* no longer allows *any* theoretical argument to freedom. Kant continues to hold that freedom (in a positive sense in us) is certain, but now he says that this can be asserted only as a consequence of the '*a priori* fact' that we see the moral law is binding.[58]

In effect no strict deduction, let alone a non-circular one, of the moral law (i.e., of the validity in general of morality, as opposed to the best formulation of its supreme principle) is offered, and no non-moral proof of freedom is given. (Thus Kant uses the term 'fact' here precisely as a contrast to what is a mere consequence of a proof.[59]) Instead of a solution to the earlier charge of a circularity in the deduction, the original project of a deduction is in effect given up. Only freedom (now called 'the keystone of the whole architecture of the system of pure reason')[60] is argued for, and this is done on the basis of the ultimately unargued for premiss of the validity of morality (and the unacceptability of compatibilism).

Instead of taking up the old problem of a vicious circle, Kant merely notes that there is no inconsistency in his present position, which takes freedom as the *ratio essendi* of the moral law and the latter as the (unique) *ratio cognoscendi* of freedom.[61] Strictly speaking, Kant is consistent here, but this does not compensate for the fact that the claim of transcendental freedom is not metaphysically secured, and that the matter which was originally primarily suspected of being only circularly grounded, namely morality, is not grounded in a deduction. Similarly, the charge of circularity in arguing to freedom can be met, but this means little. Before, the assertion of our freedom seemed to be based on the assertion of morality, which in turn rested on an appeal to freedom. Now instead of the last step, which does involve a circular grounding, no step at all and so no theoretical grounding is offered. In the place of ambitious but understandable attempts at a strict deduction Kant has fallen back into the invocation of an alleged *a priori* fact of practical reason.

The major interpreters have not been willing to accept at face value the enormous contrast between Kant's views here. Beck says that Kant's note in the second *Critique* (cited above) handles 'in a very conscise and effective manner' the problem of a vicious circle.[62] Yet, as has been just shown, this note really is not directed to and cannot offer anything in the way of a solution to the difficulties that originally came under the heading of the problem of a circle. In another and more developed analysis, Beck contends that elsewhere in the body of the second *Critique* Kant presents considerations that in effect amount to a successful completion of the original deduction and thus a resolution to the circularity problem. Paton, on the other hand, argues that the circle is a 'side issue' and that what seemed like a deduction in the *Foundations* is best understood as a set of considerations which properly also do not go anywhere without moral premisses and so are in (implicit if not explicit) harmony with the second *Critique*. I think both these lines of interpretation distort Kant's text and would not be even tempting were it not for the fact that rejecting them also leaves a very perplexing situation, namely an apparent total reversal of positions by Kant on a central issue in the heart of his supposedly mature and settled critical period.

The analysis just presented may seem only to increase this perplexity, for it implies that if Kant offers no strict deduction of freedom and morality in the second *Critique*, then this conflicts not only with what the *Foundations* attempts but also with what it clearly and properly perceives as desirable. If one looks back at the *Foundations* it is not hard to find fault with the specifics of Kant's attempt to carry out a deduction, but it is difficult to see anything very wrong with what he says about his need for one, and so it is very hard to see how later he could ignore that need (later Kant refers back only to the first two parts of the *Foundations*).[63] I suggest the only way to make sense of this situation is to face Kant's texts literally and hypothesize that earlier Kant made such a point about a deduction only because (as before) he thought one could be easily provided; that meanwhile he discovered that *the* way he believed in was not a tenable or appropriate one for him; that thus out of necessity he had to renounce the attempt metaphysically to ground freedom or morality; and that, finally, it was only to make a virtue of necessity[64] that (given his deepest beliefs of longest standing) he felt it was proper to announce that without the moral law 'we would never have been justified in assuming anything like freedom'.[65] I shall present the textual evidence for this complex hypothesis first, and then at the end will deal with the opposing interpretations.

5. How the Doctrine of the Second *Critique* Developed

If now we look back to evaluate the deduction in the *Foundations*, we first should recall that it involved three major steps. First, there is the argument to freedom in a negative transcendental sense. This step is originally based on the supposed implications of mere judging; later reference is made to a special faculty of ideas. The second step, which is filled out in the course of the reformulation of the backing for the first, is to characterize positively the transcendental self as subject to distinct rational laws (for action) of its own. Finally, it is argued these laws constitute morality and are to be obeyed because they represent one's 'proper self', one's being in itself, which is the foundation of one's mere appearance. All these steps can be severely criticized – the first for not giving a fair chance to compatibilism and to a more sophisticated treatment of subjective causal grounds (which may do what 'mere impulse' can't to explain judgements or ideas); the second for presuming too quickly that what is beyond nature must none the less be like nature in being a realm defined by a set of rational laws; and the third for drawing normative consequences from what is at best an ontological truth, and a very questionable one in any case.[66] It cannot be said that these are the only objections possible here, but I believe other familiar difficulties such as the mere comprehensibility of transcendental freedom (which is supposed to affect but not interfere with nature)[67] have been overemphasized, and so in my view these do represent the major problems.

The mere fact that there are problems in Kant's argument is not itself that significant, for although he appears to believe he has a strict deduction, he also properly indicates that all he must have are some good overriding reasons for our freedom in the strong sense that he understands it. Moreover, the weakness in the second step is not crucial for our purposes. Even in the second *Critique* Kant held that autonomy and freedom are reciprocal concepts, although he no longer needed such an argument to autonomy (since this followed from the assumed fact of morality). That is, Kant argued that 'granted that a will is free', 'the law which alone is competent to determine it necessarily' is a law of autonomy,[68] and he simply did not question that a free will must be 'determinable necessarily', i.e., that there must be some sort of law analogous to nature fully governing it.[69] Kant's later distinction between *Wille* and *Willkür* in his book on religion implies a step beyond this presumption, but in fact it was never adequately developed by him.[70] Thus, if there is any rationale behind Kant's giving up the deduction of the *Foundations*, it must be traced to a new attitude to the first and third steps, and in particular to a belief that these steps not only had not been convincingly carried out but also cannot be carried out (without an antecedent appeal to morality) with any persuasiveness.

In what follows, the key claim that there is such a rationale will be backed by evidence of this new attitude in Kant quite soon after the *Foundations*. That this attitude replaces a view which was well entrenched, even if only fully articulated shortly before, is evident already from our analysis of Kant's earlier critical writing. Although for a long time he had definitely believed he had a strict proof of transcendental freedom in hand, Kant had never before so clearly emphasized it.

For example, it has been noted already that the Antinomies, which Kant himself designated as containing the key thought of his new critical system, simply fails to make a clear statement on transcendental freedom in general. Similarly, we also know that in the Paralogisms an even less clear picture emerges, although if Kant had simply kept to the structure of his discussion of the soul in the lectures, freedom would have been the topic of his fourth Paralogism.[71] What happened instead, of course, is that he substituted the topic of the external world. At first sight this shift might seem justified by his desire to fit all discussions on to the table of categories, but as even Kant in effect concedes elsewhere, his new topic scarcely meets this desire any better. It might also be thought that the shift could be explained by saying that Kant simply lost faith in his earlier argument for freedom from the nature of the *cogito*. But now it is clear that texts even after the first edition of the first *Critique*, such as the *Foundations*, hardly indicate any basic loss of faith here, and in any case such a loss would rather have been a justification for bringing the discussion of freedom into the critical framework of the Paralogisms. Hence it is more likely that a major reason why Kant didn't directly continue with this topic was that he *did* still believe our freedom can be speculatively grounded. It cannot be said that such a belief is so much out of line with the tenor of the first *Critique* that it could not have been held then, for as was indicated earlier, even the Paralogisms does not say much against similar basic rationalist beliefs about the immateriality and simplicity of our being.[72] It is true that systematic suspicions are raised against certain ways of arguing about the soul, and in particular about making too much out of the formal requirements of unity in apperception, but Kant clearly had not thought through all the ways these suspicions could be developed. If he had, a number of his later writings would be inexplicable and the arguments to freedom in the *Foundations* would be totally mysterious. At the same time, it is understandable that Kant would not say too much in the first *Critique* to elaborate on his beliefs about our free immaterial being, for such elaboration would clearly complicate the proper critical claims he wanted to make against rational psychology, and in any case it would have seemed to Kant that this could wait until the development of the practical philosophy that he thought he would soon publish.

Given these considerations and the lack of convincing alternatives, I think it possible and preferable to take the arguments of the *Foundations* at face value, and to see them merely as a slightly more self-conscious continuation of some relatively crude beliefs about freedom that Kant had held for some time and simply had not gotten around to submitting to a thorough critique. Moreover, ascribing such a fundamentally lax attitude to Kant helps to make sense of the odd passivity argument interjected in the *Foundations*. As has been noted, this argument does not serve a valid function in the primary task of the text, namely the *deduction* of freedom and morality. It serves rather to introduce a supposedly helpful *association* between the passive and merely phenomenal on the one hand, and the active and noumenal on the other hand. Even in Kant's system this association cannot be let stand in this crude form. Although Kant seems to believe that something actively represented is necessarily seen in itself, it at no point is shown generally that something passively represented must be represented phenomenally and not as it is in itself. Furthermore, taken literally this association is not used in the rest of Kant's discussion, for what he goes on to argue is that there is an aspect of the self (spontaneity) known as it is in itself not specifically because it actively represented but rather because it (supposedly) involves an active representing.[73] Yet even though the passivity argument as such can play no valid essential role, Kant clearly needs something like it to set up the *suggestion* that instead of speaking merely negatively about what is not merely sensible, we should think there is a distinct order of non-sensible things which have their own way of being constituted, namely by themselves rather than passively or heteronomously.

Only in view of this casually developed suggestive function can the passivity argument be understood. Contrary to what some have suggested, it cannot be taken as a short summary of the first *Critique* that is inadequate simply because of a lack of space, for in fact there is no way the argument as such *could* be filled out properly to represent the first *Critique*. If it were really the case that Kant held that the mere passivity of our representations makes them merely phenomenal, then there would have been no need for him to have made the extensive arguments that he did for transcendental idealism, and to have distinguished his idealism as he did from other kinds (see, e.g., A 36/B 53). But although the passivity argument (as presented in the *Foundations*) can hardly be taken as a fair representation of the general argument of the first *Critique*, I believe it is understandable, given Kant's relatively undeveloped attitude toward the self, that he might have fallen into the idea that the passivity argument was permissible as a way of suggesting why the phenomenal/noumenal distinction can be made with respect to the self. Kant takes it as evident that we do passively perceive ourselves, and in the first edition of the *Critique* he gave no clear treatment of any other feature of self-knowledge in order to back his doctrine of the transcendental ideality of the (empirical) self, even though he knew analogues to the doctrine had already been sharply criticized.[74] It is true that originally Kant had formulated the doctrine with an emphasis on the temporality of our passive self-perception, but he never had said clearly what it is distinctly about temporal representations that entails their ideality. In particular, he did not and obviously could not argue that just as physical knowledge is supposedly merely phenomenal because it rests on a synthetic *a priori* doctrine of space, self-knowledge is merely phenomenal because it rests on a synthetic *a priori* doctrine of time. Were he to say this, Kant would have been led toward rather than away from a kind of rational psychology. The first *Critique* thus originally left unclear Kant's ground for the basic claim that we know ourselves only as phenomena, and so it made a focus on the passivity of self-perception (as a contrast to the dogmatic rationalists) tempting.

In the second *Critique* Kant admits that the doctrine of transcendental idealism when applied to the self invites one of the two 'most weighty criticisms' of his system.[75] In having to face again the weighty criticisms on this issue in the reviews of his work, Kant naturally would have become acutely aware that he had hardly given a clear treatment of it. Once this occurred, I suggest, Kant must have realized the passivity argument of the *Foundations* was especially inadequate and could give a wholly misleading picture of his doctrine of the phenomenality of physical knowledge. This realization in turn could have led Kant to see that to the extent that he had developed any specific positive arguments for transcendental idealism, they depended heavily upon reference to presumed features of spatiality,[76] and so if he were to hold to a similar idealistic position on the self, he ought to argue similarly. That is, he ought to argue explicitly that the phenomenality of our knowledge derives from the fact that for us all objective determinations are temporal and that these, even with respect to the self, always involve an implicit spatial reference.

I am hardly endorsing this line of argument, but I am saying it is the obvious one for Kant to have taken when pressed to reconsider his discussion of the self. Moreover, to see that this is exactly the line that Kant in fact emphasized right after publication of the *Foundations* (1785), one need only take a brief look at Kant's next two projects: the *Metaphysical Foundations of Natural Science* (1786) and the second edition revisions of the first *Critique* (1787). In the former work, Kant digressed to explain why there was no distinct set of first principles for psychology and the realm of the inner to match the *a priori* principles for physics that he was developing. In revising the first *Critique*, he focused almost entirely on filling out this explanation by reorganizing the fourth Paralogism and related sections. His aim was to make more prominent our dependence on spatial references in self-knowledge and to offer an explicit argument for its phenomenality because of those references.[77] The tenor of these changes and the philosophical need for them have been noted by many interpreters, but no one has adequately accounted for their historical motivation. We now can present an adequate answer here, namely that the changes were precisely what should be expected given the continued weak discussion of the self offered in the *Foundations* and the continued weighty criticisms that followed upon it.

The revising of the first *Critique* and the forsaking of the deduction of the *Foundations* take place simultaneously, and thus already in the second edition of that *Critique* there are a number of strong statements that freedom is to be argued for only *after* morality is accepted (B 428 f., B xxviii, B xxxii). Kant finally decided explicitly to block any temptation to take as (theoretically) ascribable to our personal self the spontaneity and transcendental freedom known indeterminately to have to underlie our phenomenal self. This point is made most clearly in the 'General Note' with which Kant concludes his revised section on the paralogisms. Here he brings under critique the idea that dominates the arguments of all the moral texts we have analysed, namely the spontaneity of thought. Kant does not deny that thinking exhibits a 'pure spontaneity', but now he emphasizes that this represents merely a 'logical function' and that although it does not exhibit 'the subject of consciousness as appearance', it also 'does not represent myself . . . as I am' (B 428 f.) (B 429). As Kant adds, this is not to say that there could not be other, non-theoretical means whereby there could be 'revealed a spontaneity through which our reality would be determinable' (B 430), but as the only means Kant had in mind here are obviously moral ones, they could not be used in the deduction he originally attempted.

The clear insistence that the representation of spontaneity in our thought does not yield knowledge of the self in itself gives Kant for the first time a consistently critical theory of self-knowledge and simultaneously undermines the first and third steps of the *Foundations'* deduction: now our rationality cannot get us to a free noumenal self, and whatever noumenal side the self is allowed to have, the restrictions on ascribing any personal character to it eliminate even the possibility of arguing from freedom to morality on the basis of what is (supposedly theoretically) known to be one's 'proper self'. By the time of his latest work, Kant thus had totally abandoned the distinctive points of the last section of the *Foundations*. However, in this abandonment Kant gave up not only some vulnerable points but also some valid ones. That is, Kant never gave any reason for ignoring his earlier idea that freedom should be argued for theoretically and that a mere absence of grounds against it is not adequate given the 'perplexity' our transcendental freedom presents for the system of speculative knowledge. Instead, at the very end of his career Kant frankly acknowledged his practical philosophy was 'dogmatic' and only his theoretical philosophy was to be called critical.[78]

Kant emphasized, of course, that his dogmatism was at least not mystical, that it rested on a given generally recognized cognition and not a sheer feeling or ordinary intuition. Yet although in intention his practical philosophy surely can be distinguished from the mystical excesses of the Idealists who followed him, Kant must bear considerable responsibility for the latter. Only some technical peculiarities of his system prevent labelling his position fundamentally intuitionistic, for although the '*a priori* fact' of the validity of the moral law is not a given particular, as a standard Kantian intuition should be, but is rather a kind of principle,[79] it shares the non-naturalistic ultimacy that is found explicitly and typically in intuitionistic systems. Moreover, this ultimacy is clearly taken by Kant to be a prime sign and proof of a special transcendent realm of being,[80] and to this extent he can be said to have encouraged the return, at least in Germany, to a kind of dogmatic metaphysics — notwithstanding the fact that he repeatedly insisted on the limited content of any justified transcendent claims.[81]

The only thing that could appear as an attempt at a strict foundation of the moral law (i.e., its general validity, not its specific formulation) in Kant's last work is the 'credential' for it offered in the second *Critique* as a 'substitute' for a deduction.[82] The 'credential' Kant offers comes from the observation that the supposedly established possibility of transcendental freedom in a negative sense is complemented by the 'positive definition' that the moral law can provide.[83] Kant then goes so far as to say that thereby there is an increase in 'certitude' concerning theoretical reason's 'problematic concepts of freedom', for now the 'empty place' that could not be positively characterized is given a determinable form.[84] Yet however true it may be that the moral law gives us a way to think our freedom more concretely, strictly speaking the idea of the law as such can add only to the content of that thought and not its theoretical certainty. Even if, 'to fill one of its own needs', theoretical reason must assume some transcendental freedom, nothing (theoretical) has been said (in the later writings) to show that this must be met by something noumenal *in us*. Theoretically our freedom and morality still have only a hypothetical validity, and so Kant represents his (late) position most accurately when he simply says he feels the moral law is 'firmly established by itself'[85] and can draw no support at all (not even the slightest increase by probability) from theoretical reason other than the knowledge that freedom implies no 'internal impossibility (contradiction)'.[86] Thus, Kant's statement about an increase in our certainty can be taken only in this way: although it is the theoretical, i.e., absolute, concept of freedom that one becomes certain about when one accepts the '*a priori* fact of reason', the ground of this certainty is still practical, not strictly theoretical.[87]

In saying Kant definitely moved away from an attempt at a deduction I again mean not to commend his move but only to show how it was forced on him once he chose squarely to face both the full consequences of his theoretical philosophy with respect to the self and the implications of his deepest beliefs, his principles of practical philosophy.

Although he could no longer believe he had a theoretical proof of our transcendental freedom close at hand, Kant still chose to reject compatibilism and to hold to the moral philosophy to which he had been committed longer and more intensely than his theoretical system.[88] Without denying the temptation to wish Kant had not taken these moves, my aim here has been to show that we must recognize that in fact he did take them, and that some familiarity with the history of his views can help to make the fact less surprising than most believe.

6. Contrary Interpretations

We can now finally deal directly with the traditonal interpretations that are contrary to ours and that try to reconcile the earlier and later critical texts on morality. First we will deal with a significant minority view, namely L. W. Beck's attempt to reconcile Kant's texts by arguing there is a genuine deduction of morality throughout the critical texts.[89] Generally, instead of contrasting the *Foundations'* ambitious argument for freedom with other discussions, Beck holds that the *Foundations* has the 'same argument' as the 'Review of Schulz' and that it is only 'somewhat different' from that of the second *Critique*, which (latter) supposedly even offers 'more detail on freedom'.[90] In numerous places in his *Commentary* Beck insists there is in effect a strict deduction of morality in the second *Critique*,[91] and that in it an 'independent warrant' for freedom is provided that 'breaks out of the circle' suspected in the *Foundations*.[92]

The 'independent warrant' that Beck finds turns out to be the 'need of theoretical reason' for some 'absolute beginning' outside the natural realm. But as was just noted, even if this need is granted, it hardly shows *we* must be free, and yet only then could the beginning of a deduction from freedom to morality arise. Beck says Kant is arguing 'the vacant place, into which the concept of natural causality cannot enter [apparently to answer the above 'need'] is suited for only one kind of tenant' − the moral law.[93] Yet at no point in the second *Critique* can such a strong argument be found, and in fact there can be no such argument, for there is nothing in the mere idea of transcendental freedom that requires it to be understood in such a particular way. There simply is no unique relation to morality that can be discerned here. Moral freedom can be said to 'fill' the notion of transcendental freedom with appropriate content, but this does not at all show (or even make it theoretically more probable) that transcendental freedom is realized in us, let alone that it could only be so realized.

Furthermore, it should not be forgotten that this section of the *Critique* is not said by Kant to provide a deduction of morality but rather is characterized as speaking only '*Of* the Deduction of the Principles of Pure Practical Reason'.[94] In speaking 'of' a deduction here Kant may mean simply to call attention to a significant possibility that he now thinks we cannot realize. And in fact this appears to be what Kant is doing, for he goes on to claim 'the objective reality of the moral law can be proved through no deduction'.[95] Beck is unwilling to take this text as decisive, and in various places his translation even makes Kant speak less hypothetically about a deduction than he really does.[96]

Perhaps because of an awareness of the tenuousness of his interpretation and a cognizance that this is 'the most obscure part of Kant's ethical theory', Beck attempted a further explanation in an article published shortly after his *Commentary*.[97] This explanation develops a line of thought suggested already in the *Commentary* to the effect that 'in *any* willing there is a principle which is purely rational', and therefore pure reason is practical and the moral law is binding for us.[98] In his original discussion Beck admits this line 'seems to be a rather tricky argument',[99] and in any case it is hardly fully developed. Beck quotes only Kant's statement in the *Foundations*: 'I say that every being that cannot act otherwise than under the Idea of freedom is thereby free in a practical respect'.[100] Then he says, 'But the Idea of freedom is expressed in the moral law; hence to be conscious of moral constraint, i.e., of the law — this is the fact of pure reason — *ipso facto* validates the practical claim of a moral law'.[101] Beck's analysis here is questionable in a number of respects. First, it is notable that he does not directly support his interpretation of the second *Critique* with a passage from the body of that text. Second, the passage he does use does not clearly entail the strong conclusion Beck draws. Third, the passage happens to be one we have already analysed at length, and we made sense of it in terms of an over-all theory of Kant's development that is quite at odds with Beck's.

In his later article Beck tries to develop his interpretation with a lengthy discussion that confesses going beyond Kant's explicit doctrines. Beck's aim, though, is still to present a view which he takes to be the main implicit point of the second *Critique* and which he thinks is an adequate counter to those who would call Kant an intuitionist. Part of Beck's counter rests on his overlooking Kant's admission that his practical philosophy is dogmatic. Beck claims, 'for Kant the metaphysics of the moral law is not Platonic; the moral law is a creation of reason'.[102] If this statement is stripped of metaphor, it seems to come to little more than the disputed assertion that there is a critical theoretical foundation for morality in the later Kant. The remainder of Beck's counter rests on the claim that the moral law is a fact known reflexively and not intuitively.[103] In particular, Beck argues, 'there is, in willing, a principle that is rational, whether the willing be moral or immoral, prudent or foolish. If volition appears to be independent of desires and to be morally unconditional, then there must be an unconditionally rational principle for it.'[104] Beck believes this amounts to a 'presupposition which is at least part of the answer to the external question of ethics', i.e., the general question of why one should accept any morality as valid.[105]

Although Beck's discussion is more extensive here, there are still problems in its move from the mere appearance of a moral claim to the validity of an 'unconditional' principle. For us, however, the main issue is not this but rather what Beck's argument implies for interpreting Kant, and here it still seems clearly vulnerable on at least three key points. First, Beck's newly formulated argument still adds no direct evidence for being taken as a gloss of what the second *Critique* really holds. (The only text he cites in his development of the deduction is again the passage from the *Foundations*.) Second, it is very unlikely that the argument could at all even be accepted by the later Kant, for the strategy of arguing for morality from features present in *all* willing is precisely what Kant rejects in the texts after the *Foundations* (recall the revisions of the first *Critique*). Third, even if one could show all willing presupposes an 'unconditionally rational principle', this would not of itself establish the categorical imperative, and even Beck admits it is only 'part' of the answer to the external question. Hence, even Beck's additional discussion has not been able to show how Kant offered what amounts to a deduction of morality in the second *Critique*. I conclude that although my historical explanation of Kant's rejection of the *Foundations'* deduction is complicated and does not leave him with an intrinsically satisfactory position (given his own general system), the alternative of attempting to reconcile Kant's texts in Beck's way has at least these difficulties and has a much weaker textual grounding.

The other main traditional attempt to reconcile Kant's texts has involved a strategy that is the opposite of Beck's, namely to minimize the theoretical deductive strain of the *Foundations* on the ground that in addition to its intrinsic difficulties it conflicts with the proper tendency of Kant's first two *Critiques*. The advocates of this interpretation could share my analysis (but not evaluation) of the second *Critique* but for important reasons would reject that of the *Foundations*, for they say that there Kant did not seriously assert a need for deduction, and that given his philosophy as a whole he was right. On the first point my attack of this interpretation would rest not only on the key quotation from the *Foundations* (see above, n. 57) but also on all that our analysis has done so far to show how systematically (though admittedly sketchily and probably invalidly) the (third section of the) *Foundations* is developed precisely as a response to the need for a strong theoretical deduction. The strategy of the opposing interpretation is simply to minimize the relevant passages bearing out this point. The motive for this interpretation is tied to its view on the second point, its idea that Kant's eventual declaration of morality as an '*a priori* fact' is proper and unavoidable. This view, and a desire to recast all of Kant's work in what is supposedly its best light, makes the traditional attitude here on the first point more understandable but not more acceptable.

Two versions of this interpretation will be dealt with: the well-known commentary of H. J. Paton and the more recently developed analysis of Dieter Henrich.[106] Henrich's discussion is especially sophisticated in its historical method, and it is difficult to find very much to question in it. Henrich does not deny that in the *Foundations* there is talk of a strict deduction, and he even puts this into a helpful context by comparing it with similar efforts in Kant's pre-critical writings.[107] None the less, Henrich is a reconciliationist in that he still insists that 'in effect' the *Foundations* is to be understood as recognizing that freedom and morality are strictly speaking non-provable 'facts' of reason. Originally, Henrich apparently thought this was so because he falsely believed it was implied by what Kant had to say about our inability to *explain* freedom.[108] More recently, Henrich's interpretation has been backed by a detailed analysis of the *weakness* of the *Foundations'* deduction, emphasizing that 'in effect' the deduction cannot validly reach its conclusion without reference to the experience of binding moral claims.[109] Given our previous analyses, we can now agree with Henrich that Kant's argument in the *Foundations*, even in its final filled-out form, is not adequate as a proof.[110] Yet this is hardly sufficient to show that Kant didn't take his attempt at a deduction in the *Foundations* fully 'seriously', that he didn't believe a non-circular proof of freedom and morality was needed and possible. It is after all Kant himself who raises the question of a circle so as to claim it has been fully resolved. Of course, in hindsight it is admittedly tempting to say Kant still was (at the time) in a way aware of the weakness of his arguments, but the point of our analysis has been precisely to show that we need not fall prey to this temptation. Henrich claims the awareness is implicit in Kant's remark at the end of the *Foundations*[111] that the deduction has been made for those who 'believe' themselves in possession of a will.[112] Henrich feels this remark shows Kant did not really think he was in possession of a categorical theoretical proof of freedom. However, we have shown that although in the first formulation of his deduction Kant gives no grounds for adequately asserting we have a will in the requisite sense, a central point in the rest of his discussion is precisely the insistence that we are beings who do 'find' in ourselves adequate theoretical grounds for making such an assertion.[113]

A similar point must be made against Paton's famous analysis in *The Categorical Imperative*. Although Paton generally prefers to use the *Foundations* as the model for explaining the fundamentals of Kant's entire ethical theory, it is remarkable that with respect to the themes of the last section of the text he suddenly interprets everything from the standpoint of the second *Critique*. Yet rather than simply replace (as Kant did) this section with what is said in that *Critique*, Paton dutifully records the *Foundations'* arguments while constantly insisting one ought not to 'exaggerate the differences' between them and the second *Critique*.[114] Paton can maintain this position only because he labours under the double belief that all the *Foundations* really can try to do is 'defend' freedom, not justify it (i.e., it can only argue there is no contradiction in freedom, that 'dogmatic determinism' is untenable),[115] and that Kant is arguing not that we are free but 'only' that we must act under the idea of freedom.[116] Paton's belief can be countered by our earlier analysis of what Kant meant by a 'merely practical' proof of freedom. Paton sees the relevant point here, namely that we can't explain how freedom works, but he does not see that it is the relevant point, and so he falsely infers that this means one can only defend freedom and not argue that it exists.[117] Paton's view also rests on ignoring the crucial passage from the *Foundations*[118] about the desirability of an argument establishing freedom, and on simply asserting a number of times that Kant couldn't have taken seriously such steps as appealing to a 'proper' and metaphysically primary self. Paton prefers to call this step a 'seemingly' new point and relegates it to an appendix as a mere 'additional' argument.[119]

In the end, Paton believes the justification of the categorical imperative can be and is based solely on a kind of 'direct insight'.[120] The main problem with such a view is not that it turns the moralist as such into something of a dogmatist, for it may well be that the external question of the validity of morality, if it is accepted at all, can be answered only by an appeal to some kind of direct insight. The problem is rather that in Kant's case this answer involves an enormous consequence, a commitment to an instance of transcendental freedom that at one point on his own admission creates great 'perplexity' for his whole theoretical system.

Paton concludes his interpretation by saying that he argued 'above all' that 'Kant's ethics is independent of metaphysics'. Yet he immediately adds, Kant is 'maintaining that there can be no morality, as it is understood, however obscurely, by ordinary men without the supposition of freedom'.[121] By 'freedom' Paton (like other Kantians such as Henrich, Beck, and Silber) means our transcendental freedom, freedom understood in a noncompatibilist way, and therefore he simply cannot get away with the claim that Kant's ethics are independent of a questionable kind of metaphysics that requires justification.[122] As various contemporary ethicists (for example, Marcus Singer in America and Hans Reiner in Germany) have shown, there are still many Kantian insights that can be developed into a moral system without entering into such a metaphysical project, but unfortunately for those like Paton, who profess to trying to take Kant wholly and literally, only wishful thinking stands behind the idea that such a project can be properly avoided. The same can be said, I believe, of the idea that Kant himself could and eventually did succeed in this project. We do the most justice to Kant when we face up to his dogmatism and use his own remarks to help show that it is unacceptable but ultimately historically understandable.

7. Conclusion

Our excursion into Kant's practical philosophy has obvious implications for the general interpretation of Kant's theory of mind. The great reversal in Kant's practical writings on the basic issue of freedom confirms our earlier interpretation to the effect that the Paralogisms section in the *Critique* is caught in a serious and genuine tension between Kant's rationalist inclinations and his own critical emphasis on restricting theoretical claims about the self. It is no wonder then that Kant's original presentation does not present a paralogism dealing clearly with mere substantiality, that it twists his own architectonic to exclude the related and troublesome topic of our independence, and that the second edition of the *Critique* involves an important reorganization of the treatment of these topics.

Another lesson of the excursion into Kant's practical works is that it would be a mistake to think that even Kant's latest critical position is without dogmatic attachments. In the practical sphere these attachments come out in such tendencies as the constant and immediate rejection of compatibilism. In the theoretical philosophy there are similar constant themes. In particular, Kant holds throughout to an immaterialist and idealist conception of the self in itself. Although his position is quite nuanced, the fact remains that Kant's new extra emphasis on the critical limits of self-knowledge still contains a fundamentally rationalistic motive. Although the limits eventually require some retreat from the traditional claims that Kant was still trying to argue for within his earlier critical period, the limitations have the ultimate purpose of preserving a kind of traditional dualistic distinction between the knowable, physical, and merely external world on the one hand, and the transcendent, non-physical, and ultimately significant self on the other hand. In our final chapter we will have to reflect more directly on the most sophisticated Kantian formulation of this position, and on the most challenging criticisms that have been made of it.

Notes

[1] *AA*, Vol. 18, p. 7. The 'Reflections' are found in order of their number in volumes 17–19 of the *AA*, and in the following they will be referred to by 'R' and their number, and not by the volume and page number. Otherwise, the Academy pagination will still be used, but the translations are from *Critique of Practical Reason*, tr. L. W. Beck, and *Foundations of the Metaphysics of Morals*, tr. L. W. Beck (New York, 1959).

[2] Lectures, *AA*, vol. 28, pp. 266, 268–9.

[3] By 'strict deduction' (or 'categorical proof') here I mean a 'linear' argument intended to be logically sound with premises that are all only theoretical as

opposed to practical in any Kantian moral sense. I do not claim that this is generally what Kant must mean by a 'deduction'. (For details on Kant's notion of a 'transcendental deduction' see my 'Kant's Transcendental Deduction as a Regressive Argument', and Dieter Henrich, 'Die Deduktion des Sittengesetzes', in *Denken im Schatten des Nihilismus*, ed. by Alexander Schwan [Darmstadt, 1975].) My main claim is simply that both the need for something at least approximating a strict deduction of freedom and morality, as well as a clear attempt to provide one, can be found in Kant's *Foundations of the Metaphysics of Morals*, whereas in Kant's later work this is definitely not the case.

[4] Lectures, *AA*, vol. 28, pp. 255, 257.

[5] Ibid., p. 255.

[6] Ibid., p. 267, 269.

[7] Ibid., p. 267.

[8] Ibid., p. 268.

[9] Ibid., pp. 268, 270.

[10] Ibid., pp. 267, 268.

[11] Ibid., p. 270.

[12] Ibid., p. 271.

[13] Ibid., p. 267; see B xxcii and the second *Critique*, *AA*, vol. 5, p. 97, or cf. above, e.g., Ch. IV, n. 2.

[14] Cf. A 803/B 831 and 'Review of Schulz', *AA*, vol. 8, p. 13.

[15] Some have taken Kant rather to mean *simply* that practical freedom is sufficient for practical *philosophy* in that the rules it develops can be *exposited* without entering into the issue of transcendental freedom. (See e.g., L. W. Beck, *A Commentary on Kant's Critique of Practical Reason*, p. 190.) However, Kant makes his remarks about sufficiency not in the context of clearly defining branches of philosophy but rather when speaking about what the common man needs in order to proceed properly (see especially the lectures, *AA*, vol. 28, pp. 267, 269; and 'Review of Schulz', *AA*, vol. 8, p. 13), and so a more complex explanation is called for and can be justified.

[16] Lectures, *AA*, vol. 28, pp. 267, 269.

[17] Ibid., pp. 268, 269.

[18] Ibid., p. 267 f.

[19] This is a problem that gives Kant considerable difficulty later. See the second *Critique*, *AA*, vol. 5, pp. 100 ff.

[20] Lectures, *AA*, vol. 28, p. 270.

[21] Ibid., p. 269.

[22] loc. cit.

[23] It should also be noted that the term 'practical freedom' is used with a new meaning here (cf. *Prolegomena*, *AA*, vol. 4, p. 446) which is equivalent not (as in our definition) to a mere comparative freedom, but rather to a specific kind of absolute freedom, namely spontaneity in us as an intelligent agent. This point is distinct from but consistent with our observation that a so-called 'merely practical' proof of freedom in Kant can involve a proof of transcendental freedom.

[24] Here one should keep in mind that often by the proof of the 'possibility' of something Kant means a determination of its 'real possibility', and this may be tantamount to requiring evidence of its actuality. See below, n. 87.

[25] See, e.g., the second *Critique*, *AA*, vol. 5, p. 48.

[26] Only the latter formulation saves the exact formulation of the theses at A 444/B 472, A 445/B 473, but this is not so decisive, for Kant is often careless in such formulations. In the *Prolegomena*, for example, he restates the thesis as the claim that there are free causes in the world, and the antithesis as the claim that there is absolutely no freedom (*AA*, vol. 4, p. 340) — in which case both

Independence 229

statements would be obviously false rather than true, Perhaps Kant wanted to contrast improper dogmatic and proper critical formulations here, but he hardly did this clearly.

27 *Prolegomena, AA*, vol. 4, p. 345.
28 'Review of Schulz', *AA*, vol. 8, p. 13.
29 Ibid., p. 14.
30 loc. cit.
31 Ibid., p. 13.
32 A similar point is made in W. D. Ross, *Kant's Ethical Theory* (Oxford, 1954), p. 73.
33 *Foundations, AA*, vol. 4, p. 448.
34 loc. cit. (amended translation) cf. ibid., pp. 458 ff.
35 Ibid., p. 461.
36 loc cit.; cf. ibid., p. 453.
37 Ibid., p. 447.
38 Ibid.
39 Ibid., p. 448; cf. Lectures, *AA*, vol. 28, p. 268, and 'Review of Schulz', *AA*, vol. 8, p. 13.
40 Cf. Henrich, 'Die Deduktion des Sittengesetzes', p. 67; and Rüdiger Bittner, 'Kausalität als Freiheit und kategorischer Imperativ', *Zeitschrift für philosophische Forschung*, 32 (1978), 270.
41 *Foundations, AA*, vol. 4, pp. 448-9. Cf. ibid., p. 450: 'That we ought to detach ourselves, i.e., regard ourselves as free in acting . . . we still cannot see.'
42 Ibid., p. 449.
43 Ibid., p. 450.
44 H. J. Paton, *The Categorical Imperative* (1947, reprint ed., New York, 1967), p. 225.
45 *Foundations, AA*, vol. 4, p. 450.
46 Ibid., p. 450-3.
47 Ibid., p. 447.
48 Ibid., p. 452.
49 loc. cit.
50 loc. cit.
51 Ibid., p. 457.
52 Ibid., p. 458.
53 Ibid., p. 458. Cf. the second *Critique, AA*, vol. 5, p. 42.
54 *Foundations, AA*, vol. 4, pp. 453-5.
55 Ibid., pp. 457, 461. The background of Kant's notion of an 'intelligible world' is explored in G. Tonelli, 'Kant's Ethics as a Part of Metaphysics: A Possible Newtonian Suggestion, and Some Comments on Kant's *Dreams of a Spirit-Seer*', in *Philosophy and the Civilizing Arts*, ed. by J. Anton and Craig Walton (Athens, Ohio, 1974), pp. 236-263.
56 *Foundations, AA*, vol. 4, p. 451.
57 Ibid., p. 456; my emphasis.
58 See the second *Critique, AA*, vol. 5, pp. 6, 31, 42, 43, 47, 55, 91, 104; Lectures, *AA*, vol. 28, pp. 582, 773; R 7201, R 7321, R 8105; *AA*, vol. 27, p. 48; and for other references, Beck, *Commentary*, p. 116 n.
59 Second *Critique, AA*, vol. 5, p. 31.
60 Ibid., p. 3.
61 Ibid., p. 4 n.
62 Beck, *Commentary*, p. 59.
63 See the second *Critique, AA*, vol. 5, p. 8.
64 Here I also differ with an interpretation that does not carry out a reconcilia-

tionist line, namely Karl-Heinz Ilting's 'Der naturalistische Fehlschluss bei Kant', in *Rehabilitierung der praktischen Philosophie*, vol. 1, ed. by Manfred Riedel (Freiburg, 1972), p. 126. Ilting says Kant gave up the deduction not because he saw it was 'shattered' but because he had no 'need' for it, for he thought he could replace it with a reference to the willingness of people to sacrifice their lives on moral grounds (second *Critique, AA*, vol. 5, p. 30). Ilting puts an implausible weight on this reference, and in any case does not explain why Kant does not make any use of the deduction. As I will show, the historical evidence gives us an answer here by indicating Kant did see his proof was shattered.

[65] Second *Critique, AA*, vol. 5, p. 4 n.

[66] There are also other problems here. Kant argues, 'if I were a member of only that [intelligible] world, all my actions *would* be in accord with the autonomy of the will. But since I intuit myself at the same time as a member of the world of sense, my action *ought* to conform to it' (*Foundations, AA*, vol. 4, p. 454). But a naturalist might say similarly that if he were only a member of the world of sense, all his actions would be in accord with it, and so if 'I intuit myself at the same time as a member of another world', I still ought to do what I 'otherwise' (as a naturalist) always would have done.

[67] Here Jonathan Bennett's *Kant's Dialectic* is typical. At times Bennett reads into some of Kant's ambiguous and early formulations the view that noumenal action would literally interfere in the course of the phenomenal realm (ibid., pp. 199–200). Yet he generally sees this is not Kant's view, and so he objects that freedom (in Kant's system) cannot 'act' on the world (ibid., p. 200; cf. Beck, *Commentary*, p. 192: 'If the possession of noumenal freedom makes a difference to the uniformity of nature, then there is no uniformity. If it does not, then to call it "freedom" is a vain pretension'.) This is not a sound objection, for without any literal intervention surely the noumenal can act on the phenomenal in the sense of being a (timeless) condition of it, in that were the noumenal (e.g., one's character) different, the phenomenal would have been different. (Contrary to Beck then, it is logically possible for there to be complete uniformity to our actions, and yet for us to be absolutely responsible for them. For, were we intelligibly different, we could have grounded another phenomenally uniform character, since obviously there is more than one possible way in which a being could have a 'uniform' phenomenal character. In defending this logical possibility I still, of course, do not mean to say that it, as opposed to a compatibilistic theory, points to a preferable concept of human freedom.) Bennett further complains that Kant's theory does not allow us a 'channel' to 'explain' and assess phenomenal occurrences by reference to the noumenal (*Dialectic*, p. 204), but this is precisely what Kant would regard as a virtue or at least an appropriate aspect of his theory. The consequence is not, as Bennett fears (in citing Beck, *Dialectic*, p. 188), that we must say that my freedom operates 'if anywhere, then everywhere', that it may just as well be thought to be behind my heart's beating or digestion (ibid., pp. 189, 202). Kant simply does not require that our transcendental freedom be omnipotent. Such freedom can lie in an absolute choice with respect to a restricted range of alternatives and hence within the bounds of initial conditions laid down by God and not us. A Kantian can say that the assertion of transcendental freedom (not to 'explain' anything but only to secure a supposedly necessary condition of genuine action) can be made only when (on Kant's later theory) relevant moral phenomena lead us to it, and that at least in our own case (given the validity of morality and Kant's anti-compatibilism) such an assertion is fitting. Of course, as Kant himself notes, the ultimate evaluation of the scope and intention of this freedom can remain in our own case beyond our ken, but this is no excuse for us to withhold ascribing any freedom

or to pretend that the whole notion of transcendental freedom in a lawful world is incoherent. It still can remain certain and consistent within a Kantian framework to say that, to the extent a particular matter is regarded as a moral phenomenon, to that extent one must regard it as founded in absolute freedom.

[68] Second *Critique*, *AA*, vol. 5, p. 29. Cf. ibid., p. 31.

[69] Cf. ibid., p. 43.

[70] See *AA*, vol. 6, pp. 226-7.

[71] See Lectures, *AA*, vol. 28, p. 267, and below, Ch. VII.1.

[72] See above, especially Ch. II.3-5, and A 547/B 575.

[73] *Foundations*, *AA*, vol. 4, p. 452.

[74] A 36/B 53. Cf. *AA*, vol. 10, p. 134. See also below, Ch. VII.7.

[75] Second *Critique*, *AA*, vol. 5, p. 6.

[76] See, e.g., ibid., pp. 13 f., 53 f. Cf. below, Ch. VII.10.

[77] For details on these points, see Michael Washburn, 'Did Kant Have a Theory of Self-Knowledge?' *Archiv für Geschichte der Philosophie*, 58 (1976), 43, and 'The Second Edition of the *Critique*: Towards an Understanding of its Nature and Genesis', *Kant-Studien*, 66 (1975), 277-90. Cf. also above, Ch. III.10.

[78] See *AA*, vol. 20, pp. 297, 305, 309, 311; and Josef Schmucker, *Die Ursprünge der Ethik Kants* (Meisenheim am Glan, 1961), pp. 373-93.

[79] See the second *Critique*, *AA*, vol. 5, pp. 42, 63-6.

[80] Ibid., p. 6. Cf. R 6343.

[81] Cf. Henrich, 'Die Deduktion' p. 97, n. 26, and Henrich, 'Zu Kants Begriff der Philosophie', in *Kritik und Metaphysik*, ed. by Friedrich Kaulbach and Joachim Ritter (Berlin, 1960), p. 53. A typical dogmatic development of Kant's thought can be found in Johann Henrich Abicht's 'Über die Freiheit des Willens' (1789) in *Materialien zu Kants Kritik der praktischen Vernunft*, ed. by Rüdiger Bittner and Konrad Cramer (Frankfurt, 1973), pp. 229-40. A short revealing attempt by Kant to respond to such developments can be found in his 'Von einem neuerdings erhobenen vornehmen Ton in der Philosophie', *AA*, vol. 8, p. 389 ff.

[82] Second *Critique*, *AA*, vol. 5, pp. 47-8.

[83] Ibid., p. 48.

[84] Ibid., p. 49.

[85] Ibid., p. 47.

[86] Ibid., p. 4.

[87] This is my view as to how to understand the statement at ibid., p. 48, 'Denn das moralische Gesetz beweist seine Realität dadurch auch für die Kritik der spekulativen Verstand genugtuend'. Often for Kant the determination of something's 'reality' means not a theoretical proof of its existence but a positive specification of its nature. (Thus without taking existence to be a predicate Kant can speak of different degrees of 'reality', and even Beck can translate *realisieren* as 'give content to', ibid., p. 49.) At the same time it can turn out that a particular specification may amount to what would in one sense satisfy a demand of speculative reason — as in this case when we determine a *concept* of freedom that is the concept of something free in the absolute sense that speculative philosophy supposedly desires (cf. *AA*, vol. 5, p. 3).

[88] Cf. Henrich, 'Der Begriff der sittlichen Einsicht und Kants Lehre vom Faktum der Vernunft', in *Kant: Zur Deutung seiner Theorie von Erkennen und Handeln*, ed. by Gerold Prauss (Cologne, 1973), p. 238, on evidence of the categorical imperative in Kant's notes from 1765. See also Schmucker, *Ursprünge*.

[89] Implicit sympathy for a view like Beck's, to the effect that Kant at least could have developed a successful deduction, is suggested in Gerold Prauss, *Kant und das Problem der Dinge an Sich* (Bonn, 1974), p. 174, n. 106; and Warner

Wick, 'Introduction', in Kant's *The Metaphysical Principles of Virtue*, tr. by James Ellington (New York, 1964), p. xxxiv.
    [90] Beck, *Commentary*, pp. 16, 59 n.
    [91] Ibid., pp. 52, 68–9, 111, 166–67, 172–5.
    [92] Ibid., p. 174. Cf. ibid., p. 167, n. 12.
    [93] Ibid., p. 175. Cf. Henrich, 'Die Deduktion des Sittengesetzes', pp. 73–4, 83, 87. Henrich takes Kant rather to be arguing in both the *Foundations* and the second *Critique* that these considerations show only that our transcendental freedom is not a 'wholly arbitrary assumption' — and that this is enough.
    [94] Second *Critique*, *AA*, vol. 5, p. 41. Beck somehow misses this and, in the same sentence in which he acknowledges Kant 'denies . . . there can be a deduction of the principle of pure practical reason', he adds that Kant says this 'in spite of the title of the section' (*Commentary*, p. 171).
    [95] Second *Critique*, *AA*, vol. 5, p. 47.
    [96] Thus Beck injects a too optimistic tone (about the possibility of a deduction here) by translating 'darf man nicht so gut fortzukommen hoffen' as 'we cannot hope to have *everything* as easy' (second *Critique*, translation, p. 47, line 35 = *AA*, vol. 5, p. 46). And on p. 48, line 11 of the translation, he has Kant speak of 'our deduction' where the German clearly speaks only of 'the moral law'. (Beck's error here goes back to the use of 'it' on line 6 of that page of his translation. The English reader might think — as Beck later clearly does — that here 'deduction' is the referent, but the gender of the German makes clear that 'moral law' must be the referent.)
    [97] Beck, 'The Fact of Reason: An Essay on Justification in Ethics', in *Studies in the Philosophy of Kant* (Indianapolis, 1965), p. 212.
    [98] Beck, *Commentary*, p. 169.
    [99] Ibid.
    [100] *Foundations, AA*, vol. 4, p. 448 n.
    [101] Beck, *Commentary*, p. 169.
    [102] Beck, 'The Fact of Reason', p. 210.
    [103] loc. cit.
    [104] Ibid., p. 211.
    [105] Ibid., p. 208.
    [106] Similar views can be found in Leonard Nelson, *Kritik der praktischen Vernunft*, in *Gesammelte Schriften*, vol. 4 (Hamburg, 1972), p. 44; Gerhard Krüger, *Philosophie und Moral in der Kantischen Kritik*, 2nd edition (Tübingen, 1967), p. 198; and T. C. Williams, *The Concept of the Categorical Imperative* (Oxford, 1968), p. 100.
    [107] D. Henrich, 'Über die Einheit der Subjektivität', *Philosophische Rundschau*, 3 (1955), 41; and Henrich, 'Der Begriff der sittlichen Einsicht', pp. 239–43.
    [108] D. Henrich, 'Das Prinzip der Kantischen Ethik', *Philosophische Rundschau*, 1 (1953), 34. Cf. Henrich, 'Der Begriff der sittlichen Einsicht', p. 253, n. 25.
    [109] 'Die Vernunft erzeugt die Idee sittlicher Freiheit allein in Beziehung auf einen Bezugspunkt, der selber schon die Überzeugung von der Realität der Energie des sittlichen Willens logisch impliziert: Die Deduktion muss notwending auf das Bewusstsein Bezug nehmen, das ein vernünftiges Wesen von seinen Willen hat. . . . Der Begründungsgang der *Grundlegung* bewegt sich somit zwar wirklich in einer "Art von Zirkel" ' (Henrich, 'Die Deduktion des Sittengesetzes', pp. 85–6). 'Da aber dieser zweite Standpunkt in Blick auf eine intelligible Welt kein *zureichender* Grund für die "Anmassung" sein kann, einen Willen zu besitzen, muss fur sie ein weiterer Grund geltend gemacht werden. Kein anderer könnte es sein als das Bewusstsein von Geltungsanspruch des Sittengesetzes' (ibid., p. 93; cf. ibid., pp. 77, 86, 106, and Henrich, 'Das Prinzip der Kantischen Ethik', p. 36).

¹¹⁰ See also Henrich, 'Die Deduktion des Sittengesetzes', pp. 72, 93, 97; Henrich, 'Der Begriff der sittlichen Einsicht', pp. 246-7; Paton, *The Categorical Imperative*, pp. 102, 244; Ilting, 'Der Fehlschluss', p. 124; Nelson, *Schriften*, p. 45; T. C. Williams, *The Concept*, p. 211; Robert Paul Wolff, *The Autonomy of Reason* (New York, 1973), p. 211.

¹¹¹ *Foundations, AA*, vol. 4, p. 459.

¹¹² 'Die Idee der Freiheit gilt für ein Wesen, "das sich eines Willen bewusst zu sein glaubt". Damit ist in einer für den Text der *Grundlegung* eben noch erträglichen Weise eingeräumt, dass das Freiheitsbewusstsein eine Voraussetzung im sittlichen Bewusstsein hat' (Henrich, 'Die Deduktion des Sittengesetzes', p. 93).

¹¹³ *Foundations, AA*, vol. 4, p. 452.

¹¹⁴ Paton, *Categorical Imperative*, pp. 203, 204, 221, 224, 252, 277. In all these pages Paton uses phrases such as Kant 'may seem' or 'does to some extent appear' to attempt a strict deduction. Yet no basis is given in the text for the qualifications. Instead, Paton says 'if Kant really believes' he can make such a deduction, 'he is falling into fundamental error' (ibid., p. 226). The qualifications are thus surely based on Paton's hope to find in Kant what he himself considers to be the most tenable position. It is revealing that Paton says, 'whatever be his [Kant's] view' in the *Foundations* we ought to follow what the second *Critique* says (loc. cit.), for this indicates, I believe, that here Paton is not up to explaining literally Kant's thought in the *Foundations*.

¹¹⁵ Ibid., p. 271: 'All he [Kant] has to show is that there is no theoretical reason why we should not be entitled to act' on the categorical imperative.

¹¹⁶ Ibid., p. 217. Cf. Wolff, *Autonomy*, p. 35; Ross, *Kant's Ethical Theory*, p. 6; A. R. C. Duncan, *Practical Reason and Morality* (Edinburgh, 1957), p. 139; L. W. Beck, 'Translator's Introduction', in Kant, *Foundations of the Metaphysics of Morals*, p. xv.

¹¹⁷ Paton, *Categorical Imperative*, p. 273. A similar error is made in Duncan, *Practical Reason*, p. 55: 'Kant repeatedly insists that freedom cannot be *proved*, that free causality must remain beyond the *comprehension* of the human intellect.' I have added the emphasis to make clear the contrast that Duncan and others have failed to observe adequately.

¹¹⁸ See the passage cited above at footnote 57.

¹¹⁹ Paton, *Categorical Imperative*, pp. 242, 250. Cf. Margot Fleischer's critique of Paton for playing down the latter part of the deduction ('Das Problem der Begründung des kategorischen Imperativs bei Kant', in *Sein and Ethos*, ed. by Paulus Englehardt (Mainz, 1967), p. 387; and 'Die Formeln des kategorischen Imperativs', *Archiv für Geschichte der Philosophie*, 46 (1964), 201, 226), a point on which Henrich (e.g., 'Die Deduktion des Sittengesetzes', p. 90) could also be criticized.

¹²⁰ Paton, *Catogorical Imperative*, p. 247. For a very interesting analysis of the notion of 'ethical insight', see Henrich, 'Der Begriff der sittlichen Einsicht'.

¹²¹ Paton, *Categorical Imperative*, pp. 277-8.

¹²² The desperation of the situation of the Kantians here is indicated by the move made by Beck (*Commentary*, p. 194) and John Silber ('Introduction', in Kant's *Religion Within the Bounds of Reason Alone*, p. ci), namely to deny that determinism (universally and not merely regulatively) applies to the phenomenal realm — a move that is absolutely incompatible with Kant's views at the time under discussion.

Chapter VII

Ideality

So far this study has been organized primarily in terms of Kant's categorial characterization of the soul. It has been noted in passing that this characterization takes on a number of different forms, and that the *Critique*'s explicit structure masks some of Kant's central concerns. To provide some means of completeness for our study, we now will recount more specifically how the structure of Kant's discussion of mind changed over time. This survey will confirm that we already have focused on all but one of the main topics that Kant covered in his theory of mind, namely the claim of the ideality of the self that Kant attaches to his general doctrine of the transcendental structure of our knowledge. The remainder of the chapter accordingly will be devoted to analysing this last topic.

A.1. Introduction: Historical Review of Kant on Rational Psychology

In the last chapter it was pointed out that Kant's earliest schema characterizes the human mind as (a) within the world, (b) simple, (c) free, and (d) contingent.[1] This schema is only one example of Kant's constant effort to place a four part framework on issues, even when, as here in his philosophy of mind, his characterizations never map smoothly onto his four general categorial headings: quantity, quality, relation, and modality. By attending to the peculiarities in the ways Kant reads these headings at different times, as well as to the different contexts in which he places the headings as a whole, one can gain a revealing index of the significant material shifts in his philosophy of mind.

The peculiarities of Kant's first schema are fairly obvious. The only characterization of mind in it that is maintained to the end is the ascription of simplicity. Yet even this ascription loses its importance over time (especially when it is no longer taken to entail immortality), and it never gains a clear relation to its associated category, quality. (This is not a deficiency peculiar to Kant's philosophy of mind. 'Quality' takes on very different meanings in the various parts of his philosophy, and most of these have an especially unclear relation to what Kant takes to be the underlying logical feature of judgment, namely affirmative or negative character.) Both of these points are confirmed by the fact that in its first appearance the claim of simplicity also seems to be doing service for the quantitative determination of the soul, whereas later Kant introduces separate discussions of the specific questions of our numerical identity over time, and of whether the human soul is an absolute unity rather than, as some Scholastics may have thought, a complex including a vegetative and an animal soul.[2]

A more important peculiarity of Kant's first schema is that it squeezes in two (so-called) relational determinations of the soul, namely substance and causality. As is generally the case in Kant's theory of mind, these crucial determinations are not developed very well. The characterization of the soul as intramundane rather than supramundane substance reveals Kant's typical hesitancy to focus directly on the issue of substance as such. The determination of the soul as free in its causality, as well as the extra modal claim that the self is a contingent being, are also problematic and involve claims which transgress the limits Kant's own philosophy ultimately places on theoretical assertions about the self. What is striking here is that *if* Kant had only continued to tie rational psychology directly to such claims, then the Paralogisms' discussion of the soul's categorial determinations could have been easily understood as the evaluation of a dogmatic position which is supposed to appear wholly unfounded. In fact, that discussion has been shown to be hardly this simple, and this is made possible by the very significant fact that Kant chose to replace the original categorial claims with less dogmatic and more ambiguous ones.

The main peculiarity in Kant's later or 'sceptical' period has to do not with any specific categorial list but rather with a shift to a stress on the general limits of rational psychology. These limits are easily drawn here because in this period Kant tends to understand rational psychology simply as the science of spirits, i.e., beings known to be not dependent on bodies, and, more specifically, as the science of their inner constitution. Such knowledge would require a special intuitive power, one which Kant says is 'not yet' given to man.[3]

Kant's focus here on knowledge of 'spirit' is an important anticipation of his later tendency to present his critical position on this issue as if it amounted to a wholesale rejection of rationalism in the theory of mind, whereas in reality it did no such thing. In fact, in his lectures around this time, Kant continued to call the soul 'substance, one, simple, and spirit'.[4] The exact date of these claims is not very clear (see above, Ch. II.2), and in a sense they do not amount to as sharp a contrast with the sceptical writings as one might at first think. The first characterizations are meant largely as limited determinations of the experienced human mind and not as details about the inner nature of a pure spirit. In the last characterization, which does speak of a kind of spirituality, it turns out that Kant was not taking this term in its typical sense but was simply expressing his belief in human freedom, as explained in the last chapter. The lectures further resemble Kant's sceptical writings in that they also place the categorial determination of the soul in a larger context. The doctrine expounded in the lectures is quite similar in structure to Kant's extended treatment of problems of mind in his *Dreams* essay of 1766,[5] as well as to the metaphysics of Baumgarten (see chart below). The original categorial determination of the soul becomes little more than the first part of a rational psychology which is in effect divided into an (1) intrinsic, (2) relational, and (3) comparative and transcendental study of the soul. Two important topics are introduced at the fissures of this division, where Kant provides separate discussions of immateriality and personality.

The format of the *Critique*'s section on the mind represents a synthesis of this developing complex of topics. Kant insists on holding to a fourfold categorial schema and even allows it again to dominate the structure of rational psychology. But he appends to each categorial determination a 'corresponding' predicate. Thus rational psychology is said to involve not only the soul's substantiality, simplicity, personal identity, and distinctness from the physical world, but also its immateriality and spirituality (A 345/B 403). The relational and comparative studies of mind are maintained primarily in the form of insertions about interaction, immortality, and the general nature of the representation of the I (the first topics are emphasized in the first edition, the last one in the second edition). Despite the great significance of these insertions, the categorial characterization of the soul is given overt primacy, and Kant implies this necessitates putting in the question of the external world under the category of modality. We have already developed an explanation of why Kant really was inclined to introduce the epistemological rather than the metaphysical issue of the soul's independence, and of how this move displaces an essential concern (namely freedom) of his theory of mind from the Paralogisms proper (see above, Ch. VI). We have also covered all the intrinsic and relational discussions of mind that do appear in the Paralogisms (see above, Chs. II-V). All that remains is to analyse Kant's treatment of the general peculiarities of human self-knowledge, the transcendental features that make our mind unlike other possible minds.

First, however, some general lessons should be drawn from this review of the organization of Kant's discussions of mind. Although the four determinations of the soul that Kant presents in the *Critique* are also treated elsewhere, none of them can be taken to have one clear categorial meaning even for Kant himself. None the less, the categorial table is not a passing fancy but is rather a persistent interest of Kant's, although in fact his understanding of rational psychology is clearly much broader than any one formulation of the table indicates. To display the considerable continuity in Kant's discussions, despite all the shifts that were indicated, I offer the following juxtaposed outlines of (I) the treatment of rational psychology in the Pölitz lectures and (II) in the Paralogisms, along with (III) an outline of the sequence of topics covered in our own analysis, as well as (IV), a list of the topics in Baumgarten's treatment.

238   *Ideality*

I. The Lectures	II. The *Critique*
The concept of rational psychology and the I	The concept of rational psychology and the I
Intrinsic characterizations: substance, singularity, simplicity spirithood (freedom)	Categorial determinations: substance — immateriality; simplicity — incorruptibility; personality — spirituality; distinctness from the external world
Immateriality	
Comparative determinations: animal, human, and pure spiritual consciousness	Incidental discussions: *commercium* of mind and body (in life); immortality
Personality	(Elsewhere: freedom)
Relational determinations: *Commercium* of mind and body, before, during and after life	

III. This Analysis	IV. Baumgarten
Intrinsic categorial determinations: substance, simplicity immateriality	*natura*
	commercio cum corpore
Relational determinations: interaction, embodiment, external world	*origine*
	immortalite
Personal Identity	*status post mortem*
Immortality	
Freedom	
The concept of rational psychology and the I: comparative and transcendental study of the human mind	*Comparatis animabus non humanis, brutorum spiritibus*

2. Introduction: the Critical Breakthrough

In developing his comparative and transcendental doctrine of the unique nature of the human mind, Kant came to emphasize a new and crucial idea, namely that all our knowledge must involve a combination of inner sense and apperception. With this insistence Kant achieved one of his most important breakthroughs, and in so doing also committed himself to one of his most questionable claims. The breakthrough was the critical rejection of a supposition common to nearly all his modern predecessors, the supposition that self-knowledge is relatively immediate and epistemologically primary. The questionable claim was that in our self-knowledge we have no more theoretical insight into things in themselves than elsewhere, and hence we cannot determine the self in itself.

There are, of course, a number of qualifications that must be added immediately to the claim of a breakthrough. First of all, Kant's move hardly emerges full-blown in the *Critique*. On the contrary, as the last chapter revealed, there is evidence that the passages in the original version of the *Critique* that hold back from the full implications of the critical turn are not accidental but rather reflect deep and even (temporarily) growing commitments on Kant's part. Secondly, the principal means by which Kant makes his critical move are hardly uncontroversial, for the central concepts of 'inner sense' and 'apperception' are extraordinarily difficult to understand, even when compared with other terms in Kant's philosophy. Finally, even if it is allowed that here Kant did point to a kind of breakthrough, and that the basic terms of his doctrine can be defined, there are still important objections to be met from those who have argued that in general the Kantian position on self-knowledge is vitiated by inconsistencies or a kind of idealism that is transparently absurd.

The rest of this chapter will seek to meet these difficulties, and accordingly it will be divided into two main parts. The first part begins by tracing the historical background of Kant's notion of self-awareness up to the point at which the term 'inner sense' is introduced. The ambiguity of this term is noted, three theories of its meaning are distinguished and evaluated in detail, and important distinctions are developed with respect to the key terms 'apperception' and 'affection'. It is concluded that primacy is to be given to a view that takes 'inner sense' in a much less restricted fashion than most interpreters have and that construes it as whatever can be immediately and passively revealed to a reflective self. (Given Kant's idealism, it could also be called that faculty in us which allows there to be such a revelation, but I shall abstract from this meaning and will focus on the nature of the content of inner sense.) It is then argued that although this view is tied by Kant to the notion that we can have only phenomenal knowledge of ourselves, this need not imply, as some have believed, that Kant is committed to a radical claim that in self-awareness we merely fabricate the self.

The remainder of the chapter pursues in more detail the idealistic claim that we can know the self only as phenomenon. Two main types of justification for this general claim — the 'passivity argument' and the 'time argument' — are examined, and the latter is treated as more typically Kantian and more promising, although not fully convincing. The general meaning of Kant's idealism is explained in terms of a doctrine called the 'species theory', but it is also pointed out that Kant may have had other doctrines in mind, and one in particular, the 'essence theory', is given separate attention. Finally, recent general and radical objections to Kant's idealism are surveyed and rejected. The upshot of our analysis will be that even the best of Kant's recent interpreters (e.g., Strawson, Bennett, Wolff, Walker) have much exaggerated the weakness of Kant's doctrine of the ideality of self-knowledge. They have construed Kant's doctrine of transcendental idealism in different ways, but they have all concluded that when it is applied to the self Kant immediately is caught in a wholly untenable position. I will argue that a patient understanding of the development and nature of Kant's doctrine of our ideality can save him from their objections, although this will not establish that Kant's position is ultimately satisfactory. To this extent I will be endorsing only Kant's critical breakthrough, and not the questionable claim of ideality that is appended to it.

B.3. Three Theories of Inner Sense

Before he arrived at the notion of the necessary and unique synthesis of inner sense and apperception in human self-knowledge, Kant's concept of the powers of the mind underwent considerable development. In 1747 his position was formulated in Leibnizian terms:

Now the entire inner condition of the soul is nothing other than the collection of all its representations and concepts, and in so far as this inner condition is directed to what is external it can be called a *status representativus universi*.[6]

This definition does not distinguish the human soul in kind from possible lesser souls. It is consistent with this view that later in his empiricist period Kant remarks:

Man gets all his concepts and representations from impressions, which the universe arouses in his soul through the body. For the clarity of these as well as the capacity to compare and combine them, which is called thought, he is entirely dependent upon the composition of matter.[7]

Here matter is regarded as an essential condition of all aspects of human knowing, and there is as yet no sign of the Kantian doctrine that central to knowledge is a synthesis of data that cannot be given or explained materialistically but must be produced *a priori*.

It may be that Kant could remain comfortable as long as he did with this view because at this time he still felt human uniqueness was obviously preserved by man's status as a free being. The *Nova Dilucidatio* of 1755 is devoted to showing how a thoroughgoing (not merely phenomenal) determinism is compatible with giving man a special place by saying he is still free in that he governs himself on the basis of 'inner' grounds. There are considerable difficulties with Kant's presentation of this position. It is unclear how it proves a difference in kind between man and beast, especially because Kant says that all souls, even those inwardly determined, implicitly reflect and thus react to the whole universe.[8] Kant later strongly rejected his early position, and although he continued to believe it is freedom above all that distinguishes man, he went on to make it a central point in his philosophy that this freedom could not be given a compatibilist interpretation.

By the time of his second period Kant had developed the rudiments of a more sophisticated epistemological ground for differentiating souls. He remarked that although animals are capable of 'physically distinguishing' two items (he uses the example of a dog who regularly takes meat rather than bread), this does not mean that they are capable of 'logically distinguishing' them.[9] Kant understands even the first kind of capacity as involving not only behavior but also inner representations: different behaviour is to be explained as being cued by different conscious representations. He says that although we are aware of only the 'outer acts' of animals, we can ascribe to them some inner awareness, but we cannot go so far as to attribute to them explicit powers of judgment.[10] He does not go into detail about the basis of this claim, but elsewhere he affirms the principle that theoretical postulates are warranted only where they add an explanatory factor unattainable otherwise, and so apparently with respect to animals we are justified in making the first but not the second ascription.[11] What is important here is not this controversial thesis but rather what Kant meant by the capacity he believed distinguishes man. At first he ventured only a hypothesis as to what is implied in ascribing the capacity for making 'logical distinctions':

[If only one could know] what the secret power is whereby judgment is possible. . . . My present opinion inclines toward regarding this power or ability as nothing other than the faculty of inner sense, that is, of making one's own representations the object of one's thoughts.[12]

Kant's hypothesis here is especially significant because it involves the introduction of the term 'inner sense'. Kant's definition of inner sense undergoes considerable revisions over time, and there are a variety of interpretations of its ultimate critical meaning. Kant calls inner sense that form of consciousness which is laid bare when one abstracts from all that is 'outer' in consciousness,[13] but this is a very ambiguous characterization. Such 'outer consciousness' might mean spatial as opposed to non-spatial consciousness, but it could also mean direct as opposed to reflexive consciousness, or the content of our representations as opposed to the acts of representing. Corresponding to these options, I shall distinguish three main theories of inner sense: the *independent stream theory,* the *reflection theory*, and the *act theory.* These theories have never been systematically compared, although the importance of determining exactly what Kant meant by 'inner sense' is surely obvious for any attempt to understand and evaluate Kant's mature theory of self-knowledge. This failure is understandable, however, for as will soon be evident, it is no easy matter to determine Kant's precise meaning here, or to make a case for one theory over the other. Versions of the reflection theory will be discussed first, for it is the one implicit in Kant's original use of the term 'inner sense'.

4. The Reflection Theory and the Independent Stream Theory

The form of the reflection theory that is supported by probably most interpreters holds that inner sense consists in nothing other than reflections on our past acts of consciousness, which themselves must be all (at least originally) directed towards a spatial content. N. Kemp Smith and T. D. Weldon have developed this theory in perhaps the most detail, but it is also implicit in H. J. Paton's belief that outer sense is possible without inner sense but not vice versa.[14] The main backing of this interpretation is Kant's statement that outer sense provides all the material for our knowledge (B 67, B xxix n.). The interpretation also appears to be supported by Kant's remarks that the mind thinks by reference to figures or schemata. He suggests that when we think of abstract entities (e.g., numbers) it is via consideration of non-abstract items such as images (B 16, A 240/B 298), and that these in fact always involve an interaction with our spatial being.[15] Indirect support for the theory is provided by Weldon, who points to the fact that Tetens, whom Kant read closely, held such a theory of inner sense.

The evidence for this version of the reflection theory, which shall be called the *extreme reflection theory* of inner sense, can be challenged. Kant's statement that outer sense provides all the material for our knowledge could be understood as primarily a claim not about 'material' but about 'knowledge', and about it in a strict sense. It may be that all our determining empirical judgments about concrete objects (see B 147) require reference to spatial items (B 243), but this by itself does not mean that no acts of mind can take place without reference to such concrete objects or that Kant must have believed so. It is notable that Kant says only that it may be that without spatial items our inner sense would not continue.[16] What he means is that this capacity of our mind might depend, in some unknown metaphysical way, on spatial objects, or, more precisely, on the ultimate substrata of such objects.[17] If Kant had held the extreme reflection theory he should have said that without spatial items obviously there would be no inner sense, for then there could be no content for reflection. Also against the theory is Kant's belief that we might have an afterlife with a kind of inner sense although we then would not have or be aware of a body.[18]

Kant's first reference to inner sense does not restrict it to reflection on spatial consciousness, but it does hypothesize that such reflection depends on a capacity which is equivalent to the power of judgment. This thesis defines what shall be called the *cognitive reflection theory* of inner sense, and it too seems unduly restrictive. It is true that Kant does argue for a tight connection between reflection and judgment in one direction by claiming that a being cannot be credited with understanding unless it can reflect upon itself. Kant's argument is that genuine understanding, as opposed to mere association of images, involves a recognition of rules, and that only beings who can reflect on representations can appreciate rules.[19] Yet even if this argument is allowed to stand, no reason is given to accept a connection in the other direction, that is, that the capacity for reflection entails a capacity for judgment. Various interpreters have in effect ascribed such a belief to Kant. For example, Ewing and Paton say that for Kant there cannot occur unsynthesized internal impressions.[20] On this theory, all internal impressions are reflected upon and thereby synthesized in judgment. R. P. Wollf has recently formulated and endorsed the interpretation (and combined it with the extreme reflection theory) in these terms:

The self becomes conscious of itself and gains knowledge of itself by seeking out and bringing to self-consciousness its own contents. Now these contents are spatial perceptions, and the act of bringing them to consciousness is simply the act of synthesizing them.[21]

The evidence for this version of the reflection theory can also be challenged. Smith seems to believe that without implicit commitment to the theory Kant could not maintain his idealism.[22] He says that if Kant were to allow 'immediate consciousness' (i.e., unmediated by apperception), this would be to admit that the self is knowable in itself and not merely as a phenomenon. But surely there could be a consciousness of self which precisely by being immediate would not be cognitive (e.g., religious feeling), and so it would yield no knowledge in conflict with the doctrine of transcendental idealism.

Ewing ties the cognitive reflection theory to Kant's claim that animals don't have understanding. They supposedly lack understanding simply because they have no capacity for reflection.[23] This is of course what Kant is saying in his first discussion of inner sense (cited above, but not by Ewing), but it is easy to see that discussion as not representative of his ultimate teaching. Kant's primary claim about animals is that they have 'bare intuitions' and so are incapable of judgment or discursive consciousness.[24] He says that although they may even have a capacity to reproduce mental contents, this would not involve any self-conscious synthesis but would be done automatically according to laws of association.[25] He can use this point alone as sufficient to distinguish between men and animals, without getting involved in the claim that the latter must be incapable of all reflection.[26]

It is the unique capacity for judgment that Kant is pointing toward in his systematic differentiation of souls:

All thinking being has three dimensions:
1) representation, e.g., the monads of Leibniz;
2) representation and feeling, and thus desire and action but nothing more: . . .

3) consciousness of the entire condition of representations and feelings. Man is the only being we know with these three capacities, and we cannot think of more.[27]

Here Kant means to be criticizing an earlier (and Wolffian) view that judgment (in contrast to sensation) involves merely a clearer mode of representation rather than an irreducibly distinct kind of act.[28] Kant frequently expresses criticism of the general Wolffian strategy of attempting to understand things in terms of one fundamental power or *Grundkraft*. He argues that matter has a plurality of irreducible powers (attraction and repulsion) and so also may mind.[29] As Heimsoeth and Henrich have pointed out,[30] Kant was here following Crusius and others who had attacked the Wolffian project — but he was also going beyond them. The doctrine of the uniquely human and distinct power of judgement is the root not only of the notion that the reduction of various powers of the mind to one must remain but a 'regulative idea' (A 634/B 712), but also of the Paralogisms' restrictions on knowledge of the self, and of the basic critical distinction between sensible and conceptual representations.[31]

One reason for rejecting the cognitive reflection theory of inner sense is thus that, contrary to what some have thought, Kant did not need it in order to hold to his idealism or the doctrine that (mere) animals have a different kind of mind than men. However, the main reason for rejecting the theory is that Kant eventually distinguished inner sense from apperception in a way that obviously allows the possibility of reflection without cognition. He defines apperception as the conceptual determination of the intuitions of the self provided through inner sense (B 154). There is no evident logical necessity prohibiting bringing such intuitions to consciousness without simultaneously synthesizing them in cognition. The latter consciousness in turn should be distinguished from the fully developed self-consciousness that is had when, instead of merely judging a particular inner state, one rather synthesizes broad stretches of experience so as to come to a concept of the concrete situation and character of the self. Kant generally does not stress this latter distinction (as in the passage cited above at n. 27), but he seems to be drawing attention to something like it eventually in differentiating what he calls 'noting' and 'observing' oneself.[32]

An express emphasis on the distinction between mere reflection and cognition can be found in a late manuscript that develops the argument that 'the [mere] consciousness of having a thought' is by itself 'no experience', for 'experience' is 'judgement that expresses empirical cognition'.[33] This is an important distinction, and we will employ it not only in (a) differentiating inner sense and apperception, and (b) distinguishing animal and human consciousness, but also (c) to distinguish two senses of 'affection' (see below, Ch. VII.4), and (d) to distinguish two senses of 'experience' and thus two ways of reading the premiss of the transcendental deduction (namely as asking for necessary conditions of empirical knowledge as opposed to conditions of lesser awareness; see below, n. 70). Implicitly, the distinction has already been used (e) to distinguish two ways of reading the Refutation of Idealism (namely as asking for conditions of self-knowledge as opposed to lesser kinds of self-awareness; see above, Ch. IV, nn. 66 and 74), and (f) to distinguish two senses of personal identity (see above, Ch. V.9).

In the lectures of the 1770s Kant uses a similar distinction in a way that suggests a reflection theory of inner sense unencumbered by the specific weaknesses of the extreme and cognitive versions. Kant distinguishes between the straightforward 'logical consciousness' involved in such acts as counting, and the reflexive 'psychological consciousness' involved in focusing on acts of counting.[34] Although he doesn't expressly call the latter inner sense, he may well have understood it as such at the time, for he calls it 'consciousness of self' as opposed to 'consciousness of objects'. There are still difficulties, however, in allowing inner sense to be immediately identified with reflection in even such a minimal sense. Given Kant's language in his distinction between inner sense and apperception (B 154), it seems clear that he wants inner sense to be understood not as the active consciousness reflecting on or judging the self but rather as the conveyer of the data of the self which are thus acted upon.

This point suggests that the reflection theory might be

presented in a further weakened version in which inner sense would be identified not with acts of reflection but with what is directly revealed when reflection is carried out. Inner sense could then be described as the material (here it need not be decided whether it is physical or psychic stuff) provided for and acted on by reflective thought. There is a difficulty with even this version, however, for it seems to entail that man has an inner sense only when he reflects upon himself. This is in tension with Kant's basic doctrine that all representations belong to inner sense (A 34/B 51; A 155/B 194; B 220). The tension might be lessened in either of two ways. First, one could adjust further the definition of inner sense so that it becomes identified not with only what is actually reflected upon but instead with whatever can be (directly) reflected upon (this shall be called the *weak reflection theory*). On the other hand, one could argue that implicitly all consciousness is simultaneously reflective, and so there need be no worry about inner sense being treated as merely an occasional occurrence.

The first of these alternatives is the more appealing and eventually will be defended at length, but it should be noted that there may be some ground for seeing Kant as committed to the latter and stronger claim. At a crucial point in the transcendental deduction he argues that all our perception, simply by its being in one spatio-temporal framework, must be in effect subject to a comprehensive unification by the intellect and hence to apperception and reflection (B 160 n.).[35] It is not clear, however, that such apperception would have to involve reflection in the sense of constant self-consciousness. Although the capacity for apperception may require a capacity for reflecting on one's representations, it would seem that particular unifying apperceptions, e.g., judgements about external things, might take place without reflection on the self. In any case, Kant does not expressly argue (as a clear substantiation of this interpretation would need) that inner sense arises only on reflection but is *none the less* not merely occasional, and at times he does seem to concede that inner sense need not be thought of as taking place only when there is actual apperception. He speaks of children, for example, as going through a period in which they have not yet attained a capacity for apperception (though they are obviously enjoying temporal awareness), and it seems only proper to leave room for such childlike phases in adult life.[36]

These considerations further support development of the weak version of the reflection theory, but first the other interpretations deserve to be explained. Unlike some notions of inner sense studied, so far, the second or 'independent stream' theory[37] has the means for readily allowing a very frequent occurrence of inner sense. Here the term 'inner' is taken more literally and inner sense is equated with all consciousness of items that are non-spatial. It certainly appears to be this understanding of 'inner sense' that is behind Kant's remarks that pure spiritual beings would exist with only an inner sense,[38] and that we would be using inner sense if we were directly conscious of God[39] or of other spiritual beings as such.[40] The independent stream theory would further ascribe to inner sense consciousness of abstract items, as well as immediate consciousness of feelings and inclinations, and acts of reflection of one's perceptual states. Kant's pre-critical suggestion that philosophical knowledge can be gained via 'certain inner experience'[41] could be seen as a reference to another facet of inner sense on this theory. In direct contrast to the extreme reflection theory, this theory holds that there are two separate streams of consciousness, one presenting spatial contents and one presenting contents which may have no direct reference to spatial characteristics. Here the theory (which is supported primarily by texts prior to the *Critique*) generates new difficulties though, for in construing inner sense sheerly in contrast to spatial sense it reveals no positive common bond characterizing the inner as such, that is, nothing clearly tying it to self-consciousness.

At this point the main difficulties of the first two theories of inner sense can be summarized. The reflection theory entails that all and only reflective consciousness is inner sense. The 'all' claim, combined with the cognitive version of the theory, goes against Kant's basic doctrine that apperception is to be distinguished from inner sense, and it thereby requires the theory at least to be weakened to identifying inner sense with reflected and not reflecting consciousness. The 'only' claim goes against Kant's equally basic doctrine that all representations belong to inner sense — *unless* the theory is finally weakened to be only a claim about what is possibly reflected upon. The corresponding 'all' claim of the independent stream theory conflicts with the tie Kant obviously wants to make between inner sense and self-consciousness. The corresponding 'only' claim of this theory is defeated by the fact that it can in no way do justice to Kant's doctrine that all representations belong to inner sense. This last weakness is easily overlooked because it is tempting to see inner and outer senses as exclusive domains, especially if the former is understood as consciousness of self and the latter as consciousness of what is not self.[42] But this goes directly against what Kant says (see again A 34/B 51), and it makes mysterious the fact that he globally contrasts transcendental apperception merely with inner sense.

5. The Act Theory

With these difficulties in mind we can begin to evaluate the third or act theory of inner sense. On this theory something is said to belong to inner sense whenever it is spoken of as a representing as opposed to a represented. Inner sense is thus conceived of not as a separate set of occurrences of consciousness but as a constant aspect of it. This way of looking at inner sense has not been developed much in the literature, but it is suggested in a remark by Jonathan Bennett that the inner aspect of inner sense should not be thought of as primarily having to do with what the sense is of or about.[43] Rather, a representation's being inner has to do simply with its (possibly) belonging to someone's psychic history or stream of consciousness. On this theory it is easy to see that there is no danger of turning inner sense into a mere occasional occurrence, and it is also easy to see how Kant can say that all our representations, as belonging to inner sense, are temporal. Moreover, the act theorist can agree with the reflection theorist that inner sense adds no new content to consciousness, and he can do this without having to deny the independent stream theorist's belief that there can be non-spatial contents of consciousness. At the same time the act theory has a response to the difficulty the liberal independent stream theory ran into when it permitted many representations to be assigned to inner sense which did not have a relation to self-consciousness. On the act theory all that is ascribed to inner sense has a relation to self-consciousness in that it is always the case that, no matter what the content of one's representations, these representations, *qua* representing, do belong to one's self. Inner sense can be said to involve self-consciousness, in the sense of constituting one's consciousness, without its necessarily involving awareness of a self as a distinct item. The theory thus fits well with Kant's remark that inner sense 'yields no intuition of the self itself as an object' (A 22/B 37), as well as his description of inner sense as a 'modification of the mind' (A 98), and his characterization of apperception's turning to inner sense as a matter of 'seeking out that which lies in the mind' and is a 'manifold which is antecedently given in the subject' (B 68). This theory also can explain Kant's frequent characterization of inner sense as but a 'shapeless flux'.

Despite this kind of support there are objections to the act theory. One text that at first might be cited against the theory is Kant's remark in his lectures that animals entirely lack an inner sense.[44] On the act theory it would follow that to the extent that animals have conscious representations – and Kant is quite steadfast in his belief that they do – they would have to be spoken of as having an inner sense. Here it simply must be admitted that the remark does not support the act theory, but like others from Kant's early lectures it is not decisive because it comes before his mature differentiation of apperception and inner sense. In saying animals lack 'inner sense' Kant probably meant only that they lacked the judgmental capacity that he later designated as apperception. As has been noted, this would be sufficient for him to make the distinction he wants between mere animals and men.

A better and, I believe, persuasive objection to fully accepting the act theory is that it still does not explain to the reflection theorist's satisfaction Kant's frequent mature remarks about inner sense being what is disclosed upon reflective affection of the mind. Of course, the act theorist can also say that inner sense is what is revealed upon affection, for in reflecting upon experience what we become aware of as such is precisely our experiencing. The act theorist can further note that his account of inner sense is superior to those versions of the reflection theory that make it either a merely occasional event or, absurdly, require that we are in a state of constant reflection. But ultimately the weak reflection theorist has the option of saying that inner sense is simply whatever may be the direct object of reflection. In that way all of our experience can belong to inner sense, and at the same time inner sense can be understood as involving not merely consciousness had by a self but consciousness which is of a self. Given the obvious traditional link between inner sense and introspection, as well as Kant's own remarks, it seems only proper to define inner sense in terms of some relation to reflection — and the weak version of the theory makes this possible. Moreover, it can still be granted (to adherents of stronger versions of the theory) that generally when speaking of inner sense Kant understands it to be the object of actual cognitive reflection. Given that self-consciousness is cognitively significant only when there is actual apperceptive reflection, it is natural that Kant would emphasize such events and that it might appear that such reflection is essential to inner sense.

6. Affection

The weak version of the reflection theory attempts to do justice to the relation to affection or possible reflective stimulation that Kant sees as essential to inner sense, while at the same time not taking that affection to be either a constant or rare occurrence with a too limited (as in the extreme reflection theory) or too unlimited (as in the independent stream theory) range of content. The theory also does not require understanding affection as a metaphysically creative event. This is important because on at least some versions of the cognitive reflection theory the mind, in its apperceptive affection of itself, is thought to be responsible for bringing inner sense to consciousness and thereby for first giving it a temporal character. In Wolff's words, 'the result of the affection is to set the self-awareness of the spatial manifold in a temporal order. That order is the *subjective* order of the empirical consciousness of outer objects'.[45] This seems to conflict with Kant's theory in the Analytic of the *Critique* that apperception, through the categories, synthesizes and determines a non-objective but already temporal manifold. Wolff's response is to charge Kant with inconsistency and with having a theory that 'tends to slip toward the idealist doctrine that the self spins the world, *in toto*, out of itself'.[46]

If we drop the cognitive version of the reflection theory, we need not charge Kant with inconsistency or extreme idealism, for we can say apperception gives inner sense only its cognitive, objective temporal form. *Qua* representings capable of being reflected upon by us, representations belong to inner sense and as such can be already temporal. But only upon apperception do we genuinely cognize their temporality as such, and then upon further comparative reflection we can assign a temporal order to our acts of representing which fits a general objective picture of events.[47] This explanation is alone consistent with the distinction Kant makes between inner sense and apperception as a contrast between intuitive and conceptual capacities. If apperception were itself entirely responsible for giving temporality to consciousness, there would be no way to explain the fact that Kant calls time an intuition. He describes intuition as that which precedes all thought (B 132), and as he describes time as the form of inner sense, we can presume that inner sense, precisely as temporal (though indeterminately so), 'precedes' apperception (as an actual, conceptually determinative process).

Even if it is admitted that the affection that brings about self-consciousness is not to be understood as a kind of creative generation, it is not yet clear how that affection is to be understood positively. Here, just as we have generally distinguished the capacity for reflection and that for apperception, it is helpful specifically to distinguish at least two senses of affection, a reflective and an apperceptive one. Kant says that to know oneself one 'must affect the mind and only in this way can it give rise to an intuition of itself'

(B 68). This statement can be taken as indicating a complex of activities. Within this complex, a first aspect can be distinguished, namely affection in a first sense, which brings one's representings to explicit consciousness (B 68, B 64, B 153, B 157) but in so doing need not bring them to knowledge. This 'reflective affection' generates (or spotlights) an intuition (of the self's state) or sequence of them; it does not thereby synthesize them to bring them under a concept. This latter work is done by what may be called 'apperceptive affection' or what Kant calls 'pure apperception': He therefore says that prior to apperception there may be 'no determinate intuition of the self' (B 154) — not that there may be no intuition at all.

Because Kant also calls this conceptual work of apperception, this judgmental determination of inner sense, 'affection' (B 154, B 155),[48] and he does not bother clearly to distinguish reflection from apperception, it is very easy to pass over or misunderstand the first, mere reflective sense of 'affection'. Perhaps Kant prefers the term 'apperception' because it especially connotes spontaneity, and in both cases of affection a spontaneous capacity of mind is exhibited — in the first case, in the power of directing oneself to one's thoughts, and in the second case in that of determining them. However, in dwelling upon 'affection' in his theory of self-consciousness, I believe Kant ultimately wants to emphasize precisely its implications of passivity rather than spontaneity,[49] for he sees it as a limitation on our part that we know ourselves only as affected. This implies what he calls the seeming contradiction that we are in a passive relation to ourselves (B 153). We are passive here because, first of all, when reflection provokes one of our representings into consciousness so that we become self-conscious, that which reflection acts on must be our own mind. Our mind thus suffers the activity or affection of reflection. But this affection reveals our passivity in at least two more fundamental ways.[50] These ways are brought out in Kant's contrast of our self-knowledge with the active kind an 'intuitive intelligence' may have. Unlike such an intelligence,[51] to know ourselves we require given data, that is, contents of experience which are not self-created; and, secondly, (here the specifically apperceptive or judgmental aspect of affection becomes central) we must be not only in intuitive contact with these data but must undertake a special act of synthesis in order to know them (B 68).[52] Here Kant already has moved beyond prior empiricist and rationalist accounts.

The two points about affection that Kant makes here correspond to his belief in a twofold structure of self-knowledge involving inner sense and apperception, and they reinforce the interpretation of inner sense as being a manifold given independently of actual apperception. Nothing in Kant's text requires us to assume that the affection of ourselves in self-knowledge involves a generation of matters *'in toto'* in the extreme idealistic way that Wolff suggested. This interpretation is understandable, though, in view of the different senses that Kant has for the term 'affection', and especially in view of the very different meaning he gives it in other contexts. When Kant speaks of our being affected through outer sense, he does imply that the very material of such (outer) representations is generated by what does the affecting, and yet for the reasons just given this cannot be what he means by the term in the context of self-consciousness.

C.7. Interpretations of Transcendental Idealism: the Passivity Argument

Although the doctrine that we know ourselves only as we inwardly affect ourselves need not be taken to have an extreme idealistic meaning, there can be no doubt that it is meant to have an idealistic significance of some kind. In particular, the doctrine obviously is connected to Kant's thesis that we can know ourselves only as phenomena. In presenting this aspect of his transcendental idealism Kant appears to employ various different justifications which, to begin with, can be divided into what shall be called the *passivity argument* and the *time argument*. The former was already discussed briefly in the last chapter. The latter appears in a variety of versions involving what will be termed the *epistemological*, the *relational*, and the *flux arguments*. To determine the meaning of Kant's specific doctrine of the transcendental ideality of self-knowledge, we will examine these arguments in turn and place them within the context of his general doctrine that we can know only phenomena. This general doctrine of transcendental idealism will itself be interpreted in terms of what will be called the *species theory*.

The claim of the passivity argument is that I know something only as phenomenon when I can know it only through representations that affect me. Traditionally, the argument is extended by claiming that to know of something only through representations that affect one is to be aware of it not directly but only through its effects, and the effects may always in some indiscernable way fail to reflect the thing in itself. Precisely because of this extension, the prime advocates of the argument, those who held a representationalist theory of perception, generally excluded it from applying to the self. The notion that captivates the representationalist, namely the notion of the representations being securely held and directly intuited in the mind while what is represented remains outside the mind, never directly accessible, is a notion that can provoke the feeling that what is within is absolutely certain whereas what is without can never be really known. This feeling involves a conflation whereby the indisputable internality of representations, *qua* acts, becomes elevated into an indisputable and self-sufficient cognitive access to the internal in the sense of one's intrinsic nature as a self. Here Kant's general epistemology and his Refutation of Idealism do a valuable service by countering that merely having a representation in one's self (and thereby being in an admittedly more than merely causal relation to it) hardly amounts to having knowledge of the self, for the latter requires some reference to other items that can provide means for an objective determination of one's situation (see above Ch. III.10). In particular, Kant would find these representationalists guilty of violating the distinction of inner sense and apperception (B 153), that is, of forgetting that the first or possessive aspect of consciousness is but a part of what is needed for knowledge.

The representationalists felt that in self-consciousness at least the key condition they held necessary for knowledge, namely immediacy, was satisfied. They did not reflect adequately on whether sufficient conditions were thereby met. Conversely, it may appear that Kant did not reflect enough on whether passivity is not only a necessary (if that) but also a sufficient condition for being restricted to knowing only phenomena. That is, Kant rejected not only the representationalist view of what is sufficient for self-knowledge, but also the general view that we can have knowledge at least of the self in itself, and at first it would seem he did so merely by returning to the original passivity argument. He not only emphasized that in self-knowledge, as in knowledge of what is outside the self, we are affected, but he also seemed to suggest that we know ourselves only as phenomena precisely because we intuit ourselves 'only as affected' (B 68, B 153). As thus stated, the argument obviously could also amount to an argument for transcendental idealism in general. It would merit a special place in a discussion of mind only as a challenge to those who might think knowledge of the self presents an exception to the broader thesis. Kant seems to believe the most natural way this challenge would be mounted would be not by an empiricist representationalist but by someone who holds that we can gain direct cognition of the self by a kind of non-sensible intuition (or pure act of apperception). Although such a challenge is hardly to be expected today, it was a real concern for Kant, and, as we now know, he was for a while quite sympathetic to its main idea,[53] as were probably most philosophers in the rationalist environment of his era. Here again Kant's eventual distinction between inner sense and apperception is vital, for it implies that our self-consciousness involves passivity and that whatever active aspects of consciousness we have are not by themselves cognitive.

Despite these considerations, the passivity argument alone is obviously too weak and cannot be taken to be Kant's prime ground for holding to the transcendental ideality of our self-knowledge. Kant's use of 'affection' in the context of self-knowledge has just been analysed, and none of the meanings disclosed so far are such as to justify concluding we can know ourselves only as phenomena. The fact that we do not generate our own experiences and do not by intuition alone know them may help in the fight against dogmatism, but it does not establish idealism. It would have to be shown that our mere passivity rules out any view whereby the intrinsic nature of what is represented could be properly determined. That is, because Kant's view is not merely that we are uncertain about what is more than phenomenal, but is rather that we cannot (theoretically) know it, it would have to be proven that our passivity makes impossible a corrected or even accidentally adequate representation of what is in itself. Such a proof is difficult to imagine, for Kant cannot be held to the Berkeleyan view that representations, as ideas, cannot ever be taken as causally reflecting and in some way resembling objects. Kant does not argue in this way and rather remarks, 'If the representation contains merely the way in which the subject is affected by the object, it is easy to understand how it corresponds to the object.'[54] Moreover, whether or not Kant thought that in general a representationalist view requires that we can know only phenomena or the direct objects of perception and not things themselves, he could have agreed that in self-knowledge we aren't dealing with something that has to be a mere effect and numerically distinct from the object, as may be the case in outer perception. So the argument that we cannot know things in themselves because we are in contact only with their effects is in general a suspicious inference and apparently not one Kant believed in, and in any case it seems inapplicable to self-knowledge. But without such an argument the route from the remarks about affection to the ideality of self-knowledge is hard to explain in any traditional terms. It presents, as Kant himself says, 'the greatest difficulty'.[55]

There is another sense of 'affection', not previously discussed, which might seem relevant here because in using it Kant does argue for essential limitations in our self-knowledge. He employs, as an example of the affection that takes place in self-consciousness, the modification of the self that attention can evidently bring about (B. 158 n.). In this sense we are 'affected' in self-knowledge not only because we are dependent on given data and having to combine them, but also because we always may disturb that which we are seeking to know. But although Kant did not mean to minimize this aspect of 'affection', he used it only to suggest the impossibility of a science of self-knowledge, not to show we can never at all know the self in itself.[56]

The apparent sympathy in the *Critique* for the passivity argument thus remains in need of explanation. Earlier we noted that the argument has some point, even if it lacks validity, in the context of Kant's discussion of freedom, and so it is not a mere slip but is repeated in the *Foundations of the Metaphysics of Morals*. But this explanation cannot cover the brief suggestions of the argument that continue in the second edition. To handle this problem I will argue eventually that if the argument is supplemented by many other considerations, then there is a sense in which the statement that we know ourselves 'only as affected' can be seen to imply (for Kant) the ideality of the self (see below at n. 89). But for now it should be reiterated that we must reject the idea that the passivity argument alone can justify this implication. Not only is the argument too weak, but it is also clear that Kant could not have taken it to be adequate. In his early work he did claim that we know ourselves most truly as free and active beings, and this might lead to the idea that to know the self passively or as passive is not to know the true self.[57] But there is no reason to ascribe this odd inference to Kant in his ultimate critical theory, especially after his rejection of the idea that our freedom can give us theoretical knowledge of ourselves.

Perhaps the best way to show Kant could not have taken the bare passivity argument to be adequate is to note again that it is not restricted to knowledge of the self, and therefore if it is to be the key to the way Kant argued for the transcendental ideality of our knowledge it should also function in his general argument for that ideality. But it does not do this, for in characterizing his transcendental idealism Kant is quite clear that the ideality he argues for does not rest on the mere passivity and variability of our representations (A 30/B 45, A36/B 53). If it did, he obviously would not have needed to go into the special arguments that he introduces for ideality. The whole complex discussion of *a priori* intuitions and synthetic *a priori* knowledge would be unnecessary, and yet it is clearly around such knowledge that Kant's general argument for ideality — which will be called the *epistemological argument* because it posits ideality as an explanation of the possibility of synthetic *a priori* knowledge — revolves. If all this is granted though, it becomes hard to see what the basis for the ideality claim that concerns us could be, for Kant indicates that with respect to the self he does not believe there is a proper body of *a priori* knowledge. Fortunately, however, these last points need not defeat or make incongruous Kant's specific doctrine of the ideality of self-knowledge. To make the doctrine comprehensible, it need only be shown that Kant argues such knowledge is relevantly dependent upon something that (he believes he can show) is merely phenomenal, and that he argues this on the basis of considerations at least like those of the epistemological argument. This is what it appears Kant tries to do in various versions of the time argument.

8. The Time Argument

The time argument for our ideality involves two main steps. First, it is held that all our concrete knowledge of the self involves knowledge of its temporal characteristics,[58] and then it is argued, in accord with the general doctrine of transcendental idealism, that all such characteristics are merely phenomenal. It is the first point that receives special attention in Kant's specific discussion of the self, and it explains the emphasis he puts on the notions of inner sense and apperception. First, he presumes that inner sense and apperception are the only means we have for gaining cognition of the self. Then he claims that the data of inner sense are the only ones we have to go on for (theoretical) self-knowledge, and that they are all temporal. Finally, apperception is characterized as being for us only the conceptual complement to the intuition provided through inner sense, as being a mere faculty for synthesizing temporal representations (B 158-9). From all this it is to be concluded that for us there can be no non-temporal self-knowledge.

Kant's argument can be disputed, for it has to be shown that even if all our consciousness is temporal (something which in his view isn't necessarily true for all consciousness, nor even for our own in itself),[59] we cannot abstract from this feature so as to know ourselves intrinsically and independently of time. Fortunately, Kant filled out his Paralogisms with a detailed critique of the main way this abstraction has been attempted, namely through a metaphysical and categorial determination of the soul. However, there remains an obvious and classical objection to Kant here, namely first-person present tense psychological statements. In saying, 'I feel depressed', for example, it would seem that one can know something about oneself that is certain and even transcendentally valid, no matter what Kant may be able to prove about rational psychology and the phenomenality of time.

Kant is not at a loss for a reply here. He would emphasize that such statements are cognitive only to the extent that they are determinate and are uttered by a being who can employ with some justification the concepts that provide determinateness. He would add, of course, that one does not come justifiably to use a concept simply by having a feeling, for mere intuitions are 'blind'. How then does one come to have a concept of something like depression or pain? Kant unfortunately says little positively and directly about the acquisition of any empirical concepts,[60] let alone psychological ones, but if pressed he no doubt would have said that for us it would have to involve acquiring the ability to use a term in a variety of contexts (A 68/B 93). Here what needs to be claimed is not that this ability can arise only through the teachings of a public language, but merely that some compared and comprehended multiplicity of experience is needed, and so for us some temporal self-consciousness is required to say properly even what inner state one is in now.[61]

Furthermore, for Kant not only would the attainment of the concept of pain or depression involve temporal self-consciousness, but the concept itself would involve facts of the spatio-temporal world. In so far as pain (or depression) designates an occurrence or process and is not regarded as a mere emotional stance or behavioural capacity, the most consistent line for Kant to take is that what it designates is an ordinary physical process, and so for him knowledge of it would be knowledge of the spatio-temporal and phenomenal realm.[62] There may be difficulties here, as in general (see above, Ch. III.10) with Kant's idea that for us knowledge of anything temporal must involve knowledge of something spatial, but these would not save the claim that first-person present tense psychological statements may be exempt from Kant's idealism merely by being not expressly temporal. Of course, one could still argue that when one has a feeling the knowledge one attains about oneself is not so much about a bodily process but is rather simply that one seems to have a mental episode of a certain kind. But even the mere belief that one has such a mental episode is empty unless something is said about the kind of episode it is or about its place in one's history, and both these considerations play into Kant's hands.

Roderick Chisholm has recently tried to argue that such episodes are immediately certain and so presumably provide transcendentally valid knowledge of the self, but I think the vulnerability of his argument helps show the strength of Kant's position. What Chisholm claims is that 'I feel depressed' is known simply because it is a 'self-presenting state'. Such states supposedly cannot obtain without one's knowing them, and their being known consists in the fact that, for anyone in such a state, there is 'no more reasonable thing' for him to believe than that he is in that state.[63]

This claim may seem already suspect on the ground that even if it were most reasonable for a depressed person to believe he is depressed, he still need not have this belief at all. Children have all kinds of feelings without knowing that they do, simply because they don't have any adequate concepts. Furthermore, it is notorious that even adults can fail to believe they are depressed when this is precisely what they are and is even the reason for their failing to believe it (and for tending, for example, to believe someone else is depressed). However, for Chisholm to defeat Kant here it is not necessary for him to make good on a strong claim that all psychological states are known immediately; he need only produce some that are so known. But here the content of feelings becomes crucial again. Kant hardly needs to argue in a sceptical way that one can never say whether it is, for example, depression or anxiety that one is really feeling. Rather, he can argue again that even when one can justifiably commit oneself to some specific description of one's state, it is only on the basis of some command of a rudimentary psychological theory, and for us that theory must at the least be a theory of beings with temporal states. It is surely by reference to such a rudimentary theory and not mere momentary feelings that we ordinarily and justifiably distinguish similar psychological states. This point could even be made when one focuses on statements of the form 'it seems to me that I am depressed', rather than 'I feel depressed', for they still involve a classification that could go astray (although this is no doubt less likely).

Even if all this were disputable, Kant's doctrine would still be remarkable in holding that, to the extent that all our consciousness has been overtly temporal, it cannot give us knowledge of ourselves in ourselves. This leaves the second step of the time argument, the theory of the transcendental ideality of time, as our prime concern. Although this theory seems to be simply borrowed from Kant's general argument for transcendental idealism, it is not out of place to examine the theory here, for that broader argument does not contain an adequate discussion of time. The epistemological argument for ideality is given much more attention in the discussion of space, and Kant has obvious difficulties applying it to time for he is not even clear what the body of synthetic knowledge is that allegedly must be assumed and can be explained only on the doctrine of transcendental idealism. None of the likely candidates — arithmetic, pure mechanics, psychology, general axioms of time — presents us with relevant propositions (that Kant himself would recognize) of a clearly synthetic *a priori* type.[64] The difficulty here should not be surprising though, if it is recalled how Kant must stand in an ambiguous position with respect to *a priori* knowledge of time. On the one hand, his general doctrine of transcendental idealism requires him to posit such knowledge in order to argue for the mere phenomenality of time. On the other hand, once time is identified as the form of inner sense, Kant's anti-rationalist limitations on self-knowledge must lead him to restrict *a priori* knowledge of time. As might be expected, his final position tries to have it both ways — *to hold both that there is such a thing as a pure form of time* (structuring and limiting all our self-knowledge), *and that by itself* (i.e. without reference to features such as spatiality which do not apply to the self as a distinct being) *it doesn't yield any pure knowledge*.

Before evaluating this strategy it is best to have some understanding of how Kant's discussion of the self fits in with how the rest of the *Critique* argues about *a priori* knowledge. This is a complicated topic, and as I already have developed my view on it elsewhere, only a brief outline will be presented here.[65] In the Aesthetic, Kant's argument is: (Ia) there is synthetic *a priori* knowledge of space and time (this is the definitive premiss of what is meant by the 'original epistemological argument'), but (Ib) this is possible only if there are pure intuitions of space and time, and (Ic) this is possible only if space and time are merely phenomenal. In the Analytic, his argument is (IIa) there is experience, i.e. empirical knowledge,[66] but (IIb) this is possible for us only if there are synthetic *a priori* principles for spatio-temporal objects, and (IIc) this is possible only if these principles (and thus the schematized categories) are merely phenomenally valid. Now in his Dialectic and critical discussions of self-knowledge, Kant can be seen as arguing that (IIIa) although there is empirical knowledge of the self, (IIIb) this is possible for us only on the basis of a pure form of time, and (IIIc) this is possible only if time (and so our self-knowledge) is merely phenomenal.

It is notable that throughout Kant employs a regressive argument scheme, moving from presumed types of knowledge to their necessary conditions, and that as the *Critique* goes on, these presuppositions appear weaker and the arguments in turn less speculative and less dependent on the original epistemological argument. Whereas the first argument involves a presumption (viz. Ia) that many see as incoherent or so strong as to beg the important issues; and whereas the second argument employs a more acceptable premiss but moves to a conclusion (viz. IIb) that still may seem incoherent or dependent upon a questionable metaphysical apparatus;[67] the third argument appears to have an acceptable premiss (viz. IIIa) and a conclusion free from the controversial assertion of specific synthetic *a priori* principles. However, the argument still uses the disputable notion of a pure form of time. Such a notion is needed for Kant to get to the claim of the ideality of our self-knowledge and to connect the argument for it with the rest of his philosophy, and yet his argument clearly appears less objectionable the less specifically connected it is to the just noted controversial steps of that philosophy. The notion that Kant employs here seems to be nothing more than the general idea that time is an articulated and universal feature of experience, but one that is given and not logically necessary, and in that sense is a mere form. It has a structure with a necessity that is held to be transcendental because it is stronger than the physical necessity of the particular laws of nature in that they all presume that structure. They thus could all be imagined to be different without (supposedly) changing the species of our experience. It is on this ground, and not because of any biological considerations, that Kant would say non-spatio-temporal knowers would be another kind of being, whereas beings who know differently but still in terms of a spatio-temporal framework would differ from us only in degree.

Kant's notion of a pure form of time is thus a fairly austere but uneliminable part of his general doctrine of transcendental idealism. To get a grip on this doctrine I propose that it be understood in terms of a relatively modest thesis that will be called the species theory. This theory confronts the objection that the temporality of experience is absolutely real by holding that to say something has a characteristic which is merely phenomenal is to say only that the perception of the characteristic is dependent upon the limitations of the perspective of a certain species. That is, if there is any *fundamentally more adequate* perspective from which the characteristic would not be perceived, then the characteristic can be said to belong to the object only as phenomenal. It does not belong to the thing in and of itself independently of the limited ways in which it might be perceived.[68] At the core of this theory is the notion that there can be a quasi-divine perspective on all things (which has no forms of sensibility and so no species limitations like ours), and that the nature of things in themselves just is what would be perceived from such a perspective.[69] It seems that Kant understood this theory to hold in such a way that a characteristic is phenomenal only if it *would* not be perceived from such a perspective. It is not necessary that a being with such a perspective be known to exist, nor even that the being simply exist, although I believe Kant would require that we can say the perspective exists, that is, not merely that we not know it (the non-phenomenal aspect) to be impossible but that we have reason to believe it is there.[70]

This understanding of transcendental idealism has the virtue of saving one from having to regard Kant as committed to theological claims or a phenomenalistic equation of things with collections of perceivings.[71] According to the species theory, characteristics are merely phenomenal simply because through them things are in principle less than adequately seen by us, and this because they are seen indirectly through a form of sensibility. This is, of course, an interpretation close to the traditional 'two worlds' view of Kant, but I don't think it requires one to get involved in the intricacies of a 'double affection' theory and to claim that in addition to each ordinary and empirical causal or affection relation there is a specifiable transcendental affection relation between things in themselves and appearances (see below, Ch. VII.12). Rather, things in themselves might be said to affect or be affected simply in that they underlie (as having the properties that give a more adequate view of) the things that are involved in empirical affection.[72]

9. The Essence Theory

Although the species theory has advantages over many other ways of taking Kant's transcendental idealism, it still has obvious problems and there is reason to attempt to find alternatives to it. Before completing the presentation of the species theory, I shall exposit one such alternative, which will be called the *essence theory*. It offers a neglected and, I believe, attractive and almost convincing explanation of the nature and background of Kant's route to claiming our transcendental ideality. According to the essence theory, a thing's properties are merely phenomenal simply if and only if they are contingent, that is, do not belong to the real essence of the thing. Given that all one can know of oneself is temporal, and that temporality does not attach to oneself by necessity,[73] our transcendental ideality follows.

One way to see how this theory could be relevant is simply to reflect on what Kant could mean by saying spatio-temporal properties are merely phenomenal. First, he surely can't mean that they are phenomenal in a subjective, individual way. To believe this would be, as Kant stresses, to misunderstand their phenomenality in empirical terms rather than to conceive it in a proper transcendental way (see again A 30/B 45; A 36/B 53). Yet this transcendental aspect of 'phenomenal' cannot be given a sheerly objective meaning either. That is, Kant can't be taken to mean simply that the characteristics are phenomenal in that they do appear to us;[74] rather he holds they are merely phenomenal.[75] Here he cannot mean only that although they appear in a certain way to us they could appear in other ways to other beings — for this much could be said of things in themselves. So the claim must be that spatio-temporal properties are merely phenomenal because there is some other basically more adequate way of (theoretically) perceiving things. But here Kant rejects the traditional, Leibnizian way of understanding 'more adequate'. When Leibniz treats characteristics as merely phenomenal, he apparently means there is another perspective from which things can be perceived without these characteristics as such, because through it the more basic properties to which the sensible characteristics can be reduced would be perceived. For Kant, however, the more adequate view of things in themselves cannot be a view of basic properties to which the merely phenomenal ones can be reduced. As he emphasizes, this would be to treat these characteristics as 'confused' conceptual ones, and so to reject his whole theory of space and time as irreducible forms of sensibility (B 67; A 261/B 216 f.). This also explains why Kant treats Leibniz as an 'objectivist' about space and time, for as he sees it Leibniz still regards space and time as at least wholly rooted in things in themselves (A 23/B 38-9; A 33/B 49).

The problem then is to find a basis on which Kant can believe there can be an intuition of things in themselves that gives a better but not merely 'clearer' perspective (on the very same things) than that given by (even *a priori*) sensible intuition. The former sort of intuition must in some general way be more basic than the latter without the latter being implied by it. Now just this sort of relation is manifested when the former is taken to reveal the necessary aspects of things and the latter their contingent aspects. Of course, this still gives only the suggestion of a more basic perspective on things; it doesn't show that there is such a perspective, for it still might be that things have only contingent properties, in which case our view may be one of many views but not thereby a merely phenomenal one. How then could Kant say that there not only may be but are real non-spatio-temporal essences? One answer that he might have had in mind is that we are familiar with the essences of certain operations, and that in particular logic gives us the essence of our acts and thoughts. Thus Kant says that although it may be that I am aware of myself only as temporal, it is possible that the (theoretical) characteristics I have *qua* mind, which are just those I have through the acts of synthesis I carry out according to the categories, could in a sense be had without temporality because the categories have a meaning that is non-temporal (B 305).[76] This is, of course, not a new or incidental doctrine for Kant. It is merely a reflection of his theory of the logical forms of judgement, a theory that he takes to be the key to his entire (theoretical) philosophy.[77] This doctrine ties in directly with the ideality thesis that concerns us, for in claiming there is a (theoretical) non-spatio-temporal essence of mind, it provides precisely what is needed to give meaning to the claim that the perceived spatio-temporal properties of the self are merely phenomenal.

It appears to be precisely this non-essentiality of the temporal that is at the heart of Kant's understanding of our ideality when he directly raises the problem that the

> I that thinks can be distinct from the I that intuits itself (for I can represent still other modes of intuition at least as possible) and yet, as being the same subject, can be identical with the latter. (B 155, amended translation.)[78]

Further support for the theory can be gained from the fact that often the contrast Kant makes between what a thing is in itself and what it is as phenomenon is a contrast between a thing *qua* its substantiality and *qua* what merely attaches to it;[79] and he can be taken to understand this substantiality in turn as equivalent to the individual's essential nature. This is because if he meant to distinguish substance from all accidents, even essential ones, his theory would become opaque, for at that point there would be no link between thinghood and substantiality. An item without any properties at all would become not an absolutely pure and bare item but rather not a thing at all (cf. A 187/B 230). Kant appears to acknowledge as much in his lectures, when he states it is absurd to expect to know a substance apart from its properties.[80] There he further supports the essence theory by saying that what we can know of things, i.e., the whole phenomenal realm, are always contingent properties, whereas the necessary properties of things' real essences remain for us unknowable.[81]

Despite the surprising support the essence theory may have, there are serious objections to taking it ultimately to be the key to the meaning of Kant's transcendental idealism. The theory requires that contingency be not only a necessary but also a sufficient condition of a property's being merely phenomenal. Unfortunately the evidence given supports only the first claim, and this invites the objection that it seems perfectly possible for things to have contingent properties that could reveal themselves to other species of knowers, and that could do so directly because those species might not have any overarching forms of sensibility. In that case no conclusive reason prevents our saying such properties belong to the thing in itself. The properties would, after all, be seen not merely from another perspective but from a more direct one, and this could constitute the more adequate view that would justify labelling our own merely phenomenal. Of course, one could stipulate that 'merely phenomenal' means 'non-essential', but Kant does not clearly do this and in any case there remains a crucial second objection, namely that the essence theory wholly severs Kant's idealism from the epistemological argument. This may have its philosophical advantages, but it leaves the essence theory hard to accept as an interpretation of Kant. There appears to be no reason why it could not have been invoked at the beginning of the *Critique*, in which case the phenomenality of our knowledge would follow without the complex strategies that Kant actually employed.

There are of course counterarguments to these objections, or at least some ways of indicating further affinities between the essence theory and a Kantian philosophy. As has been noted, the theory has difficulty with the possibility of intrinsic contingent properties. Yet such a possibility may have been one that Kant was not at all inclined to take seriously. Working in a Leibnizian tradition, his starting point could have been the view that all intrinsic properties of a thing have a necessary attachment to it. It is notable that Kant's doctrine of space and time as irreducible contingent forms led him to say that *contra* Leibniz, we do ascribe properties which are not essential to objects — but not that such properties are intrinsic. Because the moment Kant took space and time to be contingent he also proved them to be phenomenal, he may well have believed that there are no properties which turn out to be contingent and intrinsic — especially because he held that in any case we would not know any.

This belief could also be supported by taking Kant's own transcendental deduction (or even the passivity argument) in such a way as to be a proof that knowledge had by any sensible intuitors must be merely phenomenal. In fact, the transcendental deduction does not proceed in that way but eventually requires reference to presumed forms of intution.[82] It thus shows at most only that all empirical knowledge must be merely phenomenal when knowers have a form of intuition as we do (which is not to say they have the specific forms of space and time). But although this is the logical status of Kant's deduction, his exposition is so complicated that the deduction has often been thought of as (supposedly) proving the mere phenomenality of all possible empirical knowledge. Whether or not Kant really inclined to this view, the Kantian philosophy can certainly be taken to be very close to it, and it may be that the transcendental deduction could even be modified (or the passivity argument shored up) along this line. Once the view is taken, the first objection to the essence theory may be met, for, given the assumption that contingent properties can't be non-sensibly known, the classes of phenomenal and contingent properties would coincide. To back this assumption it could be held that Kant identifies things in themselves not with just any direct view of things but with a divine view,[83] and that God would create things only with (intrinsic theoretical) properties that are necessary. Finally, it could be argued that only when it can be said that things have essential properties, and not merely that they can be more directly seen, is there enough of a ground to warrant calling certain views merely phenomenal. Given that knowledge is mediated in so many ways, a mere difference in one level of directness may seem inadequate to bear all the significance that the species argument attaches to it.

These counterarguments are still not conclusive, and they do nothing to meet the second objection. Whatever embarrassing implications the epistemological argument may have, and whatever may be the restrictions it may appear to need to be consistent with Kant's theory of self-knowledge, it is still of such significance that it must be allowed for in any interpretation of transcendental idealism. The species theory at least makes the epistemological argument relevant. Like that argument, however, the theory does not of itself prove that time is merely phenomenal. That is, even if it can make comprehensible how all our empirical knowledge is temporally ordered, it doesn't show that this order must be merely phenomenal in the sense of non-intrinsic and not merely in the sense of 'known via the mediation of a form'. Even if there is a subjective form of time, Kant also needs to establish the claim that time cannot characterize items apart from this form. He recognizes this by offering further arguments for precisely this claim in the Antinomies, arguments which appear dubious to many today, but which definitely were regarded by Kant himself as the starting point of his critical philosophy and as the conclusive proof for his transcendental idealism.[84] In studying Kant's philosophy of mind we may not need to trace those arguments, but we must at least acknowledge that they block taking the essence theory as the primary means for understanding Kant's transcendental idealism. We shall now continue the case for the primacy of the species theory by noting how it fares in the context of evaluating Kant's other versions of the time argument.

10. The Relational Argument and the Flux Argument

One very terse Kantian argument for the phenomenality of time involves a line of thought that can be called the relational argument (B 67). It begins with a fact that Kant and his opponents can both acknowledge, namely that all concrete knowledge about time can be (and for our purposes at least must be) relationally expressed. It is also agreed that such relations require some backing. That is, the fact that an item appears, e.g., later than another item, must rest ultimately not on something which is as it were suspended between two items, but rather on either intrinsic non-temporal features of the two objects or on the incidental position of the items in an overarching matrix or form of time. As has been noted, Kant believes the former (Leibnizian) option is closed, but on the latter option there remain two alternatives. The form could be understood either as an absolute objective structure (as by the Newtonians) or as a subjective form. Against the former option the obvious Kantian move would seem to be to refer to the epistemological argument that we have *a priori* knowledge of time, and that this in turn is comprehensible if it is knowledge simply of a form of our sensibility (see A 33/B 49). But this type of argument (as was just noted) does not show that the form cannot be objective ('transcendentally real'), and in fact Kant prefers to invoke it against Leibnizians rather than Newton (A 39/B 56). His general objection to the Newtonian view is rather the metaphysical doctrine that the view involves an absurd commitment to treating time as either an objective substance or accident (ibid.). The latter alternative is unappealing, for what sort of thing time could be an accident of is hardly clear. But aside from remarking on the peculiarities of such a substance (A 32/B 49), Kant has only theological objections against the former alternative (B 70). These objections appear at best to hold against the objectivity of space but not time, for it is not evident that God must be thought of as beyond time. The relational argument thus needs completion by the species theory (via the epistemological argument, in excluding the Leibnizian view) and ends with only a weak indirect ground (against the Newtonians) for asserting the phenomenality of time. It hardly represents an independent line of thought that can be taken as Kant's primary ground for that thesis.

Kant's final strategy for asserting our ideality by establishing the phenomenality of time involves what can be called the flux argument. According to it, (i) our temporal being is in constant (and as such unintelligible) flux; and so (ii) our knowledge of (concrete) temporal characteristics ultimately is entirely dependent on that of spatial ones; therefore given (iii) the phenomenality of spatiality (as established, supposedly, by the epistemological argument), it is to be concluded (iv) that our temporality is only phenomenal (B 156).

The original nature of this argument lies entirely in the second point, one that Kant emphasized only with the second edition of the *Critique*. It is very difficult to say whether Kant's main interest in developing the argument was his attachment to idealism or rather a desire to overcome certain kinds of rationalist dogmatism (see above, Ch. VI.5) or empiricistic scepticism (see above, Ch. III.9). In any case, the flux argument was not stressed in Kant's original belief in our transcendental ideality, and the new emphasis on it implies a concession that this belief requires further grounding.

What makes it especially tempting to give the argument a primary role is the fact that it appears best to respond to the problem noted earlier of the ambiguity of Kant's relation to *a priori* knowledge of time. That is, the argument seems to be just the way for Kant to accept such knowledge without thereby opening the way for rationalist claims about a pure mind. (It would be a great irony if this laudable critical objective was in fact pursued by Kant because of a dogmatic attachment to idealism.)

The basic premiss of the flux argument, that inner sense by itself offers only a 'shapeless flux', with nothing constant in it merely as such, is something that Kant had already claimed repeatedly in the first edition of the *Critique* (A 23, A 33, A 381). In the second edition the extra point is then made that therefore we can have no knowledge through representations considered only as belonging to inner sense (i.e., merely *qua* being representations that may be directly reflected on) but must refer to spatial characteristics of representations (B 242, B 297).[85] Kant concludes that because these spatial characteristics are only phenomenal, all that we know by means of them must be only phenomenal too. It is this last step that will be questioned here. Steps (i) and (ii) have been treated earlier, and step (iii) is borrowed from another part of the *Critique* not being put into question here, but even if all these steps were allowed it is not evident that step (iv) is thereby entailed.

The problem is as follows. My temporality is merely phenomenal only if I could be perceived more adequately without it. But the fact that I can perceive x (my temporality) only through y (spatiality), which is itself presumed to be merely phenomenal because I can be perceived more adequately without it (y), does not by itself prove that I really can be more adequately perceived without x (my temporality). This can be spelled out by reference to either the essence or the species theory. Consider first the species theory. Even if a certain form (in this case, space) always mediates *my* knowledge of a situation (in this case, temporal), nothing yet clearly excludes the possibility of other beings better knowing that situation without reliance on such a form. Similarly, the essence theory would lead to step (iv) only if it could be proven that *our* reliance on knowing a certain kind of property (in this case, temporality) only through another and contingent property (in this case, spatiality) requires that the first kind of property be itself contingent. This is hardly evident though, for one can imagine a species that would have to rely on something contingent, for example an algorithmic mechanism, in order to know properties which are themselves necessary, as for example mathematical truths. It seems the only way left for Kant to prove our ideality here would be to take step (ii) to mean that not only do I know my temporality only through spatiality, but moreover my temporal characteristics are simply a species of or reducible to spatial ones. Yet such a claim appears both ungrounded and not in line with Kant's beliefs. So even if it were granted that all our self-knowledge is temporal, and all our temporal knowledge requires spatial knowledge, as well as that all our spatial knowledge is phenomenal, it still doesn't follow that all our self-knowledge must be merely phenomenal.

The disturbing idea here that a being like God could be able to know our temporality (or what underlies it) without relying on spatiality points up not only a difficulty in the flux argument but also some complicated implications for the species theory and the issue of God's knowledge of our situation. This is not a minor issue, for the question of how God can know our spatio-temporal characteristics was a central problem for Kant and his time.[86] Kant himself seems to accept Leibniz's rebuke of the Newtonians for making God in effect spatio-temporal so He could know such characteristics (B 70). But the rationalist tradition in which Leibniz stood could allow God the privilege of non-spatio-temporally knowing our spatio-temporality, for it believed in a hierarchy of properties such that God could be said to know us through the more eminent non-spatio-temporal properties on which the spatio-temporal ones are based. Through such sheerly intellectual knowledge God would be knowing us better than we know ourselves, just as a blind physicist can know light better than a child — which is not to say that he has the child's awareness of light, any more than God has our awareness of things. This traditional explanation of God's knowledge is undercut by the species theory and its doctrine of irreducible and merely phenomenal sensible properties.[87] Thus not only is Kant's major argument (the flux argument) for the species theory in our own case unconvincing, but it also appears that we are left without a natural way to fill out the meaning of that theory.

Although these problems are serious, they do not disprove Kant's claim of our ideality but only indicate difficulties in establishing it or explaining its implications. Moreover, the difficulty in seeing how our temporality could not be intrinsic, given its ubiquity in our knowing, should not be taken as evidence that it must be intrinsic after all. For, if it were claimed that Kant must say temporality intrinsically characterizes us, since he believes we must use it in all our knowing, then it should similarly, and surely unsuccessfully, be argued that spatiality intrinsically characterizes us. The mere fact that I must refer to certain kinds of properties (spatial or temporal) in carrying out one type of activity (determining my temporality) does not entail that in myself I am in a literal way characterized by those properties.

Similar considerations can be used to defend Kant against a familiar objection recently expressed by Strawson:

Each human being . . . *is* a thinking being, a seat of the categories, and to that extent a source, and not merely an outcome, of the conditions of experience. . . . After all, it seems, a good deal can be known about the noumenal self . . . if the being that thinks in us [a phrase used by Kant at B 402] is under the impression that its understanding affects its sensibility in the production of a temporal succession of connected perceptions, feelings and thoughts (including this one), then, apparently, the being that thinks in us is not deluded at all, but is absolutely right![88]

Strawson's main claim is that Kant must on his own grounds concede considerable specific information about the noumenal self, namely the 'absolutely right' information that human knowledge is a product of sensibility and understanding in the way the *Critique* says. There is a fallacy behind this claim, for it does not follow that we must learn something literally about our noumenal *selves* whenever we learn 'absolutely right' propositions about the structures of phenomenal knowledge. The fact that these structures are in one sense about a self (in that they apply to the phenomenal self) and that they do have in one sense, an absolute validity (just as there can be absolute truths about the structures of unicorns, without there even being real unicorns) does not entail that they give us knowledge about what our selves are like in themselves. The fallacy here is no doubt understandable in view of Kant's frequent metaphorical talk about the structures as being due to 'us' (this talk could be understood as a proper corrective to the assumption that they *must* be in *things* in themselves distinct from us). None the less, the whole programme of the Paralogisms is to remind us how we need not jump to the conclusion of identifying the source of the structures with any personal being, and especially not with a human self. It would clearly be contradictory for Kant to speak (as Strawson does) of the *human* self as the source of its own structures, although it still could be that these structures have their metaphysical ground in the being(s) who *appears* as a human self.

11. The Species Theory Supported

Before moving on to other important objections to Kant, we should complete the case for taking the species theory to be the key to understanding what Kant meant in claiming our ideality. This can be done by finally analysing the major unexamined passage of the *Critique* that bears on the claim of our ideality and its relation to inner sense and apperception. In the second edition Kant added a long special exposition of the claim of our ideality:

This [phenomenality] also holds true of inner sense . . . because the time in which we set these representations, which is itself antecedent to the consciousness of them in experience, and which underlies them as the formal condition of the mode in which we posit them in the mind, itself contains [only] relations of succession, coexistence, and of that which is coexistent with succession, the enduring. Now that which, as representation, can be antecedent to any and every act of thinking anything, is [1] intuition; and if it contains nothing but relations, it is [2] the form of intuition. Since this form does not represent anything save in so far as something is posited in the mind, it can be nothing but the mode in which the mind is affected through its own activity (namely, through this positing of its representation), and so is affected by itself; in other words, it is nothing but an [3] inner sense in respect of the form of that sense. . . .

In man this [self-]consciousness demands inner perception of the manifold which is antecedently given in the subject, and the mode in which this manifold is given in the mind must, as non-spontaneous, be entitled [4a] sensibility. If the faculty of coming to consciousness of oneself is to seek out (to apprehend) that which lies in the mind, it must affect the mind, and only in this way can it give rise to an intuition of itself. But [4b] the form of this intuition, which exists antecedently in the mind, determines, in the representation of time, the mode in which the manifold is together in the mind, since it then intuits itself not as it would represent itself if [4b, a] immediately self-active, but as it is affected by itself, and therefore as it appears to itself, not as it is (B 67–8; cf. B 153 f.).

At least four stages of argument can be distinguished in this difficult passage. First, Kant wants to say that because time in some way precedes thought it is an *intuition*.[89] Secondly, he adds that because it is merely relational it is a *form* of intuition. This is probably because he implies the relations are in some way *a priori*, all inclusive, and not reducible to the matter of individual objects. Thirdly, as such a form of intuition, it is also the form of *inner* sense. This is because the stimulation of consciousness here has an internal source, and because it is only when there is something within the mind, some matter which we can attempt to determine, that we can say that there can be something objectively and temporally represented. Presumably, time would otherwise be a bare intuitive form, just as Kant believes the pure intuition of space, without a sensible manifold, is a bare form that cannot be said objectively to represent anything. Fourthly, Kant argues that (a) the notion of inner sense implies that our self-consciousness rests on a *sensible* intuition which, as previously noted, relies on data that are given, not made, and so (b) that are known *not immediately* but only via forms of synthesis specific to our kind of being. Thus Kant concludes that through inner sense we know ourselves not in an 'immediately self-active' manner but merely as phenomenal.

The species theory can be taken to be fundamental here because Kant does not stop after the first step or the first half of the fourth step, as he might if he took the passivity argument to be decisive, nor does he stop after the second step, as he might if he thought a relational argument alone were sufficient. Rather, he stresses that in our self-consciousness we are subject to a form which pre-determines 'the mode in which the manifold is together in the mind'. The point of his argument is that I know myself as a phenomenon not simply because in order to know myself I need to do something, viz., exert reflection (and so be 'affected'), but rather because even after I am affected through reflection, self-knowledge is not achieved until data I am given are subsumed under conditions (temporal forms) beyond my doing — conditions from which other types of beings (operating on the very same things) might be free. This also indicates that ultimately the species theory can be seen as incorporating the defensible spirit of the passivity argument — the notion that self-knowledge is fundamentally receptive, limited, and dependent on our affectibility — without involving any commitment to the dubious associated ideas of representationalism and a process of distortion.

In Kant's late *Anthropology* there is an interesting exposition of the species theory along this line:

I as a thinking being am indeed one and the same subject that I am as a sensible being. But as an object of inner empirical intuition, that is in so far as I am *affected* by representations in time that are contemporaneous or sequential, I know myself only as I appear to myself, not as a thing in itself. For this (knowledge) *depends on a condition of time which is not a concept* of the understanding (and so not of sheer spontaneity), thus on a condition with respect to which my capacity for representation is passive (and thus receptive).[90]

Here one can discern another Kantian sense of 'affection'. In this case it is the form of time itself with respect to which we might be said to be affected, simply in the sense that it is something contingent to which we are subject, something that limits and demarcates our self-knowledge. It may well be that this understanding of the term was largely responsible for Kant's speaking often as if the fact that we can know ourselves 'only as affected' is tantamount to the claim of our ideality; at least this would finally provide a proper Kantian route from those statements to that claim.

D.12. Radical Objections to our Transcendental Ideality

Having clarified the meaning and basis of the Kantian thesis of the ideality of our self-knowledge, we turn to the major radical objections that have been offered against it. Unlike the points raised so far, which primarily concern difficulties in positively establishing and defining the thesis, these objections take the thesis to be clearly false, absurd, or trivial. The first kind of objection to be considered holds that the type of self-knowledge that Kant does allow has absurd implications that undermine his whole theory. Such an objection has been made by P. F. Strawson, who attacks Kant for (allegedly) holding that in our self-consciousness our empirical self appears to a transcendental or noumenal self.[91] Strawson notes that here the term 'appears' must be given either a temporal or a non-temporal meaning. In the former case he claims (1) that what is appeared to must then also be temporal and hence cannot be the noumenal subject that Kant seems to believe it is. In the latter case, Strawson's argument is not so clear. He may be saying (2a) that it is not understandable how one can be non-temporally aware of something which (as in this case) is temporal, namely one's empirical self. Or, his main point may be (2b) that even if there were a noumenal subject to whom an empirical subject non-temporally appears, such a subject, with a 'non-history', would have nothing 'to do with us' and so could not constitute the essential reality of the self as Kant claims.

Stawson himself does not directly back (2a), and it seems dismissable, for we can imagine a quasi-divine being with a non-temporal intuition of a phenomenal temporal situation, as for example in an image about the course of a fabulous event.[92] Before determining whether the remaining points, (1) and (2b), can be pressed, it should be determined which involves the sense of 'appears' most likely to be favoured by Kant in this context. Fortunately, there is a text (not cited by Strawson) in which Kant speaks directly about the 'transcendental subject' and the appearance of the empirical self:

Even the inner and sensible intuition of our mind (as object of consciousness) which is represented as being determined by the succession
of different states in time, is not the self proper, as it exists in itself —
that is, is not the transcendental subject — but only an appearance
that has been given to the sensibility of this, to us unknown, being
(A 492/B 520).

All that Kant commits himself to here is the idea that the
appearance of the temporal self is 'given to the sensibility'
of a being which is in some sense unknown to us and is
presumably the self in itself. This does not commit him to
holding it is appropriate to speak directly of an *epistemic*
appearance relation between the empirical and noumenal
self. The noumenal subject can be identified not sheerly
as a knowing ('appeared to') as opposed to known being,
but rather as the being to whom the 'sensibility' is ultimately
due. This is helpful because it would be incredible for Kant
to hold that it is literally the noumenal self that is appeared
to when we know ordinary things. For, in any case of self-
consciousness where x is knowing y, we can hardly hold
y alone to be phenomenal, because, as Kant himself reminds
us, there is always a possible iterated self-consciousness of
the form, z is knowing x is knowing y. So unless Kant were
absurdly to hold that an act of knowing cannot at all be
known, in any particular case of self-consciousness the subject can in principle be regarded as empirical just as can
the object.

All this merely confirms the fact that when a person knows
himself he is, as a knowing subject, also in principle an
empirical object, and so the appearing whereby this knowledge is mediated is an ordinary temporal appearing (that is,
an appearing in time, if not necessarily one that takes time).
The distinction between the noumenal and the phenomenal
subject may still have a defensible Kantian meaning even
if — and indeed precisely because — the subject to whom
the temporal self appears is also temporal. For, all Kant
needs to hold is that there is a subject (a being which underlies the process and object of self-consciousness) which
'in itself' is responsible for the sensibility in which the
appearing takes place (and so the noumenal subject would
have something 'to do with us'). On the species theory,

this is only to say that the temporality of the self is merely phenomenal because (although it does characterize the content of our self-observation) it is something that being could have lacked and without which it could be more adequately perceived. Because our temporality is something through which we do actually see ourselves but need not be seen (especially given the rejection of (2a)), it can be spoken of as something that merely attaches to us from one view, something had by a being that may be characterized by different features that are intrinsic and essential.

If this solution does not appear wholly convincing, the problem may be that although it is understandable that the various contents of consciousness could all be merely phenomenal, it seems that temporality is a feature of consciousness *qua* act and not merely *qua* content. Here it must be granted that we do often take temporality to be central to the act as opposed to the content character of a particular consciousness (for it is properly thinkings and not thoughts that we time). None the less, as was just noted, consciousness can always be iterated, and so whatever are the specific features a particular consciousness has *qua* act, these are features that can be reflected in the content of another instance of consciousness. (This is not to deny that, as Kant notes (B. 429), the mere existence of an act of consciousness can't be made merely phenomenal because of a relativity attaching to its contents.) Moreover, Kant holds that whatever temporal features are epistemically significant in this content are ones that can be modelled or adequately represented by mere spatial or pure logical manifolds. This confidence may be ill-founded, but it is not incoherent, even though it is peculiar in not resting on any idea that the features can be fully reduced.

The critic of Kant here may still object to the fact that with transcendental idealism properties are classified as merely phenomenal simply because there is some fundamentally more adequate view of things without them. Whether that view be described as more direct or as essential, it still follows that something we actually undergo will be missed by the view, namely the formal (in a transcendental sense) or contingent properties of our experience. Yet it is precisely this fact that Kant is willing to accept in saying the basic phenomenal properties of space and time are irreducible.[93] The question then is simply whether it is absurd to label these irreducible but actually 'experienced' features as merely phenomenal. This is where the critic may insist experience can't be 'merely' anything, for it is rather the most full-blooded form of reality we have. But here the Kantian can reply that if 'experience' means the sheer felt quality of existence, then that is not being denied (although it may be epistemologically empty); whereas if 'experience' means what is known, then the claim is simply that the content we attend to in our cognitive determinations attaches to something that (in principle) can be interpreted in a much better way.

Sometimes objections to Kant here seem to rest on the thought that with transcendental idealism the very appearing of the self in self-consciousness is somehow claimed to be unreal. Strawson speaks as if for Kant the noumenal subject is alone real, and what is phenomenal is simply false.[94] Kant was quite aware of this objection.[95] Something like it was already raised against his *Dissertation*, and the objection is surely part of what motivated the added discussion of self-consciousness in the second edition of the *Critique*. Here Kant clearly emphasizes that by saying the temporality of experience is wholly phenomenal ('only appearance'), he doesn't mean to say that it only appears to be the case *that* we have experience, or it only appears that this experience has a temporal *nature* (B 69).[96] Strawson claims that if it is after all Kant's position that 'I really do appear to myself temporally' (although I do not really-temporally appear to myself, i.e., my appearing isn't something noumenally temporal), then (in the context of transcendental idealism) the meaning of 'really do appear' cannot be determined, for 'the bounds of intelligibility have been transgressed, on any standard'.[97] But why can't Kant say that there is experience, and this experience really is temporal (i.e., that is the nature of its content), but this experience itself, as the particular form of empirical knowledge that it is, has only a phenomenal reality? Once again this is not to say that the experiencer is entirely phenomenal, but only to deny that the sensible and cognizable features of this self-consciousness are more than phenomenal, in the sense laid out by the species theory. That our temporality is in this sense ultimately a guise or ornament may be a remarkable idea, but not one that clearly transgresses all 'bounds of intelligibility'.

Another notion that many, including Strawson, see as involving the phenomenality thesis in absurdity is that of an affection relation between things in themselves and appearances. The most recent major presentation of this objection has been an extensive criticism of Kant by M. S. Gram. Strawson's original objection could be met by showing there is no need to spell out a peculiar appearance relation (between phenomena and noumena), such that our self-knowledge is not to be understood in terms of a temporal subject grasping a temporal object, even if Kant is committed to saying that empirical things appear to something which is also a thing in itself. Gram's objection can be handled in a similar fashion if it can be shown that Kant is not committed to spelling out a peculiar affection relation between phenomena and noumena, even if it cannot be denied that he speaks about affection involving items which are also things in themselves. Kant's thus speaking need only be explained in such a way that it does not have to involve absurdly specifying a mysterious metaphysical process in addition to familiar empirical causation or affection. This explanation can be made most easily via the essence theory, although the point could also be made in terms of the species theory. If we only think of the thing in itself as an aspect of the object underlying it as a real essence may, then when an empirical object affects another, it is also true that something that has an essence and so is a thing in itself has affected something, but there is no need to specify a mysterious machinery of transcendental or essence affection.

Problems naturally arise *if* it is claimed that Kant is committed to specifying such a machinery as well as to holding that it must be distinct from empirical affection and unknowable. Gram's attack on Kant is based on such a claim. He begins by saying Kantian things in themselves must fulfill an 'affection condition', which he defines as meaning that they generate what we do perceive by acting in a certain way on our modes of intuition.[98] He takes this condition as tantamount to holding not merely that there is something that underlies phenomena, but also that there is a 'relevant epistemic relation' between things in themselves and what we perceive, such that things in themselves must appear to us.[99] Gram then finds Kant in contradiction because allegedly he is committed to something that must appear but cannot be known, given the doctrine of the unknowability of things in themselves. On our interpretation there is no contradiction, for things in themselves need not and in fact cannot appear to us *as such*, although this *need* not make them things numerically distinct from what does appear (viz., phenomena) nor put them totally out of relation to our experience. Rather, as (for example) the real essence of those things that do appear to us, they can be ultimately not distinct from such things and so ('relevantly') related to our experience, and yet unknowable for us.

At one point Gram seems to attend more directly to something like this kind of reply when he shifts from objecting to things in themselves as such to objecting to their failing to provide a full ground for phenomena. That is, he objects that 'we are still obligated to explain how it is that we perceive the spatio-temporal part of what we intuit',[100] and he thinks that here the thing in itself must still be brought in, now as in some way accounting for the very forms of space and time. This is again to forget that for Kant space and time are irreducible phenomena, and that things in themselves are not posited as sufficient explanations of all that appears to us. The latter can be independent from the former just as contingent properties may be underivable from essential ones.[101]

A quite different kind of objection to the claim of our ideality is to be found in the interpretation of Jonathan Bennett. Bennett in a sense accepts 'transcendental idealism', but according to him, 'properly expressed, transcendental idealism about any concept *C* says that it is only because of the way our experience is that we have any use for the concept *C*'.[102] He believes this makes our ideality 'not false but trivial', for instead of explaining, as 'idealism' is supposed to, how we can come to apply the concept of time even to our own inner states, Kant always 'assumes that our inner states can be set in a temporal order'.[103] For Bennett, inner states can yield an interesting 'idealist' account of how through them we come to concepts such as those of external objects, but not an interesting account when the concept is one of time that supposedly has a meaning 'no matter how' our inner states are.

The species theory also provides means for replying to Bennett's objection. Bennett presupposes that proper 'idealist' accounts must be in effect explanations of the empirical conditions under which concepts have a meaning due to the peculiarities of our temporal experience. Such a presupposition leaves little special significance for the term 'transcendental', for the accounts are always ultimately empirical (although they may be distinguished in that at least the *explanandum* is always epistemic). But Kant surely wants 'transcendental' to contrast with 'empirical' in a more basic way. When he calls something merely phenomenal or transcendentally ideal, he ultimately cannot be speaking about something that has to do with dependence on a temporal process, for obviously he doesn't take the form of time itself, which is the transcendentally ideal item *par excellence*, to be due to such a process. On our interpretation, to call something transcendentally ideal is not so much to explain how it functions as rather to note the ultimate contingency of its functioning. This contingency comes out in the fact that Kant would deny (and his idealism just is this denial) that temporality characterizes us 'no matter what' our inner states are. His theory is that on the contrary there is a perfectly coherent sense of 'inner state' — namely the intrinsic (e.g., essential) qualities of oneself — such that we could have such states without time applying to them. This leaves us with no explanation of a process whereby time is attached to our experience, but surely that is just as well.[104]

Bennett's interpretation also involves a view of transcendental idealism in general that gives a very peculiar and textually indefensible slant on Kant's philosophy. Bennett properly notes that when Kant calls something an 'appearance', he (generally) doesn't mean to say that it is something that merely seems to be the case, as in the manner of illusions and hallucinations. But Bennett jumps from this point to claiming that for Kant appearances are *not at all* 'to be contrasted with some unextended and unperceivable reality'.[105] Such a comment may have some value as a balance to difficulties of the 'double affection' theory, but it still goes directly against Kant's central claim about contradictions in taking space and time intrinsically to characterize things. Against these and other texts that refute his interpretation, Bennett can say only that they represent 'Kant at his worst'.[106] Although they admittedly represent an unpopular aspect of Kant's philosophy, it should be clear now that at least they do represent his position and that it is not an absurd, trivial, or demonstrably false one.

A final recent objection to Kant's theory of our ideality is found in R. C. S. Walker's work on Kant. Unlike interpreters such as Strawson, Walker is rather sympathetic to the general idea of transcendental idealism. He balks, however, at Kant's application of it to the self, and he contends that here Kant becomes entangled in patently false and contradictory views. According to Walker:

Kant's views about the limits of human knowledge commit him . . . to denying he can properly claim that he exists even simply as the subject of "*cogito*", whatever else he may or may not be.

And this is an uncomfortable position. Uncomfortable for anyone, but especially so for Kant. For the existence of the self, as subject if not as enduring and independent substance, is a condition of the possibility of experience. In the transcendental deduction appeal is frequently made to the part the self must play in synthesis . . .[107]

Despite the general acuteness of Walker's study of Kant, I think it can be easily shown that here it is his own views and not Kant's that are in trouble, and that the way to see this is precisely through an appreciation of the basic point Kant was making in the Paralogisms. That basic point is simply that we ought not to conflate the transcendental conditions of knowledge with properties of the self in itself (this point is admittedly not aided when Kant sometimes conflates the terms 'transcendental' and 'transcendent'). That is, it is one thing to say that the structure of human knowledge depends on 'our' categories and forms of intuition, in the sense of the species theory, and something else to say that it literally depends on the existence or action of any known individual human selves. Although it may be hard to believe that Walker would confuse these points, it can be shown that his objection involves such confusion.

As Walker himself appears to concede, nothing in Kant's transcendental theory commits him to holding one is an 'enduring and independent substance'. Thus the supposed transgression of the limits (that Kant himself sets) on self-knowledge must lie in what Walker calls the denial 'of the self as subject', or 'simply as the subject of "*cogito*" '. Yet if our being a subject is simply our being something that actually exists, then Kant clearly does not deny that, for, as Walker also concedes, Kant states that we can be absolutely sure that we exist.[108] But then what is left in claiming one is a subject, if it is to claim something more than merely being an existent item but not to claim as much as that one is an 'enduring' or 'independent' substance? I think that here Walker can only be understanding the phrase 'self as subject' as tantamount to the claim that noumenally one is a *mental* being and the ultimate subject of one's thoughts, just as one at first *appears* to be. But to claim this is just to fall prey to the fallacies of rational psychology, and especially the second paralogism, as analysed above (Chapter II). Thus, in the only relevant sense in which Kant could be denying the self is a subject, the denial would seem to be not an absurdity but rather a point in line with his best critical observations.

Walker would be unwilling to accept this response because he believes that this kind of denial of the self as subject is inconsistent with Kant's general doctrine of how knowledge is constituted. Thus he says, 'one's own mind . . . must be more than a quasi-phenomenalist construction; it must exist to carry the construction out', and 'the mind cannot read itself and its own spontaneity into the world of appearances'.[109] Walker's idea here is that Kant's idealism forces him to speak simultaneously and absurdly about the self as the agent and object of acts of spontaneous construction. The trouble with this idea is that Kant's idealism does not need to be, and should not be, understood in terms of an *empirical* self *literally* constructing a world and then, some-how, doing the same for itself. Rather, the 'spontaneity' of the subject that Kant speaks of refers basically to the fact that there are structures of experience that precede objects in that they cannot be understood as mere consequences of individual experiences in a typical empiricist fashion. Despite some ambiguity, especially in the first edition trans-cendental deduction, it is clearly essential to Kant's theory that this spontaneity is not to be identified with the capacity of any empirical being as such. On the contrary, all empirical beings, including human minds with their phenomenal structures as such, must be understood as being due to this spontaneity, or, better said, must reflect certain *a priori* conditions. Thus the mind that is part of 'the world of appearances' is simply not the agent of spontaneity in Kant's sense, and in fact we have no ground for asserting there is an 'agent' here, or in any case that it is literally mental, literally a self. There are certainly peculiarities and difficulties in justifying details of this Kantian doctrine, but there is still no absurdity or necessary self-contradiction in it, which is only to be expected given that it represents the most sophisticated aspect of Kant's philosophy.

I conclude that it is only because of an uncharitable understanding of the notion of 'spontaneity' that Walker could suggest that Kant is in any trouble in speaking of our self as itself (i.e., as a determinable phenomenon, not as a thing in itself) due to spontaneity. There is, however, one way left that Walker might mean to press his objection to Kant's doctrine of our ideality. This would be to observe that although it may be allowed that the belief in trans-cendental structures (which are not asserted to be due to a literal and personal action) can be said not to involve inconsistent claims about access to the *self* in itself, none the less the belief still may appear to involve instances of noumenal knowledge that are contrary to the general pro-hibitions of Kant's transcendental idealism. Thus Walker believes that with Kant's admission that there are things in themselves, and that we do exist, 'the flood-gates are opened; the principle that I can have no knowledge regarding things in themselves has been breached.'[110]

This common objection was touched on before (see above, Chs. I.2 and II.9), and here we will emphasize only how Walker himself ironically provides the best materials for refuting it. As Walker reminds us, 'Kant does not think the speculations of the dogmatic metaphysicians are unintelligible'.[111] That is, there is a meaning the categories have which is independent of their justified use in our spatio-temporal world. Of course, Kant believes that this bare meaning can be put to no great theoretical use by us; we cannot determine specific noumenal causes, substances, quantities, etc. But all this is consistent with allowing indirect arguments that there exist things in themselves, and that in some way, which we cannot determine specifically, they are categorized as causal, substantial, etc. Or more precisely, in view of Kant's practical philosophy, the point is that there definitely are such meanings, but their use in specific determinations must for us rest on some non-theoretical premisses (B 430). The careful way Kant proceeds here indicates that he has consistent means to prevent breaching his idealism without having to deny all claims about reality in itself.

13. Conclusion

The last section was meant to show that Kant's claim that we cannot know the noumenal nature of our being is a claim that remains meaningful despite the severe objections that philosophers have made against it, and despite questions our own study has raised about the claim's justification. Thus, even if Kant's theory of mind is at remarkably many points infected by his pre-critical commitments, it at least is not guilty of nonsense or egregious rationalist claims about the self. Even if it is not ultimately compatible with empiricism in any common-sense form, it at least provides an imaginative alternative and a possible object of belief.

At this point a last and rather different kind of objection remains to be considered, namely that in view of our own claim that considerable rationalism remains behind Kant's critique of rational psychology, it may be that there are still various kinds of questionable *a priori* but *phenomenal* claims about the self that Kant intended to develop. As Michael Washburn has noted, 'students of Kant . . . have incorrectly assumed that his criticism of (dogmatic) rational psychology was tantamount to a rejection of psychology as a genuine *a priori* science'.[112] Just as we know Kant's critique of dogmatic cosmology was no bar to his developing a rational science of external phenomena, so it would seem he could have developed an *a priori* doctrine of inner phenomena. Washburn claims that this was in fact Kant's intention, and he cites Kant's discussion of an 'immanent physiology' of the 'object of inner sense' in the *Critique's* 'Architectonic' (A 846/B 874), as well as a promise by Kant in a letter of 1785 to add an 'appendix' on the soul to his *Metaphysical Foundations of Natural Science*.[113]

Washburn's references are significant, but they cannot be taken to prove a serious intention on Kant's part. The former reference is taken from a part of the *Critique* generally considered to have been written quite early, (cf. the peculiar outline of 'the whole system of metaphysics' at (A 846/B 874)), and in any case it gives no sign of what Kant really meant to do. His mention here of the idea of a science of the soul is compatible with believing that not much of a science could really be developed. It is notable that this science is described as using the same datum — 'the concept of a thinking being' (in the empirical representation 'I think') (A 848/B 876) — that in the Paralogisms is said in principle severely to restrict psychology. Moreover, in the same section Kant lists other sciences, e.g., 'the transcendental knowledge of God', which he also does not criticize here although we know he takes them to be quite limited at best (A 846/B 874). Finally, the fact that Kant intended to write an 'appendix' on the soul is no proof that he meant to put into it much more than is found in the very critical 'preface' that he eventually published.

Whatever Kant's intentions were, Washburn realizes and even emphasizes that it was no accident that Kant did not develop a detailed *a priori* doctrine of the soul.[114] This point is consistent with our study, for we have explained how Kant came to insist on severe limitations with regard to knowing the self independently of reference to spatial items. Our major thesis has been that this insistence was understandable given the frustration Kant experienced in his own attempts to demonstrate our freedom, and given his simultaneous realization that the flux argument was the best tool he had for meeting the objections that continued to be made about the claim of our ideality. None the less, even if this explains how Kant came to argue the way that he did for limitations in our self-knowledge, it does not fully explain why in general he was so committed to these limitations. It is natural to continue to ask why he appeared so thoroughly opposed to rational psychology and why he was so attracted to the idea that, just because (so he thought) our Newtonian paradigms of scientific knowledge are of merely phenomenal validity, all our determinate knowledge must also have this status.

There are some obvious partial answers here: Kant's concern for a neat architectonic, the fact that an emphasis on spatiality gave him a nice way to respond to certain kinds of extreme scepticism and dogmatism, the fact that his own reference to transcendental structures appears most palatable when distinguished from all metaphysical claims about a personal self and, above all, the fact that putting the ultimate being of our self wholly beyond our theoretical determination leaves a place open for the practical hopes Kant wanted to encourage.

Important as these facts are, they still seem compatible with some allowance of an *a priori* determination of the self, especially at the phenomenal level. Unfortunately, as time went on Kant shortened rather than extended his treatment of mind, and he never presented a final clarification of all that could and could not be said *a priori* about the mind in his philosophy. This situation is demonstrated not only by the very limited progress in the late lecture notes, but also by the conflicting trends in his last published expressions on the topic. In the *Metaphysical Foundations of Natural Science*, for instance, Kant begins by expressing the idea that in one sense a detailed *a priori* determination of the soul remains unproblematic, namely in so far as the soul, like all phenomena, should be thought of as subject to the *general* principles that are to be understood as applying irrespectively of whether one is dealing with objects of outer or mere inner sense.[115] Yet Kant also adds remarks that seem to exclude the soul from being subject to at least the first and third Analogies.[116] He is less clear about the application of the second Analogy. Speaking for it is his already noted belief in a perfect psycho-physical parallelism[117] and his remarks in the Antinomies about the complete determination of 'empirical character' (A 549/B 577).[118] Counting against it is the opening provided by his new formulation of the principle as not reasonably applicable to all kinds of change (B 232).[119]

The easiest way to try to save Kant from inconsistency here is to ascribe to him the view that strictly speaking (phenomenally) only spatial things are substantial, and so inner changes that prima facie do not seem to be instances of the Analogies would turn out to be so after all; phenomenally they ultimately would represent perfectly regular changes in bodily substance.[120] In this way it would not matter that the soul doesn't fall under the Analogies, for the soul as such could be a mere appearance, and all that (phenomenally) really happens in it would then be in principle accounted for in terms of Kant's general *a priori* (and thoroughly spatial) framework. This approach, however, was never worked out in detail by Kant himself, and, as noted earlier, (cf. above, Ch. II.3) it appears to be in tension with his stress on 'scientific immaterialism' and his repeated claims that the soul as traditionally understood is a proper regulative idea for psychological research. These claims are perhaps to be balanced by his eventual pessimism about the value of such research, but they do seem to offer a final illustration of the common pattern we have found in Kant's philosophy: the promise of a very modern and radical theory of mind, surrounded and often held back by powerful rationalist sympathies.

In conclusion, it seems that Kant should be faulted not so much for making questionable *a priori* claims about the soul as rather for not being willing enough to pursue such claims. Even with respect to the specific range of topics covered by Kant's categorial characterization of the soul, there is an obvious way in which the field of rational psychology can be taken to emerge alive from the Paralogisms — namely if it is conceived of not as a dogmatic pattern of syllogistic assertions stemming from the mere representation of the I, but rather as a critical and non-empirical debate between a sophisticated naturalism and a properly qualified rationalist view of mind.

Unfortunately Kant himself does not appear clearly to see the future or value of this debate, for he seems rather to be under the impression that here little more can be said after his *Critique*. This opinion need not be taken too seriously, however, for Kant also speaks as if practically all the other branches of philosophy reached their basic limits in his work. More important is the fact that the Kantian philosophy allows one to develop either of the two basic philosophical options just mentioned, and that Kant provides much that can be said in favour of these views as against their less developed predecessors. Yet it is also true that Kant was found to have nothing decisive to say against some versions of these views when he really needed to say some such thing in order to complete a particular argument he was advancing (e.g., against scientific materialism) or appeared to accept. Thus with respect to future work, we are left with a difficult twofold challenge: to build up a theory of mind that will avoid the specific errors Kant committed, and to maintain a perspective that will be broad enough to do as much justice as Kant did to both our immaterialist and materialist traditions.

Notes to Chapter VII

[1] *AA*, vol. 18, p. 7, R 4849.

[2] Kant calls this the problem of the singularity of the soul. *AA*, vol. 28, pp. 683, 267, 754.

[3] *AA*, vol. 2, p. 371.

[4] *AA*, vol. 28, p. 265.

[5] See also above, Ch. III.2, and R 4230, as well as *AA*, vol. 28, p. 263, and *AA*, vol. 27, p. 467.

[6] *AA*, vol. 1, p. 21. I will not distinguish here between 'mind' and 'soul'.

[7] Ibid., p. 355; cf. p. 356.

[8] Ibid., p. 408. Later Kant suggests being 'inwardly determined' is just being absolutely free, in which case it would not have degrees (*AA*, vol. 17, p. 313, R 3855).

⁹ *AA*, vol. 2, p. 59. Cf. *Kant: Selected Pre-Critical Writings and Correspondence with Beck*, p. 16 = *AA*, vol. 5, p. 464 n.

¹⁰ This is all that Kant means in his frequent statements that animals lack 'consciousness' (*AA*, vol. 28, pp. 277, 449, 594, 689).

¹¹ See *AA*, vol. 28, p. 277; and *Critique of Judgment*, p. 315 n. = *AA*, vol. 5, p. 464 n.·

¹² *AA*, vol. 2, p. 60.

¹³ *AA*, vol. 28, p. 671; cf. pp. 265, 279. Note that this is not to equate it with what takes place *when* one abstracts the outer.

¹⁴ H. J. Paton, *Kant's Metaphysics of Experience*, vol. 2 (London, 1936), p. 389; N. Kemp Smith, *A Commentary to Kant's 'Critique of Pure Reason'*, p. 294; T. D. Weldon, *Kant's Critique of Pure Reason*, second edition (Oxford, 1958) p. 259. Cf. also R. P. Wolff, *Kant's Theory of Mental Activity*, p. 193 f. In Germany, the theory appears to be held by Gerhard Krüger, whose version is less clear: 'Das Mannigfaltige des inneren Sinnes ist also das mannigfaltige Gefühl davon, dass und wie wir äusserlich affiziert werden'. ('Über Kants Lehre von der Zeit', in *Philosophie und Moral in der Kantischen Kritik*, second edition [Tübingen, 1967], p. 276.) For a critique of Krüger's interpretation and of his further claim that the inner, *qua* temporally given, is the thing in itself, see Dieter Henrich, 'Zur theoretischen Philosophie Kants', *Philosophische Rundschau*, 1 (1953–4), 144.

¹⁵ 'Thus nothing can take place in the soul if the body does not come into play' (*AA*, vol. 28, p. 259).

¹⁶ *AA*, vol. 20, p. 309; cf. vol. 28, p. 755.

¹⁷ This point is closely related to Kant's rejection of spiritualism. See, e.g., above at n. 3.

¹⁸ *AA*, vol. 28, p. 296. Cf. also vol. 17, p. 418 (R 4108), where Kant speaks of our 'later' having a 'non-corporeal sensibility'.

¹⁹ *AA*, vol. 28, pp. 276, 449.

²⁰ A. C. Ewing, *A Short Commentary on Kant's Critique of Pure Reason*, p. 124; Paton, *Kant's Metaphysics*, p. 389. They think Kant leaves this possibility open for outer impressions.

²¹ Wolff, *Kant's Theory*, p. 200.

²² Smith, *Commentary*, p. 296.

²³ Ewing, *Commentary*, p. 124; cf. Smith, *Commentary*, p. xlviii.

²⁴ *AA*, vol. 28, p. 594.

²⁵ *AA*, vol. 8, p. 414; vol. 28, pp. 275 ff., 689 f. Cf. also vol. 9, p. 65, and *Kant's Philosophical Correspondence 1759–1799*, ed. and tr. by Arnulf Zweig (Chicago, 1970), p. 154 = *AA*, vol. 11, p. 52 (letter to Herz, 26 May 1789). There is a problem here because Kant also says that animals, unlike 'lifeless' matter, 'conform' to an inner principle that they in a sense 'know' although not through reflective judgement. Although Kant's discussion is too brief, it does seem important here (as in practical philosophy in general) somehow to mark the basic distinctions he is after between (i) merely conforming to a principle, (ii) guiding oneself implicitly in view of that principle, and (iii) acting in explicit heed of the principle.

²⁶ Tetens questions Reimarus on just this point. J. N. Tetens, *Sprachphilosophische Versuche*, ed. by H. Pfannkuch (Hamburg, 1971), p. 105.

²⁷ *AA*, vol. 28, p. 117.

²⁸ Ibid., p. 145.

²⁹ *AA*, vol. 7, p. 140 n.; vol. 8, p. 180; vol. 28, p. 262.

³⁰ Heinz Heimsoeth, 'Metaphysik und Kritik bei Chr. A. Crusius', in *Studien*

zur Philosophie Immanuel Kants; D. Henrich, 'Über die Einheit der Subjektivität', *Philosophische Rundschau*, 3 (1955), 28–69.

[31] The distinction is already nicely made at *AA*, vol. 28, p. 234.

[32] *AA*, vol. 7, p. 131.

[33] *AA*, vol. 18, p. 319 (R 5661), in 'Beantwortung der Frage, ist es eine Erfahrung dass wir denken?' from notes of Kiesewetter, 1788–90. The value of the distinction between mere awareness and judgement experience is often overlooked, even in fine interpretations such as, e.g., S. C. Patten, 'An Anti-Sceptical Argument at the Deduction', *Kant-Studien*, 67 (1976), 557.

[34] *AA*, vol. 28, p. 227.

[35] For a discussion of this passage see my 'Kant's Transcendental Deduction as a Regressive Argument', p. 285. Cf. Paton, *Kant's Metaphysics*, p. 407, who says that according to Kant, 'in being aware of physical objects and their changes I am also . . . aware of a succession of ideas in my mind'.

[36] *AA*, vol. 7, p. 127.

[37] These two theories are implicitly distinguished in Smith, *Commentary*, p. 293. See also John Locke, *An Essay Concerning Human Understanding*, Bk. II, Ch. 1, § 4; Graham Bird, *Kant's Theory of Knowledge*, pp. 43–6, 169; and H. J. Paton, *The Categorical Imperative*, p. 233.

[38] *AA*, vol. 28, pp. 276–7.

[39] Ibid., p. 112.

[40] *AA*, vol. 28, p. 113.

[41] *Selected Pre-Critical Writings*, p. 18 = *AA*, vol. 2, p. 286.

[42] This temptation is succumbed to by G. Bird, *Kant's Theory*, p. 169. In the *Critique* Kant often does say things such as, 'I, as thinking, am an object of inner sense, and am called soul. That which is an object of the outer senses is called body' (A 342; amended translation). But this is not to rule out that representations of bodies can belong to inner sense too.

[43] J. Bennett, *Kant's Analytic*, p. 45.

[44] *AA*, vol. 28, p. 276.

[45] Wolff, *Kant's Theory*, p. 199.

[46] Ibid., p. 202.

[47] Kant's theory is more complicated than suggested here, but the facts require at least as much complexity. On his theory it is only through a focus on the spatial content of our representations that we discern the real temporal order of our representings, and yet it is also only as objects of possible representings (organized by the Principles) that we can discern the spatial order of these contents, *qua* objective.

[48] Indeed, this is all that Paton (*Kant's Metaphysics*, p. 389) and Ewing (*Commentary*, p. 124) think Kant can mean by the term in this context. Wolff is right against them in seeing that in self-knowledge Kant uses 'affection' to mean more than mere conceptual determination. That is, he is right to see that here the mind operates as more than a mere formal cause, but wrong to think it is therefore a sufficient material cause rather than simply an efficient cause of one's representation of oneself.

[49] On Kant's emphasis on our passivity, cf. W. Sellars ('This I or He or It (the Thing) Which Thinks'), pp. 19–21.

[50] I think these ways are more fundamental because they are present even if we drop Kant's questionable suggestion that we can become aware of ourselves only by *our* bringing our representations to consciousness.

[51] For one philosopher's picture of what such an intelligence might be like, see

Harry Frankfurt, 'Descartes on the Creation of the Eternal Truths', *Philosophical Review*, 86 (1977), 36-57.

[52] As J. Bennett (*Kant's Analytic*, pp. 58-9) notes, it is admittedly difficult, given the central insights of Kant's own philosophy, to see how we can ever call such a mere intuitive being an 'intelligence'.

[53] *AA*, vol. 28, p. 226; 'This is the only case in which we can intuit substance directly.'

[54] *Selected Pre-Critical Writings*, p. 112 = *AA*, vol. 10, p. 124 (letter to Herz, 21 February 1772); cf. A 92/B 125, B 167.

[55] *AA*, vol. 28, p. 654.

[56] *Metaphysical Foundations of Natural Science*, p. 8 = *AA*, vol. 4, p. 471. Cf. *AA*, vol. 20, p. 270.

[57] See, e.g., *AA*, vol. 17, p. 668, R 4723: 'Die Vorstellung von unsrer [freyen] Selbsttätigkeit ist eine solche, da wir nicht affiziert werden, folglich ist nicht Erscheinung, sondern Apperception.' Cf. *AA*, vol. 28, p. 264.

[58] Kant is also often thought to hold that all temporal knowledge is self-knowledge (see, e.g., W. Sellars, *Science and Metaphysics*, p. 235), that is, that not only is time the only form of inner representings, but also that it is only the form of such representings and not of distinct outer representeds. I will not presume that Kant is committed to such a strong thesis, for it appears to involve a conflation of the empirical and transcendental subject.

[59] This seems to have been forgotten by T. E. Wilkerson (*Kant's Critique of Pure Reason*, p. 24) and others who sometimes evaluate Kant as if he were trying to argue that space and time are logically necessary for all experience. Bennett also goes too far at one point in saying simply that Kant holds 'experience must be temporal' (*Kant's Dialectic*, p. 54).

[60] See R. Pippin, 'Kant on Empirical Concepts', *Studies in History and Philosophy of Science*, 10 (1979), 1-19.

[61] Cf. Bennett, *Kant's Analytic*, p. 207.

[62] See above Ch. III, n. 59, and W. H. Walsh, *Kant's Criticism of Metaphysics*, p. 187. How Kant himself was not entirely clear on this point is explained in the first part of my 'Kant and the Objectivity of Taste', *British Journal of Aesthetics*, 23 (1983), 3-17. See also below, Ch. VII.13.

[63] R. Chisholm, *Person and Object*, p. 27; cf. ibid., pp. 24-5. See also H. D. Lewis, *The Elusive Mind* (London, 1969), p. 269: 'We find our knowledge of essentially non-material processes in *having* such processes.'

[64] I take it that regarding space it can be said that there are such, although there remains the question of there being any specifiable set of them about whose objective validity we have certainty. See S. Körner, 'On the Kantian Foundation of Science and Mathematics', in *The First Critique*, ed. by T. Penelhum and J. MacIntosh (Belmont, California, 1969), pp. 97-108, and Paul Henle, 'The *Critique of Pure Reason* Today', *Journal of Philosophy*, 59 (1962), 225-34.

[65] See my 'Kant's Transcendental Deduction as a Regressive Argument'; my review of R. Walker's *Kant, Teaching Philosophy*, 3 (1980), 358-63; and my 'Recent Work in Kant's Theoretical Philosophy', *American Philosophical Quarterly*, 19 (1982), 1-24. I there argue that the deduction is meant as a weaker form of argument (i.e., not aimed against total scepticism) than many have presumed, and yet it can still be a significant proof. (My interpretation is closest to the views of W. Sellars, 'Some Remarks on Kant's Theory of Experience', *Journal of Philosophy*, 64 (1967), 646, and W. D. Stine, 'Self-Consciousness in Kant's *Critique of Pure Reason, Philosophical Studies*, 28 (1975), 189-97.)

I do not take it to be as weak as some hold, that is, as being 'designed not to prove any concepts to be categories or to be objectively valid, but to explain the notions of a category or of objective validity' (Bird, *Kant's Theory*, p. 114; cf. ibid., pp. 84–6). One reason why Bird and others have been driven to such a view is that they believe the Analytic of Principles alone proves specific categories. But rather than saying the deduction is not (meant as) a proof at all, or is only a general proof that some categories are needed, we can say it means to prove precisely that the categories set out by the metaphysical deduction are valid (see B 143, B 160–1), while leaving open for the Principles the demonstration of the specific schematizations the categories take for us.

⁶⁶ On the notion of 'experience' in this sense as the premiss of Kant's deduction see also B 147 and *Kant's Philosophical Correspondence*, p. 184 = *AA*, vol. 11, p. 302 (letter to Beck, 20 January 1792).

⁶⁷ Given the reconstruction I have offered of the transcendental deduction, it follows that the completion of the deduction of the categories ultimately does depend on a form of what has been called the 'definitive premiss of the original epistemological argument', that is, the *a priori* determinable objective validity of some mathematical system. The source of that premiss in turn seems to be Kant's excessive reaction to scepticism about the application of geometry to the phenomenal world. He appears to have believed it necessary that not only in some ways do idealized geometrical manifolds apply to that realm but that some such *a priori* determinable manifold is perfectly instantiated by it. (This is not the same as presuming the manifold is Euclidean; see Rolf Horstmann, 'Space as Intuition and Geometry', *Ratio*, 28 (1976), 17–29.) See B 128, as well as Sellars, *Science and Metaphysics*, p. 54, and Philip Kitcher, 'Kant on the Foundations of Mathematics', *Philosophical Review*, 84 (1975), 23–50.

⁶⁸ See *AA*, vol. 7, pp. 142, 396 f; A 378, B 155, A 37/B 54.

⁶⁹ Moreover, the content of what is so perceived is to be determined as a 'limitation' of the concept of that superior being. This is Kant's direct answer to the objection that the notion of things in themselves is too empty for us to say even indirectly what they could be like. See *AA*, vol. 8, p. 154, and vol. 23, p. 34: 'Man muss Dinge an sich selbst durch den Begriff von einem realsten Wesen denken, weil dieses alle Erfahrung ausschliesst.' Cf. Allen Wood, *Kant's Rational Theology* (Ithaca, 1978), p. 81.

⁷⁰ This point is contrary to H. Allison, 'Kant's Concept of the Transcendental Object', *Kant-Studien*, 68 (1959), 165–86.

⁷¹ It is only texts suggesting this that keep writers such as Strawson and Wilkerson from accepting the interpretation of transcendental idealism set forth here. But the texts they cite (A 369–70) occur only in the first edition and need not be taken in a subjectivistic way (see above, Ch. III.8), and if so taken obviously contradict other things Kant says even in that edition (A 190/B 235) about the difference between representations and appearances.

⁷² There are admittedly problems of individuation here. See above, Ch. III, n. 77.

⁷³ By 'necessary' here I mean metaphysical necessity in the sense explained, e.g., by Alvin Plantinga (*The Nature of Necessity* [Oxford, 1974]), and not physical necessity or even the necessity Kant says our epistemic forms and principles provide.

⁷⁴ Nor can he mean they are phenomenal merely because our knowledge of them involves conceptual and sensory activity on our part. Prauss has recently offered a careful interpretation along this line, but it has difficulties as an exposition of Kant's view because, as Prauss admits (*Kant und das Problem der*

Dinge an sich, pp. 175 ff.), it forces one to regard all of Kant's own comments about our being 'restricted' to phenomenal knowledge as inappropriate and even incoherent.

⁷⁵ For this reason, although I shall try to make Kant's transcendental idealism not appear too exotic, I cannot make it out to be as innocuous as some believe. Bird, for example, says appearances and noumena are 'two ways of looking at the same thing only because, on Kant's view, there is only one thing at which to look, namely appearance' (*Kant's Theory*, p. 29; cf. above, Ch. II, n. 100). Admittedly noumena need not be different things from appearances, nor can we look at them as such, but they still constitute for Kant a more fundamental, though unknowable for us, layer of reality. It is precisely appearances which for Kant are not things in a full substantial sense (see below, n. 79).

⁷⁶ Cf. P. Lachièze-Rey, 'Das Kantische und das Kartesische *Cogito*', in *Materialen zu Kants Kritik der reinen Vernunft*, ed. J. Kopper (Frankfurt, 1975), pp. 177 ff. There is an obvious though controversial analogue of this idea for acts of practical reason.

⁷⁷ *Metaphysical Foundations of Natural Sciences*, p. 12 n. = *AA*, vol. 4, p. 474 n. Cf. A 67/B 92.

⁷⁸ Cf. *AA*, vol. 7, p. 399: 'Now as these forms [whereby I know myself] cannot be assumed to be valid for all beings conscious of themselves, therefore in the knowledge that man has on the basis of inner sense, he represents himself not as he is in himself (*because* this is not a condition valid for all thinking beings, for otherwise it would be a representation of the understanding). Rather, this is merely a consciousness of the mode whereby man appears to himself through inner observation of himself.' (My emphasis.) See also vol. 18, p. 680 (R 6354).

⁷⁹ Generally, instead of directly equating substances with things in themselves and mere determinations with phenomena, Kant distinguishes things in themselves from mere determinations, and substances from phenomena: 'Das Substrat oder Grund der Seele kennen wir nicht, blos ihre Erscheinungen . . . die Körper sind aber keine Substanzen, sondern nur Erscheinungen' (*AA*, vol. 28, p. 591). 'Ein Phänomen ist an sich keine Substanz' (ibid., p. 682; cf. p. 671). '. . . der behauptet dass die Seele keine besondere Substanz sey, sondern nur eine Kraft, also ein Phänomenon und Accidens' (ibid., p. 261). 'Das Substantiale ist das Ding an sich selbst und unbekannt' (*AA*, vol. 18, p. 145, R 5292) '. . . we begin with the category of substance, whereby a thing in itself is represented' (A 344/B 402). 'For it is obvious that a thing in itself is of a different nature from the determinations which constitute only its state' (A 360). 'Matter, therefore, does not mean a kind of substance . . . but only the distinctive nature of those appearances of objects . . . the representations of which we call outer' (A 385). For an early linking of substance and essence, see *AA*, vol. 28, p. 25. Cf. *Kant's Philosophical Correspondence*, p. 140 = *AA*, vol. 11, p. 37 (to Reinhold, 12 May 1789).

⁸⁰ *AA*, vol. 20, p. 270, and vol. 28, pp 411, 429, 511, 563. Cf. Sellars, 'The I Which Thinks', pp. 8–9. Apparently overinfluenced by the fact that things in themselves as such have no determinable sensible properties, Bird goes too far in saying that in Kant's view 'no predicates belong to these things in themselves as they are in themselves' (*Kant's Theory*, p. 29).

⁸¹ *AA*, vol. 28, pp. 553, 493, 629; vol. 9, p. 61. Kant's ground for this is not so clear, but unlike Leibniz's it would no doubt have to do more with passivity than the mere finitude of our mind.

⁸² See above, n. 35.

⁸³ See M. Westphal, 'In Defense of the Thing in Itself', *Kant-Studien*, 59 (1968), 118–41.

84 Cf. B xxix n. For criticism of the arguments, see P. F. Strawson, *The Bounds of Sense*, pp. 171 ff.; Bennett, *Kant's Dialectic*, pp. 114 ff.; and M. S. Gram, 'Kant's First Antimony', *The Monist*, 51 (1967), 511 ff.

85 The reference to space is important, for as R. Walker demonstrates, Kant's argument needn't be taken as meaning one could know things only by reference to material items ('The Status of Kant's Theory of Matter', in *Kant's Theory of Knowledge*, ed. by L. W. Beck, pp. 151–6).

86 Kant's difficulty with the issue is still evident in his remarks on creation in the *Critique of Practical Reason*, p. 106 = *AA*, vol. 5, p. 102.

87 In general Kant may have been too impressed by the idea that if a concept is 'confused' it is not thereby sensible (A 43/B 61). He does not argue as convincingly against the corresponding notion that if a representation is sensible it is in a sense a confused concept.

88 Strawson, *Bounds of Sense*, pp. 173–4. Cf. below at n. 107.

89 For a good explanation of how Kant can say time as a pure intuition can precede thought, see A. Melnick, *Kant's Analogies of Experience* (Chicago, 1973), pp. 7–14.

90 *AA*, vol. 7, p. 142; my emphasis. Cf. *AA*, vol. 20, p. 270, where Kant says the apprehension of the self is 'according to the mode in which the subject is affected, that is, the condition of time'.

91 Strawson, *Bounds of Sense*, p. 249; cf. ibid. p. 39. Here the term 'transcendental' is used in a deviant way by Strawson (and Kant at A 492/B 520), namely as meaning supersensible ('transcendent') and noumenal, and not in its primary epistemological meaning.

92 See e.g., R. C. S. Walker, *Kant*, p. 59, and St. Thomas, *Summa Theologiae* Ia, q. 14, art. 13, ad. 9.

93 Sellars introduces an interesting alternative here when he says that although the spatio-temporal phenomenal realm cannot be reduced to what is 'ultimately real', still there must be (and Kant must believe in) some analogy between the phenomenal and the transcendentally real, and so the latter must be constituted of quasi-spatio-temporal elements which replace the phenomenal ones in an ultimate account of things, without the latter being analysable into them and yet also without anything significant for explanatory purposes being thereby missed (*Science and Metaphysics*, p. 56 f; cf. *AA*, vol. 28, p. 493, where Kant speaks of real essences 'explaining' phenomena).

94 Strawson, *Bounds of Sense*, p. 249.

95 See *Selected Pre-Critical Writings*, p. 97 (letter from Lambert, 13 October 1770 = *AA*, vol. 10, p. 102), and ibid., p. 116 (letter to Herz, 21 February 1772 = *AA*, vol. 10, p. 128), where Kant speaks of what 'seems to be the most essential objection that can be raised against the system'.

96 Cf. *AA*, vol. 7, p. 142, and A 37/B 53: 'I really have the representation of time and of my determinations in it.'

97 Strawson, *Bounds of Sense*, p. 39.

98 M. Gram, 'How to Dispense with Things in Themselves', *Ratio*, 28 (1976), 107.

99 Ibid., p. 108.

100 Ibid., p. 109. Cf. ibid., p. 11.

101 Gram deals with something like this further reply when he attacks transcendental idealism even when taken simply as a 'distinction between two ways in which the same thing is regarded' (ibid., p. 6). His objection is only that the 'object which we perceive must satisfy descriptions appropriate to things in themselves and appearances at the same time: And this is obviously impossible' (ibid.,

p. 7). Gram just does not prove that the descriptions are incompatible, and it surely seems possible that something could both be spatio-temporally perceived (and described) by us and not so by God. Cf. B xxvii–xxviii.

[102] Bennett, *Kant's Analytic*, p. 51. Cf. Bird, *Kant's Theory*, p. 148: 'Transcendental idealism holds then that all our knowledge is based upon experiences, and that we have no knowledge of anything that cannot be experienced, but that this is compatible with our empirical discrimination of what we experience into inner and outer objects . . . The force of transcendental idealism is only to suppose that we have experiences, and that these play an essential part in our knowledge.' Such an interpretation may do justice to Kant's empirical realism but does not at all account for the fact that he distinguished this in meaning from transcendental idealism.

[103] Bennett, *Kant's Analytic*, p. 51.

[104] Bennett says, 'The minimal objection to "temporality is stamped upon experience by inner sense" is that it speaks of what is *done* by inner sense and it therefore presupposes temporality' (ibid., p. 49). Here our earlier characterization of inner sense is directly helpful in countering a misunderstanding of Kant's idealism. Such a sense is taken by Kant to be precisely a sign of our passivity, something we're limited by before we can do anything, even conceptually.

[105] Bennett, *Kant's Dialectic*, p. 49.

[106] Ibid., p. 56. Bennett there also claims that for Kant the 'extended world is not contrasted with any possible subject even of conjecture'. Compare Kant B xxvi, B 427–8.

[107] Walker, *Kant*, p. 133. Cf. ibid., pp. 12, 274, and P. Strawson, *Bounds of Sense*, p. 174.

[108] Walker, *Kant*, p. 132. See B 158, B 423.

[109] Walker, *Kant*, pp. 131, 12.

[110] Ibid., p. 134.

[111] Ibid., p. 131. See above, n. 69, and Ch. II, n. 99.

[112] Michael Washburn, 'Did Kant Have a Theory of Self-Knowledge?' p. 43.

[113] Ibid., pp. 45, 51.

[114] See Michael Washburn, 'The Second Edition of the Critique: Towards an Understanding of its Nature and Genesis', pp. 277–90.

[115] See, e.g., *Metaphysical Foundations of Natural Science*, p. 6 = *AA*, vol. 4, p. 469.

[116] Ibid., p. 103; B 256. The application of the first categories, quantity and quality, is not so problematic, but at times Kant does question the full applicability of mathematics to inner sense, and it also might be argued that quality applies only to the inner and isn't a genuine category.

[117] Cf. B 437, B 292, *Metaphysical Foundations of Natural Science*, p. 8 = *AA*, vol. 4, p. 471.

[118] This is stressed by A. C. Ewing, *Kant's Treatment of Causality* (London, 1924), p. 139.

[119] Cf. T. Mischel, 'Kant and the Possibility of a Science of Psychology', p. 608.

[120] Cf. Ewing, *Kant's Treatment of Causality*, Chapter 6. Kant need not say, of course, that the laws for these changes, understood in mere bodily terms, are very accessible or interesting.

Postscript: Kant and Mind:
Mere Immaterialism

I

Andrew Brook's very valuable book, *Kant and the Mind*[1] draws attention to a number of aspects of Kant's account of mind that deserve a more thorough treatment than could be given in *Kant's Theory of Mind*. Two topics in particular deserve more attention: the nature of apperception, and the issue of the underlying metaphysics of Kant's theory. Since the topic of Kantian apperception and self-reference has already become the focus of so many other recent discussions (e.g., by Patricia Kitcher, C. T. Powell, Dieter Sturma, and Manfred Frank, as well as myself),[2] on this occasion I will return to the relatively neglected topic of Kant's metaphysics of mind, and the issue of whether it is closer to immaterialism, or materialism, or something neutral. This issue is pressing now not only because of the effect of Brook's study, but also because of several references to Kant in some of Colin McGinn's important recent work in the philosophy of mind. Like Brook, McGinn has devoted considerable attention to the privileges of self-reference, but what his invocation of Kant stresses is the metaphysics of mind and a defence of what he calls 'noumenalism', the view that there are in principle obstacles to our access to the self's underlying nature.[3] I will be arguing that, while Brook and McGinn each nicely stress important ways in which Kant's theory avoids the limitations of traditional forms of materialism, their interpretations ultimately are unsustainable at certain points because of an inclination to neutrality or materialism that leads them to miss the meaning and force of Kant's immaterialist metaphysics.

II

I will begin with a response to Brook and his challenge to a key part of the main thesis of my work, the thesis that Kant's theory of mind was closer to traditional metaphysics than has been allowed by most interpreters, especially in English. Brook details a series of functional and epistemic features of mind that he shows Kant's philosophy deserves special credit for clarifying. Brook then takes it as a significant advantage of his account that, even with all these features, Kant's theoretical philosophy is supposedly saddled with no 'positive theory', i.e., no ontological account, of what the mind is. Taking Kant's philosophy to be 'neutral' in this way is recommended in part because it leaves room, Brook stresses, for allowing the ultimate truth of materialism without bringing materialism into the very analysis of features of our experience, such as there being a subject and apperception. My interpretation of Kant is faulted precisely for missing this point: 'Ameriks' book . . . makes the mistake of thinking that Kant is presenting a positive theory.'[4] In particular, I am faulted for attributing an immaterialist metaphysics to Kant; for not seeing that, although Kant admittedly favoured immaterialism on practical or moral grounds, he supposedly did not have a theoretical attachment to it: 'Commentators such as Ameriks who urge that Kant had a positive doctrine of immaterialism rest a lot of weight on it. Though [Kant] certainly accepted immaterialism as an item of faith . . . [there are] powerful reasons to doubt that Kant's *theory* contained any such doctrine.'[5]

I agree that a practical commitment to immaterialism does not of itself show that there is a theoretical basis for immaterialism. I also agree with Brook's 'neutralism' to the extent that it suggests that a commitment to the truth of what Kant holds on the basis of practical reason does at least imply that one also should not expect in the *Critique* a theoretical basis for materialism (for then our two basic kinds of reason would be in conflict). Furthermore, against the suggestion of some interpreters,[6] I would also agree with Brook that the Kantian analysis of such functions of the mind as apperception does not have a genuinely immaterialist thesis built into it. All this still leaves it open that somewhere in Kant's mere theoretical philosophy there is a basis for asserting the immateriality of mind, which is just what Brook is at pains to deny. Who is right?

The crucial text from the *Critique of Pure Reason* that Brook relies on here is B 420: 'if materialism is disqualified from explaining my existence, spiritualism is equally incapable of doing so.'[7] I happen to have cited this text as well,[8] and I would still contend that it does not show Kant is blocked from a theoretical doctrine such as mere immaterialism. It is crucial to keep in mind that 'spiritualism' is a technical term here, and it is not the same as immaterialism. As I noted in my book, for Kant a spirit is a being that is not only immaterial but also has the property of being in its existence necessarily independent of material beings.[9] There might, after all, exist beings that are immaterial (e.g., human minds) but that would come and go out of existence when certain material beings ceased (e.g., human bodies). Moreover, the possibility of such beings that would not be spirits is extremely relevant for Kant. He is concerned with them precisely because what he wants to show above all, against certain rationalists, is that, even if immaterialism were conceded, the crucial traditional claims of our necessary persistence, let alone personal immortality, would not yet follow. Hence, reservations expressed against spiritualism do not at all carry over against immaterialism.

Secondly, note that at B 420 Kant is stressing problems with 'explaining one's existence'. The use of the terms 'existence' and 'explaining' reveals the limitations of Kant's point here. The question of the ultimate origin of the existence of particular finite things is a notorious philosophical problem— but there is nothing here that implies a *special* problem for immaterialism. There are ways in which either materialism or immaterialism could be true and inescapable even if by themselves they were each too general, and hence insufficient, to 'explain' the origin of particular beings. Recall also that Kant goes into some detail about how the 'explanatory' and 'ontological' status of various features can differ considerably, just as regulative and constitutive claims can differ. Thus, mechanism may work as a general theory of the empirical constitution of matter and yet fail for us as a sufficient account or 'explanation' of specific, organic comings into existence (e.g., Newton 'can't explain' a blade of grass).[10] Hence, the 'explanatory' weaknesses of a doctrine such as immaterialism or materialism need not rule out its being an unavoidable theory to assert—especially if the alternative turns out to be, as Kant believes, demonstrably contradictory.

At some points (especially in the *Prolegomena*), Kant also stresses that there are some phenomena, notably apperception, for which a specifically materialistic explanation is never to be expected (hence the first clause in the quote above from B 420). However, I am not resting my argument for ascribing immaterialism to Kant on this point, for the point is made precisely in a context in which one is supposed to recall that the explanatory and regulative limitations of a certain framework (in this case, materialism) are secondary and by themselves do not rule out the ultimate truth of the theory.[11] I also am not resting my position on the interpretation of the second paralogism; for, although I stressed in my book that Kant does not adequately spell out the exact flaw in the rationalist's arguments towards simplicity and immateriality, I realize that this is still not to say that in the second Paralogism Kant is himself arguing for immaterialism (parallel considerations hold for the oddly presented thesis of the second antinomy).[12]

So far, all that I have meant to show is that there is nothing in Kant that counts *against* immaterialism in the way that Brook suggests; this does not yet show what there is in Kant's theory that counts *for* immaterialism. There is definitely more to be done, for although I hold that it is extremely important to show how little is meant to follow immediately from Kant's immaterialism, I do mean to claim a theoretical Kantian commitment to immaterialism. Moreover, by 'immaterialism' I mean more than the restricted doctrine that not every concrete thing is material; I mean the unrestricted doctrine that every concrete thing is basically non-material. So, even with all the limitations and qualifications that I want to stress, immaterialism remains on the table as a fairly strong claim, one most philosophers now certainly do not think can be defended, and hence it must be acknowledged that the burden is on those who admire Kant and yet would commit him to such a claim.

The claim also has the problem of seeming to conflict with what Brook calls 'the doctrine of the unknowability of the mind as it is'.[13] This is a much discussed 'doctrine', but Kant does not put matters so simply. Everyone, after all, agrees that the mind is not in all respects unknowable; its appearance and empirical features can be known in all sorts of ways. So the alleged doctrine is, of course, to be understood as a claim about the mind as it is 'in itself', as a thing in itself. And here one runs into the thorniest general problems of Kant exegesis. One has to take a stand here, and either insist that for Kant there is absolutely no knowledge of things in themselves, or contend that his position is more complex than it at first appears. I contend that some complexity is inescapable here. For example, even Brook allows adding that Kant wants a kind of *practical* knowledge of things in themselves. The big question then is whether some kind of relatively *indeterminate theoretical* knowledge of things in themselves can also be attributed to Kant. I am of the view that it can, for charity alone demands that we see Kant as not only allowing but even theoretically asserting that at least there exists some thing in itself, even if we cannot say much about it, not even about its quantity.[14] Once this much is said, though, a breach is made, and if one is led by specific Kantian arguments to some other relatively indeterminate claims that do not conflict with the most basic Kantian doctrines, then I think such claims should also be allowed. Kant does not have to be bound down by the fanatical purity of his interpreters. If, in the route to the weak kind of knowledge of things in themselves that is conceded here, there is nothing clearly endangering the specific traditional objects of attack (e.g., theoretical proofs of immortality) of the Critical philosophy, what is the problem? As long as there are specific Kantian reasons for allowing a weak theoretical claim about things in themselves, why not allow it? The alternative of claiming that absolutely nothing can be known of things in themselves does not escape problems itself, for one can ask how such a strong claim could itself be backed, and one can note that, once this claim is made, however it is backed, it appears to undermine itself; for then of things in themselves we would still know something absolute, namely that they cannot be known.

More generally, I think we should take the doctrines of the Dialectic one at a time. It is no good to assume the following common three-step procedure, i.e., to argue that:

   (i) in general, nothing can be known about things in themselves,

  (ii) this particular, apparently convincing, argument for such things being F (e.g., immaterial) has implications for things in themselves,

 (iii) so, the particular argument just has to be bad.

Such a procedure begs the question, for, until one knows more, one could rather take the second step (= ii), the apparently convincing particular argument, as precisely a strong sign of a flaw in the general argument of the first step (= i). Hence there is a need in each case for a flaw to be demonstrated in the specific arguments presented, and Kant usually does provide this extra step.[15]

Rather than running away from things in themselves, a Kantian can start by conceding that, even before we begin to ask about the mind as such in itself, we do know something about it 'in itself', namely that there is some thing in itself there, though not necessarily in some way 'isomorphic' with appearances.[16] This is, of course, pretty 'thin' knowledge, for, as Kant stresses—in a passage that turns out to be central to McGinn's interpretation—the thing in itself of mental appearances and the thing in itself of non-mental appearances may even be the same, at least in character (B 428). Yet all this leaves open the possibility that we could know something else very general about it, and that we could be led to an immaterialism that does not rest on outdated rational psychology.

How is this possible? The answer is that Kant's immaterialism does not rest essentially on claims specifically about the mind. It can remain in harmony with his Critical theory because it is presented not as a specific consequence of rational psychology, let alone as a sufficient ground of its crucial traditional doctrines, but rather as something forced on us by more general aspects of Kantian ontology.

What are these aspects? The main argument underlying my position is simply that immaterialism follows from Kant's general doctrines of space, time, and matter. If matter is defined as the moveable in space, and if Kant's transcendental idealism is committed to the doctrine of the non-spatiality of things in themselves, then it surely appears to follow that things in themselves are non-material because they are not even spatial. And then they are also immaterial, for on my (not uncommon) usage to say that something is immaterial is nothing other than to say that it is non-material.[17] (The mediating connection here between spatiality and materiality is not trivial, but at least on Kant's view things certainly have to be in some way spatial in order to be material—although it is true that over time Kant modified the details of his view by reconsidering what is meant by 'filling a space'. At first, he thought material things could be simply items that have spatial effects—such as monadic point forces, or 'physical monads'—and they need not themselves be spatially extended, but, ultimately Kant came to the view that they need to be extending over a space themselves.[18])

It might be thought that Kant is not an immaterialist because theoretically he holds that things in themselves cannot be said to be mental in the sense of having 'ordinary' psychological properties as such, i.e., of consisting of 'pneumatic' stuff, any more than they can consist of physical stuff. But this rejection of what can be called 'pneumatism' is not tantamount to a rejection of 'mere immaterialism'. For a Kantian, things in themselves are non-pneumatic simply because they are non-temporal, for temporality is essential to what he understands by one's 'pneumatic' or ordinary psychological properties.[19] That is, since things in themselves, whatever they are, cannot be spatial or temporal as such, they cannot be like *ordinary* minds—but they are still immaterial, because as non-spatio-temporal they are definitely not physical. Moreover, they are in some way also like minds, for they do turn out in part to be a locus of rational principles, to be such that they *can* be morally 'determined' by explicit principles. This is all consistent with the fact that the 'noumenal' proof that all things are immaterial does not show specifically that there is a noumenal immaterial 'soul-substance', but merely that whatever underlies the phenomenon of the mind is immaterial. A reason for not calling it a 'soul-substance' (A 359: 'the thesis that only souls (as particular kinds of substances) would have to be given up') is simply that this immaterial item might be, for all we know theoretically, indistinguishable in kind from whatever it is that underlies other things (e.g., all matter). This indeterminacy can lead to misunderstandings, as will become clear when we turn to McGinn's interpretation, but it still does not count against Kant's mere immaterialism (cf. B 428, and below at n. 23).

There remains one popular way to try to escape this interpretation, namely to turn the non-materiality of things in themselves into a triviality by holding that things in themselves are not material simply because there are not any such 'things'. To speak of something 'in itself' on this account is not to speak of a thing of a certain sort but rather precisely to avoid speaking of a thing; i.e., it is simply to abstract from how we supposedly know things, namely by relating them to us and not leaving them 'in themselves'—for leaving them that way would mean having *by definition* nothing really to say about them. It is obviously possible and interesting to consider such an abstraction, but the crucial question is whether this move can *exhaust* what Kant does and must mean by talk of things in themselves. I have explored and criticized this interpretation elsewhere;[20] for now, suffice it to say that not only does this interpretation cause huge problems for understanding the preconditions of Kant's own moral philosophy, but it also offers a very suspicious 'high road' to idealism, one that makes the non-spatio-temporality of things in themselves an all too immediate result, something not requiring the complex arguments in the Aesthetic and the Antinomies that Kant actually uses to ground his doctrine. (Note that no part of my discussion involves endorsing these particular arguments.)

All this is relevant because at times Brook seems to indicate a sympathy with what I would call the 'trivializing' view of things in themselves that would block my strategy of allowing there to be something substantive, even if very limited, that can and must be said of things in themselves, and a fortiori of minds, namely that they are not material. I take it that this trivializing view should not be presumed, and that if it were held as a general position it would make impossible the practical claims that even Brook concedes. But, if the trivializing view is left aside, and we still can and should see Kant as a theoretical immaterialist, what then of Brook's objection that going so far would impose a 'positive' theory of the mind on Kant, something that is supposedly definitely ruled out? My response is simply that little hangs on calling Kant's immaterialism a 'positive' theory. It is obviously introduced in negative terms; it just says things in themselves (which must exist) are not spatial or temporal or physical or mental in the ordinary sense. But it still can be a substantive theory; it can leave room for all those general characterizations that are asserted later in the practical philosophy, as when we say that, as moral self-determiners, we are substantive and causal, although not in a directly spatio-temporal way.

At one point Brook does recognize and challenge a line of thought found in Kant that goes to immaterialism from general considerations like those I have stressed; he even calls them considerations 'we could imagine Karl Ameriks making'.[21] He admits that there appears to be some support for them, and an 'apparent contradiction' of his own reading, in passages from Kant like the following: 'Neither the transcendental object which underlies outer appearances nor that which underlies inner intuition, is in itself either matter or a thinking being . . .' (A 379–80).[22] How Brook means to go on from here to counter my interpretation is very unclear, though, for his comment is simply that Kant's conclusion follows 'only on his own, very peculiar conception of matter'.[23] But note that this means there is hardly a merely 'apparent' contradiction of Brook's interpretation—there is rather a real contradiction with Kant's own view—and this is already to take back any challenge to my reading. It is to admit that Kant did argue for immaterialism, and to add only that his argument had weaknesses—which is something that I have also stressed. Moreover, the considerations which Brook himself implies are lying behind the cited passage are not really so 'very peculiar'. They are basically Kant's considerations about how matter is supposedly bound to the property of infinite divisibility, which is just a reminder of how the features of space and time, and hence their ideality, are crucial to the ideality of matter and thus the immaterialism of things in themselves.[24] Hence, to save his reading of matter and things in themselves Brook would have to jettison Kant's basic theory of space and time—which is hardly an option where the issue is the interpretation and not yet the revision or evaluation of Kant's theory.

Brook does introduce two further problems with the immaterialist position. The first is that 'Kant is not entitled to any view about the real nature of appearances, any more than about anything else'.[25] Supposedly, after the Critical turn, all Kant can do is hypothesize about appearances, and not say anything about a 'real nature'. But, I would counter, if we do run into contradictions about ascribing certain features to the ultimate real nature of things—as Kant insists we do with the features of space and time—then we simply cannot avoid at least this much of a view: that the 'real nature' of things is not spatio-temporal, and a fortiori it is not material.

A second objection Brook develops claims that the immaterialistic interpretation 'overphenomenalizes' Kant and even suggests solipsism.[26] But on my version it does no such thing. To assert, as A 379 does, that there is a non-material ground, something without the features of 'inner' or 'outer' intuition as such, is precisely to deny what phenomenalism asserts, viz., that reality is merely a representation (for all representation is intuition or concept, and the 'ground' is neither), and it is not at all to suggest that there is only one person's set of representations.

I take all this to vindicate my claims to the effect that Kant is best read as committed to an immaterialist metaphysics, and that this commitment is not subject to the common objections of intrinsic absurdity or internal inconsistency. But this still does not show that Kant's metaphysics of mind is on a par with other options today, or that it deserves more than the neglect or transformation into 'neutrality' that Brook advocates. To provide some indication of the continuing relevance of Kantian metaphysics, I turn to a comparison of Kant and McGinn.

III

I have been emphasizing how much Kant is theoretically committed both to a genuine metaphysical nature of the mind, and to a very indeterminate picture of that nature. It is precisely this combination of metaphysical commitment and non-specificity that has attracted Colin McGinn to Kant's theory. Like Kant and Thomas Nagel, McGinn holds that we do not have determinate knowledge about the mind's ultimate nature, and that we should reject 'domesticating' reductions of mind (via functionalist or contemporary materialist definitions), as well as eliminativist theses or the assertion of brute miracles or irreducible relations between mind and body.[27] McGinn's alternative is a 'noumenalist' view of mind, which says that our consciousness has a 'hidden structure', that this structure ultimately grounds the mind's features and accounts for mind–body relations, and that the reason why we cannot actually explain how such relations operate is simply that our mind is itself so constructed that *in principle* it cannot attain to a knowledge of how its hidden structure operates.[28] With the 'in principle' claim McGinn has moved into transcendental philosophy, and has gone beyond a position like Nagel's, for even Nagel's 'pessimism' on resolving the mind–body problem is *not* necessarily permanent.

This view certainly has deep similarities with the most radical aspect of Kant's transcendental idealism, its doctrine specifically about our knowledge of the mind, for, like Kant, this view holds that the mind in itself is responsible in a fundamental way for our not being able to know specifically the mind in itself. Moreover, here the mind in itself is initially understood negatively, just as it is by Kant, as that which is at least not structured in terms of the physical and psychological principles with which we are familiar.

I find such a stark view to be realistic and intrinsically attractive, especially since the other basic alternatives do seem to have the very defects that McGinn recites. It is hard to believe in any known physical or functional definition of mind, and it just as hard to allow that the mind itself can be wholly 'eliminated' as a mere appearance, as witches have been from our ontology. It also seems too odd to accept that there is no underlying metaphysical connection between what we grasp as mind and as body, no connection at all directly between these items, as opposed to just some 'harmony' or miraculous link provided by a third being, e.g., God. McGinn's 'solution' is to assert that there must be some underlying rational connection here, and yet that there is also a fundamental 'cognitive closure' that keeps us from being able to get to know what the connection is. Rather than adopt any of the extreme alternatives just canvassed, we need to keep in mind that 'epistemic limits never entail ontological fissures or fishiness',[29] and 'there is, after all, no a priori reason to suppose that the nature of consciousness is fully revealed to conscious beings themselves'.[30]

McGinn's solution is also like Kant's in another way. He proposes that we assume that whatever the hidden structure of mind is, it should be thought of as at least somehow fitting in with what our basic theoretical knowledge has already revealed: if we could get all the way down, we would see that mind and its basis are 'homogeneous' and in accord with the overall framework of our theoretical philosophy. Here he invokes Kant's familiar response at B 428 to the difficulty of dualism: 'if we consider that the two kinds of objects thus differ from each other, not inwardly but only in so far as one *appears* outwardly to another, and that what, as thing in itself, underlies the appearance of matter, perhaps after all may not be so heterogeneous in character, this difficulty vanishes.'[31] In McGinn's approving words: 'From the perspective of objective noumenal reality, then, matter and mind may not be so disparate at they appear to our limited human viewpoint.'[32]

Despite all these similarities, McGinn senses that his position must differ from Kant's somewhere, and he points out two apparent differences. Unfortunately, with both of these points he goes astray.

One of these alleged differences is not of major importance. McGinn believes that Kant assumes that diverse items such as matter and consciousness 'have to be fundamentally *identical* in nature if they are to be linked perspicuously'.[33] Here it appears McGinn is simply misunderstanding Kant's not so unusual notion of 'homogeneity'. It can be easily inferred from Kant's discussion of the schematism (B 176/A 137) that his condition of 'homogeneity' between two hard-to-relate items requires only that the items share something in common, not that they have everything in common and end up being identical. Of course, it is also probably (and unfortunately) true that Kant still presumes a much higher degree of 'homogeneity' is needed for intelligibility than what most of us now believe—but there is nothing in his philosophy that need keep him from accepting McGinn's proposal that there be merely some kind of hidden third property, which is not identical with but does underlie and 'link' the mental and bodily items that we are incapable of joining in an explanation.

The other alleged departure from Kant that McGinn mentions does turn out to reveal deep differences, but they are quite unlike what McGinn directly cites. McGinn contends that Kant 'here attributes the problem-resolving structure to matter, not to mind'.[34] McGinn's solution is supposedly just the opposite: that mind has a hidden structure that makes it homogeneous with matter. Here I believe there is a fundamental misunderstanding in this whole way of trying to express the difference between himself and Kant. McGinn is presuming that the Kantian proposal of an underlying homogeneity has to do with a likeness between (1) mind *as we know it* and (2) a hidden *structure of matter*. This misses in a twofold way what Kant really means within the broader context of his philosophy. (A somewhat similar misunderstanding was generated some time ago by Sellars, who took this passage to suggest that 'men', as we ordinarily know them, as 'Strawsonian' persons, may be the ultimate grounds of mental and physical properties.[35]) The homogeneity that ultimately concerns Kant here must rather be the homogeneity of (1) the *noumenon underlying mind* and (2) the *noumenon underlying matter*. (He is also interested in passing in the phenomenal homogeneity of mental and material appearances, but this is established trivially, for these two kinds of items are both 'mere representations', and the whole metaphysical problem, which concerns heterogeneity between distinct interacting ultimate natures, does not even arise, since there are no distinct ultimate natures at this level.)

The 'homogeneity' proposed at B 428 cannot start from the *phenomenon* of mind, because for Kant that is something essentially temporal, and it would have in that way to be fundamentally unlike the essentially atemporal stuff that he claims 'underlies the appearances of matter', and so we would still be in just as heterogeneous a situation as we were in when dealing with spatial and non-spatial items. And as soon as we see that it is rather the *noumenon* underlying mind that Kant wants to start with, we can see how he can propose that there could be a significant homogeneity here, for there is absolutely no reason to suppose this noumenon is fundamentally unlike what 'underlies' matter. Indeed, given the Kantian considerations reviewed in our previous section, we can be more specific: what underlies mind and what underlies matter can be said to be fundamentally alike in that they both must be immaterial.

This basic point also reveals that there is something wrong with the other part of McGinn's assumption, that Kant is aiming to find something homogeneous with a 'hidden structure of matter'. This is an incorrect way of putting Kant's aim, because what Kant speaks of is rather something that 'underlies' matter, not something that is merely its 'structure'. Here McGinn has been passing over the most fundamental difference between his approach and Kant's. Contrary to Kant, for McGinn the ultimate nature of both mind and matter must be something natural (hence he also calls his position 'transcendental naturalism', not 'transcendental idealism'), i.e., something somehow material, even if it is unlike any laws of matter that we can know. For him, the 'hidden structure' of consciousness will have to be what is for us some incomprehensible way of arranging the natural, material things that are accessible to us. Thus McGinn says we can 'refer' to the basic range of material things (viz., brains) that have this structure, even though its 'sense' remains inaccessible to us in so far as we do not have the ability to identify in these material things what are the relevant features that are identical with consciousness.[36]

In the end, McGinn's and Kant's positions appear to have a crucial and neglected difference in substance that outweighs their noted agreement in form. In form they were said to agree, because they both propose that the ultimate nature of mind transcends anything like matter as we can ever expect to know it. In substance, however, they can be said to disagree, because McGinn insists that at least this structure will have to be material in some way, whereas Kant insists that at least it will have to be definitely immaterial. However, despite this undeniable and significant disagreement in substance, I will conclude by indicating how there is a sense in which for us there is not so much difference after all in the content of these positions, and thus in the end their strength as well is remarkably similar.

Recall that Kant's insistence on immaterialism rests not on a general presumption but a whole complex of arguments for the ideality of space and time. McGinn's position, in contrast, rests entirely on a heavy metaphysical presumption, namely that matter provides the only feasible ontological framework. When we realize the highly speculative level of the discussion here, and when we also keep in mind the many transformations that the notion of matter has gone through, from pre- to post-Newtonian science, the undeniable substantive differences between McGinn and Kant can turn out after all to be secondary to their agreement in form. Both positions are, as McGinn says, 'noumenalist', and whether one favours a 'transcendental naturalist' or a 'transcendental idealist' version of this noumenalism, one is still rejecting all the other main current options in philosophy of mind.

Thus, despite all the complications that have been noted, McGinn is right to regard his position as being in special proximity to Kant's. Moreover, I would contend that these positions are on a par when we evaluate their persuasive power. Kant's mere immaterialism rests on specific arguments that, like most traditional metaphysics, have been attacked sharply, but his arguments are at least manifold and relatively detailed. McGinn's noumenalism can appear more appealing at first sight, but it is expressed in terms of a 'transcendental naturalism' that not only depends on a presumption that thoroughgoing naturalism must be true, but that also concedes how this is an extremely remarkable presumption, for it is advocated in combination with a claim that nature 'as we can conceive it' is precisely in principle unable to explain the

character of mind.[37] Undoubtedly McGinn deserves credit for
reminding us that such a 'transcendental naturalism' is a *possibility*, as well as for noting that the deep shortcomings in
other forms of naturalism *could* reflect only our own cognitive
weaknesses, and that these weaknesses are *perhaps* only to be
expected given the very truth of naturalism. None the less,
McGinn's position, like Kant's, remains only one perplexing
option among others, and the advantages that it claims for
itself *vis-à-vis* immaterialism must diminish significantly when
we recall that now the matter which is supposed to explain
mind is going to have to be matter that is very different from
anything specific that we can understand by 'nature'.

Wilfrid Sellars, whom McGinn cites at one point, recognized this difficulty probably better than anyone else. When
Sellars put forth his version of scientific realism, he was careful to distinguish between two levels of nature, or the 'physical', and to allow that the terms in the ultimate level (the
ideal final science, 'physical$_1$', 'part of the spatio-temporal
order') that would explain mind would have to include some
features incompatible with, and not only supplementary to,
our present notions of matter ('physical$_2$', what is 'necessary
to and sufficient for the scientific description and explanation
of non-living matter').[38] In making specific proposals about
how science would have to introduce entities with a special
'homogeneity' (to account for the smooth 'grain' of our sense
experience) quite unlike the matter we know now, Sellars took
himself to be presenting a modified version of Kantianism, a
Hegelian Kantianism wherein all 'noumena' would eventually
come within the scope of our theoretical reason. But in the
absence of even such specific 'optimistic' proposals, McGinn
and those who are sympathetic to him cannot so easily claim
that Kantian mere immaterialism is more 'miraculous' than
their position. McGinn's strongly pessimistic position seems to
require precisely that *we cannot* outline, even in a Sellarsian
proto-scientific way, what the basic shape of the mind must
turn out to be. Once it is conceded, as it is by McGinn, that
the phenomena of mind are ineliminable and that they do not
at all appear to be material, then the Kantian claim that ultimately they are not material is at least no more mysterious
(especially when it is backed by specific arguments and the

'conservative' principle that we should not start out by *pre-suming* things are very unlike how they appear) than the sheer claim that they are material in some necessary and yet forever 'I know not what' way.

In sum, despite what Brook contends, Kant really was a theoretical immaterialist;[39] and, despite what McGinn contends, this immaterialism points to a metaphysics of mind worth taking at least as seriously as its latest and best transcendental competitor, namely naturalistic noumenalism.

Notes to Postscript: Kant and Mind: Mere Immaterialism

[1] Andrew Brook, *Kant and the Mind* (hereafter = *KM*) (Cambridge, 1994). I am indebted to Prof. Brook's response to an earlier version of a part of this paper at a session on his book at a meeting of the Canadian Philosophical Association. On that occasion, the participation of William Seager and Tom Vinci was also quite helpful. For recent help on these issues I am especially indebted to Dieter Sturma, Manfred Frank, Eric Watkins, and Leopold Stubenberg. It should be noted that my discussion of Brook's book here picks up on only one very small theme, and is not at all representative of the main interest of his very valuable book. I focus on the theme simply because I think his formulations are an especially direct way of expressing an influential view that many interpreters share implicitly.

[2] The main issue here is whether, apart from its relation to Kant's general metaphysics, the doctrine of apperception reveals a privileged and immediate kind of awareness of one's self as a particular. In recent works I have fleshed out my views on this issue, and have discussed how my interpretation relates to important contributions by Kitcher, Sturma, Powell, Dieter Henrich, and especially Manfred Frank, who in a number of works has developed an account that has remarkable and valuable parallels to Brook's treatment of apperception. See my 'Understanding Apperception Today', in *Kant and Contemporary Epistemology*, ed. by P. Parrini (Dordrecht, 1994), pp. 331–47; 'The Ineliminable Subject: From Kant to Frank', in *The Modern Subject: Conceptions of the Self in Classical German Philosophy*, ed. by Karl Ameriks and Dieter Sturma (Albany, 1995), pp. 217–30; and 'Kant and the Self: A Retrospective', in *Figuring the Self*, ed. by David Klemm and Günter Zöller (Albany, 1997), pp. 55–72. Cf. Dieter Sturma, *Kant über Selbstbewusstsein. Zum Zusammenhang von Erkenntniskritik und Theorie des Selbstbewusstseins* (Hildesheim/Zurich/New York, 1985); Manfred Frank, *Selbstbewusstsein und Selbsterkenntnis* (Stuttgart, 1991), and 'Is Subjectivity a Non-Thing, an Absurdity (Unding)? On Some Difficulties in Naturalistic Reductions of Self-Consciousness', in *The Modern Subject*, pp. 177–97. A major theme of my analyses corresponds to a main point of Brook's interpretation: that whatever special self-reference is guaranteed by the Kantian notion of apperceptive self-awareness, this should not be conflated with the steps crucial to Kant's transcendental deduction of the categories; for the purposes of the main line of that deduction, mere cognitive awareness in general, as opposed to specific self-awareness, is all that is needed. See, e.g., *KM*, p. 60; and cf. my 'Kant and Guyer on Apperception', *Archiv für Geschichte der Philosophie*, 65 (1983), 174–86, cited at *KM*,

p. 278, n. 28. Similar points are made in passing in Patricia Kitcher, *Kant's Transcendental Psychology* (New York, 1990) and C. Thomas Powell, *Kant's Theory of Self-Consciousness* (Oxford, 1990).

[3] C. McGinn, *The Problem of Consciousness* (hereafter = *PC*) (Oxford, 1991), p. 82. An initial formulation of McGinn's view can be found in 'Can We Solve the Mind–Body Problem?', *Mind*, 98 (1989), 349–66, reprinted with an Afterword in *The Mind–Body Problem*, ed. by Richard Warner and Tadeusz Szubka (Oxford, 1994), pp. 99–120.

[4] *KM*, p. 262, n. 18.

[5] Ibid., p. 177; cf. p. 263, n. 25.

[6] See, e.g., Henry E. Allison, 'Kant's Refutation of Materialism', *Monist*, 72 (1989), 190–208; Robert Pippin, 'Kant on the Spontaneity of Mind', *Canadian Journal of Philosophy*, 17 (1987), 449–75; William Hasker, 'Emergentism', *Religious Studies*, 18 (1974), 473–88. The most challenging and radical defence of Kant against materialism is to be found in the works of Gerold Prauss, e.g., 'Kant als Deutscher Idealist', in *Metaphysik nach Kant?*, ed. by D. Henrich and R. P. Horstmann (Stuttgart, 1988), pp. 144–54, and *Die Welt und wir*, 2 vols. (Stuttgart, 1990, 1993).

[7] Cited at *KM*, p. 263, n. 23.

[8] See above, p. 78, n. 41.

[9] See above, p. 36.

[10] See Kant, *Critique of Judgment*, §77.

[11] Here my account is meant to be even more cautious than that of others; see above, n. 7.

[12] Cf. *KM*, Ch. II.

[13] Ibid., p. 263, n. 23.

[14] See the discussion of the refutation of idealism, above, Ch. III. C.

[15] Cf. my 'The Critique of Metaphysics: Kant and Traditional Ontology', in *The Cambridge Companion to Kant*, ed. by P. Guyer (Cambridge, 1992), pp. 249–79.

[16] See my discussion in 'Recent Work on Kant's Theoretical Philosophy', *American Philosophical Quarterly*, 19 (1982), 10. The term 'isomorphic' has been used in this context by John Findlay, *Kant and the Transcendental Object* (Oxford, 1981), and in some forthcoming work by James van Cleve.

[17] For more details, see my 'Kantian Idealism Today', in *History of Philosophy Quarterly*, 9 (1992), 329–42.

[18] See above, Ch. II, esp. pp. 37–47; and cf. Alison Laywine, *Kant's Early Metaphysics and the Origins of Critical Philosophy* (North American Kant Society Studies in Philosophy, vol. 3; Atascadero, 1993).

[19] Cf. above, p. 36.

[20] Cf. my 'Recent Work on Kant's Theoretical Philosophy'; 'Kantian Idealism Today'; 'Kant, Fichte, and Short Arguments to Idealism', *Archiv für Geschichte der Philosophie*, 72 (1990), 63–85; and 'Kant and Hegel on Freedom: Two New Interpretations', *Inquiry*, 35 (1992), 219–32.

[21] *KM*, p. 16.

[22] Why does Kant say that what underlies appearances is not a 'thinking being'? This may seem odd, especially on my immaterialist interpretation, but I think the explanation is simply that what is 'in itself' cannot be a 'thinking being' in our ordinary understanding, i.e., something with 'inner sense' and states taking place in time. Again, what Kant is rejecting is 'pneumatism', not immaterialism. See above, at nn. 13 and 20.

[23] *KM*, p. 17.

[24] See Kant, *Metaphysical Foundations of Natural Science*, Ch. 2, Prop. 4.

[25] *KM*, p. 17.

[26] Ibid., p. 17.

²⁷ See Colin McGinn, *Problems in Philosophy* (hereafter =*PP*) (Oxford, 1993), ch. 2. Cf. Thomas Nagel, *The View from Nowhere* (Oxford, 1986); *Mortal Questions* (Cambridge, 1979). McGinn explains some of the parallels and differences between his view and Nagel's in 'Can We Solve the Mind–Body Problem', nn. 2, 4, 8, 9, 11, 12, 15, and 24.

²⁸ McGinn, *PC*, ch. 3; cf. his *The Subjective View* (hereafter = *SV*) (Oxford, 1983), pp. 106–9.

²⁹ *PP*, p. 37.

³⁰ Ibid., p. 39.

³¹ Cited at *PC*, p. 81.

³² Ibid., p. 82.

³³ Ibid.

³⁴ Ibid.

³⁵ See above, pp. 62–3; and W. Sellars, '. . . This I or He or It (the Thing) Which Thinks', *Proceedings of the American Philosophical Association*, 44 (1970–1), 12.

³⁶ Cf. *PP*, pp. 40–3.

³⁷ The position is also remarkable because at an earlier time McGinn had written that we are 'entitled—or perhaps driven—to the conclusion that the self should be conceived as a simple mental substance', *The Character of Mind* (Oxford, 1982), p. 122. This position hardly fits easily with his later assertions that naturalism is not only true but also an inescapable presumption for those who do not believe in magic or miracles. Whatever else can be said for it, the notion of a simple substance does not have a clear common-sense connection with materialism.

³⁸ McGinn refers to Sellars at *SV*, p. 111, n. 1. See Wilfrid Sellars, *Science, Perception, and Reality* (London, 1963); and Michael J. Loux, 'The Mind–Body Problem', in *The Synoptic Vision: Essays on the Philosophy of Wilfrid Sellars*, ed. by C. F. Delaney, M. J. Loux, G. Gutting, and W. D. Solomon (Notre Dame, 1977), pp. 124–5. For some sober observations against recent presumptions of materialism, cf. Tyler Burge, 'Philosophy of Language and Mind: 1950–1990', *Philosophical Review*, 101 (1992), 39.

³⁹ Many passages bearing out Kant's immaterialism can also be found in his lectures. See *Lectures on Metaphysics/Immanuel Kant*, ed. and tr. by Karl Ameriks and Steven Naragon (Cambridge, 1997).

Bibliography

Further References

For this second edition, the extra references below (with full citations given in the expanded Bibliography) are provided as a *starting* point for *new* (or previously omitted) literature *directly* on Kant's treatment of the main topics taken up in each of the old chapters. Except for corrections of errors, I have not changed the first-edition footnotes or references to primary texts. For translations of Kant's works, there are now many new versions that can be recommended, especially in the Cambridge Kant in English series, but the Bibliography here lists only items that are cited in this volume.

For background information on topics in all chapters one should now employ the extensive index of *Lectures on Metaphysics/Immanuel Kant* as well as the notes to the new translation of the *Critique of Pure Reason* by Guyer and Wood (1997), especially pp. 737–41, and 756. Further information on all topics and extensive bibliographies can be taken from the overviews provided by Ameriks (1982, 1998), Scott-Taggart (1966), Sturma (1995, 1998), Watkins (1995), Zöller (1993), and the bibliographical updates issued by Manfred Kuehn for the Newsletter of the North American Kant Society. The latest background information on Kant's development in general can be found in Stark (1993) and Kuehn's *Immanuel Kant: A Life* (Cambridge, 2000).

Chapter I. Introduction

For a separate listing of highlights of the new literature on Kant's philosophy of mind, see the works cited in the notes above for the Preface to the Second Edition.

Chapter II. Immateriality

The First Paralogism (critiques of our substantiality): Allison (1983), 283–4; Grier; Heckmann; Horstmann; Kitcher, 183–95; Klemme 312–15, 361–70; Powell, 65–90.

The Second Paralogism (critiques of our simplicity and unity): Brook, 152–78; Hurley; Kitcher, 198–204; Klemme, 316–28; Powell, 91–109; Rosas, 82–9.

Materialism and immaterialism: Allison (1990), 92–106; Brook, 14–23; Cassam (1997), 2–3; Hasker; Laywine, 43–54; Melnick (1989); Mendonca; Prauss (1988); Rosas, 51–70, 90–107.

Chapter III. Interaction (Fourth Paralogism)

Mind–body interaction: Rosas, 108–16; Friedman 2–9, 30–9; Laywine, 25–42; McGinn (1989); Shell, 31–80; Watkins; as well as Ameriks (1992), 249 ff.

Embodiment: Butts, 117–45; Cassam (1997), 56–90; Hurley, 85–7; Klemme, 50–4; Robinson.

The first edition Fourth Paralogism: Guyer (1987), 279–82; Klemme, 339–50; Powell, 174–99.

The Refutation of Idealism: Allison (1983), 294–309; Aquila (1979); Cassam (1997), 35–9, 51–5, 173–82; Förster; Guyer (1987), 272–329; Hurley, 88–102; Vogel; Walker (1989).

Immortality: Perovich; Powell, 110–29.

Chapter IV. Identity (Third Paralogism)

Kant's critique of arguments for personal identity: Blackburn; Brook, 179–95; Kitcher, 195–8; Klemme, 329–38; Powell, 130–73; Shoemaker (1984); Strawson (1987).

On Kantian considerations supporting the idea of our unity or identity: Allison (1983), 148–58; Brook, 24–45, 122–51, 195–201; Cassam (1997), 91–111, 183–98; Chisholm (1981), 75–91; Guyer (1987), 132–48; Hurley, 57–71, 102–33; Kitcher, 117–23; Klemme, 180–213; Henrich (1989); Korsgaard (1996), 363–97; Piper; Powell, 11–64; Sommer; Sturma (1985), 62–82.

Chapter V. Independence (freedom)

Spontaneity in general in Kant: Allison (1983), 310–29; (1990), 11–84; (1996), 109–42; Baumgarten, 77–88; Carl (1998); Klemme, 76–94; Hudson; Hurley, 73–85; Mohr (1995); Pippin (1987); Prauss (1983); Wood (1984); as well as Ameriks (1990), (1992), 219 ff.

Freedom in Kant's moral texts: Allison (1990), 201–49; Brandt (1988); Hill; Korsgaard (1996), 159–87; Korsgaard *et al.* (1996),

94–8; Rawls (1989); Rosas 157–63; Schönecker; as well as Ameriks (1992), 219 ff.

Chapter VI. Ideality

The idea of rational psychology: Carl (1989), 115–26; Grier; Hatfield; Klemme, 13–36, 46–9, 102–17, 234–9, 298–307; Makkreel; Satura.

Inner sense: Allison (1983), 255–63; Aquila (1983), 147–70; (1997); Brandt (1994); Brook, 47–54; Falkenstein; Mohr (1991); Zöller (1989).

Apperception: Allison (1983), 272–93; (1996), 41–66; Bermúdez; Brook, 79–94; Castañeda; Cramer; Evans, 72–80; Guyer (1987), 47–52; Kitcher, 91–110; Thiel; as well as Ameriks (1983), (1994), (1995).

The ideality of self-knowledge: Allison (1983), 263–71; Brook, 223–33, 246–56; Hurley, 71–3; Kitcher, 139–41; Srzednicki.

Transcendental idealism in general: Adams (1997); Allison (1983), 3–34; (1996), 3–26; Aquila (1983), 83–118; Findlay; Guyer (1987), 333–84; Langton; Melnick (1989); Strawson (1994); van Cleve; as well as Ameriks (1992), 329 ff.

Bibliography of Works Cited

I. Works by Kant

Critique of Judgment, tr. by J. H. Bernard (New York: Hafner, 1951).

Critique of Practical Reason, tr. by L. W. Beck (New York: Bobbs-Merrill, 1956).

Critique of Pure Reason, tr. by N. Kemp Smith (London: Macmillan, 1929).

Critique of Pure Reason, tr. and ed. by Paul Guyer and Allen Wood (Cambridge: Cambridge Univ. Press, 1998).

'Eine neu aufgefundene Reflexion Kants "Vom Inneren Sinne" (Loses Blatt Leningrad I)', in *Neue Autographen und Dokumente zu Kants Leben, Schriften und Vorlesungen,* ed. by Reinhard Brandt and Werner Stark (Hamburg: Meiner, 1987), pp. 1–30.

Foundations of the Metaphysics of Morals, tr. by L. W. Beck (New York: Bobbs-Merrill, 1959).

Immanuel Kant: Leçons de metaphysique, ed. and tr. by Monique Castillo (Paris: Librarie Générale Francaise, 1993).

Kant's Gesammelte Schriften, ed. by the Royal Prussian (later German) Academy of Sciences (Berlin: Georg Reimer (later Walter de Gruyter), 1900–).

Kant's Philosophical Correspondence 1759–99, ed. and tr. by Arnulf Zweig (Chicago: Univ. of Chicago Press, 1970).

Lectures on Ethics/Immanuel Kant, ed. by J. B. Schneewind and tr. by Peter Heath (Cambridge: Cambridge Univ. Press, 1997).

Lectures on Logic/Immanuel Kant, ed. and tr. by J. Michael Young (Cambridge: Cambridge Univ. Press, 1992).

Lectures on Metaphysics/Immanuel Kant, ed. and tr. by Karl Ameriks and Steven Naragon (Cambridge: Cambridge Univ. Press, 1997).

Lectures on Philosophical Theology, ed. by Allen Wood, and tr. by Allen Wood and Gertrude Clark (Ithaca: Cornell Univ. Press, 1978).

Metaphysical Foundations of Natural Science, tr. by James Ellington (New York: Bobbs-Merrill, 1970).

'On a Discovery According to Which Any New Critique of Pure Reason Has Been Made Superfluous by an Earlier One', in *The Kant–Eberhard Controversy,* ed. and tr. by H. E. Allison (Baltimore: Johns Hopkins Univ. Press, 1973).

Prolegomena to Any Future Metaphysics, ed. by L. W. Beck (New York: Bobbs-Merrill, 1950).

Religion Within the Bounds of Reason Alone, tr. by T. M. Greene and H. H. Hudson (New York: Harper, 1960).

Selected Pre-Critical Writings and Correspondence with Beck, tr. by G. B.

Kerferd and D. E. Walford (Manchester: Univ. of Manchester Press, 1968).

'The End of All Things', tr. by Robert Anchor, in *Kant on History*, ed. by L. W. Beck (New York: Bobbs-Merrill, 1963), pp. 69–84.

II. Other Works

Abicht, Johann Heinrich, 'Über die Freiheit des Willens' (1789), in *Materialen zu Kants Kritik der praktischen Vernunft*, ed. by Rüdiger Bittner and Konrad Cramer (Frankfurt: Suhrkamp, 1973), pp. 229–40.

Adams, Robert M., 'Moral Arguments for Theistic Belief', in *Rationality and Religious Belief*, ed. by C. F. Delaney (Notre Dame: Univ. of Notre Dame Press, 1979), pp. 116–40.

—— 'Things in Themselves', *Philosophy and Phenomenological Research*, 57 (1997), 801–26.

Allison, Henry E., 'Kant's Concept of the Transcendental Object', *Kant-Studien*, 68 (1959), 165–86.

—— 'Locke's Theory of Personal Identity: A Re-Examination', *Journal of the History of Ideas*, 27 (1966), 41–58.

—— 'Kant's Critique of Berkeley', *Journal of the History of Philosophy*, 11 (1973), 43–63.

—— 'Things in Themselves, Noumena, and the Transcendental Object', *Dialectica*, 32 (1978), 41–76.

—— *Kant's Transcendental Idealism: An Interpretation and Defense* (New Haven: Yale Univ. Press, 1983).

—— 'Kant's Refutation of Materialism', *Monist*, 72 (1989), 190–208 (reprinted in *Idealism and Freedom*, pp. 92–106).

—— *Kant's Theory of Freedom* (Cambridge: Cambridge Univ. Press, 1990).

—— *Idealism and Freedom: Essays on Kant's Theoretical and Practical Philosophy* (Cambridge: Cambridge Univ. Press, 1996).

Ameriks, Karl, 'Recent Work on Wittgenstein and the Philosophy of Mind', *New Scholasticism*, 43 (1975), 94–118.

—— 'Personal Identity and Memory Transfer', *Southern Journal of Philosophy*, 14 (1976), 385–91.

—— 'Criteria of Personal Identity', *Canadian Journal of Philosophy*, 7 (1977), 47–69.

—— 'Husserl's Realism', *Philosophical Review*, 86 (1977), 498–519.

—— 'Kant's Transcendental Deduction as a Regressive Argument', *Kant-Studien*, 69 (1978), 273–87.

—— 'Review of R. C. S. Walker's *Kant*', *Teaching Philosophy*, 3 (1980), 358–63.

Ameriks, Karl, 'Kant's Deduction of Freedom and Morality', *Journal of the History of Philosophy*, 19 (1981).
—— 'Chisholm's Paralogisms', *Idealistic Studies*, 11 (1981).
—— 'Recent Work on Kant's Theoretical Philosophy', *American Philosophical Quarterly*, 19 (1982), 1–24.
—— 'Contemporary German Epistemology', *Inquiry*, 25 (1982), 125–38.
—— 'Kant and Guyer on Apperception', *Archiv für Geschichte der Philosophie*, 65 (1983), 174–86.
—— '*Kant's Transcendental Idealism*, by H. E. Allison', *Topoi*, 3 (1984), 181–5.
—— '*Kant über Freiheit als Autonomie*, by G. Prauss', *Review of Metaphysics*, 38 (1984), 136–9.
—— '*Kant's Theory of Form*, by R. Pippin', *International Studies in Philosophy*, 18 (1986), 74–6.
—— 'Kant, Fichte, and Short Arguments to Idealism', *Archiv für Geschichte der Philosophie*, 72 (1990), 63–85.
—— 'Kant on Spontaneity: Some New Data', *Proceedings of the VII International Kant-Kongress 1990* (Berlin: de Gruyter, 1991), pp. 436–46.
—— '*Imagination and Interpretation in Kant*, by R. Makkreel', *Man and World*, 25 (1992), 227–34.
—— 'Kant and Hegel on Freedom: Two New Interpretations', *Inquiry*, 35 (1992), 219–32.
—— 'Kantian Idealism Today', *History of Philosophy Quarterly*, 9 (1992), 329–42.
—— '*Kant's Theory of Freedom*, by H. E. Allison', *Ethics*, 102 (1992), 655–7.
—— 'The Critique of Metaphysics: Kant and Traditional Ontology', in *The Cambridge Companion to Kant*, ed. by P. Guyer (Cambridge: Cambridge Univ. Press, 1992), pp. 249–79.
—— '*Kant's Theory of Self-Consciousness*, by C. T. Powell', *International Studies in Philosophy*, 26 (1994), 143–4.
—— 'Understanding Apperception Today', in *Kant and Contemporary Epistemology*, ed. by P. Parrini (Dordrecht: Kluwer, 1994), pp. 331–47.
—— 'The Ineliminable Subject: From Kant to Frank', in *The Modern Subject: Conceptions of the Self in Classical German Philosophy*, ed. by Karl Ameriks and Dieter Sturma (Albany: SUNY Press, 1995), pp. 217–30.
—— 'Kant and Mind: Mere Immaterialism', *Proceedings of the Eighth International Kant Congress 1995*, ed. by H. Robinson (Milwaukee: Marquette Univ. Press, 1995), vol. 1, pp. 675–90.

—— 'Kant and the Self: A Retrospective', in *Figuring the Self: Subject, Absolute, and Others in Classical German Philosophy*, ed. by David Klemm and Günter Zöller (Albany: SUNY Press, 1997), pp. 55–72.

—— 'The First Edition Paralogisms of Pure Reason', in *Immanuel Kant: Kritik der reinen Vernunft*, ed. by Georg Mohr and Marcus Willaschek (Berlin: Akademie Verlag, 1998), pp. 369–88.

—— 'I. Kant, *Vorlesungen über Anthropologie*', *Journal of the History of Philosophy* 37 (1999) 368–70).

—— '*Idealism and Freedom*, by H. Allison', *Philosophy and Phenomenological Research* 49 (1999) 825–8.

—— 'Introduction', *Cambridge Companion to German Idealism* (Cambridge: Cambridge Univ. Press, 2000).

—— *Kant and the Fate of Autonomy: Problems in the Appropriation of the Critical Philosophy* (Cambridge: Cambridge Univ. Press, 2000).

—— 'Kant's Lectures on Metaphysics and his Pre-Critical Philosophy of Mind: Unearthing the Unsaid', in *Kant's Pre-Critical Philosophy*, ed. by Thomas Rockmore (forthcoming).

—— 'The Practical Foundation of Philosophy in Kant, Fichte, and After', in *The Reception of Kant's Critical Philosophy: Fichte, Schelling, and Hegel*, ed. by Sally Sedgwick (Cambridge: Cambridge Univ. Press, 2000) forthcoming.

Anderson, James C., 'Kant's Paralogism of Personhood', *Grazer Philosophische Studien*, 10 (1980), 73–86.

Anscombe, G. E. M., 'The Intentionality of Sensation: A Grammatical Feature', in *Analytical Philosophy*, 2nd ser., ed. by R. J. Butler (New York: Barnes & Noble, 1968), pp. 58–80.

Aquila, Richard, 'Personal Identity and Kant's Refutation of Idealism', *Kant-Studien*, 70 (1979), 259–78.

—— *Representational Mind: A Study in Kant's Theory of Knowledge* (Bloomington: Indiana Univ. Press, 1983).

—— 'Self as Matter and Form: Some Reflections on Kant's View of the Soul', in *Figuring the Self: Subject, Absolute, and Others in Classical German Philosophy*, ed. by David Klemm and Günter Zöller (Albany: SUNY Press, 1997), pp. 31–54.

Armstrong, David, *Bodily Sensations* (London: Routledge & Kegan Paul, 1962).

Ayer, A. J., *The Concept of a Person* (London: Macmillan, 1963).

Balowitz, Victor, 'More on Persons and their Bodies', *Philosophical Studies*, 27 (1975), 63–5.

Baumgarten, Hans-Ulrich, *Kant und Tetens: Untersuchungen zum Problem von Vorstellung und Gegenstand* (Stuttgart: Metzler, 1992).

Beck, L. W., *A Commentary on Kant's Critique of Practical Reason* (Chicago: Univ. of Chicago Press, 1960).

330   *Bibliography*

Beck, L. W., 'The Fact of Reason: An Essay on Justification in Ethics', in *Studies in the Philosophy of Kant* (Indianapolis: Bobbs-Merrill, 1965), pp. 200–14.

Bennett, Jonathan, *Kant's Analytic* (Cambridge: Cambridge Univ. Press, 1966).

——*Kant's Dialectic* (Cambridge: Cambridge Univ. Press, 1974).

Bermúdez, José Luis, 'The Unity of Apperception in the *Critique of Pure Reason*', *European Journal of Philosophy*, 2 (1994), 213–39.

Bird, Graham, *Kant's Theory of Knowledge* (London: Routledge & Kegan Paul, 1962).

Bittner, Rüdiger, 'Kausalität als Freiheit und kategorischer Imperativ', *Zeitschrift für philosophische Forschung*, 32 (1978), 265–74.

Blackburn, Simon, 'Has Kant Refuted Parfit?', in *Reading Parfit*, ed. by Jonathan Dancy (Oxford: Blackwell, 1997), pp. 180–201.

Bobien, Susanne, 'Die Kategorien der Freiheit bei Kant', in *Kant: Analysen-Probleme-Kritik*, ed. by Hariolf Oberer and Gerhard Seel (Würzburg: Königshausen and Neumann, 1988), vol. 3, pp. 193–220.

Borst, C. V. (ed.), *The Mind/Brain Identity Theory* (London: Macmillan, 1970).

Brandt, Reinhard, 'Der Zirkel im dritten Abschnitt von Kants Grundlegung zur Metaphysik der Sitten', in *Kant: Analysen-Probleme-Kritik*, ed. by Hariolf Oberer and Gerhard Seel (Würzburg: Königshausen and Neumann, 1988), vol. 3, pp. 169–92.

——'Rousseau und Kants "Ich denke"', *Kant-Forschungen*, 5 (1994), 1–18.

——*Kritischer Kommentar zu Kants Anthropologie in pragmatischer Hinsicht* (Hamburg: Meiner, 1998).

Broad, C. D., 'Immanuel Kant and Psychical Research', in *Philosophy, Religion, and Psychical Research* (London: Routledge & Kegan Paul, 1953), pp. 116–55.

——*Leibniz: An Introduction* (Cambridge: Cambridge Univ. Press, 1975).

——*Kant: An Introduction* (Cambridge: Cambridge Univ. Press, 1978).

Brook, Andrew, *Kant and the Mind* (Cambridge: Cambridge Univ. Press, 1994).

Burge, Tyler, 'Philosophy of Language and Mind: 1950–1990', *Philosophical Review*, 101 (1992), pp. 3–51.

Butts, Robert, *Kant and the Double Government Methodology* (Dordrecht: Reidel, 1984).

Carl, Wolfgang, *Der schweigende Kant. Die Entwürfe zu einer Deduktion der Kategorien vor 1781* (Göttingen: Vandenhoeck & Ruprecht, 1989).

—— 'Ich und Spontaneität', in *Philosophie in synthetischer Absicht*, ed. by Marcelo Stamm (Stuttgart: Klett-Cotta, 1998), 105–22.

Carr, David, *The Paradox of Subjectivity* (New York: Oxford Univ. Press, 1999).

Cassam, Quassim, 'Introduction', in *Self-Knowledge*, ed. by Quassim Cassim (Oxford: Oxford Univ. Press, 1994), pp. 1–18.

—— *Self and World* (Oxford: Oxford Univ. Press, 1997).

Castañeda, Hector-Neri, 'The Role of Apperception in Kant's Transcendental Deduction of the Categories', *Nous*, 24 (1990), 147–57.

Chalmers, David, *The Conscious Mind* (Oxford: Oxford Univ. Press, 1996)

Chisholm, Roderick, 'The Loose and Popular and the Strict and Philosophical Senses of Identity', in *Perception and Personal Identity*, ed. by N. S. Care and R. M. Grimm (Cleveland: Case Western Reserve Press, 1969), pp. 82–139.

Chisholm, Roderick, *Person and Object* (London: Routledge & Kegan Paul, 1976).

—— *The First Person* (Minneapolis: Univ. of Minn. Press, 1981).

Coder, David, 'Strawson, Particulars, "No-Subject" and "No-Ownership"', *Philosophical Studies*, 23 (1972), 335–42.

Cohen, Gerald, 'Reason, Humanity, and the Moral Law', in *The Sources of Normativity*, ed. by Christine Korsgaard *et al.* (Cambridge: Cambridge Univ. Press, 1996), pp. 167–88.

Cramer, Konrad, 'Über Kants Satz: Das: Ich denke, muss alle meine Vorstellungen begleiten können', in *Theorie der Subjektivität*, ed. by K. Cramer, H. Fulda, R.-P. Horstmann, and U. Pothast (Frankfurt: Suhrkamp, 1987), pp. 167–202.

Daniels, Charles, 'Personal Identity', in *Philosophers in Wonderland*, ed. by Peter French (St Paul: Llewellyn, 1975), pp. 203–16.

Davidson, Donald, 'Mental Events', in *Experience and Theory*, ed. by L. Foster and J. Swanson (Amherst: Univ. of Massachusetts Press, 1970), pp. 79–102.

—— 'Psychology as Philosophy', in *Philosophy of Psychology*, ed. by S. C. Brown (London: Macmillan, 1974), pp. 41–52.

De Man, Paul, *Aesthetic Ideology* (Minneapolis: Univ. of Minn. Press, 1996).

Dennett, Donald, 'Conditions of Personhood', in *The Identities of Persons*, ed. by A. O. Rorty (Berkeley: Univ. of California Press, 1976), pp. 175–96.

Duncan, A. R. C., *Practical Reason and Morality* (Edinburgh: Nelson, 1957).

Düsing, Klaus, *Selbstbewusstseinsmodelle* (Munich: Fink, 1997).

Eldridge, Richard, *On Moral Personhood: Philosophy, Literature, Criticism, and Self-Understanding* (Chicago: Univ. of Chicago Press, 1989).

bibliography

Evans, J. Claude, *The Metaphysics of Transcendental Subjectivity: Descartes, Kant and W. Sellars* (Amsterdam: Grüner, 1984).

Ewing, A. C., *Kant's Treatment of Causality* (London: Routledge & Kegan Paul, 1924).

——*A Short Commentary on Kant's Critique of Pure Reason* (Chicago: Univ. of Chicago Press, 1938).

Falkenstein, Lorne, *Kant's Intuitionism: A Commentary on the Transcendental Aesthetic* (Toronto: Univ. of Toronto Press, 1995).

Findlay, John, *Kant and the Transcendental Object* (Oxford: Clarendon Press, 1981).

Fleischer, Margot, 'Das Problem der Begründung des kategorischen Imperativs', in *Sein und Ethos*, ed. by Paulus Englehardt (Mainz: Matthias-Grünewald, 1963), pp. 387–404.

——'Die Formeln des kategorischen Imperativs', *Archiv für Geschichte der Philosophie*, 46 (1964), 201–26.

Fodor, Jerry, *Psychological Explanation* (New York: Random House, 1968).

Förster, Eckart, 'Kant's Refutation of Idealism', in *Philosophy, Its History and Historiography*, ed. by A. J. Holland (Dordrecht: Reidel), 295–311.

Frank, Manfred, 'Fragmente zu einer Geschichte der Selbstbewusstseinstheorien von Kant bis Sartre', in *Selbstbewusstseinstheorien von Fichte bis Sartre*, ed. by Manfred Frank (Frankfurt: Suhrkamp, 1991), pp. 415–599.

——*Selbstbewusstsein und Selbsterkenntnis* (Stuttgart: Reclam, 1991).

——'Vorwort', in *Analytische Theorien des Selbstbewusstseins*, ed. by M. Frank (Frankfurt: Suhrkamp, 1994), pp. 7–34.

——'Is Subjectivity a Non-Thing, an Absurdity (Unding)? On Some Difficulties in Naturalistic Reductions of Self-Consciousness', in *The Modern Subject*, ed. by Karl Ameriks and Dieter Sturma (Albany: SUNY Press, 1995), pp. 177–97.

Frankfurt, Harry, 'Descartes on the Creation of the Eternal Truths', *Philosophical Review*, 86 (1977), 36–57.

——*The Importance of What We Care About* (Cambridge: Cambridge Univ. Press, 1988).

Friedman, Michael, *Kant and the Exact Sciences* (Cambridge, Mass.: Harvard Univ. Press, 1992).

Ginet, Carl, *Knowledge, Belief and Memory* (Dordrecht: Reidel, 1976).

Gochnauer, Myron, 'Kant's Refutation of Idealism', *Journal of the History of Philosophy*, 12 (1974), 195–205.

Gram, Moltke, 'Kant's First Antinomy', *The Monist*, 51 (1967), 511–18.

——'How to Dispense with Things in Themselves', *Ratio*, 18 (1976), 1–16, 107–123.

Grice, H. P., 'Personal Identity', *Mind*, 50 (1941), 330–50.

Grier, Michelle, 'Illusion and Fallacy in Kant's First Paralogism', *Kant-Studien*, 83 (1993), 257–82.

Guyer, Paul, *Kant and the Claims of Knowledge* (Cambridge: Cambridge Univ. Press, 1987).

——*Kant and the Experience of Freedom* (Cambridge: Cambridge Univ. Press, 1993).

Harrison, Jonathan, 'The Embodiment of Mind, or What Use is Having a Body?' *Proceedings of the Aristotelian Society*, 74 (1973–4), 35–55.

Harrison, Ross, *On What There Must Be* (Oxford: Oxford Univ. Press, 1974).

Hasker, William, 'Emergentism', *Religious Studies*, 18 (1974), 473–88.

Hatfield, Gary, 'Empirical, Rational, and Transcendental Psychology: Psychology as Science and as Philosophy', *The Cambridge Companion to Kant*, ed. by P. Guyer, (Cambridge: Cambridge Univ. Press, 1992), pp. 200–27.

Heckmann, Heinz-Dieter, 'Kant und die Ich-Metaphysik', *Kant-Studien*, 76 (1985), 385–404.

Heimsoeth, Heinz, *Studien zur Philosophie Immanuel Kants* (Cologne: Kölner Universitätsverlag, 1956).

——*Atom, Seele, Monade* (Mainz: Verlag der Akademie der Wissenschaften und Literatur, 1960).

Henle, Paul, 'The *Critique of Pure Reason* Today', *Journal of Philosophy*, 59 (1962), 225–34.

Henrich, Dieter, 'Zur theoretischen Philosophie Kants', *Philosophische Rundschau*, 1 (1953–4), 124–49.

——'Das Prinzip der kantischen Ethik', *Philosophische Rundschau*, 2 (1954–5), 20–37.

——'Über die Einheit der Subjektivität', *Philosophische Rundschau*, 3 (1955), 28–69.

——'Zu Kants Begriff der Philosophie', in *Kritik und Metaphysik*, ed. by Friedrich Kaulbach and Joachim Ritter (Berlin: de Gruyter, 1960), pp. 40–59.

——'The Proof Structure of Kant's Transcendental Deduction', *Review of Metaphysics*, 22 (1968), 640–59.

——'Der Begriff der sittlichen Einsicht und Kants Lehre vom Faktum der Vernunft', in *Kant: Zur Deutung seiner Theorie von Erkennen und Handeln*, ed. by G. Prauss (Cologne: Kiepenheuer & Witsch, 1973), pp. 223–57.

——'Die Deduktion des Sittengesetzes', in *Denken im Schatten des Nihilismus*, ed. by Alexander Schwan (Darmstadt: Wissenschaftliche Buchgesellschaft, 1975), pp. 55–112.

——*Identität und Objektivität* (Heidelberg: Carl Winter, 1976).

Henrich, Dieter, 'The Identity of the Subject in the Transcendental Deduction', in *Reading Kant*, ed. by Eva Schaper and Wilhelm Vossenkuhl (Oxford: Basil Blackwell, 1989), pp. 250–80.

—— *The Unity of Reason: Essays on Kant's Philosophy*, ed. by Richard Velkley (Cambridge, Mass.: Harvard Univ. Press, 1994).

Hesse, Mary, *Forces and Fields* (New York: Nelson, 1961).

Hill Jr., Thomas E., 'Kant's Argument for the Rationality of Moral Conduct', in *Dignity and Practical Reason in Kant's Moral Theory* (Ithaca: Cornell Univ. Press, 1992), pp. 97–122.

Hortsmann, Rolf-Peter, 'Space as Intuition and Geometry', *Ratio*, 28 (1976), 18–30.

—— 'Kants Paralogismen', *Kant-Studien*, 84 (1993), 408–25.

Hübner, Kurt, 'Leib und Erfahrung in Kants Opus Postumum', *Zeitschrift für philosophische Forschung*, 7 (1953), 204–9.

Hudson, Hud, *Kant's Compatibilism* (Ithaca: Cornell Univ. Press, 1984).

Hurley, S. L., *Consciousness in Action* (Cambridge, Mass.: Harvard Univ. Press, 1998).

Ilting, Karl-Heinz, 'Der naturalistische Fehlschluss bei Kant', in *Rehabilitierung der praktischen Philosophie*, vol. 1, ed. by Manfred Riedel (Freiburg: Alber, 1972).

Kalter, Alfons, *Kants vierter Paralogismus* (Meisenheim: Anton Hain, 1975).

Keller, Pierre, *Kant and the Demands of Self-Consciousness* (Cambridge: Cambridge Univ. Press, 1998).

Kitcher, Patricia, *Kant's Transcendental Psychology* (New York: Oxford Univ. Press, 1990).

Kitcher, Philip, 'Kant and the Foundations of Mathematics', *Philosophical Review*, 84 (1975), 23–50.

Klemme, Heiner, *Kants Philosophie des Subjekts* (Hamburg: Meiner, 1996).

Körner, S., 'On the Kantian Foundation of Science and Mathematics', in *The First Critique*, ed. by T. Penelhum and J. MacIntosh (Belmont, Calif.: Wadsworth, 1969), pp. 97–108.

Korsgaard, Christine, 'Morality as Freedom', in *Creating the Kingdom of Ends* (Cambridge: Cambridge Univ. Press, 1996), pp. 159–87.

—— 'Personal Identity and the Unity of Agency: A Kantian Reply to Parfit', in *Creating the Kingdom of Ends* (Cambridge: Cambridge Univ. Press, 1996), pp. 363–97.

—— 'The Authority of Reflection', in *The Sources of Normativity* , ed. by C. Korsgaard *et al.* (Cambridge: Cambridge Univ. Press, 1996), pp. 90–130.

Krüger, Gerhard, *Philosophie und Moral in der Kantischen Kritik*, 2nd edn. (Tübingen: Mohr, 1967).

Kuehn, Manfred, *Immanuel Kant: A Life* (Cambridge: Cambridge Univ. Press, 2000).

Lachièze-Rey, Pierre, 'Das Kantische und das Kartesische *Cogito*', in *Materialen zu Kants Kritik der reinen Vernunft*, ed. by J. Kopper (Frankfurt: Suhrkamp, 1975), pp. 173–204.

Langton, Rae, *Kantian Humility* (Oxford Univ. Press, 1998).

Leibniz, G. W., *Selections*, ed. by Philip Wiener (New York: Scribner's, 1951).

Lewis, David, 'Survival and Identity', in *The Identities of Persons*, ed. by A. O. Rorty (Berkeley: Univ. of California Press, 1976), pp. 17–40.

Lewis, H. D., *The Elusive Mind* (London: Allen & Unwin, 1969).

Locke, John, *An Essay Concerning Human Understanding*.

Long, Douglas, 'The Bodies of Persons', *Journal of Philosophy*, 71 (1974), 291–301.

Loux, Michael J., 'The Mind–Body Problem', in *The Synoptic Vision: Essays on the Philosophy of Wilfrid Sellars*, ed. by C. F. Delaney, M. J. Loux, G. Gutting, and W. D. Solomon (Notre Dame: Univ. of Notre Dame Press, 1977), pp. 105–26.

McGinn, Colin, *The Character of Mind* (Oxford: Oxford Univ. Press, 1982).

—— *The Subjective View* (Oxford: Clarendon Press, 1983).

—— 'Can We Solve the Mind–Body Problem?', *Mind*, 98 (1989), 349–66, reprinted with an Afterword in *The Mind–Body Problem*, ed. by Richard Warner and Tadeusz Szubka (Oxford: Blackwell, 1994), pp. 99–120.

—— *The Problem of Consciousness* (Oxford: Blackwell, 1991).

—— *Problems in Philosophy* (Oxford: Blackwell, 1993).

Maddell, G., 'Ayer on Personal Identity', *Philosophy*, 51 (1976), 47–55.

Maddy, Penelope, 'Is the Importance of Identity Derivative?', *Philosophical Studies*, 39 (1979), 151–70.

Madigan, P. S., 'Time in Locke and Kant', *Kant-Studien*, 67 (1976), 20–50.

Makkreel, Rudolf, *Imagination and Interpretation in Kant* (Chicago: Univ. of Chicago Press, 1990).

Medonca, W. P., 'Der Psychophysiche Materialismus in der Perspektive Kants und Wittgensteins', *Kant-Studien*, 81 (1990), 277–97.

Meerbote, Ralf, 'Kant's Functionalism', in *Historical Foundations of Cognitive Science*, ed. by J. C. Smith (Dordrecht: Reidel, 1989), 161–87.

Melnick, Arthur, *Kant's Analogies of Experience* (Chicago: Univ. of Chicago Press, 1973).

Melnick, Arthur, *Space, Time, and Thought in Kant* (Dordrecht, Reidel, 1989).

Mijuskovic, Ben, 'The Premise of the Transcendental Analytic', *Philosophical Quarterly*, 23 (1973), 156–61.

—— *The Achilles of Rationalist Arguments* (The Hague: Nijhoff, 1974).

Mischel, Theodore, 'Kant and the Possibility of a Science of Psychology', *The Monist*, 51 (1967), 599–622.

Mohr, Georg, *Das sinnliche Ich: Innerer Sinn und Bewusstsein bei Kant* (Würzburg: Königshausen und Neumann, 1991).

—— 'Freedom and the Self: From Introspection to Inter-subjectivity', in *The Modern Subject: Conceptions of the Self in Classical German Philosophy*, ed. by K. Ameriks and D. Sturma (Albany: SUNY Press, 1995), pp. 31–45.

Nagel, Gordon, *The Structure of Experience: Kant's System of Principles* (Chicago: Chicago Univ. Press, 1983).

Nagel, Thomas, 'Brain Bisection and the Unity of Consciousness', *Synthese*, 22 (1971), 396–413.

—— *Mortal Questions* (Cambridge: Cambridge Univ. Press, 1979).

—— *The View from Nowhere* (Oxford: Oxford Univ. Press, 1986).

—— 'Universality and the Reflective Self', in *The Sources of Normativity*, ed. by C. Korsgaard *et al.* (Cambridge: Cambridge Univ. Press, 1996), pp. 200–9.

Naragon, Steve, 'Die Metaphysikvorlesungen Kants in der Akademie-Ausgabe', in *Kants Gesammelte Schriften (Akademie-Ausgabe)—Eine Kritische Bestandsaufnahme* (forthcoming).

Nelson, Leonard, *Kritik der Praktischen Philosophie*, in *Gesammelte Schriften*, vol. 4 (Hamburg: Meiner, 1972).

Noland, J., 'Kant on Meaning: Two Studies', *Kant-Studien*, 70 (1979), 113–30.

O'Neill, Onora, 'Space and Objects', *Journal of Philosophy*, 73 (1976), 29–45.

Parfit, Derek, 'On "The Importance of Self-Identity"', *Journal of Philosophy*, 68 (1971), 683–90.

—— 'Later Selves and Moral Principles', in *Philosophy and Personal Relations*, ed. by Alan Montefiore (Montreal: Queen's Univ. Press, 1973), pp. 137–67.

—— 'Lewis, Perry, and What Matters', in *The Identities of Persons*, ed. by A. O. Rorty (Berkeley, 1976), pp. 91–108.

—— 'Personal Identity' (revised version), in *The Philosophy of Mind*, ed. by Jonathan Glover (Oxford: Oxford Univ. Press, 1976), pp. 142–62.

Paton, H. J., *Kant's Metaphysics of Experience* (London: G. Allen & Unwin, 1936).

—— 'Self-Identity', in *The Defence of Reason* (London: Hutchinson, 1953), pp. 99–116.

—— *The Categorical Imperative*, reprint edn. (New York: Harper, 1967).

Patten, S. C., 'An Anti-Sceptical Argument at the Deduction', *Kant-Studien*, 67 (1976), 550–69.

Penelhum, Terence, *Survival and Disembodied Existence* (London: Routledge & Kegan Paul, 1970).

Perovich, Anthony N., 'Immortality, *Religion*, and "The End of all Things"', in *Kant's Philosophy of Religion Reconsidered*, ed. by Philip J. Rossi and Michael Wren (Bloomington: Indiana Univ. Press, 1991), pp. 165–80.

Perry, John, 'The Problem of Personal Identity', in *Personal Identity*, ed. by J. Perry (Berkeley: Univ. of California Press, 1975), pp. 3–30.

—— 'Personal Identity, Memory, and the Problem of Circularity', in *Personal Identity*, ed. by J. Perry (Berkeley: Univ. of California Press, 1975), pp. 135–55.

—— 'The Importance of Being Identical', in *The Identities of Persons*, ed. by A. O. Rorty (Berkeley: Univ. of California Press, 1976), pp. 67–90.

Piper, Adrian, 'Xenophobia and Kantian Rationalism', in *Feminist Interpretations of Immanuel Kant*, ed. by Robin May Schott (University Park: Penn State Univ. Press, 1997), pp. 21–73.

Pippin, Robert, 'Kant on Empirical Concepts', *Studies in History and Philosophy of Science*, 10 (1979), 1–19.

—— 'Kant on the Spontaneity of Mind', *Canadian Journal of Philosophy*, 17 (1987), 449–75.

Plantinga, Alvin, *The Nature of Necessity* (Oxford: Oxford Univ. Press, 1974).

Powell, C. Thomas, *Kant's Theory of Self-Consciousness* (Oxford: Oxford Univ. Press, 1990).

Prauss, Gerold, *Erscheinung bei Kant* (Berlin: de Gruyter, 1971).

—— *Kant und das Problem der Dinge an Sich* (Bonn: Bouvier, 1974).

—— *Kant über Freiheit als Autonomie* (Frankfurt: Klostermann, 1983).

—— 'Kant als Deutscher Idealist', in *Metaphysik nach Kant?*, ed. by D. Henrich and R.-P. Horstmann (Stuttgart: Klett-Cotta, 1988), pp. 144–54.

—— *Die Welt und wir*, 2 vols. (Stuttgart: J. B. Metzler, 1990, 1993).

Pucetti, Roland, 'Memory and the Self: A Neuro-Pathological Approach', *Philosophy*, 52 (1977), 147–53.

Putnam, Hilary, *Philosophical Papers*, 2 vols. (Cambridge: Cambridge Univ. Press, 1975).

Rawls, John, 'Kantian Constructivism in Moral Theory', *Journal of Philosophy*, 77 (1980), 515–72.

—— 'Themes in Kant's Moral Philosophy', in *Kant's Transcendental*

Deductions, ed. by Eckart Förster (Stanford: Stanford Univ. Press, 1989), pp. 81–113.

Rescher, Nicholas, *Conceptual Idealism* (Oxford: Oxford Univ. Press, 1973).

Rey, Georges, 'Survival', in *The Identities of Persons*, ed. by A. O. Rorty (Berkeley: Univ. of California Press, 1976), pp. 41–66.

Robinson, Daniel, 'What Sort of Persons are Hemispheres? Another Look at "Split-Brain" Man', *British Journal of the Philosophy of Science*, 27 (1976), 73–9.

Robinson, Hoke, 'Kant on Embodiment', in *Minds, Ideas, and Objects*, ed. by Phillip D. Cummins and Guenter Zoeller (Atascadero: Ridgeview, 1992), pp. 329–40.

Rosas, Alejandro, *Kants idealistische Reduktion. Das Mentale und das Materielle im transzendentalen Idealismus* (Würzburg: Königshausen und Neumann, 1996).

Ross, W. D., *Kant's Ethical Theory* (Oxford: Clarendon Press, 1954).

Russell, Bertrand, *Logic and Knowledge*, ed. by R. C. Marsh (London: G. Allen & Unwin, 1956).

Satura, Vladimir, *Kants Erkenntnispsychologie in den Nachschriften seiner Vorlesungen über empirische Psychologie* (Bonn: Bouvier, 1971).

Schlick, Moritz, 'Meaning and Verification', in *Readings in Philosophical Analysis*, ed. by H. Feigl and W. Sellars (New York: Appleton Century Crofts, 1949), pp. 146–70.

—— Moritz, *General Theory of Knowledge*, tr. by A. Blumberg from the second German edn. (New York: Springer, 1974).

Schmucker, Josef, *Die Ursprünge der Ethik Kants in seinen vorkritischen Schriften und Reflexionen* (Meisenheim: Anton Hain, 1961).

Schneewind, J. B., *The Invention of Autonomy* (Cambridge: Cambridge Univ. Press, 1997).

Schönecker, Dieter, 'Zur Analytizität der Grundlegung', *Kant-Studien*, 87 (1996), 348–54.

Scott-Taggart, M. J., 'Recent Work on the Philosophy of Kant', *American Philosophical Quarterly*, 3 (1966), 171–209.

Sellars, Wilfrid, *Science, Perception and Reality* (London: Routledge & Kegan Paul, 1963).

—— 'The Identity Approach to the Mind–Body Problem', *Review of Metaphysics*, 18 (1965), 430–51.

—— 'Some Remarks on Kant's Theory of Experience', *Journal of Philosophy*, 64 (1967), 633–47.

—— *Science and Metaphysics* (London: Routledge & Kegan Paul, 1968).

—— '". . . This I or He or It (the Thing) Which Thinks"', *Proceedings of the American Philosophical Association*, 44 (1970–1), 5–31.

—— 'Metaphysics and the Concept of a Person', in *Essays in Philosophy and its History* (Dordrecht: Reidel, 1974), pp. 214–43.

—— 'Kant's Transcendental Idealism', in *Proceedings of the Ottawa Congress on Kant in the Anglo-American and Continental Traditions*, ed. by P. Laberge, F. Duchesneau, and B. Morrissey (Ottawa: Univ. of Ottawa Press, 1976), pp. 165–81.

Shell, Susan Meld, *The Embodiment of Reason* (Chicago: Chicago Univ. Press, 1996).

Shoemaker, Sydney, *Self-Knowledge and Self-Identity* (Ithaca: Cornell Univ. Press, 1963).

—— 'Persons and their Pasts', *American Philosophical Quarterly*, 7 (1970), 269–85.

—— 'Embodiment and Behavior', in *The Identities of Persons*, ed. by A. O. Rorty (Berkeley: Univ. of California Press, 1976), pp. 109–38.

—— 'Personal Identity: A Materialist's Account', in *Personal Identity*, by Sydney Shoemaker and Richard Swinburne (Oxford: Blackwell, 1984), pp. 67–132.

Sidgwick, Henry, *Lectures on the Philosophy of Kant and Other Philosophical Essays and Lectures* (London: Macmillan, 1905).

Silber, John, 'Introduction', in I. Kant, *Religion Within the Bounds of Reason Alone*, tr. by T. M. Greene and H. H. Hudson (New York: Harper and Row, 1960), pp. lxxix–cxxxiv.

Smart, Brian, 'Diachronous and Sychronous Selves', *Canadian Journal of Philosophy*, 6 (1976), 13–33.

Smith, Norman Kemp, *A Commentary to Kant's 'Critique of Pure Reason'*, 2nd edn. (London: Macmillan, 1923).

Smythe, T. W., 'Chisholm on Person Identity', *Philosophical Studies*, 26 (1974), 351–9.

Sommer, Manfred, *Identität im Übergang: Kant* (Frankfurt: Suhrkamp, 1988).

Srzednicki, Jan, 'On Strawson's Criticism of Kant's "Transcendental Idealism"', *Kant-Studien*, 75 (1984), 94–103.

Stark, Werner, *Nachforschungen zu Briefen und Handschriften Immanuel Kants* (Berlin: Akademie Verlag, 1993).

Stine, William, 'Self-Consciousness in Kant's *Critique of Pure Reason*', *Philosophical Studies*, 28 (1975), 189–97.

Strawson, P. F., *Individuals* (Garden City, NY: Anchor, 1963).

—— *The Bounds of Sense* (London: Methuen, 1966).

—— 'Review of Jonathan Bennett's *Kant's Dialectic*', *Philosophical Quarterly*, 25 (1975), 165–9.

—— 'Kant's Paralogisms: Self-Consciousness and the "Outside Observer"', in *Theorie der Subjektivität*, ed. by K. Cramer, H. Fulda, R.-P. Horstmann, and U. Pothast (Frankfurt: Suhrkamp, 1987), pp. 203–19.

—— 'The Problem of Realism and the A Priori', in *Kant and Contemporary Epistemology*, ed. by P. Parrini (Dordrecht: Kluwer, 1994), pp. 167–74.

Sturma, Dieter, *Kant über Selbstbewusstsein. Zum Zusammenhang von Erkenntniskritik und Theorie des Selbstbewusstseins* (Hildesheim/Zurich/New York: Olms, 1985).

—— 'Self-Consciousness and the Philosophy of Mind', in *Proceedings of the Eighth International Kant Congress 1995*, ed. by H. Robinson (Milwaukee: Marquette Univ. Press, 1995), vol. 1, pp. 661–74.

—— *Philosophie der Person* (Paderborn: Schöningh, 1995).

—— 'Die Parologismen der reinen Vernunft in der zweiten Auflage', in *Immanuel Kant : Kritik der reinen Vernunft*, ed. by G. Mohr and M. Willaschek (Berlin: Akademie Verlag, 1998), pp. 391–411.

Swinburne, Richard, 'Personal Identity', in *Proceedings of the Aristotelian Society*, 74 (1973–4), 231–47.

—— 'Persons and Personal Identity', in *Contemporary British Philosophy*, ed. by H. D. Lewis, 4th ser. (London: Allen & Unwin, 1976), pp. 221–38.

Tetens, J. N., *Sprachphilosophische Versuche*, ed. by H. Pfannkuch (Hamburg: Meiner, 1971).

Thiel, Udo, 'Between Wolff and Kant: Merian's Theory of Apperception', *Journal of the History of Philosophy*, 34 (1996), 213–32.

Thomas Aquinas, *Summa Theologiae*.

Tonelli, Giorgio, 'Kant's Ethics as Part of Metaphysics: A Possible Newtonian Suggestion, and Some Comments on Kant's *Dreams of a Spirit-Seer*', in *Philosophy and the Civilizing Arts*, ed. by J. Anton and Craig Walton (Athens, Oh.: Ohio Univ. Press, 1974), pp. 236–63.

Van Cleve, James, *Problems from Kant* (Oxford: Oxford Univ. Press, 1999).

Van Inwagen, Peter, *Metaphysics* (Boulder: Westview, 1993).

Vogel, Jonathan, 'The Problem of Self-Knowledge in Kant's "Refutation of Idealism": Two Recent Views', *Philosophy and Phenomenological Research*, 53 (1993), 875–87.

Walker, R. C. S., 'The Status of Kant's Theory of Matter', in *Kant's Theory of Knowledge*, ed. by L. W. Beck (Dordrecht: Reidel, 1974), pp. 151–8.

—— *Kant* (London: Routledge, 1978).

—— 'Introduction', in *The Real and the Ideal* (New York: Garland, 1989), pp. vii–xv.

Wallace, R. Jay, *Responsibility and the Moral Sentiments* (Cambridge, Mass.: Harvard Univ. Press, 1996).

Walsh, W. H., *Kant's Criticism of Metaphysics* (Chicago: Univ. of Chicago Press, 1975).

Washburn, Michael, 'The Second Edition of the *Critique*: Towards an Understanding of its Nature and Genesis', *Kant-Studien*, 66 (1975), 277–90.

—— 'Did Kant Have a Theory of Self-Knowledge?', *Archiv für Geschichte der Philosophie*, 58 (1976), 40–56.

Watkins, Eric, 'Kant's Theory of Physical Influx', *Archiv für Geschichte der Philosophie*, 77 (1995), 285–324.

—— 'Recent Developments in Kant Scholarship: Kant's Philosophy of Mind', *Eidos*, 12 (1995), 83–107.

Weldon, T. D., *Kant's Critique of Pure Reason*, 2nd edn. (Oxford: Oxford Univ. Press, 1958).

Westphal, Merold, 'In Defense of the Thing in Itself', *Kant-Studien*, 59 (1968), 118–41.

Wick, Warner, 'Introduction', in I. Kant, *The Metaphysical Principles of Virtue*, tr. by James Ellington (New York: Bobbs-Merill, 1964), pp. xi–lxii.

Wiener, Norbert, *The Human Use of Human Beings* (New York: Houghton Mifflin, 1971).

Wiggins, David, 'Locke, Butler, and the Stream of Consciousness, and Men as a Natural Kind', in *The Identities of Persons*, ed. by A. O. Rorty (Berkeley: Univ. of California Press, 1976), pp. 139–74.

Wilkerson, T. E., *Kant's Critique of Pure Reason* (Oxford: Oxford Univ. Press, 1976).

Wilkes, Kathleen, 'Consciousness and Commissurotomy', *Philosophy*, 53 (1978), 185–99.

Williams, Bernard, 'Knowledge and Meaning in the Philosophy of Mind', *Philosophical Review*, 77 (1968), 216–28.

—— 'The Self and the Future', *Philosophical Review*, 79 (1970), 161–80.

—— *Problems of the Self* (Cambridge: Cambridge Univ. Press, 1973).

Williams, T. C., *The Concept of the Categorical Imperative* (Oxford: Oxford Univ. Press, 1968).

Wilson, Margaret, 'Kant and "the *Dogmatic* Idealism of Berkeley"', *Journal of the History of Philosophy*, 9 (1971), 459–75.

—— 'Leibniz and Materialism', *Canadian Journal of Philosophy*, 4 (1974), 495–513.

—— 'On Kant and the Refutation of Subjectivism', in *Kant's Theory of Knowledge*, ed. by L. W. Beck (Dordrecht: Reidel, 1974), pp. 208–17.

—— 'Leibniz on Self-Consciousness and Immortality in the Paris Notes and After', *Archiv für Geschichte der Philosophie*, 58 (1976), 335–52.

Wolff, Robert Paul, *Kant's Theory of Mental Activity* (Cambridge, Mass.: Harvard Univ. Press, 1963).
—— *The Autonomy of Reason* (New York: Harper, 1973).
Wood, Allen, *Kant's Moral Religion* (Ithaca: Cornell Univ. Press, 1970).
—— 'Kant's Dialectic', *Canadian Journal of Philosophy*, 5 (1975), 595–614.
—— *Kant's Rational Theology* (Ithaca: Cornell Univ. Press, 1978).
—— 'Kant's Compatibilism', in *Self and Nature in Kant's Philosophy*, ed. by A. Wood (Ithaca: Cornell Univ. Press, 1984), pp. 73–101.
—— 'Kant's Historical Materialism', in *Autonomy and Community*, ed. by Jane Kneller and Sidney Axinn (Albany: SUNY Press, 1998), pp. 15–37.
Woods, M., 'Reference and Self-Identification', *Journal of Philosophy*, 65 (1968), 568–78.
Young, Robert, 'The Resurrection of the Body', *Sophia*, 9 (1970), 1–15.
Zelazny, Miroslaw, and Stark, Werner, 'Zu Krystof Celestyn Mrongovius und seinen Kolleghcften nach Kants Vorlesungen', *Kant-Forschungen*, 1 (1987), 279–97
Zöller, Günter, 'Making Sense out of Inner Sense', *International Philosophical Quarterly*, 29 (1989), 263–70.
—— 'Main Developments in Scholarship in the *Critique of Pure Reason*', *Philosophy and Phenomenological Research*, 53 (1993), 445–66.

Index

Abicht, J. H., 231
'Act theory', 243, 250 (definition),
    251-2
Adams, R. M., 188
Affection, 22, 94, 240, 247, 252-5,
    257-9, 266, 279, 284-6, 296
Allison, H. E., v, xiii, xxxi, xxxii, 81,
    126, 127, 173, 298, 320
Analogies of Experience, xxix, 79, 80,
    120, 293
Analytic/synthetic distinction, 48, 52,
    56, 117, 131-3
Anderson, J. C., 172
Animals, 28, 42, 86, 179, 181, 241-2,
    245-7, 251, 295
Anscombe, G. E. M., 125
Anthropology From a Pragmatic Point of View,
    279
Antinomies, xxxv, 96, 170, 197, 213,
    228, 272, 293
    Second Antinomy, xxi, xxv, xxix, 43,
        51-3, 80, 82, 306
    Third Antinomy, 198
Appearance, 20, 30, 33, 44, 50, 77, 80,
    102, 113, 158, 161, 298
Apperception/inner sense distinction,
    17, 21, 31, 130, 239-57, 260, 277
Aquila, R., v, xxxi
Aristotle, 82-3
Armstrong, D., 125
Axinn, S., xxxiii
Ayer, A. J., 125

Balowitz, V., 126
Baumgarten, A. G., xvi, 124, 236-8
Beck, L. W., xxxiii, 187-8, 192, 210,
    220-3, 226, 228-33
Bennett, J., v, x, xxxiii, 1, 2, 24, 26,
    60-1, 69, 76, 78-83, 87, 124,
    126-8, 137-8, 146-8, 171-3, 230,
    240, 260, 285-7, 296-7, 300-1
Berkeley, G., 109, 112, 126
Bird, G., 77, 83, 127, 142, 172, 296,
    298-9, 301

Bittner, R., 229
Brain bisection, 61, 81, 146, 153, 161,
    163
Brandt, R., v, xxxi, xxxii, xxxiii, xxxvi
Brentano, F., 125
Broad, C. D., 77, 83, 124-5
Brook, A., v, vii, 303-12, 319-20
Burge, T., x, 321

Cadava, E., xxxii
Carl, W., v, xxxi, xxxiv
Carr, D., xxxii
Cassam, Q., v
Castañeda, H.-N., vi
Castillo, M., xxxiii
Categorical Imperative, xi, 183, 186,
    193-4, 205, 223, 225, 231
Categories, 16, 54, 67, 82, 109, 129,
    189, 190, 234-8, 261, 268, 290,
    293, 298, 301
Causality, 13, 85, 92, 107, 109, 124,
    152, 235
Chalmers, D., xxxiv
Chisholm, R., v, x, xxxii, 1, 26, 71-2,
    82-3, 170-2, 174-6, 262-3, 297
Clark, G., xxxiii
Coder, D., 174
Cohen, G., xxxiii
Compatibilism, 13, 85, 129, 193, 200,
    207, 210, 212, 220, 226-7, 230,
    241-2
Conner, P., xxxii
'Copernican image', 5-8
Cramer, K., xxxi
Critical period in Kant, xxi-xxii, xxvi,
    3, 11, 15-17, 22, 24, 35-6, 182,
    239, 246, 272
Critique of Judgment, 78, 187-8, 295, 320
Critique of Practical Reason, xviii, 16, 21,
    185-8, 191-3, 210-12, 216,
    219-33, 300
Crusius, C. A., 77, 100, 125, 246, 295

Daniels, C., 175

Davidson, D., vi, 40, 79
Delaney, C. F., 321
De Man, P., xxxi
Dennett, D., 176
den Ouden, B., xxxi
Descartes, R., xvi, xxvi, 61
'Divisibility argument', 34–8, 39
     (definition), 40, 42, 45, 50, 53, 77–9
Dreams of a Spirit-Seer, 14, 28–32, 187, 236
Duncan, A. R. C., 233

Eldridge, R., xxxi
Embodiment, 19, 84, 95–108, 125, 166
Empirical apperception, 42
Empirical concepts, 261
Empiricist period in Kant, 3, 13, 85–6,
     95, 109, 241
Empirical psychology, xxiii, 44, 195
End of All Things, 176, 188
'Epistemological argument', 255, 260
     (definition), 261, 263–4, 270–1,
     273, 298
*Essay Concerning the Clarity of the Principles
     of Natural Theology and Ethics*, 14
'Essence theory', 240, 267 (definition),
     268–72, 274, 284–5
Euler, L., 125
Ewing, A. C., 78, 127, 244–5, 295–6,
     301
'Experience', xxviii, 115–17, 247, 264,
     283, 298
External world, xviii, 12, 13, 15, 17, 19,
     25, 84, 108–23, 213, 237

Findlay, J., x
'Flux argument', 255, 272, 273
     (definition), 274–6, 292
Fodor, J., 79
Förster, E., xxxi, xxxiv
Foundations of the Metaphysics of Morals,
     xviii, 21, 191–3, 201–33, 259
Frank, M., v, xxxi, xxxii, 303, 319
Frankfurt, H., xxxiv, 297
Freedom, xi–xiii, xiv, xvi–xix, xxxv, 12,
     13, 17, 21, 22, 26, 29, 86,
     189–223, 234, 236, 241–2, 259,
     292, 294, 324–5
Fulda, H.-F., xxxi

Ginet, C., 175
Gochnauer, M., 122, 126–7
God, 14, 86–8, 96, 109, 145, 179–80,
     183, 185, 188–9, 193, 195–7, 200,
     230, 249, 271, 273, 275, 291, 301

Gram, M., 284–5, 300–1
Grice, H. R., 160, 175
Gutting, G., 321
Guyer, P., v, x, xxxi, xxxii, 320

'Harmony theory', 87–91
Harrison, J., 100–6, 125–6
Harrison, R., 24
Hasker, W., 320
Hatfield, G., xxxiii
Heath, P., xxxiii
Heidegger, M., x
Heimsoeth, H., 77, 80, 125, 246, 295
Henle, P., 297
Henrich, D., v, xi, xii, xxxii, xxxiii,
     xxxiv, 128, 140, 172, 192, 224,
     226, 228–9, 231–3, 246, 255,
     295–6, 319
Hesse, M., 79
Horstmann, R., v, xxxi, 298, 320
Hübner, K., 126
Hume, D., 6, 151, 156–7, 171
Hurley, S. L., xxxii
Husserl, E., 176

'I' (bare representation of), 16, 31, 44,
     54–6, 69–70, 72, 80, 134, 179,
     190, 217, 237, 294
Identity, personal, v, vi, xvi, 9, 14,
     19–20, 23, 25, 77, 99, 125,
     128–75, 182, 184, 235–7, 247
Ilting, K. H., 229, 233
Immaterialism, vii, xv, xvii, xxi–xxiii,
     xxvi–xxviii, 14–16, 18, 20, 25–84,
     91, 96, 107–8, 119, 123, 129, 146,
     166, 180, 187, 214, 227, 236–7,
     303–21, 324
  'appearance immaterialism', 33
     (definition), 37, 42–3, 46, 65–6, 74,
     78, 90
  'noumenal immaterialism', 35
     (definition), 37, 43, 45–6, 59, 62–3,
     66, 74, 79, 81, 90, 93, 99
  'phenomenal immaterialism', 33
     (definition), 34–5, 37, 42, 46, 62,
     66, 74, 90
  'scientific immaterialism', 34
     (definition), 37–8, 40–1, 45–6, 60,
     63, 66, 74, 76–7, 81, 293–4
  'transcendental immaterialism', 34
     (definition), 45–7
Immortality, xvii, xxiii, 13, 14, 16, 20,
     68, 73, 75, 82, 99, 173, 177–88,
     235, 237, 304, 324

Impenetrability, 14, 29–30, 32, 33, 77, 79, 126
Inaugural Dissertation, xvi, xxvii, xxix, 16, 86, 109, 283
Incorruptibility, 18, 20, 25, 27, 50, 63, 65, 68, 71, 78, 80, 136, 143, 199
'Idependent stream theory', 243, 249–52
'Influx theory', 14, 86–92, 94
Inner sense, xxxv, 44, 107, 114, 121, 130, 132, 139–40, 184, 239–55, 264, 274, 278, 296, 301, 325
'Inner sense argument', 30, 32 (definition), 33–4, 37

Judgement vs. mere reflective awareness, 167, 244–51, 253–5, 296

Kalter, A., 1, 68, 80, 82–3, 126–7
Kant-Eberhard Controversy, 76, 78, 124, 126
Keller, P., xxxiii
Kim, J., x
Kitcher, P., v, x, xxxi, xxxii, 303, 319–20
Klemm, D., xxxi, 319
Klemme, H., v, vii, xii, xxiii–xxx, xxxii, xxxiv–xxxvi
Kneller, J., xxxiii
Körner, S., 297
Korsgaard, C., vi, xiii, xxxiii
Kripke, S., x
Krüger, G., 232, 295

Lachièze-Rey, P., 299
Laywine, A., 320
Lectures of Kant, vii–x, xiii–xxiii, xxv, xxx, 3, 12, 13, 16, 24, 28, 31–7, 66, 79, 91–2, 97, 130, 137, 179–82, 190, 193–5, 236–8, 247, 269, 292, 321, 323
Leibniz, G., 28, 30, 36–7, 77, 81, 87, 90, 110, 125, 148, 150–2, 172–3, 245, 267–8, 270, 272–3, 275, 299
Leibnizian idealism, 36–7, 45, 78
Levine, J., xxxiv
Lewis, D., x, 154, 159, 167, 173–5
Lewis, H. D., 297
Life, 15, 28, 79, 179, 181
Location of soul, 13, 29, 77, 95–6, 99–100, 107, 126
Locke, J., 87, 123, 130, 148–52, 156, 161, 164, 166, 171, 173, 296

Long, D., 125
Loux, M., 321

Maddell, G., 174
Maddy, P., 174
Madigan, P. S., 173
Makkreel, R., v, xxxi, xxxii
Malebranche, N., 87
'Material elements' (or 'physical monads'), 14, 15, 28–33, 35, 38–9, 43, 53, 78, 96, 309
Materialism, xv, xvii, xxii–xxiii, xxvi–xxvii, 303–21, 324
'Materialism in an extended sense' (or 'transcendental materialism'), 35–7, 62, 77, 97
McDowell, J., vi
McGinn, C., vi, vii, 303, 308, 310, 312–21
Meerbote, R., v, xxxi
Melnick, A., x, 300
Mendelssohn, M., xvii, 184
Metaphysical Foundations of Natural Science, xxii, 16, 40, 50, 65, 78, 87, 125, 188, 191, 216, 291–2, 297, 299, 301, 320
Mijuskovic, B., 82, 172
Mischel, T., 79, 301
Mistaken Subtlety of the Four Syllogistic Figures, 13
Mohr, G., v, xxxi, xxxvi
Moral law (its deduction), 191–4, 202–26, 230, 232
Multiple embodiment, 101 (definition), 104–7, 126, 145, 158
Multiple inhabitation, 101 (definition), 158, 174

Nagel, G., x
Nagel, T., vi, xi, xxxiii, 81, 313, 320
Nancy, J.-L., xxxii
Naragon, S., xxxii, xxxiii, xxxvi, 321
Nelson, L., 232–3
Newton, I., 272–3, 275
Nietzsche, F., x
Nolan, J., 82
Noumenal self, 8, 71–3, 80, 99, 185, 208, 212, 218, 225, 276–7, 280–1, 315–16
Nova Dilucidatio, 13, 14, 241

Oberer, H., xxxi
O'Neill, O., 126–7
Origin of soul, 97, 125, 180

Paralogisms:
First Paralogism, xxix, xxxv, xxxvi, 18, 25–6, 64–6, 84, 131, 199, 323; *see also* substantiality of soul
Fourth Paralogism, 19, 76, 84, 92, 111–23, 132, 213, 217, 324; *see also* external world
revisions by Kant, xvii–xviii, xxviii–xxix, xxxvi, 4, 10, 16–19, 21, 48–9, 56, 68–70, 108, 111, 114–15, 117, 184, 191, 198, 216, 223, 227, 237, 273–4
Second Paralogism, 18, 25–6, 32, 47–52, 67–76, 84, 129, 131, 288, 306, 324; (*see also* simplicity)
Third Paralogism, 19, 60, 76, 128–40, 324; *see also* identity
'Passivity argument', 208, 214–15, 240, 255–9, 270–1, 279
Parfit, D., 128, 149, 154–6, 159–60, 163, 173–5
Parrini, P., 319
Paton, H. J., 172, 192, 205, 210, 224–6, 229, 233, 243–4, 295–6
Patten, S. C., 296
Penelhum, T., 174
Perry, J., 128, 149, 154, 156, 159–60, 162, 173–5
Phenomenal/noumenal distinction, xxvii, 7, 10, 16, 19–20, 23, 33–5, 44, 51, 57, 66–73, 80–3, 89, 92, 94, 98–9, 106, 111–12, 128, 144–6, 152, 158–9, 161, 163, 168–70, 172, 184, 198, 215, 230, 281, 299, 308
Physical Monadology, 13, 14
Physical monads *see* 'material elements'
Physics, 13, 17, 23, 83, 85
Pippin, R., v, xiii, xxxi, 297, 320
Plantinga, A., 298
Plato, 179
'Pneumatism', 36 (definition), 37, 45, 78, 91, 97, 120, 146, 182, 309
Pothast, U., xxxi
Powell, C. T., xxxii, 303, 319–20
Prauss, G., v, xiii, xxxii, 77, 79, 231, 298–9, 320
'Principle of life argument', 179–83
Prolegomena to any Future Metaphysics, 16, 38, 65, 78, 82, 87, 143, 172, 193, 199, 228–9, 306
Pucetti, R., 174
Putnam, H., 79

Rationalism in Kant, xi, xv, xxii, 3, 4, 10, 12–14, 17–19, 20–1, 23, 26, 28, 31–2, 55, 76, 86, 97, 119, 178–81, 189–92, 217, 218, 227, 236, 257, 290, 293
Rational psychology, xiii–xvi, xix–xx, xxiii, xxviii, 11, 13–16, 18, 20–1, 23, 25, 38, 44, 49, 54, 65–6, 68, 73–5, 109, 111, 115, 117–18, 131–3, 137, 143, 177, 181–2, 189, 195, 214, 216, 235–8, 261, 290–3, 308, 325
Rawls, J., xi, xxxiv
Reflections, xvi, xxiii, 189, 196–7, 200
'Reflections theory', 243–52
Refutation of Idealism, 19, 43, 110, 115–23, 137, 143, 169, 247, 256, 324
Reimarus, H. S., 255
Reiner, H., 226
'Relation argument', 65, 67, 255, 272 (definition), 273, 279
Religion Within the Bounds of Reason Alone, 212
Representation (faculty of), 14, 15, 27, 241
Rescher, N., 81
Resurrection, 98
Review of Schulz, 193, 199–201, 220, 227–9
Rey, G., 160, 175–6
Robinson, D., 174
Robinson, H., xxxii
Rockmore, T., xxxvi
Rosas, A., v, xxxi
Ross, W. D., 229, 233
Russell, B., 174

Satura, V., xxxiii
Sceptical period in Kant, 3, 14, 16, 30, 235–6
Schlick, M., 124, 174, 176
Schmucker, J., xi, xxxiii, 231
Schopenhauer, A., 125
Schott, R. M., xxxiii
Schneewind, J., xi, xxxiii
Schultz, J., 199
Scott-Taggart, M. J., 77
Sedgwick, S., xxxii
Seel, G., xxxi
Selected Pre-Critical Writings, 77, 123, 125, 295–7, 300

Sellars, W., v, xxxiii, 1, 26, 45, 60, 62–3, 79–83, 126, 172, 176, 296–300, 315, 318, 321
Shell, S. M., xxxiii
Shoemaker, S., 125, 128, 148, 164–7, 173, 176
Sidgwick, H., 49, 79, 171
Silber, J., 226, 233
Simplicity, xiv, xvi–xvii, xix, 14–16, 18, 25–32, 39, 43–4, 47–66, 71, 74–5, 77–8, 80, 82, 97, 119, 131, 140, 146, 179, 181, 184, 190, 214, 234–7, 324
Singer, M., 226
Smart, B., 174
Smith, Norman Kemp, 80, 111, 126–7, 171–2, 243, 245, 255, 295–6
Smythe, T. W., 175
Solomon, W. D., 321
Spatiality (its role in self-knowledge), xxxv, 17, 23, 43, 79, 96, 108, 110, 120–3, 144, 169, 216–17, 262, 264, 301–2
'Species theory', 93, 112–13, 240, 256, 265 (definition), 266–7, 271, 273–9, 281–4, 288
'Spiritualism', xv, xxii–xxiii, 14, 16, 19, 23, 36 (definition), 37, 45, 47, 78, 97, 117–19, 133, 146, 182, 186, 236, 295, 304
Stamm, M., xxxi
Stark, W., xxxii–xxxiii, xxxvi
Strawson, P., v, xxxiii, 1, 2, 6, 24, 62, 78, 80–1, 92–4, 124, 126–8, 138, 144, 148, 171–4, 176, 240, 276–7, 280–4, 287, 298, 300–1
Stine, W. D., 297
Sturma, D., v, xxxi, 303, 319
Substance, 27, 31, 50–1, 51, 53–4, 65, 67–8, 80, 82–3, 89, 97, 138, 146, 184, 188–9, 195, 198, 235, 249, 293, 299
Substantiality of soul, xiv–xv, xvi–xvii, xix, xxix, xxxv, 14, 16–18, 25–7, 29–31, 46–8, 64–74, 83–4, 131, 138, 190, 198, 227, 236–7, 288, 309–10, 323
Survival, 149, 152–64, 173–4
Swinburne, R., 144–5, 149, 152, 172–3

Tetens, J., 243, 295
Thiel, U., v, xxxi
Things in themselves, xxvii, 2, 7, 35, 65, 79, 89, 106, 120, 258, 266–71, 277, 284–5, 290, 295, 298–9, 307–10, 314
Thomas Aquinas, 300
Thoughts on the True Estimation of Living Forces, 13, 85
'Time argument', 240, 260 (definition), 261–6
Tonelli, G., 229
Transcendental deduction of categories, xviii, 2, 5, 6, 8, 10, 19, 128, 139, 142, 169–70, 172, 228, 247–8, 264, 270–1, 287, 289, 297–8
Transcendental idealism, xxvi, 5, 7, 8, 9, 13, 15–16, 19–20, 22, 40, 46, 72–3, 78–9, 84, 87, 92–4, 96, 98, 110–13, 117, 126, 132, 145–6, 153, 169–70, 172, 197–8, 214–16, 239–40, 255–90, 299–301, 313, 316, 325
Transcendental ideality of self, 3, 7, 9–10, 17, 21–2, 169, 216, 255–90
Transcendental unity of apperception, xvi, 15, 140–2, 163, 303, 304, 306, 325

Unity of thought, 15, 29–30, 38, 41–2, 53–4, 82, 135, 141–2, 147–8
'Unity argument', 29, 32 (definition), 37–8, 42, 44, 48–9, 53–65, 80–2, 152, 181
Universal Natural History and Theory of the Heavens, 13, 85–6

Van Cleve, J., x, xxxii, 320
Van Inwagen, P., xxxiv
Velkley, R., xxxiii

Wallace, R. J., xxxiv
Walker, R., 6–8, 24, 26, 71–2, 83, 127, 240, 287–90, 300–1
Walsh, W. H., 127, 297
Washburn, M., 231, 291, 301
Watkins, E., v, xxxi, xxxvi, 319
Weldon, T. D., 243, 295
Westphal, M., 299
Wick, W., 232
Wiener, N., 173
Wiggins, D., 160, 175–6
Wilkerson, T. F., 126–7, 297–8
Wilkes, K., 175
Willascheck, M., xxxi
Williams, B., 173, 176

Williams, T. C., 232–3
Wilson, M., 26, 59–60, 62, 81, 126, 173
Wittgenstein, L., 127, 176
Wood, A., x, xxxi–xxxiii, 68, 83, 138, 172, 185, 187–8, 298
Woods, M., 176
Wolff, C., xvi, xxxiii, 246

Woff, R. P., 142, 172, 233, 240, 244, 253, 255, 295–6

Young, R., 175

Zelaszny, M., xxxiii
Zöller, G., v, xxxi, 319